Mrs. Henry Wood

Dene hollow

A Novel

Mrs. Henry Wood

Dene hollow
A Novel

ISBN/EAN: 9783337042967

Printed in Europe, USA, Canada, Australia, Japan

Cover: Foto ©ninafisch / pixelio.de

More available books at **www.hansebooks.com**

CALLING ON SANDY BLACK

DENE HOLLOW.

A Novel.

BY

MRS. HENRY WOOD,

AUTHOR OF "EAST LYNNE."

LONDON:
RICHARD BENTLEY & SON, NEW BURLINGTON ST.
Publishers in Ordinary to Her Majesty.
1872.

LONDON:
PRINTED BY J. OGDEN AND CO.,
172, ST. JOHN STREET, E.C.

CONTENTS.

Part the First.

CHAPTER		PAGE
I.	SIR DENE	1
II.	HAREBELL FARM	12
III.	MARIA OWEN	24
IV.	AN EPISODE IN THE LIFE OF MARY BARBER	34
V.	THE SHADOW ON THE HOLLOW	56
VI.	IN ST. PETER'S CHURCH	67
VII.	ENCOUNTERING THE STORM	79
VIII.	JONATHAN DREW'S MIDNIGHT RIDE	88
IX.	SIR DENE'S PERPLEXITY	100
X.	THE BAILIFF'S LODGE	110
XI.	IN THE SAME SPOT	116
XII.	THE MORNING DREAM	121
XIII.	AT THE TRAILING INDIAN	133
XIV.	HAREBELL POND	148
XV.	ONLY SADNESS	154
XVI.	SEEN BY MOONLIGHT	163
XVII.	VERY MUCH OF A WAIF	173
XVIII.	GUESTS AT BEECHHURST DENE	182
XIX.	FRIGHTENING THE PONY	192
XX.	MISS MAY	204
XXI.	DRIVEN FROM HAREBELL FARM	215

Part the Second.

XXII.	AFTER THE LAPSE OF YEARS	225
XXIII.	SIR DENE'S REPENTANCE	236
XXIV.	SENT TO THE TRAILING INDIAN	246
XXV.	MISS EMMA GEACH	258
XXVI.	AN EVENTFUL EVENING	260
XXVII.	AT SIR DENE'S SECRETAIRE	285
XXVIII.	BACK FROM BRISTOL	296

CHAPTER	PAGE
XXIX. Miss Emma gone	306
XXX. Selling out	314
XXXI. Better to have let the Doubt lie	321
XXXII. Seen through the Venetian Blinds	333
XXXIII. Been with the Old Squire in the Night	346
XXXIV. Over the Claret Cup	355
XXXV. An Arrival at the Trailing Indian	362
XXXVI. The Snow-storm	372
XXXVII. At Beechhurst Dene	379
XXXVIII. A Dish of Tea at the Forge	389
XXXIX. The Wedding Day	399
XL. The Last of Randy Black	411
XLI. With Sir Dene	422
XLII. The Ordering of Heaven	433
XLIII. The New Master	441
XLIV. Conclusion	452

DENE HOLLOW.

Part the First.

CHAPTER I.
SIR DENE.

A FAIR scene. None fairer throughout this, the fairest of all the Midland counties. Winter had turned. The blue of the sky was unbroken; the sunshine shed down its bright and cheering warmth; it was the first day of real spring.

Standing on a somewhat elevated road, as compared with the ground in front, was a group of gentlemen talking earnestly, and noting critically the points of the landscape immediately around. They stood with their backs to the iron gates of the lodge; gates that gave admittance to a winding avenue leading up to a fine old seat, Beechhurst Dene. Before them—the ground descending slightly, so that they looked down on it and saw all the panorama—were sunny plains, and groves of towering trees and sparkling rivulets; a farm-house here and there imparting life to the picture. The little village of Hurst Leet (supposed to be a corruption of Hurst Hamlet) lay across, somewhat towards the right as they gazed. Beyond it, at two or three miles' distance was the city of Worcester, its cathedral very conspicuous, on this clear day, as well as the tapering spire of the church of St. Andrew's. Amidst other features of the beautiful scenery, the eye, sweeping around the distant horizon on all sides, caught the long chain of the Malvern Hills; the white houses (very few in those days) nestling at their base like glittering sea-shells amidst moss. The hills, rising up there, looked very close, not much further off than Worcester. They were more than double the distance—and

B

in a totally opposite direction. Nothing is more deceiving than perspective.

A quick walker taking the fields and the stiles; that is, direct as the crow flies; might walk to the village of Hurst Leet in ten minutes from the lodge gates of Beechhurst Dene. But if he went by the road—as he must do if he had either horse or vehicle—it would take him very considerably longer, for it was a roundabout way, part of it very hilly. He would have to turn to his left (almost as though he were going from the village instead of to it) and sweep round quite three parts of a circle: in short, make very much of what Tony Lumpkin calls a circumbendibus. The question now occupying these gentlemen was whether a straighter and nearer road should not be cut, chiefly for the accommodation of the family residing at Beechhurst Dene.

The chief of the group, and most conspicuous of it, was Beechhurst Dene's owner—Sir Dene Clanwaring. By the Clanwaring family—and consequently by others—it was invariably pronounced Clannering: indeed, some of the branches had long spelt it so. Sir Dene was a tall and fine man of fifty years; his features were noble and commanding, his complexion was fresh and healthy. He was of fairly good family, but nothing *very* great or grand, and had won his baronetcy for himself after making his fortune in India. Fortunes were made in those bygone days, when the East India Company was flourishing, quicker than they are in these. It was nothing for the soldier, resident there for long years, to unite with his duties the civilian's pursuits, so far as moneymaking went; and Dene Clanwaring had been one who did this. He was a brave man, had won fame as well as money, and at a comparatively early age he returned home for good, with a fortune and a baronetcy. People told fabulous tales of his wealth—as is sure to be the case—augmenting it to a few millions. He himself could have testified that it was about six thousand pounds a year, all told.

Looking out, on his return from India, for some desirable place to settle down in for life, chance directed Sir Dene Clanwaring to Beechhurst Dene in Worcestershire; of which county he was originally a native. Whether it was the estate itself that attracted him, or whether it was the accidental fact that it bore his own name, Dene, certain it was that Sir Dene searched no farther. He purchased it at once, entailing it on his eldest son, John Ingram Clanwaring, and his heirs for ever.

Shortly after entering into possession of it, his wife, Lady Clanwaring, died. Sir Dene—standing there in the road before us to-day—is, as may be seen, in deep mourning. It is worn for her. He was very fond of her, and the loss was keenly felt. Close by his side is his second son, Geoffry; a tall, fair, golden-haired, pleasant looking young fellow, who is in black also. Near to them bends an old and curious looking little man, very thin and undersized; his hard features are pinched, his few grey hairs scanty. It is Squire Arde of the Hall. He wears a suit of pepper-and-salt; breeches, waistcoat, gaiters and coat; with silver knee and shoe-buckles, and a white beaver hat. Over his clothes is a drab great-coat of some fluffy material, but the Squire has thrown it quite back, and it seems to lodge on the tips of his narrow shoulders. The only other individual, completing the party, is Jonathan Drew, Sir Dene's bailiff; a hard man also, but a faithful, trustworthy servant. Sir Dene took him over from the previous owner of the estate, Mr. Honeythorn, and had already found his value. Drew managed the land and the tenants well, though complaints were murmured of his severity. He was turned sixty; a lean maypole of a man, in a long, fustian coat, and high-crowned brown hat, looking altogether not unlike a scarecrow in a corn-field. The bailiff was uncommonly ugly, and appeared at the present moment more so than usual from an access of ill-temper: which is plainly perceptible as he addresses his master.

"'Make my duty to Sir Dene, Mr. Drew, please, and tell him that I can't be turned out o' my house nohow; I've got the paper,' says she to me. 'Then, why don't you perduce the paper, Mrs. Barber?' says I, bantering at her. ''Cause I can't find it, sir; I've mislaid it,' goes on she. 'Mislaid what you've never had,' says I, as I flung away from her. And she never did have it, Sir Dene," wound up Drew; "don't you believe it, sir. Obstinate old granny!"

"When she sees that there are other cottages to be had; when she knows that it will be to the advantage of all her neighbours, I must say that I think it is unreasonable of her to refuse to go out," remarked Sir Dene, his brow contracted, his face severe just then. Accustomed all his life to command he brooked no opposition to his will.

"Onreasonable, Sir Dene!" echoed Drew. "It's a sight worse nor onreasonable: it's vicious."

The new road that Sir Dene purposed making to the village,

had been the subject of much planning and consideration between himself and his agent, Drew. One or two sites had been thought of, but the best attainable—there could be no doubt of it—the most convenient and the shortest was one that would open nearly immediately opposite his own gates. The line that would have to be cut through was his own property, every field of it, every hedge; and a footway, for a part of the road, seemed to point out its desirability. If they cut this line, it would be at quite a third less cost, both as to money and trouble, than any other. Naturally, Sir Dene wished it to be fixed upon; and Drew, who was red-hot on the new scheme, knowing it must improve the property, would not tolerate any complaints against it.

But there was an obstacle. About a hundred yards down the path just mentioned stood a cottage of the better class: a dwelling of five rooms, with masses of yellow jasmine climbing up its outer walls. It had once belonged to a farmer-proprietor of the name of Barber, who came to it in right of his wife. He had died in earlier life (several years ago now), leaving his widow and two daughters. His affairs were found to be in disorder—that is, he had died in hopeless debt. The widow and daughters took immediate steps to extricate themselves and uphold their late father's integrity. The cottage, with the bit of land attaching to it, was sold to Mr. Honeythorn, then the owner of Beechhurst Dene, who had been long wishing to possess it. Widow Barber remained in the occupancy of the dwelling and one field as tenant, paying an easy yearly rent; and she said that Mr. Honeythorn had given her a paper, or covenant, promising that she should not be turned out while she lived.

To make the road in the track contemplated by Sir Dene this cottage would have to come down, for the projected line ran right through it. Drew, acting for Dene, served Mrs. Barber with a formal notice to quit. Mrs. Barber met it by a verbal refusal (civilly and tearfully delivered) to go out; and an assertion to the above effect: namely, that she held the granted right to stay in the cottage for the term of her natural life, and that she possessed a paper in Mr. Honeythorn's own writing to confirm this right. In fact, this paper alone constituted her right, for nothing in relation to it had been found amidst Mr. Honeythorn's effects, though his executors had searched minutely. Jonathan Drew told Mrs. Barber to her face that there had never been any such paper, save in her imagination; Mrs. Barber had retaliated, not only that there was such a paper, but that Drew knew of it as well as she did, for that he had known of it at the time it was given. However, Mrs. Barber, search as she would, could not find this paper; she had either lost or mislaid it, or else had never possessed it. Matters, therefore, stood at this point, and Mrs. Barber retained the notice to quit at Lady Day—which was fast approaching.

The affair had vexed Sir Dene; it was at length beginning to enrage him. Fully persuaded—partly by Drew, partly by the fact of absolute non-evidence—that no such right had ever been conceded to the widow Barber, he could not see why the old woman's obstinacy should be let stand in the way of his plans. One dwelling-house was surely as good for her as another! But he had not quite fully decided on this thing: he was standing out there now, talking it over with his son and Drew, with a view to arrive at some decision. Squire Arde had come up accidentally.

"It would be but the work of a month or two," cried Sir Dene in his enthusiasm, standing with his arms on the fence, and looking across to the village. "See, Mr. Arde, it seems but a stone's throw."

"And nothing in the way of it but that dratted cottage!" put in Jonathan Drew.

Geoffry Clanwaring was sending his good-natured blue eyes roving here and there in the landscape, apparently in thought. Presently he addressed his father.

"Would it not be possible, sir, to carry the cutting a few yards on this side," moving his right hand, "and so leave the cottage standing?"

"No," replied Sir Dene. "The road shall be cut straight, or not at all."

"If you was to make a in-and-out road, like a dog's leg, as good stick to the old un, Mr. Geoffry," spoke up Drew. "Besides, there'd be the stream in the way lower down. No: there ain't no line but this—and Sir Dene'll hardly let a pigheaded old widow stand in the light of it."

"There's the smoke a-sprouting out of her chimney," struck in Squire Arde—who in familiar life was not very particular in his mode of speech, after the fashion of many country gentlemen of the period.

"A biling of her pot for dinner!" cried Drew. "Miserable old cat!"

"I mind me that something was said about that paper at the time," resumed the Squire.

"What paper?" asked Sir Dene, sharply.

"The one given her by Honeythorn."

Sir Dene drew a long breath. He would never have committed an injustice in the teeth of facts.

"*Was* such a paper given to her?"

"I don't know myself," replied Squire Arde, gazing out at the smoke with his watery eyes. "Some talk on't was abroad. 'Twas said Tom Barber's widow had got such a paper—had got it out of Honeythorn. On t'other hand, it might ha' been all lies. Drew, here, ought to know which way 'twas."

"I've told Sir Dene which way 'twas—that there warn't none," spoke Drew, tilting his hat up on his bald head. "Mr. Honeythorn did nothing o' that kind without me—not likely to. And if he had—put it that way—ought it to be binding on Sir Dene? Why in course not. Old Granny Barber's one of them cantankerous idiots that thinks nobody's turn is to be served but their own."

"Well, I must be going—or I shall not get there and home again by two o'clock, and that's my dinner hour," observed the Squire, pulling his light coat forward over his contracted chest. "I have got a goose to pluck with Black, up at the Trailing Indian. He was seen in my woods a night or two ago; and he'll have to tell me the reason why."

Drew threw back his long neck in a kind of mockery. "If you can keep Randy Black out o' your woods, Squire, you'll be cleverer nor other people."

"Well, I'm going up to him to have a try at it," was the old man's answer. "Good day to ye, Sir Dene."

"A moment yet, Squire Arde," said the baronet, detaining him. "Tell me truly what your opinion on this subject is. Should I turn the old woman out, or not?"

But the curious little man seemed to shrink into himself at the question; to become smaller than ever, if that were possible; as he avoided Sir Dene with a shake of the head.

"No, no, Sir Dene Clanwaring—no good to ask *me*. I've lived long enough to know that to thrust one's fingers into one's neighbour's pie brings often nothing but heart-burning in the long run. If I said to you 'turn her out,' and you came to repent of it later, why you'd lay the blame on me. 'Arde advised me' you'd be muttering to yourself night and morning, and give me anything but a blessing. Take t'other view. If

I said to you '*don't* turn her out; make the road elsewhere,' and you took the advice, you'd be ever hankering after this track that you'd missed. The cottage would become an eyesore; you'd call yourself a fool, and a double fool, to have been guided by old Arde. No, no. You must act upon your own judgment, Sir Dene; not mine. It's nothing to me. The old roads have done for me my time, and they'll do to the end. Good day."

He moved away with brisk steps towards the left, stooping forward, as was his wont. Another minute, and there met him three individuals: a gentleman and two young ladies. At least, if not a gentleman he entirely looked like one. It was Robert Owen; a farmer who had but recently come to live in the neighbourhood, renting a farm of Sir Dene. He was of notable appearance. Sir Dene was a handsome man, but not so handsome as Robert Owen. He would have been of distinguished presence amidst kings. Of noble height, slender and upright, his face, with its clearly cut features of the highest type, its pure complexion, bright even yet as a woman's, and its very dark blue eyes, presented a picture beautiful to look upon. But what caused him to be more remarkable than aught else was the fact that he had a soft, silvery white beard, falling over his white top coat: and in those days beards were very uncommon. In years he might have numbered about as many as Sir Dene. His two daughters had inherited his beauty—but not his height. Lovely girls they were, with dimpled, blushing cheeks, and of modest, simple, retiring manners; generally called, both in this neighbourhood and the one they had left, "the pretty Miss Owens." Mary, the elder of them, had been a wife for some months now: George Arde, a relative of the Squire, had married her. Maria, the younger, was Miss Owen still.

"How d'ye do, Owen?" cried the Squire, carelessly.

Robert Owen touched his hat as he answered that he was well—and "hoped the Squire was." None could be more sensible than he of the social distance that lay between him and Squire Arde; he was but a humble, working farmer. The young ladies stood blushing; Mary not venturing to speak, unless the Squire should first notice her. They wore hooded scarlet cloaks, the fashion in those days, and white straw gipsy hats, their beautiful brown hair falling in curls underneath.

"It's you, is it?" cried he, nodding to Mary. "How's George?"

"He is quite well, thank you, sir," she replied, with a slight courtesy.

"Over here?"

"No, sir. He is at home. My father came into Worcester yesterday and brought me back: my mother's not well. George is coming over for me to-morrow."

With a slight general nod from the Squire, to which the young ladies courtesied and the farmer again touched his hat, they pursued their respective ways. The foot steps caused Sir Dene and his party to turn their heads, which were still bent over the fence. Jonathan Drew vouchsafed an ungracious nod to the farmer; Sir Dene a more pleasant one; but Geoffry Clanwaring went up, spoke cordially to the farmer in his free, good-natured way, and shook hands with Mrs. Arde and Maria Owen.

It was but a slight episode. They went on, and Mr. Geoffry Clanwaring returned to the fence again.

But Sir Dene had become tired of standing still; perhaps a little tired of his indecision. Saying something about business at Hurst Leet, he suddenly turned alone down the narrow path before mentioned—which would take him straight by the cottage in dispute.

Perhaps few cottages could boast less of a look-out in front. This had none. The door nearly abutted on the path: there was not more than a yard and a half of ground between, but that little space was redolent of sweet-scented gillyflowers— as they are called in Worcestershire. On the other side of the path, the bank rose as perpendicularly as though it had been a cutting; a high bank, whose elm trees, towering above it, threw the shadow of their branches over the cottage roof. This fine grove of trees—which began at the top of the path, opposite Sir Dene's gates—was the pride of Sir Dene's heart. He'd not have had any one of the trees cut down for the world. The cottage—as Sir Dene walked—lay on the right hand, the bank and trees on his left. The door was standing open as he passed, and he caught a vision of a plump old woman inside it in grey stockings, who was stooping to skim a pan of cream in the passage.

"Old Mother Barber," said Sir Dene to himself.

Old Mother Barber, hearing the footsteps, looked up. When she saw whose they were, a tremor, as if an ice-shaft had darted through her heart, took her, and she ran into her kitchen like a frightened hare. She wore a short black gown of rough flannel cloth, its sleeves cut off at the elbow, a cotton print handkerchief crossed upon her shoulders, the ends, back and front, confined under her check apron, and a mob-cap, tied round with black ribbon, the bow in front. What little hair could be seen was grey. A cleanly looking but timorous old woman, five or six years past seventy. To be turned out of the cottage in which she was born, and had lived all her life, seemed to her the very worst evil that could by possibility fall on her in this world. The old cling to their resting-places; and it is in the nature of age to exaggerate discomforts and misfortunes.

The kitchen-window at the back looked out upon a fair scene: it was just as pleasant as the front was dull: sunny plains near, Worcester in the distance. Also—morning after morning, as that old woman awoke, her eyes had fallen on the familiar Malvern hills (for she could catch a glimpse of them slantwise from her own front chamber), on the white dots of houses underneath, glistening in the early sun, and on the sloping vale of wood and dale descending in one great expanse.

"Lord, be good to me," she murmured, her hands crossed upon her bosom, that was beating so fast underneath the cotton handkerchief. "Let not my poor homestead be reft from me while I live!"

Her glance fell on her cherished out-door belongings; on the one pig in the sty; on the cow in the meadow, by whose produce, the milk, she was helped to exist; on the patch of cabbage and potato ground. The brook, winding along nearly close to her back-door (and which brook, perhaps, caused Sir Dene's difficulty in regard to taking the road a few yards farther off, as his son had suggested, for the water, widening into a stream lower down to feed the mill, might not be interfered with) was dancing in the sun, its gentle murmurings falling lightly on the ear. Time had been when that murmuring soothed her to peace; latterly, since this horrible fear had oppressed her, it seemed to suggest nothing but woe. Suddenly, another sound drowned it—a sharp knock, as with a stick, at the front door. Looking out of her kitchen, she saw Sir Dene.

And whether she stood on her head or her heels, the poor woman could not have told, had she lived to be a hundred. The sight scared her senses away. At the most favourable of times, and when she was a younger woman, she would have been struck into incapability at the presence of a great man like Sir Dene Clanwaring: regarding him now as a powerful enemy, it increased the feeling tenfold. Saying he had stepped back to speak to her, he walked, of his own accord, into the open small front room, or parlour, which had a sanded floor, and a bright painted tea-tray lodged against the side wall for ornament. She followed him in, courtesying and shaking visibly. Without any circumlocution, Sir Dene inquired whether she was in possession of the paper that she professed to be.

What with the abrupt question and its nature, what with her own startled fears and her innate timidity, Mrs. Barber behaved like a lunatic. She could get out no answer at all. When it did come, it was strangely hesitating, and given in a whisper.

She "believed" she had got such a paper somewhere—and she hoped "his honour" would not be hard upon her.

Sir Dene Clanwaring curled his lip. An honourable man himself, he regarded deception as the worst fault on earth. This old woman before him was shaking from head to foot; her speech and manner were alike uncertain, and he believed she was telling him a falsehood. From that moment he regarded the plea she had put forth, not as a mistake on her part, but a pure invention.

"Look here, Mrs. Barber, he said, sternly. "The road I purpose making will be of great benefit to myself and the public: it ought not to be stopped by any private interests. If you have the paper you speak of, bring it to me, and I will consider it—though I do not promise, and do not at present intend, mind, to be swayed by it. This is Tuesday: if, on Friday, I have not the paper before me, I shall give orders for the work to go on. Lady-Day will fall about a week afterwards; and I must request that you will be out of this on, or before, that day when it shall come. Good morning, ma'am."

She closed the door after him with trembling hands, when he had got to a proper distance. And then she sat down on the nearest seat—which happened to be a milk-pail turned bottom upwards—and wiped her face with her apron.

Sir Dene went on down the path. In a short while it widened considerably, and branched off into the open fields. Had the cottage stood as low down as this, there would have been no absolute necessity to raze it. But it stood where it did stand; nothing more could be made of it than that. Bearing to the right, after stepping over the little bridge, and passing his bailiff's house, which was nearly hidden amidst some trees, Sir Dene crossed a stile at the end of the field, and the village was before him, the church lying rather far beyond it. As he went by the village stocks (used often then), the village doctor, James Priar — a little man in spectacles, who looked ten years older than his real age, which was but thirty—crossed his path.

"Have you decided about the new road, Sir Dene?" the doctor asked, when they had talked for a minute or two.

"Yes; in a week's time from this you will see it begun," was the baronet's firm answer, as he pursued his way.

Just a minute we must take, to follow Drew, before closing the chapter. Not for any particular purpose as regards *him*, but to afford the reader a little more insight into the locality.

Mr. Jonathan Drew, then, when his master quitted him, and Geoffry Clanwaring had disappeared within his father's gates, betook himself about his business. He pursued the road to the right—in the opposite direction to that taken by Squire Arde—and soon came to some farm-houses and cottages. Some half mile, or more, from the gates of Beechhurst Dene, there stood back, on the left, a substantial stone house, its front facing Hurst Leet, with good gardens and farm buildings around it. This was Arde Hall. The road here was open, and the village underneath the hall (underneath, so to say, for the ground still sloped a little) could be more plainly seen. *Here* would have been the best spot to make the new road, if one must have been made at all: but Squire Arde, to whom the ground belonged, would as soon have thought of making a bull-run. Jonathan Drew came to a stand-still, as if tracing it out, for the road was what his thoughts were running upon.

"Ay, this 'ud ha' been the right track to hollow it through," ran his reflections. "Catch old Arde at it! When Sir Dene does it, though, Arde won't be back'ard to reap the benefit. A downright good move it'll be for Sir Dene's property. My old bones 'll be spared a bit, too, when I can ride straight up, 'stead o' going round, or trapesing it afoot. The Squire gets more niggardly as he grows older. Wonder who'll come in for his savings, and his estate? Shouldn't wonder but he'll leave all to a mad-house! I'll lay a crown on't. As to that cross-grained old stupe, Granny Barber, who's she, that she should put in her spoke again' the public good? One place is just as good as another, for the short time she'll want a place at all. One foot must be in the grave now, and t'other's hardly out on't."

With this, Mr. Drew brought his comments to a conclusion. There was a pathway down to the village from hence, just as there was nearer Beechhurst Dene; and he appeared undecided whether or not to take it. But finally he continued his way on the road. We need not follow him: the highway took a sudden turn just above here, and branched off, between rich pasture lands and homesteads large and small, far away from Hurst Leet.

CHAPTER II.

HAREBELL FARM.

In turning to the left, on emerging from the gates of Beechhurst Dene, the road continued to run in a tolerably straight line for about the third of a mile. It then branched off, almost at right angles, in two directions: that to the right being the continuance of the road; that to the left soon becoming nothing but a solitary lane. We may have occasion to follow the road later, so just now we will take the lane.

As dismal and shadowy a place at night, this Harebell Lane, as you would care to enter. On the right, lying back, stood a very moderately sized dwelling, with its fold-yard, ricks, and barns. This was Harebell Farm, in the occupancy of Robert Owen. Not far on, on the left, were two wooden gates side by side; one for carts, one for people on foot—they were the back or side entrance to Beechhurst Dene. The lane wound on, getting narrower and darker. Its banks were tolerably high, its overhanging trees shut out the daylight. But soon it widened considerably, in one part forming on the right hand a capacious curve, in which lay a rather deep pool, green with slime within and rushes without, and known as "Harebell Pond." A plantation of firs was fenced in on the bank rising immediately above it. Altogether, in spite of its space, this was the most dreary part of the lane. A few yards onwards, the lane, narrowing again, took a sharp turn to the right, and led direct to an inn of not too good reputation, called the Trailing Indian. The man keeping this inn was named Randolf Black. His brother, Moses Black, had died about a twelvemonth ago at Harebell Farm. They had come strangers to the place some years back, evidently moneyed men; at any rate, flush of ready money; and became tenants of Mr. Honeythorn. Moses took Harebell Farm; Randolf the solitary public-house, known then as the Plough, but which he re-named the Trailing Indian. After a few years Moses Black died. Randolf immediately applied to Sir Dene Clanwaring (who had just become his landlord through the purchase of Beechhurst Dene) to be allowed to take the farm as well as the inn; evincing unmistakable eagerness that it should be so. His character, however, had developed itself by this time, and Sir Dene, instructed on the point, refused. Robert Owen then presented himself to Sir Dene as a tenant for the farm, and to him it was leased. A little beyond the Trailing Indian, Harebell Lane was crossed by a high road, in fact, was terminated by it; and it was to the chance of the travellers on the highway turning aside to the inn, that the Trailing Indian trusted—or assumed to trust—for its support.

But we must go back to Harebell Farm. Entering at the small wooden gate (that, and the large one by its side, looked like twin brothers of those of Beechhurst Dene on the other side of the lane) and passing round by the barns, the ricks, and the fold-yard, we come to the front; for the dwelling faced the opposite way. The house was full of angles; the red brick of which it was built had become dark and dingy with age. A square patch of lawn and flower-garden was before the door; beyond it stretched out the expanse o meadow and corn-fields; with the tips of the Malvern hills bounding the horizon in the distance.

It was a day or two after the one mentioned in the last chapter; and the sky was as blue as then, and the sunshine as bright. In a homely room, partaking somewhat of the kitchen as well as of the parlour, save that cooking was not done in it, sat Mrs. Owen after dinner; a delicate-looking woman of low voice and gentle manners. She had on a warm gown of purple stuff, a large collar of muslin-work—the mode then—and white lace cap. Her feet rested on a footstool; her thin hands were busy with a heap of stockings, sorting those that wanted darning from those that did not. At the window, preparing to embroider a strip of fine cambric that was to form a portion of an infant's cap, sat Maria Owen— prettier without her bonnet even than with it. She wore a dress of light, checked green silk, its sleeves finished with a ruffle and a fall of lace just below the elbow. Her hair fell in glossy curls; her fresh, bright, dimpled face was something good to look upon. The floor was of red brick—squares—but a carpet covered it to the edge of the chairs; the furniture, plain, old, but of substantial mahogany, was polished to brightness. This was the parlour in ordinary use; there was a handsomer one, called the best parlour, for high-days and holidays. The terms dining-room and drawing-room were too grand for a farm-house in those unpretentious days.

Maria looked up to speak: some eagerness on her beautiful face. "Mamma, how long do you think I shall be working this cap?"

"That depends, my dear, upon the time you are able to give to it," was Mrs. Owen's answer. "You cannot neglect your necessary home occupations for fancy work."

"Oh, I know that. I won't neglect anything. I should like to get it done in two months."

"You have chosen so very intricate a pattern, Maria."

"But it will be all the more beautiful. I should not like Polly to be buying a best cap. Rather than that, I would tell her I am working this one: though I want it to be a surprise. I think you can give me some old lace for it, mamma."

"I shall see, when the cap's finished—whether it is worth it."

Standing by the fire, having come in during this colloquy, was a rather tall and somewhat hard-featured woman, with a strange look of perplexity on her sensible face. She wore the costume of the day, a print gown straight down to the ankles, white stockings, and tied shoes. This was Mary Barber: the faithful upper servant of the house—indeed, there was but one maid kept besides—but regarded more as a friend than a servant. Her features were well formed; her hair, worn in small curls on either side of her face beneath the cap-border, was of a bright brown yet. What Mary Barber's age was, could not be guessed from her appearance. At thirty years of age she had looked middle aged; she looked it still; she would probably look it for thirty years to come. Perhaps she was now not very much turned forty. Her mother was the old woman you saw skimming the milk.

"Have you done that bit of ironing, Mary?" asked Mrs. Owen.

"No, missis."

A shade of surprise passed over Mrs. Owen's features. But she said nothing.

"I can't settle to anything, missis; and that's the plain truth," burst forth the woman, flinging up her hands. "It is a cruel, wicked thing, that my poor old mother should come to this when she's close upon her grave."

"It is very grievous to be turned out of one's home," remarked Mrs. Owen, a sad, far off look in her lifted eyes.

"It's worse to have her word disputed: at least, I think it so. Jonathan Drew told me to my face last night, missis, that mother must be in her dotage to fancy she had ever had the paper."

"But you told me Mr. Drew knew of her having the paper."

"Mother says he knew of it; she always said he did. I wish Sir Dene Clanwaring had stayed where he was, afore he'd ever come here to trouble us."

"When once your mother's out of the place—if she has to go out—I daresay she won't mind it, Mary Barber," observed the young lady. "One home is as good as another."

"Much you know about it, Miss Maria! If you had to be turned out of your home, you'd tell a different tale."

"Why I have been turned out of it. We all have. That is, my father chose to leave. I can tell you, Mary Barber, I was sad enough at the time: but I like this one best now."

Mary Barber gave a rather significant sniff, as if she thought there might be some special cause for the young lady's liking the new one best.

"You don't understand it, Miss Maria. The young can't be expected to know how much old people become attached to their homes, so that they seem like just a part of themselves, and that it gets as hard to part with 'em as it is to part with a limb. I am sure of this," concluded Mary Barber emphatically, "that if mother is drove out, she'll go straight to the graveyard."

Maria dropped her cambric in consternation. "Do you mean that it would—kill her?" she asked in a low tone.

"Just as certainly, Miss Maria, as that the Lord's looking down upon us to note the injustice. And He *will* note it—if it's done."

"Hush, Mary," interposed her mistress. "Let us hope for the best. She may be let stay in it yet."

"Well, I'll hope it, missis, as long as I can: and I'll do my best to further it. But it won't be none the nearer coming to pass, for all that: I've not had these bad dreams lately for nothing. And poor mother, always in distress, is first and foremost in every one of 'em."

There was a short silence: the cuckoo clock against the wall ticking out lazily the minutes of the afternoon. Mary Barber resumed.

"If it warn't for that bit of ironing, missis—and I know it ought to be done when to-morrow's Friday and cleaning-day —I'd ask you to spare me."

"What for?" questioned Mrs. Owen.

"To go to Sir Dene Clanwaring," said the woman in a decisive tone, and both her auditors looked up in amazement. "When I was at mother's last night I told her to have one good last hunt for the paper, and to send it me this morning if she could find it. It hasn't come; which is a pretty safe sign that it's not found. But perhaps if we both go together to Sir Dene, she and me, and I speak up quietly for her to him—for she'd never have the courage to speak for herself— he may listen to us, and let her stay. The ironing——"

"I'll do the ironing for you, Mary," cried Miss Owen, starting up with sweet good nature. "I'll go and set about it now."

Mary Barber made ready for her errand; and came down stairs dressed in her best, surprising her mistress. A cinnamon-brown gown of soft cashmere, and grey twilled-silk shawl, with a handsome border of bright colours. She had had the shawl for half her life, and it looked as good as new now. The straw bonnet, of the "cottage" shape, had gay ribbons on it.

"You have dressed yourself up, Mary!"

"Yes, missis. If I had gone in my rags, Sir Dene mightn't have looked twice at me. Dress goes down with all the world. You'll wish me luck, ma'am."

But the word, rags, was merely a figure of speech. Mary Barber was always neat to a degree. And as she turned out at the back door, a folded handkerchief and her large cotton umbrella in her hand—an invariable appendage when she had on her best things, no matter how fine the weather—an old slipper and a joyous laugh came after her from Miss Maria.

She went along at a brisk pace, drawing on her gloves. In

the fold-yard she met the farmer. He regarded the dressed-up apparition with intense astonishment.

"Why, where are you off to, Mary, woman?"

She told him where. Mr. Owen shook his head a little, as if he had not much faith in the result of the expedition.

"You can try of course, Mary Barber. But great men like Sir Dene don't choose to be dictated to, or thwarted in any scheme they set their minds on."

"Sir Dene went as far as to say to mother that he'd deliberate upon it if the paper could be found, master," she observed, noting the signs.

"But the paper's not found. My opinion is, it would have been better never to have said anything about the paper, as it's not forthcoming."

"Why!—surely, master, you are not supposing that there never was any such paper?" she exclaimed.

"I feel as sure as you do that the paper was given," he answered; "I heard speak of it at the time. But Sir Dene is a stranger among us; and, to assert such a thing to him, and in the same breath to plead inability to produce the paper, gives a bad impression, you see."

Mr. Owen was in his usual working attire—for he took a very active part amidst his men: drab breeches and gaiters, and a drab coat. In his younger days, Robert Owen was fond of pleasure; had been what would now be called fast, seduced to it perhaps by his remarkable beauty. He would neglect his business to follow the hounds, to take a morning's shooting, to kill time, and spend money in many other ways. Debts had accumulated, and he had been ever since a crippled man in means. Instead of remaining a gentleman farmer, he had been obliged to degenerate into a working one, always pulled back by want of capital. None could regret that early improvidence more than he: but unfortunately regrets don't undo these things. He had taken this new farm, hoping to do better at it than he had at the old one, the lease of which was out. Mrs. Owen had been quite willing to leave the old home. They had lost their youngest son in it, Thomas, a very promising youth, under distressing circumstances; and while she stayed in it she could not forget her sorrow.

"Mary Barber will not succeed," was Mr. Owen's mental thought as he stroked his fine white beard in abstraction, and his eyes followed her through the gate to the lane. "The old woman has no doubt inadvertently destroyed that paper: and without it, she has no legal case."

"Well, mother, is it found?" began Mary Barber, entering her mother's home and kitchen without ceremony.

Mrs. Barber was bending over the fire, on which stood a large saucepan full of potato peelings that she was boiling for her fowls. She turned her head.

"Lawk a day!" was her exclamation as the vision of her smart daughter burst on her astonished view. "Whatever be you decked out for, like that, Mary? 'Taint the wake."

"No; but missis has gave me a holiday," replied Mary, sitting down on the wooden chair, which she dusted first with a cloth. "Have you found the paper, mother?"

Poor Mrs. Barber shook her head. "I've looked for it till I can look no longer: above stairs and below. I looked till I went to bed, Mary; where I got no sleep all night; and at daylight I was up, looking again. It'll wear me out, child; it'll wear me out."

Lifting the saucepan on the hob, lest its contents should burn whilst she ceased stirring, she dropped on a low wooden stool, and hid her face in her hands. Mary Barber was looking more cross than compassionate.

"To leave the place where I've lived all my life! To see my bits o' furniture turned out, sold perhaps—for where am I to put 'em?—these very pots and pans even" (ranging her eyes on the hanging tins) "that I've kept as bright as silver! My poor cow, my fowls, the pig in its sty—Mary, I'd rather the gentlefolks would kill me outright."

"Now look here, mother," said Mary—who never wasted the slightest time or sympathy upon sentiment. "That paper is in the house, or ought to be; and if it is, it must be found. First of all—where did you put it?"

"Where did I put it?" repeated Mrs. Barber, rather listlessly, for just at the moment her thoughts were running on abstract matters. "When I was looking in the press this morning—and *that*'ll have to go along o' the other things, Mary! Oh, woe's me!"

"Just carry your mind back, mother"—with a slight stamp of the umbrella—"to that back time when it was given you. Who brought it here?"

"Who brought it here?—why, Squire Honeythorn himself. He came in and sat down in this kitchen in that very chair of your poor father's. I remember being vexed because

Harebell Farm.

I'd not got on my best black with the crape bottom to it; a bombazine it was, three shillings a yard. A grand dress-maker at Worcester made it, and——"

"About Mr. Honeythorn, mother," interrupted Mary Barber, bringing her up.

"Well, he came in—I can see his pigtail now, hanging over the back o' the chair. The money for the house and land was paid over to Lawyer Haynes, he said, and he had brought to me himself the promise in his own hand that I should not be turned from the place while I lived. A great rogue that Haynes was! He buttered his own pocket smartly while he settled with your poor father's creditors."

"Mother, there's the afternoon slipping on. Where did you put the paper then?"

"In my best tea-caddy," said the old woman, promptly. "All my papers of consequence be kept in there; and nobody has never had the key of it but me. That same day, after I'd locked it up, Jonathan Drew looked in to say the money was paid—not knowing his master had been here before him. I told him of the promise I had got, and he said it was no news to him. Squire Honeythorn had told him he should give it."

"Have you seen the paper since then?"

"Yes, many a time. I've looked at it when I've unlocked the caddy for other papers."

"Will you let me look, mother? Maybe, it's there still."

Mrs. Barber was a little offended at this, asking her daughter if she thought she had no eyesight; but finally consented. The tea-caddy, a japanned one, had stood on the parlour mantelpiece, its middle ornament, as long as Mary could remember. Mary's keen grey eyes searched every paper—chiefly consisting of the half-yearly receipts for her rent—but the missing paper was not there.

"You must have put it somewhere else yourself, mother."

"I suppose I must. There was a great talk one winter of the highwaymen being about, and I know I got in a worrit over my caddy o' papers, and hid 'em away in places. But I always thought I put 'em all back again later."

"Well, there seems nothing for it but to beg grace of Sir Dene Clanwaring, as we've got no proof to show of any right. And that's where I am going, mother, and what I've made myself smart for. You must come with me."

But the astounding proposition put Mrs. Barber into a

tremor—go to Sir Dene Clanwaring!—and Mary found it was of no use urging it. So she departed alone. In the narrow pathway, almost close to the cottage, stood Jonathan Drew and a couple of men; the latter with a measuring-chain in their hands. Mrs. Barber saw them from her door, and turned as white as death.

"What be you a doing?" demanded Mary Barber, as she was passing them.

"Only a-measuring out o' the ground, a bit," said Jonathan Drew.

"For the new hollow they talk of?"

"There's nothing else we should be a measuring of it for," was his retort. And Mary Barber walked on.

Crossing the high road, she entered the gates, and proceeded up the avenue between the fine old trees. Beechhurst Dene was an ancient red brick mansion, roomy, old-fashioned, comfortable, and withal handsome both outside and in. It stood in the midst of its park, ornamental gardens immediately around it. Mary Barber had been there more than once in Mr. Honeythorn's time, and knew it well. Avoiding the grand front entrance, she bore round to her right, to the familiar one used by the servants, tenants, and, in fact, often by the family themselves. Just on this side, the look-out of the house seemed confined, so many trees and shrubs were crowded about. A pathway led direct to the gate in Harebell Lane: and Mary Barber would have made that her way of entrance at first, but for having to go to her mother's. A parlour, with a bay window opening to the ground, faced this way, and Mary saw Sir Dene sitting in it. Knocking at the open side door with her umbrella, she asked a footman if she could be allowed to see his master. The servant did not happen to know her. He told Sir Dene a lady was asking to see him: "leastways a respectable-looking woman, that might be a farmer's wife."

Sir Dene admitted her. But when she introduced herself as Mary Barber, and he found she was the widow Barber's daughter, come to bother him about the new cutting, he felt anything but pleased. Something had occurred that afternoon to vex Sir Dene: it had nothing to do with the matter in question; but it served to put him out of temper. However, he was civil enough to ask her to sit down, and did not refuse to hear her. It was a small room, the floor covered with matting: Sir Dene chiefly received his tenants here, and other business people.

Mary Barber sat bolt upright on the extreme edge of the chair: her folded handkerchief and umbrella in her hand, her back to the window. Sir Dene was on the other side of the table, near the fire, his open desk before him. He listened to what she had to say, without once interrupting her.

"Do you think this paper, that you talk of, ever had any existence?" he asked then—and his tone bore a kind of suppressed scorn, which caused Mary Barber's hard cheeks to flush.

"I am sure it had, sir."

"Did you ever see it, Mrs. Barber?"

"No, sir; never," was the straightforward answer. "My mother did not show it to me. And I never heard that my sister saw it, either," she added, in her honesty. "Neither of us was at home then. Father's affairs took a good while to arrange after his death; and before they were settled, my sister Hester and I had gone out to relieve mother of our keep and make our own way in the world. I went to service; Hester married."

"Does she—your sister—profess to remember anything of this promise?"

"She has been dead some years, sir."

"Don't you think it a strange thing that your mother should not have kept more carefully a paper of the importance she appears to attach to this?"

"My opinion is, sir, she has kept it too carefully, and put it into some out-of-the-way place for safety, that she can't now remember," was Mary Barber's independent answer. "There's no doubt she was scared with fear because of the highwaymen; and the best of us are liable to forgetfulness, especially when we grow old."

"I cannot say more than I have done," cried Sir Dene, impatiently. "Produce the paper, and its merits shall be examined. I am in ignorance as to what weight it carried, or was intended to carry. Of course, if it conferred the right *legally* that you seem to fancy—which I think almost an impossibility—we must submit it to a lawyer, and take his opinion; but I strongly suspect it was not legally worth the paper it was written upon."

"Mr. Honeythorn would not trifle with my mother, sir."

"As to Mr. Honeythorn, I don't doubt that his bare word, passed, would have been good for him to act upon to the end of his life, without need of document to confirm it. But what bound him could never be meant to bind me. No, ma'am, nor be expected to, in any sort of reason."

The manners in those past days were far more courtly than they are now. Sir Dene Clanwaring thought nothing of addressing Mary Barber as "ma'am," and did not do it ironically.

"I'm afraid you'll go on with this dreadful thing, sir," she said, her grey eyes fixed upon him.

"Dreadful thing! It will be a very good thing."

"Not for my mother. She has been a good woman, sir; her cup of sorrow brimfull."

"I should say she must be an obstinate one, Mrs. Barber. She would be as well in another cottage as this—and there are plenty to be had for the seeking."

"She cannot live long, sir," pleaded Mary Barber. "She——"

"As to that, she may live as long as I," was the interruption. "She is a tough, healthy, hearty woman, and may last for ten or fifteen, ay, for twenty years to come."

"She is in her seventy-sixth year, Sir Dene. Oh, sir, spare her! Don't turn her out to die. I'd make bold to ask, sir, how you would like to be turned out of a home where you'd lived all your days, when you shall be as old as she is. She was born in it; it was her father's before her; and she brought up her children in it, Hester and me. Sir, I know you are one of the high gentlefolks of the land, and it's not becoming of me to dare to speak to you in this free way. Heaven knows, I'd only do it for poor mother's sake."

"I thought the property belonged to your father," observed Sir Dene, on whom the pleading cry appeared to make no impression.

"No, sir; to my mother; she was Hester Drew. When she married Thomas Barber she went home to her house, which was reversing the order of things in ordinary. Father had nothing of his own, and he was somehow a bad manager; not fortunate. When he died, and it was found affairs were bad, there seemed nothing for it but selling the property, so that folks should be paid, and my sister and I turned out at once. Squire Honeythorn was sorry for mother, and he gave her the promise we tell of."

"Is your mother any relation to Drew, my bailiff?" asked Sir Dene, noting the coincidence of the name.

"His father and mother's father were second or third cousins, sir—nothing to speak of."

"Has your mother any income of her own?"

"Not a penny, sir. She sacrificed all she had to pay father's debts. The sale of her milk and poultry meets her rent, perhaps a bit over; and she has 'tatoes and other garden stuff; and her pig, which makes bacon to last her the year. And for the rest, I help her to a bit o' tea and that, and Hester's family to other trifles. We shall never let her starve, sir, whatever betides."

"At her age she ought to be glad at the prospect of being relieved from the care of a cow and pig," remarked Sir Dene.

"It is her great pleasure to be active, sir; the back is generally fitted to the burden. Mother is hale and hearty yet."

"She *is*," pointedly acquiesced Sir Dene. "I have just said so, Mrs. Barber."

He looked at his watch. Mary Barber took the hint and rose. Sir Dene politely opened the door for her.

She stood still, and curtsied to him. And then—as she was actually passing out—turned round, and clasped her gloved hands in a beseeching attitude, holding the great umbrella by one little finger.

"Oh, sir, I hope you'll please to think kindly of it! I could hardly pray harder to God—as He hears and knows—than I'm praying for this boon to you. She has no one living to take her part but me, or to speak a word for her. Be merciful to her, sir, in this her old age, and let her be! She may not stand in your way long. God will be sure to reward you for it, Sir Dene! and she will pray for blessings on you every night and morning of the few poor years of her remaining life."

Hard, matter-of-fact Mary Barber had never spoken such words in her days; never perhaps been so near to be moved by emotion. After they came forth she stood a moment looking at him, expecting perhaps some hopeful answer. But none came. Sir Dene Clanwaring steeled alike his ear and his heart.

"I am sorry this should have occurred, Mrs. Barber. In entering upon a fresh estate, one has to look I suppose for disputes and vexations. If I gave in to this exaction, others would no doubt arise: therefore, I must make a stand in my own defence. Good afternoon, ma'am."

Mary Barber, feeling that she had bitterly failed, went

straight back to her mother's cottage. There, her bonnet and shawl taken off, her gown-skirt and sleeves turned up, and the biggest apron tied round her that the place afforded, she instituted a thorough search for the missing paper. And found it not.

But Sir Dene Clanwaring, even while he gave her the last decisive answer, said to himself in his heart of hearts that he would sleep upon it. As he did.

And a very heavy sleep it was. For he dropped off the instant he got into bed, and was woke up in the morning by his hot water. During the process of shaving, he decided that Mrs. Barber, née Drew, was what his bailiff, her distant relative, was fond of calling her—an obstinate, cantankerous, troublesome old woman, who must not be allowed to stand in the light of himself and her neighbours.

And that the road should be made.

CHAPTER III.

MARIA OWEN.

It was a wild night. Clouds chased each other across the sky, darkening the face of the moon; the wind dashed along in fitful gusts with a rush and a whirl, dying away in wailing moans.

Stealing up Harebell Lane with steps that seemed to fear their own echo, went two men, carrying between them a bulky parcel, to all appearance remarkably heavy for its size. They had smock frocks thrown over their ordinary attire, and hats slouched low on their faces. A casual passer-by would have taken them for labourers, tramping home with tired feet after a day's ploughing: a keener observer, if accustomed to live amidst rustics, might have seen how uneasily those smock frocks sat, and divined by instinct that they were assumed for a purpose.

"Bear your own weight o' the load, Geach, and be hanged to ye," growled one, who was short and compact, to his taller companion.

"And don't I bear it? You be shot!" carelessly retorted the other, whose accent was somewhat superior.

The parcel was more like a bundle, its outside covering of dirty canvas, and might have been supposed to contain garments, rather untidily rolled up together. In the stout cord that confined it were left two loops at either end, by which the men carried it.

"Change hands."

They had gone a few paces further when Geach said this, and were close to the gates leading into Beechhurst Dene. Voices and steps, as if advancing from the Dene, at this moment became audible; and the men, who were in the act of changing hands, started. A moment's pause to listen: then Geach pushed his comrade into the ditch under the hedge, without the smallest compunction, and the bundle upon him.

"Keep dark for your life, Robson!" he breathed. "Hide it, man; hide it. Hang that moon!"

The offending moon, left bright by a departing cloud, was not apostrophised by any so innocent a word as "hang;" but the language really used by these men could not be allowed to appear in polite literature. Possibly believing he was too tall for any hedge or ditch to conceal him, Geach noiselessly leaped to the other side of the lane, and then went on with a bent, sauntering gait, whistling a rustic song. Two people emerged from the grounds of Beechhurst Dene.

"Good night t'ye, master," he said in the Worcestershire tone.

"Good night, my man," heartily responded Geoffry Clanwaring, who made one; the other being Simmons, his father's young gamekeeper. And they passed down the lane out of sight and hearing.

With some grumbling and grunting, the man called Robson got out of the ditch: which, fortunately for him, was tolerably dry. Taking the parcel between them as before, they stole on, Robson growling still.

"Tell ye what it is, Geach," he muttered. "This here lane ain't the place it used to be. What with these here new folks at the Dene and their crowd o' servants, and that dratted farmer in Mosy Black's farm, I'll be smothered if I call it safe."

"Where's the danger?" airily responded Geach.

"The danger! Take to-night. If them two had pounced upon us afore we'd time to get it away, they might ha' turned curious eyes on it. One was Sir Dene's son; t'other was the keeper. I know'd 'em by their voices."

"Well? They'd have seen a bundle of—anything—done up with apparent looseness, and two poor tired labourers, tramping home to their night's rest. What of that? Before there can be any danger, there must be suspicion, Robson:

and I'll take my oath there's none of that abroad yet. You were always a croaker."

"I don't care; I'm right," grumbled Robson. "The way here is not the lone way it was; and danger may come."

"Better hold your tongue just now. There may be ears behind that hedge of Owen's."

It was good advice, and they went on in silence. By the pond, Geach again demanded to change hands. He was a very tall, up-right, and apparently strong young man; yet his arms seemed to get tired quickly. Robson remarked upon it.

"I had a bad fall a week ago, and my bones haven't done aching yet," explained Geach in a whisper.

What with the natural gloominess of the lane, and the densely black cloud covering the moon, it had been for some minutes safely dark. There occurred a sudden change to light as they were changing hands: the moon shone out in all her brightness, causing the open part, where they now stood, to be almost as light as day. Robson, his mind not altogether at ease and his eyes roving everywhere, suddenly saw some object leaning over the fence above the pond. Was it a man? Starting back a step involuntarily, he hissed forth a low signal of caution. Geach was always prepared. He pushed the bundle entirely into the arms of his companion—who slightly staggered under the unexpected weight—and began whistling again, as they walked on like two unconcerned rustics.

Yes, it was a man. And one they recognised. There shone the seal-skin cap, tipped with white fur, and the whiter beard of Robert Owen. He was evidently looking at them; watching them openly. They would have gone on, pretending not to see him, but that a rather sharp cough took Mr. Owen at the same moment; and they could not assume not to hear. Geach stopped his whistling, and turned to speak.

"If ye please, master, can ye tell us whether we be in the right road for Bransford?"

"For Bransford? Why, that's a long way off," returned Mr. Owen. "You'll have to wind about a bit, my men, and traverse some cross-country before you get to Bransford. Where d'ye come from?"

"Worcester last."

"Worcester! Then, why did you not take the Bransford road direct—if it's Bransford you want?"

"Missed our way. Thank ye, master."

Resuming his whistling, and giving a pull to his hat

by way of salutation, Geach walked on. Robson had not stopped.

Mr. Owen stretched himself over the fence to look after them, until they were hidden by the winding of the lane. Geach knew, almost by intuition, that they were being watched. A very emphatic curse broke from his lips.

"What did I tell ye?" whispered Robson. "The Trailing Indian's not as safe as it was. It may have to shift its quarters."

"Shift its quarters be stifled!" retorted Geach. "Black can take care of himself; and of you too."

"Well, it's a new thing to be watched like this in Harebell Lane. I don't stomach it, Geach; I can tell ye that."

A short while, and they arrived at that solitary hostelrie: a low, two-storied old house with gables, and a dangling sign-board: it was on the left-hand side of the lane as they walked up. The turnpike road, that ran crossways and terminated the lane, was within view. It has already been said that the Trailing Indian professed to derive its support from chance travellers passing up and down it.

Save for one candle, put to stand in a casement window, the inn presented a dark appearance—which for an inn looked most inhospitable. Entering the yard, letting the parcel fall gently on the ground, Geach gave three distinct knocks on the side door, and then tapped at the window. The candle was removed from the casement, and a man's head came out.

"Who's that knocking at my window?"

"Me and Robson. Open the door, Randy."

Mr. Black hastened to do so. Amidst his friends—and foes too—his Christian name was familiarly converted into Randy: it came easier to the lips than "Randolf." He was a tall swarthy man of five or six and thirty, with a sinister look in his dark face. Catching up the bundle in his arms, he led the way through passages to a remote room, closed in with shutters: not the room of general entertainment, one entirely private to himself. The men took off their smock frocks, and the landlord called about him. A little woman, very pretty once, but pale, sad-eyed, and struck into meekness by terror long ago, came forward, in answer to his call. It was Mrs. Black.

"Get supper at once—pork chops and mashed potatoes; and put a good log on the parlour fire," said Black, imperiously. "Don't be a month over it, now: and come and knock at the door when supper's ready."

Save for an ostler, who slept over the stables, and was on very close terms with his master, no servant was kept. The ostler would give help at odd jobs sometimes, otherwise Mrs. Black had to do all the domestic work. It was not over-burthening in a general way; bonâ fide travellers at the inn were few and far between. For all the profit they brought, its master might have starved.

The inn had a bad reputation, though the suspicions cast on it were but of a vague nature. Stout sailors and boatmen occasionally made their way to it from barges coming up the Severn, striking across the country from the river by night; and it was thought their inflated appearance told of concealed brandy-skins and tobacco. Smuggling was largely pursued in those days, and brought back its profits. It is possible that Mr. Black dealt in other things: that his house had some safe hiding-places in it, where booty, the proceeds of robberies in town and country, might be stowed away in safety until the hue-and-cry after it was over. These men, at any rate, sitting round the table to-night, were neither sailors nor boatmen. A tale was current in the neighbourhood that a traveller had disappeared at this inn in a very mysterious manner. It was a pedlar, tramping the country with rather valuable wares. That he had called in at the Trailing Indian for refreshment one summer evening, there was no doubt, intending afterwards to proceed on his way to Worcester by moonlight. The landlord, and the ostler, and Mrs. Black, all declared that he had so proceeded: and there was no proof at all that he had not. However it may have been, the pedlar had not turned up at Worcester; he had never been seen or heard of since.

There was only one candle on the table; and, that, of tallow; but the articles Mr. Black was feasting his eyes upon, shone as brightly as though they had been illuminated by lime-light. Massive articles of solid silver were they; some few of gold: no wonder, packed compactly, that the two porters had found them somewhat heavy. Geach was a fair, nice-looking young man, his features small, all but the nose; that was high, shapely, and prominent. He was born to fill a better station, but evil courses had brought him down in the world. Robson had a close and contracted expression of countenance. They were telling of the encounter with farmer Owen.

"It won't do, you know, Black, to be watched by him,"

cried Robson, savagely. "If he is to pass his nights haunting the lane, the sooner the Trailing Indian knows it the better."

"I wish Sir Dene Clanwaring had been sunk before he refused to lease me the farm in Mosy's place!" exclaimed Black. "He is going to cut a hollow somewhere now to bring up waggons and carts quicker from Hurst Leet—smother him! As if we wanted more ways up here!"

"That's not much, Randy—a cutting. Owen *is*."

"Owen had better keep himself and his eyes for his own affairs; he may find himself in the wrong box if he attempts to look after mine," was Mr. Randy's comment. "The outcry's pretty hot, I hear at Worcester."

Geach laughed. "Nothing less than a gang from London, they say."

"I can't think how he could have been standing," resumed Robson, presently, returning to the subject of farmer Owen —for the encounter seemed to have made a most unpleasant impression on him. "The fence is right against the trees."

"No it's not," said Black; "there's a strip o' pathway. And my brother Mosy was fool enough to make it as a short cut to the two-acre meadow. Owen has got some sheep there; and now that the lambing season's on, he or the shepherd is everlastingly out with 'em at night. One or t'other on 'em's sure to be out."

"But why need he halt in the pathway and push his ugly beard over the fence to watch the lane?" contended Robson. "What's it for, Randy?"

"How the devil should I know?" retorted Randy. "Here; lend a hand, you two."

The articles had been placed in a box. Black then opened a closet in the room, which had apparently no other egress, pushed up one of its panels, and got through the aperture, Robson and the box disappearing after him. Soon after they were back again, and the closet door and panel had been made fast, Mrs. Black knocked to say supper was waiting in the parlour. And the three went out to it.

We must return to Geoffry Clanwaring. Passing down the lane with the gamekeeper, seeing nothing and suspecting nothing of the man hidden in the ditch, he had reached the end of the lane, when two people were observed approaching; one of whom was laughing gaily. A silvery, sweet laugh; that a little stirred the pulses of Mr. Geoffry. It was Maria

Owen's. She had been spending the afternoon at Hurst Leet, and was returning attended by the house servant—a stout red-checked and red-armed damsel, named Joan. Maria wore her gipsy cloak, its hood of scarlet drawn round her face and her pretty curls.

Geoffry Clanwaring turned back with Miss Owen; the keeper pursued his way onwards, straight down the road. Arrived at Mr. Owen's gate, they stood to talk, and Joan went in.

"Mamma was to have gone to tea with me, but she did not feel well enough this afternoon; so they sent Joan to bring me home," explained Maria, chattering and blushing, and her heart beating wildly for love of the handsome young man before her. He could see the rosy dimples in the moonlight, he could see the sweet eyes, cast down beneath the gaze of his. Every fibre within him thrilled in answer, for she was more to him than—ay, almost than heaven.

Love is no respecter of persons; the fitness of things never enters into the god's calculations. Between Geoffry Thomas Clanwaring, the baronet's son, and Maria Owen, the obscure farmer's daughter, there lay miles of that exacting gulf called social position; nevertheless, they had contrived to lapse into a passion for each other, than which nothing could be more pure and ardent. Part them, and the whole world would be to each as a blank wilderness.

Sir Dene had three sons. The heir was entirely a fine gentleman, living chiefly in London, amidst his clubs and his gaieties and his friends in high life. The youngest was a soldier, already married, and serving in India. Geoffry, the second, remained at home, looking after things on the estate, making himself quite as useful as Drew the bailiff did. Geoffry might generally be seen in velveteen shooting-coat and leather or beaver leggings, tramping about on foot, or riding on horseback, always, however, busy. It was whispered by Gander, a servant who had lived with them for years, that Sir Dene liked him the best of all his sons. The heir was cold and haughty; the soldier improvident and cross-tempered; Geoffry alone had never given anything but duty and affection to his father. Out and about the land daily, it was thus he had formed the acquaintance of Robert Owen, and thence of the family. It had become quite an ordinary matter now for Geoffry Clanwaring to run in and out of Harebell Farm at will.

"What were you laughing at, Maria?" he asked, as they stood there at the gate. "You and Joan?"

"I was laughing at Joan. She had been telling me a tale of a sweetheart she had in her last place. It was the carter. He gave her up because she threw a can of buttermilk over him in a passion. Joan says he was only angry because he happened to have on a clean smock frock · had it been a dirty one, he'd not have minded."

Geoffry laughed.

"Mr. Clanwaring, I must go in. Mamma will be sending after me."

"I saw George Arde to-day," he resumed, paying no attention to the hint—except that he held her hand a little tighter—for it lay in his.

"Oh, did you. Where?"

"At Worcester. I went in about the sale of some barley, and met him in High Street."

"Did he say anything about Mary?"

"No. Except that she was very delicate just now."

"Polly is always delicate."

"When are you going over there next, Maria?"

"I don't know," she replied in a low, half-conscious tone. For the truth was, that whenever she did go to Worcester, Mr. Geoffry invariably contrived to be there on the self-same day.

Thus they lingered, talking of one thing and another, oblivious of the lapse of time, and Maria continuing to run the risk of being sent for. No one came, however, for the best of all possible reasons—that it was not known she was there. Mrs. Owen and Mary Barber were at work together in the parlour, and Joan did not disturb them to tell of her entrance. The girl, experienced in the matter of sweethearts herself, knew what was what. But the time was really getting on.

"There has been an audacious robbery of gold and silver plate at one of the silversmiths," observed Geoffry, suddenly thinking of it. "Worcester was up in arms: the Bow Street runners are down."

"What a pity!" she cried. "I hope the thieves won't come near us. Indeed, Mr. Clanwaring, I must go indoors."

Placing her hand within his arm, he walked with her up the path and round to the front, slowly enough. At the garden gate between the tall holly hedge they halted again.

There was not the slightest necessity for this: it was not the way indoors; took them, in short, a few steps out of it. Perhaps the truth was, that one was just as ready to make an excuse for lingering as the other. The garden shone out fitfully in the night, now bright, now dark: just now it was very dark, for the moon again lay under a large black cloud. Not five minutes since, another large black one had but cleared away.

Very dark. It might have been for that reason that Geoffry Clanwaring, leaning forward on the gate, threw his protecting arm round Maria, and drew her close to him.

"I *must* go in," she whispered.

For answer, he turned up the sweet face, so lovely in its frilled scarlet hood, and took a kiss from the cherry lips. A kiss; and then another.

"Oh, Mr. Clanwaring!"

"Now you shall go in, my darling—as it must be."

The moon came out of her canopy bright as gold, flooding the garden and trees and house with her light. There ensued another minute of lingering. It was broken in upon by Mr. Owen himself. He saw his daughter run in; he saw Geoffry standing there: and he seized on the opportunity to say what it had been in his mind to say for some few days past. Namely: that, though his house was pleased and proud to receive the visits of his landlord's son, there must be no approach to intimacy with Maria.

"I understand," said Geoffry, after a pause. "Would you object to me, Mr. Owen?"

"Somebody else would, sir; and that's quite enough for me," was Robert Owen's answer.

"Who else would?"

"Mr. Clanwaring, you must know who, better than I can tell you. Your father, Sir Dene."

"Maria is one that a prince might be proud to wed," said Geoffry, in his foolish impulsiveness.

Upon that, Mr. Owen spoke; and very sensibly. Unequal marriages never did good in the end, he said. Moreover, he could not, and would not, have both his daughters wedding above their proper station.

"Your eldest daughter has not wedded above her station," said Geoffry, resentfully.

"Indeed but she has, sir. You must see it for yourself."

"I'm sure George Arde is poor enough, Mr. Owen."

"Too poor. But he's a gentleman. And—suppose he were ever to come into Arde Hall? Not that there is much chance of it."

"Not a bit of chance. Old Arde says he shall never leave it to either kith or kin—the old skinflint! It would be a jolly good thing for George Arde and his wife if they got it."

"Well, I had rather Polly had married in her own station—a farmer say, as I am. But, in regard to you, Mr. Clanwaring, there must be no thought of anything of the kind. Your father would never forgive you."

"If my father approved, would you approve, Mr. Owen?"

"Pardon me, sir, but that's a useless question to go into. Sir Dene never would approve."

"You can answer it for my own satisfaction," returned Geoffry, his pleasant, good-natured eyes going out beseechingly to the farmer's. "If things were smoothed for it in other quarters, and Sir Dene were willing, do you think well enough of me to give me Maria?"

"Yes, I do," was the honest answer. "I like you very much. But that's all beside the question, Mr. Clanwaring, as you well know, and we must go back to the starting point. There must be no thought of intimacy between you and Maria. If I saw an approach to anything of the sort, sir, I should feel that it lay in my duty to Sir Dene to forbid you my premises."

"Very well; perhaps you are right," answered Geoffry, slowly coming to reason. "I confess that I do like Maria, very much; but I should not care to bring trouble upon anybody; least of all, on my father. Time may alter things. Good night, Owen."

"You are not offended with me for speaking, Mr. Clanwaring?" said the farmer, as he met Geoffry's offered hand.

"Offended! Indeed, no. You have only done what a straightforward man would do. Good night."

"Good night, sir."

Geoffry Clanwaring set off on the run. He had told the gamekeeper to "go on slowly," and he would catch him up. They had a matter of business in hand to-night in the village—of which he had lost sight while lingering with Maria. At the corner which bounded the lane he halted for a moment, half inclined to turn along the road to the right and dash down the pathway opposite the Dene gates. But, as he knew the keeper had taken the long road—for he had to call at the farrier's, and might be waiting there—he went straight on.

A rather lonely, rather narrow, and very hilly road, this. It was but a cross-country road at best; no stage-coaches passed on it. Geoffry went up one hill and down another; the way insensibly winding round always towards the village. In fact, to go from a given point, say the entrance to Arde Hall, right round to Hurst Leet, the highway described a horse-shoe, a circuit of two miles. At the corner of the lower turning, which brought the village straight onwards in the distance, stood the premises of the farrier and horse doctor. Cole was at work in the shed; and Geoffry went to it.

"Has Simmons been here, Cole?"

"Yes, sir; about half an hour ago. He called in to say that one of the horses be ill, and I am to be up the first thing in the morning."

"Mind you are. It's Sir Dene's hunter. Good night."

He went straight on to the village now, passing sundry dwellings, most of them labourers', on either side of the road, and arrived at Hurst Leet. Simmons, however, was not to be found anywhere, and Geoffry Clanwaring had had a fruitless walk.

But it has afforded us an opportunity of seeing the road that Sir Dene was waging warfare with. That he was projecting this new cutting to avoid—to be called henceforward, as the reader will find, Dene Hollow.

CHAPTER IV.

AN EPISODE IN THE LIFE OF MARY BARBER.

THIS chapter contains an experience that may almost be called the chief event of Mary Barber's life. *She* considered it as such. It occurred some years before the epoch we are at present writing of, and was essentially supernatural. In fact, a ghost story. Not one born of the fancy or imagination, but real—at least so far as the actors and witnesses in the circumstances connected with it believed. The facts were very peculiar: for my own part I do not see how they could be reasonably accounted for, or explained away. The details are given with simple truth, and just as they happened.

The Owens were not then living at Harebell Farm, but at some few miles distance across country, in the rural village of Hallow. Their dwelling house was a commodious one: and Mary Barber the ruling power in it, under her mistress. Mrs. Owen, delicate then, as always, was not capable of active, bustling management.

One Monday afternoon in September, Mrs. Owen was seated alone in her parlour, mending soiled muslins and laces in preparation for the next day's wash, when the door opened and Mary Barber came in, neat as usual, superior in appearance, inexpensive though her attire was, to an ordinary servant. She must have been tolerably young then —say, six-and-thirty, perhaps—and yet she looked middle-aged.

"I've come to ask a fine thing, mistress, and I don't know what you'll say to me," she began, in her strong country accent. "I want holiday to-morrow."

"Holiday!" repeated Mrs. Owen, in evident surprise. "Why, Mary, to-morrow's washing-day."

"Ay, it is; nobody knows it better than me. But here's my sister come over about this wedding of Richard's. Nothing will do for 'em but I must go to it. She's talking a lot of nonsense; saying it should be the turning point in our coolness, and the healer of dissensions, and she won't go to church unless I go. As to bringing in dissensions," slightingly added Mary Barber, "she's thinking of the two boys, not of me."

"Well, Mary, I suppose you must go."

"I'd not, though, missis, but that she seems to make so much of it. I never hardly saw Hester in such earnest before. It's very stupid of her. I said, from the first, I'd not go. What do them grand Laws want with me—or Richard either? No, indeed! I never thought they'd get me to it—let alone the wash!"

"But you do wish to go, don't you, Mary?" returned Mrs. Owen, scarcely understanding.

"Well, you see, now Hester's come herself, and making this fuss, I hardly like to hold out. They'd call me more pigheaded than they have done—and that needn't be. So, mistress, I suppose you must spare me for a few hours. I'll got things forward before I start in the morning, and be back early in the afternoon; I shan't want to stop with 'em, not I."

"Very well, Mary; we shall manage, I dare say. Ask Mrs. Pickering to come in and see me before she goes. Perhaps she'll stay to tea with me."

"Not she," replied Mary; "she's all cock-a-hoop to get back again. Richard and William are coming home early, she says."

Mary Barber shut the door; she had stood holding the handle in her hand all the time; and returned to the room she had left—a great barn of a room, where the children were accustomed to play. Mary was regarded more as a friend than a servant, but she did the work altogether of any two. She was generally called "Mary Barber," one of the children being named Mary. On Mrs. Owen's sick days, Mary Barber would shut herself up with the children in the remote barn of a room, and keep them in quietness, leaving the work to be done without her.

Mrs. Pickering was older by some years than Mary. The two sisters were much alike, tall, sensible-looking, hard-featured women, with large, well formed foreheads, and honest, steady grey eyes. But Mrs. Pickering looked ill and care-worn. She wore a very nice violet silk gown, a dark Paisley shawl, and Leghorne bonnet. Mary Barber had been regarding the attire in silent condemnation; except her one best gown, *she* had nothing but cottons.

"Well, Hester, the mistress says she'll spare me," was her announcement. "But as to getting over in time to go to church, I don't know that I can do it. There'll be a thousand and one things to do to-morrow morning, and I shall stop and put forward."

"You might get over in time, if you would, Mary."

"Perhaps I might, and perhaps I mightn't," was the plain answer. "It's a five weeks' wash; and the missis is as poorly as she can be. Look here, Hester—it's just this: I don't want to come. I *will* come, as you make such a clatter over it, and I'll eat a bit o' their wedding cake, and drink a glass o' wine to their good luck; but as to sitting down to breakfast—or whatever the meal is—with the Laws and their grand company, it's not to be supposed I'd do it. I know my place better. Neither would the Laws want me to."

"They said they'd welcome you."

"I daresay they did!" returned Mary, with a sniff; "but they'd think me a fool if I went, for all that. I shouldn't mind seeing 'em married, though, and I'll get over to the church, if I can. Anyway, I'll be in time to drink health to 'em before they start on their journey."

Mrs. Pickering rose. She knew it was of no use saying more. She wished good-bye to the children, went to Mrs. Owen's parlour for a few minutes, absolutely declining refreshment, and then prepared to walk home again. Mary attended her to the door.

"It's fine to be you—coming out in your puce silk on a week-day!" she burst out with, her tongue refusing to keep silence on the offending point any longer.

"I put it on this afternoon because I was expecting Mrs. Law," was the inoffensive answer. "She sent me word she'd come up to talk over the arrangements; and then I got a message by their surgery boy, saying she was prevented. Don't it look nice, Mary?" she added, taking a bit of the gown up in her fingers. "It's the first time I've put it on since it was turned. I kept it on to come here; it seemed so cold to put it off for a cotton; and I've been feeling always chilly of late."

"What be you going to wear to-morrow?" demanded Mary Barber.

Mrs. Pickering laughed. "Something desperate smart. I can't stay to tell you."

"You've got a gown a-purpose for it, I reckon," continued Mary, detaining her. "What sort is it?"

"A new fawn silk. There! Good-bye; I've a power of things to do at home to night, and the boys are coming home to an early tea."

Mrs. Pickering walked away quickly, as she spoke. Mary Barber, enjoining the two pretty girls and little Tom to be quiet, and not go in to tease their mamma, ran to the village shop to see if by good luck she could find there some white satin bonnet ribbon. William Owen, the eldest son, was at school in Worcester.

Rather to Mary Barber's surprise, Mrs. Smith produced a roll of white satin, encased carefully in cap-paper. She didn't always have such a thing by her, she said. Mary Barber bought four yards—some narrow to match, for her cap border—and set off home again. Hearing from the children that they had been "as quiet as mice," she dived into her pocket, and produced a large mellow summer apple. Cutting it into four parts, she gave one to each.

Mrs. Pickering walked rapidly homewards. Hallow was (and is) situated about three miles from Worcester, and her house was between the two—nearer the city, however, than the village. After Hester Barber's marriage, her husband had got on in the world. A cottage and a couple of fields and a cow grew into—at least the fields did—many fields, and they into hop-gardens. From being a successful hop-grower, John Pickering took an office in Worcester, and became a prosperous hop-merchant. He placed his two sons in it—well educated youths; and on his death, his eldest son, Richard, then just twenty-one, succeeded him as its master. This was four years ago. Richard was to be married on the morrow to Helena Law, daughter of Mr. Law, the surgeon; and Mary Barber, as you have heard, considered she should be out of place in the festivities.

And she was right. Over and over again had the Pickerings urged Mary to leave service, as a calling beneath her and them, and to live with themselves. Mary declined. As to living with them, she retorted, they knew as well as she did there'd be no "getting on" together; and help from them to set up a couple of rooms for herself, or an independent cottage, was what *she'd* never accept. She said it was "their pride;" they said they only wanted her to be more comfortable. The contention ran on for years; in fact, it was continuously running on in a sort of under-current, if it did not always rise to the surface; and the result was a coldness, and not very frequent meetings. Mary Barber obstinately remained in her condition of servitude, and was called "pig-headed" for her pains.

Not much so, however, by Mrs. Pickering; she understood very little of the world's social distinctions, and cared less; and she had latterly had a great trouble upon her, beside which few things seemed of weight. For some time past there had been ill-feeling between her two sons: in her heart perhaps she most loved the younger, and, so far as she dared, took his part against the elder. Richard was the master, and overbearing; William was four years the younger, and resented his brother's yoke. Richard was steady, and regular as clock-work; William was rather given to go out of an evening, spending time and money. Trifling sums of money had been missed from the office by Richard, from time to time; he was as sure in his heart that William had helped himself to them as that they had disappeared, but William coolly denied it, and set down the accusation to his brother's prejudice. In point of fact, this was the chief origin of the ill-feeling; but Richard Pickering was considerate, and had kept the petty thefts secret from his mother. She, poor woman, fondly hoped that this marriage of Richard's would heal all wounds, though not clearly seeing how or in what manner it could bear upon them. In one month William would be of age, and must become his brother's partner; he would also come into his share of the property left by their father.

Mrs. Pickering went home ruminating on these things, and praying—oh how earnestly!—that there should be peace between the brothers. Their house was surrounded by fields; a very pretty, though small, dwelling of bright red brick, with green venetian outside shutters to the different windows; jasmine trailed over the porch, over the sills of the sitting-room windows, on either side the entrance door. Many-coloured flowers clustered round the green lawn in front; and behind was a fold-yard on a very small scale, for they kept cows, and poultry, and pigs still. The land was somewhat low just here, and no glimpse of the Severn, winding along in front between its banks, could be caught; but there was the fair city of Worcester beyond, with its fine cathedral, and the taper spire of St. Andrew's rising high against the blue sky.

The young Pickerings came home early that evening, as agreed upon: not, alas! in the friendly spirit their mother had been hoping for, but in open quarrelling. They were both fine-grown young men, with good features, dark hair, and the honest, sensible grey eyes of their mother; Richard was grave in look; William gay, with the pleasantest smile in the world. Poor Mrs. Pickering! hasty words of wrath were spoken on either side, and for the first time she became acquainted with the losses at the office, and Richard's belief in his brother's dishonesty. It appeared that a far heavier loss than any preceding it had been discovered that afternoon.

"Oh, Richard!" she gasped; "you don't know what you say. He would never do it."

"He has done it, mother—he must have done it," was the elder son's answer. "No one else can get access to my desk, except old Stone. Would you have me suspect him?"

"Old Stone" was a faithful servant, a many-years' clerk and manager, entirely beyond suspicion, and there was no one else in the office. Mrs. Pickering felt a faintness stealing over her, but she had firm faith in her younger, her bright, her well beloved son.

"Look here, mother," said Richard; "we know—at least I do, if you don't—that William's expenditure has been considerably beyond his salary. Whence has he derived the sums of money he has spent—that he does not deny he has spent? If I have kept these things from you, it was to save you pain: Stone has urged me to tell you of it over and over again."

"Hush, Richard! The money came from me."

William Pickering turned round; he had been carelessly standing at the window, looking out on the setting sun. For once his pleasant smile had given place to scorn.

"I'd not have told him so much, mother: *I* never have. If he is capable of casting this suspicion on me, why not let him enjoy it. Times and again have I assured him I've never touched a sixpence of the money: I've told that interfering old Stone so; and I might as well talk to the wind. Is it likely that I would touch it? I could have knocked the old man down this afternoon when he accused me of being a disgrace to my dead father."

It is of no use to pursue the quarrel, neither is there time for it. That Mrs. Pickering, in her love, had privately furnished William with money from time to time was an indisputable fact, and Richard could not disbelieve his mother's word. But instead of its clearing up the matter, it only (so judged Richard) made it blacker. If he had been robbing the office, he had been legally robbing his mother; words grew higher and higher, and the brothers, in their anger, spoke of a separation. This evening, the last of Richard's residence at home, was the most miserable his mother had ever spent, and she passed a great part of the night at her bed-side, praying that the matter might be cleared up, and the two brothers reconciled.

The morning rose bright and cloudless; and Mary Barber was astir betimes. Washing-day in those days, and in a simple country household, meant washing-day. It most certainly did at Mrs. Owen's; everybody was expected to work, and did work, the master excepted. Mary put her best shoulder to the wheel that morning, got things forward, and started about ten o'clock. The wedding was fixed for eleven at All Saints' Church, and Mary calculated that she should get comfortably to the church just before the hour, and ensconce herself in an obscure corner of it, as she meant to do.

She was in her best: a soft, fine, grey cashmere gown, kept for high-days, a grey twilled silk shawl with a handsome sewn-on border of lilies and roses, and a cottage straw bonnet, trimmed with the white satin ribbon, its inside border of real lace. That shawl might have been worn by a lady; it had been a present to Mary for her own wedding (which had been rudely frustrated through the faithlessness of man, and terribly sore was she upon it unto this day), and was as good as new, never coming out above once a year. She brought with her no cap, intending to be firm on the points of not remaining and not removing her bonnet; she'd step into Mr. Law's house, and drink to the bridegroom and bride, and taste the cake, and she'd start back home again.

She took the field way; it was pleasanter than the dusty road; and went quickly on with her umbrella, a large green cotton thing, tied with a string round the middle, quite a foot in diameter. The skies were serenely bright, showing no prospect of rain for days to come, but Mary Barber would not have ventured out in her best without an umbrella, to guard against contingencies, for untold gold.

She had traversed nearly two-thirds of her way, and was in the last field but one before turning into the road. It was a large field, this, called popularly the hollow field, from the circumstance of a hollow or dell being in one part of it. This part Mary Barber had left behind her, and as she walked along the path that led mid-way through it, some church clocks chiming the half-hour after ten, came distinctly to her ear in the stillness of the rarefied air. "I've stepped out well," quoth she.

It was at this moment that she discerned some one seated on the stile at the end of the path that led into the next field. Very much to her surprise, as she advanced nearer, she saw it was her sister. Mrs. Pickering was sitting sideways, her feet towards Worcester, her face turned to Mary, as if she was waiting for her, and would not take the trouble to get over. To use a common expression, Mary Barber could hardly believe her own eyes, and the proceeding by no means met with her approbation.

"Of all the simpletons!—to come and stick herself there to

wait for me. And for what she knew I might have took the road way. They be thinking to get me with 'em to church in the carriage!—but they won't. I told her I'd not mix myself up in the grand doings: neither ought I to, and Hester's common sense must have gone a wool-gathering to wish it. Ah! she's been running herself into that stitch in her side."

The last remark was caused by her perceiving that Mrs. Pickering, whose left side was this way, had got her hand pressed upon her chest or heart. The doctors had warned Mrs. Pickering that any exertion by which this pain was brought on might be dangerous. "Serve her right!" cried unsympathizing Mary Barber, who had no patience when people did foolish things.

And now she obtained a clear view of her sister's dress. She wore the violet silk gown of the previous afternoon, and a white bonnet and shawl. Mary, on the whole, regarded the attire with disparagement.

"Why, if she's not got on her puce gown! Whatever's that for? Where's the new fawn silk she talked of, I wonder? I'd not go to my eldest son's wedding in a turned gown; I'd have a new one, be it silk or stuff. That's just like Hester; she never can bear to put on a new thing; she'd rather—— If I don't believe the shawl's one o' them beautiful Chaney crapes."

It looked a very nice shawl, and was glistening in the rays of the sun. That it was a China crape was nearly certain; no other sort of shawl would have had so deep a fringe. China crape shawls in those days cost their price; and Mary Barber condemned it at once, as connected with her sister.

"I say, Hester," she called out, as soon as she got near enough for her voice to reach the stile, "what on earth made you come here to meet me?"

Mrs. Pickering made no reply, gave no token of recognition whatever, and Mary supposed she had not caught the words. Her face looked unusually pale, its expression mournfully sad and serious, its eyes turned on Mary with a fixed stare.

"Sure," thought Mary, "nothing can have fell out to stop the wedding! Richard's girl wouldn't run away as that faithless chap of mine did. Something's wrong, though, I can see, by her staring at me in that stony way, and never opening her mouth to speak. I say, Hester, is anything——Deuce take them strings again!"

The concluding apostrophe was addressed to her shoe-

strings. To be smart, Mary Barber had put new galloon ribbon in her shoes, and one or other of them had been coming untied all the way, to her great wrath. Laying down her umbrella on the edge of the grass, and her folded handkerchief, which she had carried in her hand, upon it, she stooped down and tied the shoe, giving the knot a good tug as additional security.

"Now, then, come undone again, and I'll—Bless me! where's she gone?"

In raising her head, Mary Barber missed her sister; the stile was vacant. Hastening to it, she climbed over into the next field, and there stood in what might be called a paroxysm of astonishment, for no trace whatever was to be seen of Mrs. Pickering. It was a large field, a hedge dividing it from the one she had just traversed, the path running across it before her. She looked here; she looked there; she looked everywhere: in vain. Mary Barber had once treated herself to witness the performance of a conjuror in the large room of the Bell, at Worcester; she began to think he must have been at work here.

"Hester!" she called out, raising her voice to its utmost pitch; "Hester, where *be* you got to!"

The air took away the sound, and a bird above seemed to echo it, but there was no other answer. The woman stood like one moonstruck. Was it a conjuring?—or what else was it? The hedge, a trim, well kept, cropped hedge, afforded no spot for concealment; there was no ditch or any other hiding-place—nothing but the broad open field, and no human being, save herself, stirring in it.

"Well, this beats bull-baiting," ejaculated Mary Barber, in the broad country phraseology in vogue in those days. "I'd better pinch myself to see whether I be awake or dreaming."

She turned herself about from side to side; she went back over the stile to the field she had traversed, and stared about there; but no trace could she see of Mrs. Pickering. Finally she passed over the stile again, and stood a moment to revolve matters.

"She must have gone off somewhere on the run while I'd got my eyes down on that dratted shoe," was the conclusion the woman came to. "And more idiot she, when she knows running always brings on that queer pain at her heart."

It might have been a reasonable solution had there been anywhere to run to: that is, had the field not been too broad and wide to admit a possibility of her running out of sight. In good truth there was no such possibility. Mary Barber continued her way across the field, and then, instead of pursuing her road to Worcester, she turned aside to the house of the Pickerings. That her sister could not have got back to it she knew, for the only way was the one she took. Trying the back door, she found it fastened, and, on passing round to the front, that was fastened also. There was no carriage waiting at the gate; on the contrary, everything seemed silent and shut up. Mary Barber gave a sharp knock.

"One would think you were all dead," she cried, as a maid-servant opened the door. "They are gone, I suppose."

"Yes, they are gone," was the girl's reply. "My missis left about ten minutes since."

"More than that, I know," was the answering remark. "What made her come to meet me, Betsey?"

"She didn't come," said Betsey.

"She did come," said Mary Barber.

"She did not, ma'am," persisted the servant.

"Why, my goodness gracious me, girl! do you want to persuade me out of my senses?" retorted Mary Barber in anger. "She came on as far as the hollow field, and sat herself down on the stile there waiting for me to come up. I've got the use of my eyes, I hope."

"Well, I don't know, ma'am," returned the girl, dubiously. "I was with her at the moment she was starting, and I'm sure she'd no thought of going then. She was just going out at this door, eating her bit of bread and butter, when she turned back into the parlour and put down her green parasol, telling me to bring her small silk umbrella instead: it might rain, she said, fair as it looked. 'And make haste, Betsey,' she says to me, 'for it don't want two minutes of the half-hour, and I shan't get to All Saints' in time.'"

"What half-hour?" asked Mary Barber, in a hard, disputing sort of tone.

"The half-hour after ten. Sure enough in a minute or two our clock struck it."

"Your clock must be uncommon wrong in its reckoning, then," was the woman's rejoinder. "At half-past ten she was stuck on the stile, looking out for me. It's about ten minutes ago."

It was about ten minutes since her mistress went out; but

An Episode in Mary Barber's Life. 45

Betsey did not venture to contend further. Mary Barber always put down those who differed from her.

"After all, she has not took her umbrella," resumed the girl. "I couldn't find it in the stand, off by the kitchen; all the rest of the umbrellas was there, but not missis's silk one, and when I ran back to tell her I thought it must be upstairs, she had gone. Gone at a fine pace, too, Mary Barber, which, you know, is not good for her, for she was already out of sight, so I just shut the door, and drew the bolt. It's a pity she drove it off so late."

"What made her drive it off?"

"Well, there was one or two reasons. Her new fawn gown, such a beauty it is, was never sent home till this morning—I'd let that fashionable new Miss Reynolds make me another, I would!—and when missis had got it on, it wouldn't come to in the waist by the breadth of your two fingers, and she'd got her pain very bad, and couldn't be squeeged. So she had to fold it up again, and put on her turned puce——"

"I saw," interrupted Mary Barber, cutting the revelation short. "I say, Betsey, what's her shawl? It looked to me like one o' them Chaney crapes."

"It's the most lovely Chaney crape you ever saw," replied the girl enthusiastically. "Mr. Richard made it a present to her. She didn't want to wear it; she said it was too grand, but he laughed at her. The fringe was that depth."

"And now, you obstinate thing," sharply put in Mary Barber, as the girl was extending her hand to show the depth of the fringe, "how could I have seen her in her puce gown, and how could I have seen her in the shawl unless she had come to meet me? I should as soon have expected to see myself in a satin train, as her in a Chaney crape shawl: and Richard must have more money than wit to have bought it."

"And where is she now, then?" asked Betsey, to whom the argument certainly appeared conclusive. "Gone on by herself to the church?"

"Never you mind!" returned Mary Barber, not choosing to betray her ignorance upon the unsatisfactory point. "Don't you contradict your betters again, Betsey Marsh."

Betsey humbly took the reproof.

"Why could she not have had a carriage, and went properly?" resumed Mary Barber. "It might have cost money; but a son's marriage comes but once in a lifetime."

"The carriage came, and took off Mr. Richard, and she

wouldn't go in it," said the girl. And then she proceeded, dropping her voice to a whisper, to tell of the unpleasantness of the previous evening, and of the subsequent events of the morning. Mr. William was up first, and went out without breakfast, leaving word he was gone to the office as usual, and should not attend the wedding. This she had to tell her mistress and Mr. Richard when they came downstairs; her mistress seemed dreadfully grieved; she looked as white as a sheet, and as soon as breakfast was over, she wrote a letter, and sent Hill with it into Worcester to Mr. William. "It was to tell him to come back and dress himself, and go with her to the wedding, I know," concluded the girl, "and that's why, waiting for him, she would not go with Mr. Richard when the carriage came, and why she stayed, herself, till the last minute. But Mr. William never came: and Hill's not come back either."

"Then why on earth did she come to meet me, instead of making the best of her way to the church?" once more demanded Mary Barber.

"It's what I should ha' said she didn't do," retorted the girl; "she never had no thoughts of going to meet you."

"If you say that again, I'll——Why, who's this?"

The closing of the little iron gate at the foot of the garden had caused her to turn, and she saw William Pickering. He was flushed with the rapid walk from the town—conveyances were not to be hired at hasty will in Worcester then as they are now—and came up with a smile on his good-humoured face.

"I hope my mother's gone," he called out.

"Yes, sir," answered Betsey.

"So, you and Richard have been quarrelling again, I hear, and you must go off in a temper this morning," was Mary Barber's reproving salutation. "I'm glad you've had the grace to think better of it, Master William!"

The young man laughed. "The truth is, my mother's note was so peremptory—in a sort—that I had no choice but to obey it," he answered. "I was not in the office when Hill left it, but I came as soon as I could. Some hot water, Betsey. Look sharp."

"You'll not get to All Saints' in time," said Mary Barber.

"I'll have a try for it; they may be late themselves. What time is it now?" he continued, as he bounded up the stairs.

An Episode in Mary Barber's Life.

As if to answer him, the large kitchen clock at that moment rang out the quarter to eleven. It was a clock that struck the quarters: as many kitchen clocks did in those old-fashioned days.

"Is that clock right?" asked Mary Barber, remembering her conclusion that it could not be, and why; and feeling in a maze upon the past yet. "Just look at your watch, William, and tell me."

"It's never wrong," put in Betsey, as she came hurrying out of the kitchen with the jug of hot water, probably deeming it a convenient juncture tacitly to maintain her own opinion. "It don't vary a minute in a year."

She spoke truth. Nevertheless William Pickering, in courtesy to the request, halted on the stairs midway, and took his watch from his pocket. "It is quite right," he said. "Besides, I know that must be just about the time. You wait for me in the parlour, Mary, and we'll go on together."

She turned into the parlour generally used, and waited for him. The boys had always called her "Mary," following the habit of their father and mother. On the table lay Mrs. Pickering's green parasol, just as she had put it down.

In five minutes he was downstairs again, dressed; as handsome a young man as might be—upright, frank, merry. Mary Barber told him how his mother had come to meet her, and how she had suddenly disappeared. He laughed, and said Mary must have fallen into a doze while tying her shoe. They were passing through Henwick when the clocks struck eleven.

"There!" exclaimed Mary Barber, "the wedding 'll have begun?"

"Never mind," said he, gaily, "we shall get in for the tail."

They took the lower road, as being the nearest, cutting off the corner by the suburb of St. John's, as well as the new road, crossed the bridge over the sparkling Severn, and turned off to All Saints' Church just as the tardy bridal party drove up.

"I hope they have not been waiting for me!" exclaimed William Pickering. "Which carriage is my mother in, I wonder? I shall take her in."

"She won't be in the carriage; she was going straight

into the church; Betsey said so!" snapped Mary Barber, excessively aggravated to find herself in the very midst of the alighting company. Richard Pickering drew up to his brother.

"Where's the mother?" he asked. "We have been waiting for her all this while."

"In the church, I think, if she's not with you. I am but come up myself now.

However, range their eyes as they would round the church when they got inside it, there was no sign of Mrs. Pickering. William, burying animosity for the occasion, stood by his brother at the altar, his groom's man, and the ceremony proceeded. Mary Barber ensconced herself behind a remote pillar, peeping surreptitiously round to watch the party out of church, Richard leading his very pretty bride.

"I'll let the ruck of 'em get into old Law's before me," quoth she to the female pew-opener.

And accordingly the "ruck" did get in, and then Mary Barber followed. She supposed Mrs. Pickering would be there, as did all. The conclusion drawn was, that she had not arrived in time for the ceremony, and so had gone straight to the surgeon's. His residence was not far from the church, and as Mary Barber slowly approached it, she saw quite a crowd of persons coming from the opposite way, in one of whom she recognized an officer of justice. Halting at the door to stare at these—and they seemed to be reciprocating the compliment by staring at her in a curious manner—William Pickering came out.

"What can have become of my mother, Mary?" he exclaimed. "I'm going home to see after her. She's not at Mrs. Law's."

"Why, where's she got to?" responded Mary Barber. "I'll tell you what, William Pickering," quickly added the woman, an idea flashing across her, "she's gone demented with the quarrelling of you two boys, and has wandered away in the fields! I told you how strangely she stared at me from the stile."

"Nonsense!" said the young man.

"Is it nonsense? It—whatever do you people want?" broke off Mary Barber. For the persons she had noticed were surrounding them in a strange manner, hemming them in ominously. The officer laid his arm upon William Pickering.

An Episode in Mary Barber's Life.

"I'm sorry to say that I must take you prisoner, sir."

"What for?" coolly asked William.

"For murder!" was the answer. And as the terrible words fell on Mary Barber's ear, a wild thought crossed her bewildered brain. Could he have murdered his mother? Of course it was only her own previous train of ideas, connected with the non-appearance of her sister, that induced it.

Not so, however. Amidst the dire confusion that seemed at once to reign; amid the indignant questionings of the bridal party, who came flocking out in their gay attire, the particulars were made known. Mr. Stone, the old clerk, had been found dead on the office floor, an ugly wound in the back of his head. Richard Pickering, in his terror, cast a yearning, beseeching glance on his brother, as much as to say, Surely it has not come to this!

The events of the morning, as connected with this matter, appeared to have been as follows:—Mr. Stone had gone to the office at nine o'clock, as usual, and there, to his surprise, found William Pickering, opening the letters. The latter said he was not going to his brother's wedding, and the old clerk reproved him for it. William did not like this; one word led to another, and several harsh things were spoken. So far the office servant testified; a man named Dance, whose work lay chiefly in the warehouse among the hop-pockets, and who had come in for orders. They were still "jangling," Dance said, when he left them. Subsequently to this, William Pickering went out to the warehouse, and to one or two more places. On his return, he found that his mother's out-door man-of-all-work, Hill, had left a note for him; a large brewer in the town, named Corney, was also waiting to see him on business. When Mr. Corney left, he opened the note, the contents of which may as well be given:—

"William! you have never directly disobeyed me yet. I charge you, come back at once, and go with me to the church. Do you know that I have passed three parts of the night on my knees, praying that things may be cleared up between you and your brother! "YOUR LOVING MOTHER."

After that nothing clearly was known. William Pickering said that when he quitted the office to go home, in obedience to his mother's mandate, he left Mr. Stone at his desk writing; but a short while afterwards the old clerk was found lying on the floor, with a terrible wound in the back of his head. It was quite evident he had been struck down while bending over the desk. The man Dance, who was sought for in the warehouse, and found, spoke of the quarrelling he had heard; and hence the arrest of William Pickering.

Mary Barber's first thought, amidst the confusion and the shock, was of her sister. If not broken to her softly, the news might kill her; and the woman, abandoning cake, and wine, and company, before she had seen them, started off there and then in search of Mrs. Pickering, not knowing in the least where to look for her, but taking naturally the way to her home.

"Surely she'll be coming in to join 'em, and I shall, perchance, meet her," was the passing thought.

Not Mrs. Pickering did Mary Barber meet, but Hill, the man. He was coming down the road in a state of excitement, and Mary Barber stared in blank disbelief at his news: his mistress had been found on her bed—dead.

In an incredibly short time the woman seemed to get there, and met a surgeon coming out of the house. It was quite true. Mrs. Pickering was dead. With her face looking as if it were turned to stone, Mary Barber went up to the chamber. Betsey, the servant, her tears dropping fast, told the tale.

When Mary Barber and Mr. William had departed, she bolted the door again, and went back to her work in the kitchen. By and by, it occurred to her to wonder whether the silk umbrella was safe upstairs, or whether it had been lost from the stand: a few weeks before, one of their cotton umbrellas had been taken by a tramp. She ran up into her mistress's room to look, and there was startled by seeing her mistress. She was sitting in an arm-chair by the bedside, her head leaning sideways on the back, and her left hand pressed on her heart. On the bed lay the silk umbrella, its cover partly taken off, and by its side a bit of bread and butter, half eaten. At the first moment the girl thought she was asleep; but when she saw her face she knew it was something worse. Running out of the house in terror, she met Hill, who was then returning from Worcester, and sent him for the nearest surgeon. He came, and pronounced her to be quite dead. "She must have been dead," he said, "about an hour."

"What time was that?" interrupted Mary Barber, speaking sharply in her emotion.

An Episode in Mary Barber's Life.   51

"It was half-past eleven."

There could not be the slightest doubt as to the facts of the case. While the servant was sent by her mistress for the umbrella, and delayed through being unable to find it, Mrs. Pickering must have run upstairs to her chamber, either remembering that it was there, or to look for it. She found it, and was taking off the case, putting down the bread and butter she was eating, to do so (a piece of bread and butter which the maid had just before brought to her), and must have then found herself ill, sat down in the chair, and died immediately. Her own medical attendant had warned her that any great excitement might prove suddenly fatal.

"It was the oddest thing, and I thought it at the time, though it went out of my mind again, that she should have disappeared from sight so soon," sobbed Betsey. "I don't think I was away much above a minute after the umbrella, and when I came back, and found her gone, and looked out at the door, I couldn't see her anywhere. I looked in the garden; I looked down the path as far as my eyes would go. 'Why, missis must be lost!' says I, out loud. And she had left the front door wide open, too—and that ought to have told me she had not gone out of it. And I, like a fool, never to have remembered that she might have run upstairs, but just bolted the door and went about my work."

Mary Barber made no comment; a strange awe was stealing over her. This had occurred at half-past ten. It was at precisely that time she saw her sister on the stile.

"Betsey," she presently said, her voice subdued to a whisper, "if your mistress had really gone out, as you supposed, was there any possibility of her coming in later, without your knowledge?"

"No, there was not; she couldn't have done it," was the answer to the question; and Mary Barber felt perfectly certain that it had not been possible, though she asked it. The only way to Mrs. Pickering's from the stile was the path she had taken herself, and she knew her sister had not gone on before her.

"I never unbolted either of the doors, back or front, after she (as I thought) went out, except when I undid the front for you," resumed the girl. "I don't dare to be in the house by myself with 'em open since that man frightened me last winter. No, no; missis neither went out nor come in; she just went up-stairs to her room, and died. The doctor says he don't suppose she had a moment's warning."

It must have been so. Mary Barber gazed upon her as she lay back, upon the holiday attire she wore, all the counterpart of what she had seen on the stile. The puce silk gown looked as good as new; the really beautiful shawl, with its deep rich fringe; the white bonnet, which she now saw was of plain corded silk. The doctor had closed the eyes, and put the left hand down straight; otherwise she was as she was found. On the patchwork quilt of the bed lay the silk umbrella, the cover half taken off, and the bit of bread and butter, half eaten, lay beside it. Mary Barber gazed at all; and an awful conviction came over her that it was her sister's spirit she had seen on the stile. Never from that hour did she quite lose the sensation of nameless dread it brought in its wake.

"You see, now, Mrs. Barber, you must have been mistaken in thinking my missis went to meet you," said Betsey.

Mary Barber made no answer; she only looked out straight before her with a gaze that seemed to be very far away.

What with one calamity and the other—for the news of William Pickering's apprehension soon travelled up—the house was like a fair the whole of the day. Richard Pickering, bridegroom though he was, was up there; Mr. Law was there, and, on examination, confirmed the other doctor's opinion as to the momentarily sudden death; numberless friends and acquaintances came in and went out again. For once in her life, Mary Barber was oblivious of the home wash, and her promise to return early for it. She took her bonnet off, borrowed a cap of her poor sister's, and remained.

William Pickering was taken before the magistrates in the Guildhall for examination, late in the afternoon. His brother attended it, and—very much to her own surprise—so did Mary Barber. The accusation and the facts had resolved themselves into something tangible out of their original confusion; the prisoner was able to understand the grounds they had against him; and the solicitor, whom he called to his assistance, drove up in a gig to Mrs. Pickering's, and took possession of Mary Barber.

"What's the good of your whirling me off to the Guildhall?" she resentfully asked of him, three times over, as he drove back into Worcester. "I don't know anything about

An Episode in Mary Barber's Life.

it; I never was inside that office of the Pickerings' in all my life."

"You'll see," said the lawyer, with a smile.

One thing was satisfactory—that old Mr. Stone had come to life again. The blow, though a very hard one, had stunned, but not killed him; he was, in fact, not injured beyond a reasonable probability of recovery. He had no knowledge of his assailant: whoever it was, he had come behind him, as he sat bending over his desk, and struck him down unawares.

The Guildhall was crowded: a case exciting so much interest had rarely occurred in Worcester. Independent of the station in life of the prisoner, and of his good looks, his youth, and his popularity with most people, there were the attendant circumstances—the marriage of his brother in the morning, the death of Mrs. Pickering. Of the last sad fact they did not tell him. "Let him get his examination over, poor fellow!" said they in kindness. And he stood before the court, upright, frank, unfettered by grief. "He must have done it in a moment of passion, said his sorrowing friends and the public; for the facts seemed too clear against him for disbelief—the long-continued ill-feeling known to exist between him and the old clerk, who had persistently taken his brother Richard's part; the quarrelling of the morning, as heard by Dance, and which the prisoner did not deny; and the absence of any one else in the office. Richard Pickering, his breast beating with a horrible conviction that none else could have been guilty, was not one publicly to denounce his brother. He affected to assume his innocence, and he stood by him to afford him all the countenance in his power.

The facts were testified to — those gathered on the first moment of discovery, and others since. Dance spoke of the jangling—as he still called it—between the clerk and his young master. Mr. Corney proved his visit, and that upon its termination he left Mr. Stone and William Pickering alone, and he could see that they were not friendly. This was about twenty minutes past ten. Mr. Corney added, in answer to a question, that he had heard nothing of William Pickering's intention to depart home; on the contrary, he said he should be at the office all day. Subsequently——

Yes, but then he had not opened his mother's note, interrupted the prisoner, who, up to this point, acknowledged all that was said to be correct. But, he continued, the instant he read the note he started for home, knowing how little time there was to lose: and he told old Stone that he need not be cross on Richard's account any longer, for after all he was going to be his best man. He knew no more.

Mr. Corney resumed: A little before eleven he went back to the office, to say he'd take the hops at the price offered, and was horrified to find old Mr. Stone on the ground, as he thought, dead. He raised an alarm; some people ran in from the streets, and he went himself in search of Dance, whom he found in the warehouse; somebody else ran for a constable, others for a surgeon. Of course the conclusion arrived at was, that Mr. William Pickering had done the deed.

The bench appeared to be arriving at the same.

"Not so fast, gentlemen," said William Pickering's lawyer: and he put forth another witness.

It was Mr. Kilpin, the hop-merchant, a gentleman well known in the town. He deposed that he had called in at the Messrs. Pickering's office that morning between half-past ten and eleven. Mr. Stone was alone, writing at his desk. He stayed talking to him three or four minutes, and left at a quarter to eleven. He was enabled to state the time positively from the fact, that——

"Why, then, it could not have been William Pickering; he was at home at that very time," burst forth Mary Barber.

The bench silenced her; but she saw now why she had been brought to the Guildhall.

Mr. Kilpin resumed, taking up the thread of his sentence as if no interruption had occurred—

"From the fact that, as I passed St. Nicholas Church, it chimed the three-quarters past ten. I was on my way to catch the Pershore coach, for I was going by it as far as Whittington, and it was at that moment turning the corner of Broad Street. I had to make a run for it, and to holloa out, and the coachman pulled up opposite the Old Bank. When I got back from Whittington this afternoon," added the witness, "I accidentally met Mr. William Pickering's lawyer, and learnt what had occurred."

Next came the evidence of Mary Barber, that William Pickering was in his mother's house at three-quarters past ten. Of course there could be no further doubt of his innocence after this. Meanwhile the prisoner had been writing a few lines with a pencil on a piece of paper, and it was passed over to his brother. Something in the demeanour of one of the witnesses as he gave his evidence had powerfully struck him.

"*I have an idea, Richard, that the guilty man is Dance. Take care that he does not escape. If he has done this, he may also have been the pilferer of your petty cash. Try and get it all cleared up, for the sake of the mother's peace.*"

"For the sake of the mother's peace!" echoed Richard, with an aching heart. "Poor William little dreams of the blow in store for him."

He did not dream, Richard Pickering; he acted. Giving a hint to the officer to look after Dance, he pressed up to his brother, then being released from custody.

"William," he whispered, "tell me the truth in this solemn moment—and it is more sadly solemn than you are as yet cognizant of—have you really not touched that missing money? As I lay awake last night thinking of it, I began to fancy I might have been making a mistake all through. If so——"

"If so, we shall be the good friends that we used to be," heartily interrupted William, as he clasped his brother's ready hand. "On my sacred word, I never touched it; I could not do so: and you must have been prejudiced to fancy it. I'll lay any money Dance will turn out to have been the black sheep. Both looks and tones were false as he gave his evidence."

And William Pickering was right. Dance was so effectually "looked after" that night, that some ugly facts came out, and he was quietly taken into custody. True enough, the black sheep had been nobody else. He had skilfully pilfered the petty sums of money; he had struck down Mr. Stone as he sat at his desk, to take a couple of sovereigns he saw lying in it. The old gentleman recovered, and gave evidence on the trial at the following March Assizes, and Richard and William Pickering from henceforth were more closely knit together.

But the singular circumstances attendant on the death of Mrs. Pickering—her apparition (for could it be anything less?) that appeared to Mary Barber—became public property. People talked of it with timid glances and hushed voices; and for a long while neither girl nor woman would pass through the two fields alone.

And that is the ending. If I have been unduly minute in regard to the dress, or other points, I only reiterate the minuteness given at the time by Mary Barber. She fully believed—and she was good, and honest, and truthful—that the spirit of her sister came to lead her to the house (where otherwise she would not have gone), there to meet William Pickering, and be the means of establishing his innocence: and would so believe to her dying day.

And now, the episode related, we go on with the story of Dene Hollow.

CHAPTER V.

THE SHADOW ON THE HOLLOW.

It was lovely autumn weather. The Beechhurst Dene woods were glowing with their rich tints in the October sunshine; the sky was blue and cloudless as in the sweetest day of summer.

Turning out at the lodge gates of Beechhurst Dene, was a kind of mail-phaeton; a high yellow vehicle, all the fashion at the period. The horses were iron-grey, fine, valuable animals; high steppers, but steady withal, and much like their owner, Sir Dene Clanwaring. Sir Dene sat in the carriage to-day by the side of his son Geoffry, who was driving. Sweeping out of the avenue right across the highway, Geoffrey turned the horses' heads down a road that looked newly made.

Now it was. Sir Dene Clanwaring had carried out his project—some deemed it his folly—and lost no time in completing what he had set his mind upon—a near way to the village of Hurst Leet. It was a fine, white, broad road; leading from Sir Dene's gates downwards—for the ground descended, you remember—and winding round right into the middle of the hamlet. Hurst Leet was proud of it. Sir Dene was proud of it. It had cost Sir Dene more funds than he had believed possible; a costly toy, he was apt to whisper in the privacy of his own heart; but nevertheless he could afford it, and he said complacently that the convenience of the road would well repay its outlay. Some three weeks had elapsed now since it was finished; and Sir Dene had driven down and up it nearly every day.

All trace of the widow Barber's cottage was gone. That estimable but (in the opinion of Mr. Drew) cantankerous old lady had been forced out of her life-long home. There had been a scene at her departure. Lady-day—the period by which she was ordered to be gone—came and passed; and Mrs. Barber had neither removed herself nor her chattels. Another day's grace they gave her, together with a peremptory command: but the widow did not stir. She had lived in the old place for six-and-seventy years, she pleaded; she could not, in the nature of things, last much longer—oh if they would but let her stay in it for that short remaining time! Earnestly did she pray for this boon, as though she had been praying for her life. Sir Dene was made acquainted with this contumacious behaviour—doubly cantankerous, wrathful Drew called her now—and he, Sir Dene, full of wrath also, issued the edict for her ejection. Geoffry Clanwaring, ever goodhearted, alone put in a protest, asking his father to grant the poor distressed woman's prayer, seconding her plea that it could not be for long. But Sir Dene sharply told his son not to be foolish—the new road could not wait for *her* pleasure. So, on the following morning, sundry men presented themselves at the Widow Barber's, quietly but forcibly put her goods outside the door, and turned her cow and pig and chickens into the road. She had to follow them: and she went meekly forth, weeping and wringing her hands. Mary Barber hired a couple of rooms for her mother and some of her furniture to take refuge in; and the cow and pig and fowls were sold to the highest bidder on the spot. But the fact created a great deal of scandal in the neighbourhood, and Sir Dene received some harsh blame. Sir Dene excused himself by saying that the extreme measure of ejecting her in that very summary manner belonged to his bailiff, Drew. But he could not get out of the fact that he had given his edict for her removal: and Jonathan Drew might have reasonably retorted on the grumblers with the question—How was he to get the old woman out when she refused to go?

As if tormented by the fear that she might be coming back again—after the fashion of the slippers in the Eastern tale—the men lost not a moment in commencing the work of destruction. Some bricks were out of the walls before the weeping woman was beyond view. A rumour went abroad of what was going on, and numbers of gazers came flocking up to watch. They stayed to see it, talking freely. The doors were off then, the windows out. The two chimneys could be no more seen. What with the work of dismantling, with the goods lying in a heap outside, with the let-loose cow and pig, and what with the increasing spectators, such a scene of excitement and confusion had not been witnessed by the rural population in their lives. It remained on their memories as an epoch of local history, to be talked of at convivial meetings and related by father to son: Sir Dene Clanwaring's turning out of the poor old widow Barber, when she was nigh upon her eightieth year.

Hands were quick. On the following day the rubbish of bricks and mortar was ready to be carted away; and on the subsequent morning the new road was begun. Begun at both ends: at the upper one opposite the gates of Beechhurst Dene; at the lower one at Hurst Leet. Sir Dene was all impatience for the way to be completed, and many hands made light work. Never a thought cast he to the grief of the unhappy woman who had been rudely thrust from her shell, and whose heart was breaking. Sir Dene was not by nature a hard or harsh man; but he had certainly acted both hardly and harshly in this.

"*So I returned, and considered all the oppressions that are done under the sun: and beheld the tears of such as were oppressed, and they had no comforter; and on the side of their oppressors there was power; but they had no comforter.*"

If ever there was a signal exemplification of the truthful teaching of one, to whom God had given more than earthly wisdom, it surely existed in this instance.

And now, behold the beautiful road completed—smooth, compact, level as a bowling-green. See it this early morning, as Sir Dene drives down it. The hill is at this end, commencing at the very onset; a long hill, but a gentle one: its descent not steep at all; not enough to cause good horses to slacken speed, either down or up. No more trace is to be seen of the widow's cottage, of its garden, its pig-sty, cow-shed, than if they had never existed: the new road runs right through the site. As to the meadow where her cow was wont to graze, Sir Dene has ploughed it up, fencing it in from the road. On the other side, the pathway remains still; the high bank above it remains; and the extending branches of the towering, waving elm trees cast their shadows on the road in the sunlight, just as the same shadows had used to be cast on the cottage. A fine road: and just now the pride of Sir Dene Clanwaring's heart. It had not been Sir Dene's intention to bestow upon it any particular name: he did not think about it; but the workmen when making it, began to speak of it familiarly amidst themselves as "The Hollow"—probably because they had a portion of it to hollow out. This was caught up by Hurst Leet, and converted into Dene's Hollow. The appellation grew at length into "Dene Hollow." Dene Hollow it remained.

Away they bowled, Sir Dene and his son. Geoffry, an experienced driver, had the reins well in hand. The calm, bright, lovely autumn day was good to be out in.

"Who's that, Geoffry?" asked the baronet, as a tall woman, her face nearly hidden under its large quilted bonnet of faded green silk, passed on the path, and courtesied to Sir Dene.

"It is Mary Barber, sir." And Geoffry silently wondered that the woman upon whose mother had been committed that act of injustice should continue to render active homage to Sir Dene. Manners in those days were widely different from what they are in these: reverence for the great was an institution.

"Oh, ay; servant at Farmer Owen's, I believe," remarked Sir Dene airily: for indeed the episode of the ejection, together with Mary Barber's pleading visit, had well-nigh passed from his mind: at least, it had lost its sting of annoyance. "I didn't know her in that poke-bonnet. How is that daughter of Owen's, Geoffry—she who married Old Arde's relative. Any better? You go there sometimes, don't you?"

"To George Arde's? Now and then, sir, when I am at Worcester. Mrs. Arde is ill still."

"Talking of Owen, he wants his barn—take care, Geoff."

Without the slightest warning, without any apparent cause, the horses had started. Both of them. Started violently, as if in some great terror, and sprung right across the road with a bound. It was just in the spot where the cottage had been. Geoffry Clanwaring did all that a practised driver could do; but it was as nothing. The frightened animals bounded on the bank and off again, upsetting the phaeton. There they stood, plunging and kicking.

Geoffry was on his legs in an instant; uninjured, save for a bruise on the right shoulder and elbow—which he did not feel until later. Some men, who happened to be passing on the upper road by the gates of Beechhurst Dene, came running down. The traces were cut, one of the shivering horses fell, and lay still; the other they soothed to quietness.

Which gave them time to look into the condition of Sir

Dene. He had been pitched over Geoffry's head, and was, of course, much shaken. Moreover, he could not get up without assistance. There was some damage to one of his ankles. A severe sprain, they found; not a fracture.

"It might have been worse," remarked Sir Dene. "What in the world was it that frightened the horses, Geoffry?"

"*I* don't know, sir: I am lost in wondering," was Geoffry's puzzled answer. "There was nothing whatever to startle them."

"I am sure I saw nothing."

"There was nothing. Not a creature was near us, human or animal. How shall we get you home, sir?"

"Oh, I can manage to limp up, with your arm on one side, and somebody else's on the other," returned the baronet. "I hope the horses are all right. It might have been worse for all of us, Geoff, my boy."

"Indeed, it might, father."

Yes, it might have been worse. But nevertheless one of the horses, in plunging, had fatally injured itself, and had to be shot. Cole, the farrier, had a day or two's hope over it—that he could save it—but it proved futile. Sir Dene was in a fine way, and told Cole he would almost as soon have been shot himself. The affair created nearly as much stir and talk in Hurst Leet as the turning out of the Widow Barber had done.

Two or three evenings subsequent to this, Mary Barber set off to see her mother—a small jug of buttered-ale in her hand, which Mrs. Owen had caused Mary to make. "Buttered-ale" was a cordial thought much of in those days, and often sent by the wealthy to the aged or sick. Mrs. Barber had found refuge with John Pound and his wife, renting their two upper rooms. Or, rather, one room and a loft: the last being needed to stow away the portion of her spare furniture that had not been sold. The cottage was situated on the upper road, near Arde Hall; Pound being Squire Arde's waggoner.

Mary Barber put her best foot foremost; not only because it looked likely to rain, but that the buttered-ale should reach her mother while it was hot. The old lady was seated on the bit of carpet before the fire; her head leaning sideways on a chair.

"Why, mother, you be low in the world!" was Mary's salutation. "What be you down there for?"

Mrs. Barber got up without making any particular answer, and took her seat in the chair. "It's a bit shivery to-night, ain't it, child?" she asked. And a spectator might have smiled at tall, hard, bony, middle-aged Mary Barber being addressed as "child."

"No, it's quite warm, mother."

Could it be that this poor shrunken creature was the once plump, healthy, well-conditioned woman who had lived in that disputed cottage. Was it possible that only a few months had made so great a change? Alas, yes. And the marvel was that she had lasted as long as this.

Literally she was no better than skin and bone. The face had lost its roundness, the cheeks their fresh tinge; the eyes were sunken, and dim with a sadness that might be seen and felt. Nothing had apparently ailed her to cause the change; her bodily health, save that the appetite had failed, had seemed not to suffer. But inward grief, when it is hopeless and excessive, induces decay more rapidly in the aged than sickness of body. Old Hester Barber's heart was broken.

"I've not been able to run down this last two days, mother, as we've had our big wash on," said Mary, looking rather keenly at the worn face by the help of the fire-light, for she thought it was more changed than ever. She fancied, moreover, that it had a greyish tinge on it, which she had never observed before: and she did not much like to see it now. "Here's a nice drop of buttered-ale, that the missis has sent: it'll do you good."

"The missis is over kind, Mary; carry back my duty to her and my best thanks. But I don't feel as if I could touch it, child. I don't feel to want nothing."

"That's all nonsense, mother. I'll light the candle."

Holding the candle, so that its light fell on her mother's face, Mary Barber scanned it well. Yes, it was certainly grey to-night, with a peculiar, leaden greyness. She put the buttered-ale into a basin, and reached a spoon.

"Now, then, mother, sup it up afore it's quite cold. Never mind about not wanting it: it'll cheer you up and warm you, whether you want it or not.

Holding the basin so that it rested on her knee, the dying woman—for she was dying slowly—sipped a few spoonfuls. Mary sat opposite, chatting.

"Did ye hear o' the accident to Sir Dene Clanwaring, mother?"

"Ay, I heer'd on't. Pound, he come up stairs here o' purpose to tell me."

"It's cost a sight o' money to mend the carriage, Cole's son says. And they've had to shoot the best horse."

Mrs. Barber, her spoon resting passive in the buttered-ale, shook her head in solemn silence.

"I had passed 'em not a minute afore, coming up the path from Hurst Leet, where I had been on an errand for missis," continued Mary. "All fine and grand it looked, that turn-out; the horses, for power and safety, you might have took a lease on. Before I had well got into the upper road by the gates, there was a startling noise down there, and I looked back. Mother, you might have floored me with a word when I see the carriage, and the two gentlemen lying on the ground, and the cattle plunging."

"Ay, ay," murmured Mrs. Barber.

"I didn't believe my own eyes. And what had done it I could not think, for they had been going along as steady as might be. They don't know what in the world it could ha' been that the horses started at. Young Mr. Clanwaring was at our house yesterday, and I heard him tell the master that it 'ud always be a puzzle to him. Eat the stuff, mother."

"It was the Shadow," remarked the old woman, dropping her voice almost to a whisper. "I'd lay my life, Mary, 'twas the Shadow."

"The what?" cried Mary.

"The Shadow."

Mary Barber, who had really not caught the word at first, supposed that this must allude to the shadows cast on the road by the trees. To any one but her mother she would have met the assertion with unsparing ridicule.

"'Twas not likely to have been *that*, mother. Why, the trees be there always; and their shadows, too, when the sun's behind 'em. Them horses' feet feel just as much at home amid the shadows as they do amid the stones."

"I said the Shadow, Mary. Not the shadows o' the trees."

"What Shadow?"

"The one I saw on the road."

Mary Barber believed the old mind was wandering. She stared for a minute, without speaking.

"Eat your buttered-ale, mother."

Instead of that, Mrs. Barber stretched out her withered arm and put the basin down on the table at her elbow.

"There's a shadow on that road, child. The poor dumb

animals saw it, and were frightened at it. They see sometimes what man can't see. Maybe, it'll come now and again at will, to lie on the Hollow."

Mary Barber was sufficiently superstitious herself, and had seen at least one ghost, as her friends knew; but she was wholly at fault in this. Instead of debating the point, she stared harder than before at the grey face.

"It's a shadow to frighten the best of horses, it is, an' they get to see it, Mary. It frightened me."

"Be you a wandering, mother?" demanded Mary Barber, in rather a hard tone.

"Me a wandering! What put that in your head, child?"

"Why, what else is it? A talking in this way about shadows?"

"How long is it since this new road was opened?" rejoined Mrs. Barber—and certainly, in all save the subject, she seemed to be quite as rational as usual. "What do they call it again—Hollow Dene?"

"Dene Hollow. It's more than three weeks now."

"Ay. Three weeks o' Tuesday last. John Pound, he comes up stairs the evening afore; Monday, that was; and said the workmen was a clearing off their tools, and the road 'ud be open to the parish on the morrow. When the morrow came, I thought I'd put on my old red cloak and go out and take a look at it. 'Twas a fine, sunshiny, beautiful day, warm for September. I got to the place, Mary; and I leaned my arms on the fence opposite the Dene gates, and looked at it. A fine smooth road it was, a'most fine enough to have broke an old woman's heart for. I didn't know the place again. Not a brick was there left o' the poor homestead; not as much as a stone to mark out where it had been. 'Twas all swep clean away; the walls, and the yellow jes'min that used to climb on 'em."

"It's said they've got that yellow jes'min rooted now at Beechhurst Dene," interrupted Mary Barber. "'Twas rare and flourishing always."

"But while my eyes looked this way and that," pursued Mrs. Barber, "a trying to tell whether the home had stood an inch nearer or further, they grew to see that there was a shadow lying on the road. An awful kind of shadow, Mary, just about in the spot where the house had stood. These eyes saw it child. And they'd never seen anything like it afore."

"Was it the shape of the house?" questioned Mary—perhaps as much in mockery as earnestness.

"It wasn't any shape at all. It was just as though a *darkness* lay on that part o' the hollow; or as if you were looking at it through smoked glass. Mary, I'll tell you what it put me in mind of—the valley of the shadow of death."

"Mother!"

"It did."

"I don't think it's right to say that."

"I'd not be the one to say anything wrong. But truth's truth; and the thought came into my mind as I stood there."

"What was it like?" questioned Mary Barber, in a somewhat more reverent tone.

"It was just a shadow of darkness; nothing else. But there was nothing to throw it there, and it made me tremble all over. I've trembled since when I think of it. Randy Black came by at the moment, and I asked him to look—there has been a good deal o' talk again Black in the place, but the man has always showed himself civil to me. He stopped and put his two arms on the rail beside me, and looked on to where I pointed; but he could not see it. He couldn't see it. He said it was as fine and bright all down the new road, every inch on't, as it was that day elsewhere. But the Shadow was there, Mary, all the same. You couldn't tell where it begun or where it ended: just that bit o' the road—ten or twenty yards, maybe—lay in the dark."

To hear Mrs. Barber tell this, her tone subdued to awe, her dim eyes gazing into the fire as though she could see the Shadow there, her whole manner and bearing imparting an impression solemnly earnest, brought a curious sensation to Mary.

"I will take a look myself the next time I pass by, mother."

Mrs. Barber shook her head. "You mightn't see anything. I don't think you will. I went out again the next day, and couldn't see it. Brooding over it here since, it has come to me to think that perhaps no other human eye, save mine, ever will see it. Black couldn't. But the Shadow was there all the while he looked: never a doubt of that."

"It has a curious sound to hear," was Mary Barber's answer.

"Ay. But it's true. I never was surer of anything in this world. Well, I'd a'most forgot it, Mary: I thought it was just a thing, unaccountable, that had come, and passed.

But when John Pound brought news o' the upset in that same spot, saying it was quite a mystery what had startled the horses, for there was nobody a-nigh and nothing to cause it, it flashed over me that they must have seen the same Shadow that I saw—and I don't know how I felt, so struck and dumbfounded. It's to be hoped it'll never come there again. Sir Dene turned me out," added the old woman after a pause, "but I don't wish him ill. I'd do him any good if it lay in my power."

"Well, mother, *I* feel sore at him; I can tell you that."

"Ay, so did I, at first. But the Lord has been good and shown me a bit of His light. When Heaven's opening to us, Mary, we are glad to forgive those that have injured us. I didn't think enough o' these things till I came here—mercy, and charity, and forgiveness to others—and my own sins and mistakes. I never might have thought of 'em. And so—and so, perhaps it has all happened for the best. One must get one's heart broke, as mine's been, before one can be at full love and peace with all the world, friends and enemies."

Mary Barber did not quite know what to make of her mother. She had never seen her like this. All Mrs. Barber had been noted for since she lost her home, was shrinking, silent abstraction. She would answer questions put to her, but rarely spoke of her own accord.

"I wish you'd finish that buttered-ale, mother."

Mrs. Barber took a sip or two, and then let the spoon fall again.

"I can't, Mary. The heart goes again it; and something seems wrong with my swallow. Leave it be: maybe I'll try it later."

"Shall I help you to get to bed, mother?"

"No. 'Tisn't time."

"I must be going soon. Is there anything else I can do?"

"You may read just a few verses o' the Bible, if you like. My sight's got good for nothing."

More and more amazed, for Mary had never heard such a request from her mother on a week-day, she got up to reach the Bible—one that had been in use on Sundays as long as she could remember. But she suddenly discovered that she had not brought her spectacles with her—and upon looking for her mother's could not find them. Mrs. Barber seemed disappointed.

"Oh, well, never mind. It wouldn't have took you five minutes, Mary."

"It's not the time, mother; it is that I can't see. Where's the large Bible—father's? I could see the print o' that."

It was on the top shelf of the press by the bed, and Mary had to stand on a stool to get it down. A large Bible covered with green baize, that had been Thomas Barber's; one they never used.

She dusted it, sat down, and read the chapter asked for—the 14th of St. John. Mrs. Barber listened attentively.

"Ay, ay," she murmured when it was over, "many mansions *there*. There'll be no sorrow up there, child, and no frightening Shadow."

"I wonder what's inside this cover?" cried Mary, who, in passing her hand abstractedly over the green baize, in a minute's reverie, found that something lay between it and the book.

"There's nothing there."

"There is, mother. It feels like a thickish letter. May I look?"

"You can look. I know there's nothing."

Cutting the thread that confined the covering, she took it off, and found a piece of brown paper folded together, with two or three papers inside it. Had Mary Barber's pulses been given to flutter, they had certainly fluttered then—for a sure prevision, like an instinct, told her what was coming. Two of them were old receipts for rent: the other was the missing paper, given by Mr. Honeythorn.

But the time had gone by for Mrs. Barber to be moved about anything in this world. She just looked round from the fire, but did not take the document in her hand.

"I remember now: I did put it there. I never thought o' the Bible when we were looking for it. Every other place but that. You'll show it to Sir Dene, Mary, that he may see what I said was true."

"Yes, I'll show it to Sir Dene—and to others also," was the emphatic answer.

Mary Barber wished her mother good night, again urging the buttered-ale upon her, and departed, the paper safely stowed away in her pocket. She stepped into Mrs. Pound's kitchen to say a word.

"You'll give a look upstairs to mother afore you go to bed, Matty Pound. She seems queer to-night."

"How—queer?" asked Matty Pound, who sat mending her husband's Sunday coat.

"Well, I hardly know. She don't seem like she always does. She won't drink the buttered-ale I brought."

Mrs. Pound thought the state must be serious not to take *that*. "I'll be sure and go up," said she.

"And if she should be worse in the morning, send little Jack to the farm to let me know, please. Our wash is not got up yet, and we be a-going to brew to-morrow, so I can't possibly get out afore night—unless it's for something particular. If she should become ill, we must get Mr. Priar to her. Good night, Matty Pound."

Matty Pound responded to the salutation, and Mary Barber went home. The paper in her pocket felt as good as though it had been a hundred-pound note there.

"My poor mother always said she hoped the paper would come to light before she died. Sir Dene'll see whether she was telling lies now! And Jonathan Drew, he'll see—but *he's* not worth a thought o' salt."

On the following morning Mary Barber was toasting some bacon in the kitchen for her master's breakfast, when she was surprised by the appearance of John Pound. Not little Jack; John himself. He came to bring her ill news—which he got out awkwardly. Mrs. Barber was dead.

Matty Pound had seen her to bed the night before, all comfortable. Upon going into the room in the morning, they found her dead. She had died quietly in her sleep.

"The Squire telled me to come up t'ye," cried Pound to the dismayed Mary Barber. "He was passing, and heard what 'twas, and said ' Go up at once, never mind t' work for a bit.' Matty says there bain't no call to fret too much : she must ha' gone off wi'out pain as quank as a lamb."

Ay. The broken heart was rest.

CHAPTER VI.

IN ST. PETER'S CHURCH.

IN a small but pretty house within the environs of St. Peter's parish in the suburbs of the city of Worcester, sat four people in the growing dusk of a November afternoon. George Arde and his wife; Maria Owen, and Geoffry Clanwaring.

George Arde, a man of middle height, of dark eyes and

hair, with a pale, honest, but plain face, somewhat stern in its
character, was about thirty. He had small, independent
means, derived from his hop-yards. When it was a good year
for hops, George Arde was flourishing; when the hops failed,
he had to look after his shillings as well as his pounds.
Taking one year with another, his income averaged perhaps
two hundred pounds. No great excess of means: and it may
appear singular that Farmer Owen should have regretted his
daughter's marriage to him, on the score that it exalted her
above her station. But his view of it was right. George
Arde was a gentleman by birth, and well connected; he moved
in a sphere above that of the farmer; one to which the latter
would not have been admitted on an equality. At the time
of the marriage Mr. Owen had protested against it—yielding
at last only a reluctant consent; but George Arde, a willing
captive to Mary Owen's beauty, would not hear of giving her
up. As to the remote contingency that he might succeed to
Squire Arde's wealth, none looked on it as a surer chimera
than George himself. He and the Squire were not very nearly
related; George had never received the smallest favour from
him, never the slightest intimation that he might hope to inherit as much as a mourning ring; and he certainly did not
look for it. The Squire had other relatives, as near—or,
rather, as distant—as he; but none expected to be the better
for him. As to George Arde's own prospects, he intended to
put by a little money every good hop year, buy more yards,
and so get rich that way. We all have schemes in the head for
making ourselves wealthy in course of time.

Mrs. Arde sat by the fire, a baby of some four months old
sleeping in her arms. It was very precious to the mother,
this little thing; and they had named it by her own name,
Mary. Fragile, delicate, attenuated, but exquisitely beautiful,
was Mrs. Arde. There seemed to be no strength in her, no
life-blood. A flush would appear on her cheeks towards the
close of the afternoon; but at other times her face was pale
as alabaster: you might see the blue veins underneath the
clear skin. George Arde feared the paleness less than he did
the flush: for the latter looked suspiciously like hectic.
There were moments when a horrible prevision came over him
—that he should lose her: but he strove to drive the fear
away, even from his own heart; and he never spoke of it.
Maria Owen had been staying with her sister for several weeks
now. Mr. and Mrs. Owen willingly spared her: they also

had secret fears about Mary's health. But now that Mrs. Arde seemed to be getting somewhat stronger—as in truth she did so seem—Maria was to go home: and it had been settled that her father should take her back with him when he came in to market on the following Saturday.

And that, Maria's sojourn in the house, accounted for the frequent presence in it of Geoffry Clanwaring. Hardly a day passed but upon some pretext or other Mr. Geoffry paid a visit to Worcester. Sir Dene, utterly unsuspicious, told him he was getting restlessly fond of riding. Not that Geoffry always rode in: he walked often. Just now Sir Dene, who had recovered from the sprain to his ankle, was staying in London, and Geoffry was entirely his own master in regard to his movements, accountable to nobody. He had walked in this afternoon: and he now had to walk back again. Earlier than usual, he intended to go: but he had business at home that night with Jonathan Drew.

"And you really cannot stay for tea?" asked Mrs. Arde, as he shook hands with her to leave.

"Not this evening, thank you. I wish I could. Good-night, Arde."

"Good-night, Geoffry."

"I wish you would just come as far as the gate with me, Maria. I have something to say to you."

Geoffry Clanwaring turned his head to ask this as he was quitting the room. Maria blushed painfully, and hesitated—hesitated because of the presence of the others. But Geoffry held open the door, waiting for her, and she timidly followed him. That Mr. and Mrs. Arde were tacitly aware of the state of affairs between Sir Dene's son and Maria—namely, that he was courting her, as the phrase ran—could but be a matter of course; otherwise they had possessed neither sense nor perception. They did not interfere. George Arde felt that all interference would be useless, for he remembered his own case: and it really was no concern of his, that he should make or mar. Mrs. Arde trembled a little; she saw insurmountable difficulties before them; and once she spoke just one word of warning to her sister. "Papa can never give his consent, Maria. It would put him all wrong with Sir Dene." Maria answered nothing: but the sadness that overspread her face showed to Mary Arde how perfectly she understood the hopelessness of the future: and that Mr. Owen's consent was a thing never to be looked for. And so, Mr. and Mrs. Arde had gone on, tacitly sanctioning the state of matters, inasmuch as they did not put a stop to Geoffry's visits. He had found many a moment for seeing Maria alone; for George Arde would be out and about, and the delicate young mother had often to remain in her chamber. But this was the first time that Mr. Clanwaring had gone so far as to ask Maria to go out of the room with him.

"George," whispered the wife, as the room door closed, "I do feel that we are incurring a great responsibility in suffering this. Should it ever be discovered at home, papa will say so."

"How is it to be helped?" returned George Arde. "We can do nothing, either way. It's not to be expected, Polly, that I should go off to her father, or to his father, and tell about it."

"Well—no. Of course not. At any rate, it will be over on Saturday," added Mrs. Arde, with a sigh of relief. "The responsibility, I mean. Maria returns home then, and I shall be glad of it; much as I regret to lose her."

Meanwhile Maria, a light shawl thrown over her shoulders, that she had caught up in passing out, was pacing down the path on Mr. Clanwaring's arm. George Arde could see them through the window in the dusk. It was some such a night as the one already told of, when the two men with their burden of plate had gone stealing up Harebell Lane: moonlight, but very gusty. A cold November evening.

"Everything is arranged and in readiness, Maria," began Geoffry. "I saw the clergyman this afternoon, and I've got the license. Nine o'clock, mind. You will find me at the church waiting for you."

For Mr. Geoffry Clanwaring had succeeded in obtaining Maria Owen's consent to marry him. They meant to take French leave: get married quietly, and tell the world afterwards. Such weddings were rather common in those days; and were regarded with less reprehension than they would be in these. To do Maria justice, she had at first steadily refused: but Geoffry had eloquently pointed out that there was no middle course; nothing between that, and separation. And, to separate, was beyond the philosophy of either.

"I cannot possibly see how I shall get away from here in my white dress," she answered. "The season is too far advanced for wearing white in a morning now. If they saw me, they might suspect something."

In St. Peter's Church.

"Put on a big shawl," suggested Geoffry. "Or come in a coloured dress: what does it matter?"

At the foot of the little garden there ran a sheltered walk behind the hedge, secure from observation. Geoffry turned into it.

"I want to try on the ring, love."

He had bought it that afternoon at the silversmith's. The same one from whom the gold and silver plate had been stolen: which robbery, as to its perpetrators, had never been discovered, in spite of the cunning of the Bow Street runners. Mr. Geoffry found he had guessed the size well: the friendly night hid the blushes on Maria's sweet face, as he told her so.

"Oh but, Geoffry, I scarcely dare to think of it!" she said imploringly. "I tremble for the consequences. And besides, it is *not* a right thing for us to do."

"It is quite right, my love. It can injure no one. When once my father knows you, and finds that we are happy, he will forgive all. And you are aware that Mr. Owen would give you to me himself, so far as I am alone concerned."

"I have never disobeyed my father and mother before," she said, bursting into tears.

Geoffry Clanwaring kissed the tears away. The gentle, lovely face, very sad then, lay passively against him, and he took kiss after kiss from it, as he whisperingly strove to reassure her with all the eloquence love is master of. And thus they parted—for the last time before their wedding-day.

The church of St. Peter's was open in the morning. A damp old church in the region of Frog Lane, that you stepped down into as if into a vault. The clergyman was in the vestry; the clerk fidgeted about the pews. Geoffry Clanwaring, in bridegroom's attire, stood looking anxiously from the door.

A panting, breathless girl came in. A most lovely, dimpled, timid, shrinking girl, who took off her red gipsy cloak as she entered, which had served partially to cover her. Her wedding dress was of white sprigged India muslin—the material had been a present to her years ago from her godmother—and a straw hat trimmed with a wreath of pale blush-roses.

"God bless you, my darling!" cried Geoffry, seizing upon her. "It is seven minutes past nine, and I was upon thorns."

"I was so afraid," she whispered. "I did not dare come

out of my room for fear of any one's meeting me on the stairs."

"I shall want you to stand father-in-church to this young lady," said Geoffry to the clerk, slipping a very substantial fee into that functionary's hand.

"At your pleasure, sir."

The clergyman came out in his surplice, and took his place. The clerk directed them where to kneel; standing himself at Maria's elbow. There was no bridesmaid; the clerk was to be "father-in-church" and give the bride away. It has been remarked that such weddings, unattended, were tolerably common then: and the clergyman made no fuss about this one. He saw that the license was in order, asked a question or two, and proceeded with his work.

Rarely has a handsomer couple knelt before the altar, never one more attractive. He, tall and strong, with his fair Saxon beauty, his kindly blue eyes, his golden hair; she in her gentle, shrinking, blushing loveliness. The clergyman pronounced them man and wife, and gave the bridegroom, at his own request, a certificate.

The weather had culminated into a downfall of rain when they got out again. It had been a dull, grey, threatening morning, and now the rain had commenced. Not very hard, as yet. Maria took her white India muslin up under her cloak, and tripped along on Geoffry's arm. Thanks to the umbrella—which he had had the precaution to bring from home—and the rainy streets, they got into Mr. Arde's without observation.

In consequence of Mrs. Arde's delicate state, and perhaps also of the exactions of the baby, breakfast there had recently been taken very late, more especially when she attempted to come down to it—as she had this morning. The tea was only being made; and Maria's escapade had not been discovered: it was supposed she had not yet come out of her chamber. Geoffry went in first, in his light overcoat.

"Why, Geoffry!" exclaimed George Arde, with intense surprise. "You are in town early!"

Geoffry threw his coat back, and they saw his costume—a gala one. Quite at the first moment, no suspicion as to the *why*, was aroused. George Arde, as he stared, thought there might be some grand breakfast in the town, that Mr. Clanwaring had come in for.

"Is anything going on in Worcester to-day, Geoffry?"

"Not that I know of. I have been getting married."

He turned to the door, and brought Maria in, scarlet cloak and all. Mr. Arde looked from one to the other; his wife sunk into a chair, bewildered.

"Oh, Maria!" she gasped.

Maria flew to her, and hid her face on her bosom in a passion of hysterical tears. They could not soothe her: emotion, suppressed hitherto, had its way now.

"Oh, Mary! forgive me!" came the sobbing cry.

Geoffry tenderly took off the hat and cloak, and stroked the hand with its new wedding-ring fondly within his own. Mrs. Arde was pale as death.

"You—are—surely—not really married!" she exclaimed.

"Here's the certificate," said Geoffry, handing it to Mr. Arde. "It's all in form. We were married at your parish church—St. Peter's."

"Well, you are a clever fellow!" cried Mr. Arde, half admiringly, half angrily.

"And my father and mother!—oh, what a blow it will be to them!" bewailed Mrs. Arde, weeping with Maria.

"I hope not," answered Geoffry. "They both like me."

"Who is to break it to them?"

"I; of course. I shall go over there to-day or to-morrow for the purpose. You won't refuse to give us some breakfast, will you, Arde?"

Mr. Arde, getting a little over his annoyance—for he had felt at first both dismayed and angry—told him that as much breakfast was at their service as they liked to eat. Just as he had been neuter in the matter hitherto, so he resolved, after taking a minute's inward counsel with himself, to remain. The marriage had certainly been no fault of his: none could be more surprised at it than he was; and therefore no blame could attach to him. He did not see why he should either espouse their cause, or turn against them for it: and he determined to do neither.

"It is your own concern entirely, Geoffry; I shall not make it mine. I am sorry that you have taken this step—and there's sure to be a row over it: but I don't see that *I* am called upon to resent it. And so—here's good luck to you both."

"Thank you heartily," replied Geoffry: while Maria sobbed in silence.

"But do not think I approve of what you have done—don't

run away with that notion to tell your friends," resumed Mr. Arde. "What are your plans?"

"Plans?" returned Geoffry.

"Ay. Where are you going to take Maria? Up to the moon?"

"Up to Malvern. I have engaged lodgings there for the present."

"Oh, I thought you might be going to take her to Beechhurst Dene," cried Mr. Arde rather satirically.

"I must wait for that."

But before sitting down to breakfast, Maria escaped to her chamber, unseen by either of the servants; there to remove the tell-tale attire and assume her ordinary dress. As to Geoffry, he breakfasted with his overcoat buttoned close up.

Surprises that day seemed to be the lot of Mr. and Mrs. Arde. The morning was wearing on, getting near the time that Geoffry intended to take his bride away—driving her in his open gig to avert any suspicion that a close carriage might have endangered—when Squire Arde called. The same little, stooping old man that you have already seen; in the same pepper-and-salt suit with the silver buckles at his knees and shoes; and the same fluffy greatcoat falling off his narrow shoulders. He had never honoured them with a call yet: hence the surprise. Mrs. Arde blushed as she rose timidly to receive him. As to Maria, she felt ready to sink: in the first confused moment a wild fancy came over her that her father knew all about the morning's work, and that Squire Arde had come from him, the herald of war.

"What, are *you* here!" cried he, staring at Geoffry.

"I came into Worcester this morning, Squire," was the assumingly-careless answer.

"Oh," returned the Squire, glancing at Maria, as though he had some suspicion that she might be the attraction. "When d'ye expect Sir Dene home from Lunnon?"

"In a week or two, I suppose; it's uncertain," answered Geoffry.

Squire Arde's visit this morning was not dictated by any thought of friendship or courtesy: he had but come to inquire after the character of a man who had been employed upon George Arde's hop-grounds.

"I don't know much of him, sir," was George's answer to the application. "He is steady enough, I think. Jonathan Drew could tell you more about him than I can."

"Ah, I dare say," was the old man's remark. "But Drew might not speak the truth, you know."

"Drew not speak the truth!" interposed Geoffry Clanwaring. "He'd be sure to do that, Squire. Though surly in manner sometimes, he is truthful."

"When he finds it convenient to be so," returned the Squire with composure. "He did not speak truth for Tom Barber's widow."

"How do you mean, sir?"

"In the matter of that lost paper. Drew knew it was given to her, well enough, though it suited him to forget it."

"If I thought Drew did know of it—asserting all the while that he did not; that there had never been any such paper given—I would get my father to turn him away," was the indignant remark of Geoffry.

"Let him be," said the old man. "The matter's over, and done with, and Hester Barber's gone. A curious thing, she should ha' found the paper only an hour or two afore her death, warn't it?"

He looked at Geoffry with his once bright grey eye, cold as steel. In the glance there was a strange keenness.

"Yes, it was curious," assented Geoffry. "Had the paper been unearthed in time, I hope—and I think—my father would have respected it, and not interfered with the poor old woman; although it was not binding on him. I should have done my best to beg for her. I did as it was."

"Well, it's too late by some months now," said the Squire: "the cottage is gone, and the fine new road's there instead. It's just one o' them cases, young man, that might be compared to a broken egg. Once spilt on the floor, it can never be picked up again."

"That's true," said Geoffry, a great sadness in his good-natured blue eyes. "Nobody was more sorry for poor Granny Barber than I was. It was a hard case: I told my father so. But he did not see it in the same light."

Old Mr. Arde nodded, and then shook his head from side to side, as if in strong condemnation.

"You think my father did wrong, I see, sir."

"Nay, I judge nobody, young man. But there's some plain words in an old Book that have run through my head, off and on, since the day I saw 'em demolishing her place. 'Remove not the old land-mark, and enter not into the field of the fatherless.' Sir Dene don't read his Bible, maybe."

"Oh but he does—sometimes," said Geoffry.

"Ah then he forgot 'em, maybe! Anyway the old homestead's gone, and Hester Barber's gone; and the cutting's broad and smooth, and a fine name you've given to it—Dene Hollow."

"We did not give it; I don't know who did give it, sir."

"And it don't matter," rejoined the Squire.

At that moment a young servant-maid came in with the baby. When she saw there was a stranger present, she would have retreated; but Mrs. Arde took the child from her. A very pretty, lively little baby in a clean white frock, who sat up and looked with independence on the company. The child attracted Squire Arde's attention, and he went up and patted its cheeks.

"Boy, or girl, ma'am?"

"Girl, sir," replied Mrs. Arde.

"Ho ho, pretty one: ho ho! What, are ye laughing at the old man? D'ye want to come to him?"

For the baby had broken out into a smile, and was holding forth its little fat arms. To the surprise of all present, perhaps also of himself, Squire Arde put his riding-whip on the table, and took the baby.

"What's her name?" he asked, as he sat down, and the little fingers caught hold of his hanging bunch of seals.

"It's Mary, sir."

"Mary! The same as my girl's was," muttered he, his voice dying away in a whisper. And he kissed the child fondly.

"Here, take it, ma'am; I must be going," said he, getting up. "You don't look very peart, my dear," he added, in a kind, fatherly tone, as Mrs. Arde received the child, and he chucked her under the chin. "You try and get your wife's roses back, George Arde. Good-day to ye all."

They watched him down the path in the rain, the little shrunken figure, riding-whip in hand, George Arde attending him to open the gate.

Squire Arde's had been a sad history. In the bloom of his early manhood, when life looked fair before him, he had married a young lady to whom he was much attached. She gave birth to a child—a girl—and soon afterwards symptoms of insanity developed themselves. Ever since then until her death, which only occurred three years ago, she had been the raving inmate of a lunatic asylum. The little girl lived to be ten years old: and her death nearly broke her father's heart. Since then he had been strangely altered: the kindly feelings of his nature seemed to have withered up at the grave, and he became a solitary, penurious old man. Hurst Leet was wont to say that he was Arde by name, and hard by nature. But this was mostly applied to his sociable qualities; for no one instance of oppression had ever been traced to him.

"How's hops, George?" he asked, as he was going through the gate.

"Pretty brisk, sir. Nothing much to complain of."

"I think I shall try that fellow. Good morning."

On the following afternoon Geoffry Clanwaring, leaving his wife at Malvern, went over to Harebell Farm to break the news of what he had done. Nothing, as he believed, had transpired; he took it for granted that the marriage was as yet a secret. Mr. Owen happened to be in his barn when Geoffry rode in. Leaving his horse, Geoffry found him watching the threshing. Drawing the farmer outside, for the noise was deafening, Geoffry sat down on the shaft of a barrow, and told him what he had to tell.

"I know all about it, Mr. Clanwaring."

"Know it!" repeated Geoffry, starting up. But it might have struck him that the farmer listened very quietly, without any appearance of surprise. "Why, how did you get to know it, sir?"

"From my daughter Mary. I took the pony-chaise into Worcester early this morning to fetch home Maria, her mother not being well. It could not be kept from me then."

A deprecating flush rose to the young man's ingenuous face. He held out his hand timidly.

"You will not refuse to forgive me, sir! And—to—bless us both?"

"My forgiveness will not be a material matter to you, Mr. Clanwaring," was the reply—and Geoffry could not but note with what strangely calm sadness he was speaking. "Your father's will be of more moment than mine: and that, I fear, you will never get. I cannot forgive Maria."

"Oh, but she was not to blame; it was not her fault," ardently burst forth Geoffry. "She only yielded to me after months of persuasion."

"There lies her fault—that she did yield," spoke the farmer gravely. "I had thought that I could place implicit trust in my daughters."

"She will be your dutiful daughter still, Mr. Owen, and her mother's too, although she is my wife. I'll bring her over to see you next week."

"Do you think you were justified in taking this extreme step, sir?"

"Not entirely," candidly avowed Geoffry; "but *yes* in a great degree. The only one to whom I cannot plead justification is my own father. To you and Mrs. Owen I may, and do, plead it. Had you not told me, sir, that you liked me for myself; that you would, had circumstances only been favourable, have willingly given me, Maria?"

Robert Owen drew in his refined and beautiful lips. It was true, so far.

"But the circumstances were not favourable, Mr. Clanwaring. You know perfectly well that I alluded to your father. *Only* in the event of his being willing should I have been."

"You see I was obliged to marry her as I have done," confessed Geoffry. "Had I asked my father's consent, he would have forbidden it altogether—and in the teeth of an absolute refusal I should not have liked to disobey him. As it is, nobody forbid it; and I have but taken my own way."

"I should call that three parts sophistry, sir."

"And one part good wholesome honesty," returned Geoffry, his earnest eyes full of sincere meaning. "Believe me, Mr. Owen, it will all come right. Sir Dene will be angry at first, little doubt of it; but he'll not retain anger long. I wrote to him last night, a good long letter, telling him all about it from the onset, and sent it off to-day. He'll get it to-morrow morning."

"And a fine way he'll be in," remarked the farmer. "His first act will be to give me notice of ejectment."

"How can you think he would be so unjust?" retorted Geoffry. "I have told him that you knew no more of it than he did, and would have been just as much against it. He'll make common cause with you in abusing me for a bit, I shouldn't wonder. *You* will forgive me, Mr. Owen?"—and once more the pleading eyes went out with the proffered hand.

"In one sense I forgive you, Mr. Clanwaring,—and that is, that I do not refuse my countenance to you now. The marriage cannot be undone; therefore it would serve no good end to resent it. It is not against me that you have sinned, but against your father and family."

"Thank you," said Geoffry, heartily, as his hand was at length taken. "And now, sir, I want you to hear me say that your daughter is very dear to me. By Heaven's help, I will do my best and utmost to promote her happiness."

Mr. Owen shook his head in sadness. "You think so now; I do not doubt it; but in these unequal marriages the wife generally has to suffer from neglect in the long run."

"Mine never shall," emphatically spoke Geoffry, his whole face burning red with resentment at the implied suggestion. "If I know anything of myself, Mr. Owen, of my nature, my principles, my *love*, Maria will be as dear to me and as honoured by me in the far-off years to come, as she is on this, the morrow of my wedding-day."

In the far-off years to come! Could poor Geoffry—could ill-fated Robert Owen—but have foreseen a shadow of the events that were destined to happen long before those far-off years should dawn! Astrologers have assumed to see into the future: but it is not one of the least mercies of God that all such sight is hidden from our view.

CHAPTER VII.

ENCOUNTERING THE STORM.

CLATTERING up through the gates of Beechhurst Dene in a noisy post-chaise and pair late at night, went Sir Dene Clanwaring and his eldest son. The chaise had been chartered from Sir Dene's hotel at Worcester, the Hop-pole, after the London stage-coach had deposited them in that city. Geoffry's "good long letter" was not received so soon by two or three days as it might have been, in consequence of Sir Dene's temporary absence from London. It had now brought him down in a fury, and Mr. Clanwaring accompanied him to take part in the storm. He was a little, dark man, this eldest son and heir; proud, honourable, haughtily self-conscious of his degree and position. As little like his father and Geoffry in person as he could well be; resembling, in fact, his dead mother. Bitterly wrathful, was he, against Geoffry for the (as he put it) degrading marriage: he *said* less than Sir Dene, but his anger was inwardly greater, and would be more lasting. Mr. Clanwaring intended to mate with one of high degree, himself; the youngest brother, in India, had married a title: how could they brook the disgrace on the family inflicted by Geoffry? Mr. Clanwaring's private opinion was that he deserved hanging. As a matter of course he must be discarded for ever: blotted out of the Clanwaring archives.

The housekeeper came forward in dismay as the chaise stopped: she had received no intimation of Sir Dene's return, and had been about to retire for the night. Sir Dene waved her off; said they did not want much supper; anything would do; but ordered a fire to be lighted instantly in his parlour, and Gander sent to him.

Gander was in bed. A faithful serving-man some forty years old, who had spent the last half of them with his master in India, and was now butler. Gander had a frightful toothache—which he was always having—and had gone to bed at nine on the strength of it. He was a red-faced man with obstinate dark hair that never could be persuaded by brush to lie on his head, but stood up in straight pieces like porcupines' quills, as if he were in a chronic state of fright! The popular phrase—his hair stood on end—might have been made for Gander.

"Now, then, Gander," began Sir Dene as soon as he appeared, "what is the truth of this infamous business?"

Gander knew what was meant, and wished himself miles away: he was nearly as simple as his name. The offender, Mr. Geoffry, was a great favourite of his.

"Can't you speak?" cried Sir Dene.

"Well, Sir Dene—I—I suppose you have heard on't," stammered Gander, who was a native of Worcestershire, and spoke its patois.

"Is he really married?"

"Ay, sir, I b'lieve so."

"And to one of those girls of Owen's!"

"Yes, sir, it's she. The only one left of 'em. Squire Arde's nephew married the t'other."

"Squire Arde's nephew?" Gander had thrown in that in his goodnature; a reminder that his young master was not the first gentleman by birth who had gone to Farmer Owen's for a wife.

"Has he been here since?" thundered Sir Dene.

"Mr. Geoffry?—no, sir. We hear he's staying at Malvern."

John the heir turned round: he was holding his boots, first one, then the other, to the faggots in the grate, now blazing up.

"Is it known yet in the neighbourhood, Gander?"

"Lawk, Mr. Clanwaring! Known! Why, sir, it's the talk o' the whole place—and has been since the day after the wedding, when Mr. Geoffry came over to beg forgiveness of Farmer Owen——!"

"Forgiveness of *him*!" interjected Mr. Clanwaring, with curling lips.

Gander detected the passion. "I beg your pardon, Mr Clanwaring," he resumed with deprecation. "It's said he did do it. Farmer Owen is as grieved about it as anybody else can be. He told Squire Arde that 'twas just a blow to him."

"Does he consider Mr. Geoffry Clanwaring beneath his daughter?" questioned the heir in scornful mockery.

"It is because he is so much above her, sir, and because he knows it'll put Mr. Geoffry wrong with Sir Dene—that's why *he* feels it as a blow," cried honest Gander.

"Cease this, John," stormed the baronet, bringing his hand down on the table by which he stood. "What I want to know is, how he got acquainted with the girl. They would not be married off-hand without some acquaintanceship. *Somebody* must have known that there were meetings between them."

"As to that, Geoffry was always out and about like a bailiff," spoke Mr. Clanwaring, while Gander was wisely silent.

"He had his work to do, John. Overlooking, and that."

"Yes, sir. I imagine, though, that Harebell Farm was better looked after than all the rest of the land put together."

"Harebell Farm is not in my occupation; he had no business there at all," growled Sir Dene. And his son gave a stamp to the burning wood with his right boot.

"The young lady has not been at home these five weeks past, Sir Dene—leastways, it's said so," added cautious Gander, not deeming it expedient to know too much. "The tale runs that she has been a-staying at Worcester with her sister, Mrs. Arde."

A sudden flash of enlightenment, like an illumination, darted through Sir Dene's brain. He turned on his heel.

"Then that explains his visits to Worcester! John, I thought he had gone Worcester-mad. He was always there."

"And no one could open their lips to tell Beechhurst Dene of it!" said John bitterly. "Did *you* know nothing of it, Gander?"

"Not a word, Mr. Clanwaring. Of course, sir, I knowed it was as Sir Dene says—that Mr. Geoffry was often going to Worcester. But it never came into my head to wonder why he went."

Sir Dene was biting his hot lips. "Let's see—which day was it that he made this shameful marriage, Gander?"

"'Twas last Thursday, sir—a week ago to-morrow. I wondered what business could be taking off Mr. Geoffry so soon in the morning: his gig was waiting at the door a'most afore 'twas light. He had a cup o' coffee took to his room, and came down with his top-coat on. 'If I am not at home by nine o'clock to-night, don't expect me, Gander,' says he. Upon that I asked whether he had got the key of the cellaret—for I had been looking for it, Sir Dene, and couldn't find it. He unbuttoned his coat to feel in his pockets, and then I see he was dressed up."

"Saw he was dressed up!" echoed Sir Dene. "And ought not that to have given you a suspicion of what was agate?"

"Why no, sir; how should it?" returned Gander.

"A man does not go out dressed up at dawn for nothing," stormed the baronet.

"I thought it might be the mayor's feast at Worcester, Sir Dene—if I thought anything: it's held in November. But, sir," added the man with reason, "put it that I had suspected the truth—what end would it ha' served? I could not have stopped Mr. Geoffry from getting married—or attempted to stop him. He is my master, sir."

"You are a fool, Gander," growled Sir Dene.

To what use the discussion? Of what avail to dispute as to what might have been? It could not undo the fact of the marriage, or part Geoffry Clanwaring from the young girl he had made his wife.

On the following day, Thursday, Geoffry drove his wife over from Malvern to Harebell Farm. And there, happening to meet one of his father's servants, he learnt the fact that Sir Dene had come thundering home in a storm of passion. Leaving Maria with her mother, he went at once to Beechhurst Dene.

There was a distressing and turbulent scene. Geoffry found more enemies than he had bargained for. Not only were his father and brother there: but his mother's sister, Miss Clewer, a precise maiden lady of more than middle age, had also arrived. The news of her favourite nephew's escapade had reached her at her home in Gloucestershire, and she posted over in a chaise-and-four in dire consternation.

Going in by the back way, Geoffry met Gander in the passage. The butler started back when he saw who it was; and took the opportunity to whisper a word of warning.

"They be all in the library, Mr. Geoffry," he said; "making a frightful outcry against you. The master, and Mr. Clanwaring, and Miss Ann Clewer—*she's* come over, sir. I've just carried in a pitcher o' water to keep her out of a fit of the 'sterics."

"Great cry and little wool, Gander," said Geoffry, with light goodhumour. But nevertheless he shrank from the task before him. He would not so much have minded Sir Dene alone; but there was the wrath of his haughty brother in addition to be encountered; not to speak of his aunt's hysterics.

The room called the library was a charming one. Not large, with a bay-window opening on the side of the house opposite to that of the Harebell Lane entrance. It looked on the green park; on its beautiful old trees scattered here and there; on the herd of tame deer. It had been the favourite sitting-room of the late Lady Clanwaring, and was lightly and tastefully furnished, the carpet bright with roses, the chairs and curtains of pale green brocade.

Geoffry opened the door quietly, and they did not see him. Sir Dene was pacing the floor in a fume; John Clanwaring stood with his face to the window; Miss Clewer (a very thin lady with a flaxen "front") sat on a sofa, her bonnet and shawl on, just as she had got out of the postchaise; her eyes dropping tears.

"Sir Dene! Father!"

They saw him then; and a commotion set in. What Gander had called a frightful outcry became more frightful. Sir Dene raved, Ann Clewer sobbed; John Clanwaring stared contemptuously in his brother's face, his thin lips compressed, his arms folded. Geoffry stood his ground before them, hoping for a hearing; upright, noble, his fair Saxon face quite remarkable in its beauty. He strove to make the best defence he could: but it was not a moment calculated to enhance an offender's courage. Sir Dene interrupted him at every second word, utterly refusing to listen.

"Aunt Ann, will *you* hear me—will you let me tell you how sweet and gentle she is?" pleaded Geoffry. "She is as much a lady in mind, manners, and appearance as ever my dear mother was."

"Oh!" cried Miss Clewer with a shriek and a sob. "To bring your mother's name in with *hers!* The world must be coming to an end, I think. If my dear Lady Clanwaring could come out of her grave, she'd die again with the shame."

It was of no use. Not a word of reason could any one of them be brought to hear. Abuse drowned Geoffry's voice. Sir Dene ranted out hot things; Mr. Clanwaring quieter ones, that stung ten-fold deeper with their scorn; Miss Clewer sobbed and choked and shrieked. Geoffry managed to put his hand into his father's, as he whispered forth a plea to be forgiven.

Forgiven! Sir Dene flung away the hand with a passionate force that sent Geoffry staggering: and ordered him out of the house.

"Go," he thundered, his arm stretched out to indicate the door. "Get your living in the best way you can. I cast you off from this hour."

And Geoffry went. Finding that the longer he stayed the worse it got, he went. At the angle of the passage stood Gander, with a face as red as a turkey's comb.

"It has been a'most as bad as bull-baiting, hasn't it, Mr. Geoffry?" he whispered.

"There has been as much noise, Gander."

"Ay. But look here, sir—don't you be down-hearted. Sir Dene's temper's up—and nobody knows better than me the lot of swearing it takes to cool it down again. One has to swear, living in India. Just let Mr. Clanwaring get away from the place—he is the hottest against you, sir, and it edges on Sir Dene. When he's safe off and the house is clear, you come again, Mr. Geoffry, and try then. I can tell you one thing, sir—your father likes you better than he does *him.*"

Geoffry nodded. He knew all this just as well as Gander. While he was giving directions for his clothes to be sent to him, the library door opened, and Mr. Clanwaring came out.

"You will shake hands with me before I go, won't you, John?" he asked when he had finished what he had to say to Gander—and the tone was a somewhat piteous one.

But Mr. John Clanwaring rejected the held-out hand quite as unmistakeably though less demonstratively than Sir Dene had done: and passed on, leaving a few cold and cutting words behind him.

So Geoffry went out of his father's home by the nearest and

least ceremonious way. As he crossed Harebell Lane, he saw Robert Owen leaning on his gate.

"Well, how have you sped?" were the words that greeted him.

"Badly to-day," was the young man's candid answer. "It was to be expected I should, this first time. Things will come all right later, Mr. Owen—at least with my father. I am sure of it."

"Is Sir Dene very much incensed?" questioned Mr. Owen.

"Yes. Old Aunt Ann has come posting over—to make matters worse still. Between them all, I had not fair-play. No play at all, in fact. It will be different—when I can get to see my father alone."

"And, meanwhile, what are you to do for ways and means, Mr. Clanwaring?"

Geoffry smiled. "That need not concern me yet, sir: I am not reduced to my last ten-pound note. Never having had ill outlets for my allowance, as some young fellows have, I saved it."

Robert Owen shook his head. "The time may come when you will rue the day for your foolish marriage with Maria."

"It never will," said Geoffry with emphasis. "She is a great deal too precious to me for that to come to pass."

Mr. Owen sighed. Others had thought the same, and lived to find themselves bitterly mistaken. They were leaning with their arms on the gate while they talked.

"Did Sir Dene say anything about me, Mr. Clanwaring?"

"Not a word. Who's that?"

Geoffry Clanwaring's "Who's that" applied to a man who was passing down the lane. An ill-looking fellow with a slouching gait, and slouching hat.

"I don't know who it is," was Robert Owen's answer when the man was beyond hearing, "but I suspect it is one of Mr. Randy Black's choice customers. Had this business of yours, sir, not come between me and Sir Dene, I might have found it my duty to give him a hint as to what I think of the Trailing Indian."

"Give it to me," said Geoffry.

"I have nothing very tangible to say. Only that I feel sure evil doings of some kind are carried on in the house. I am out a good deal late in an evening with my stock, and hardly a night passes by but I see ill-looking men slink up this lane on their way to the place. Sometimes they have bundles with them."

"Bundles!" cried Geoffry.

"Bundles that they try to hide. I'd not like to make an affidavit that they don't contain stolen goods."

"No!" uttered Geoffry in surprise. "Stolen goods! You mean smuggled goods, don't you?"

"I mean what I say, Mr. Clanwaring. I have had my strong suspicions for some time now, that the Trailing Indian is a receiving place for them."

"Oh but, you know my father would never allow anything of that kind on his estate," returned Geoffry, unconsciously drawing himself up with a touch of the pride of the Clanwaring family. "He would shut up the Trailing Indian to-morrow, and send Black to the right-about."

"He would have to prove it first," dissented Robert Owen. "Black holds his lease, and cannot be turned out lightly. Put it down at smuggling only: it's not very reputable to have such a man for one's next-door neighbour."

"Black must be uncommonly bold if it is anything beyond smuggling. Do you think he'd venture on it?"

"There never was a safer place for it than the Trailing Indian has been," observed Mr. Owen. "Moses Black occupied this farm, and of course was in his brother's interests; Mr. Honeythorn kept but three or four servants at the Dene in his old age—and they mostly women. Why, a gang of smugglers, or what not, might have gone up this lane nightly, and not be met or seen once in a twelvemonth! And you know how lonely the field way is across from Worcester!"

Geoffry Clanwaring took out his watch. "What time do you dine, Mr. Owen?"

"I expect dinner's ready now, sir."

"Then I'll go up to the Trailing Indian after dinner, before we start for home. Mr. Randy Black must get a hint, from me, to mind his manners."

"I should have given him a hint myself long ago, only that I possess no right to interfere," said Robert Owen. "You may tell him so if you like, Mr. Clanwaring."

When dinner was over (served in the best room, and in the best style that Harebell Farm could venture on—which was but a homely, comfortable style at the best—for this was the first time it had had the honour of entertaining Sir Dene's son) Geoffry started for the Trailing Indian. He took the short cut over the fields—not much above five minutes' walk that way—and leaped the little stile at the end of the farm's grounds, which brought him out opposite the inn. Black was standing at his door, and watched the exit. He touched his hat to his landlord's son.

"I want to speak to you, Black. Will you walk about with me in the lane for a minute or two?"

"Won't you come in, sir?"

"No, I've not the time."

Pacing the lane before the house, beyond the chance of eaves-droppers, Geoffry Clanwaring gave the hint that he had come to give. He did not accuse Black outright of unorthodox doings: only said that doubts had been aroused whether all things enacted at the Trailing Indian would bear the light of day. And he emphatically recommended Black to amend his ways, if they required amending—or he would hear more of it from Sir Dene.

"Robert Owen has been putting you up to say this!" was Black's first comment, spoken with suppressed fierceness.

"No one has put me to say it—I come of my own accord. Though I may tell you, Black, that Mr. Owen has just the same opinion of the Trailing Indian that I have. He sees queer people stealing up here often enough at night."

A change passed over Black's evil face. It settled into a sneer.

"Owen has taken a spite against me, Mr. Geoffry Clanwaring. I've knowed it long. My belief is, he wants to get me out of the Trailing Indian that he may have the place himself; that's why he invents these lies."

"Don't be absurd, man," rebuked Geoffry.

Black said he was not absurd. He denied all insinuations, out and out, giving the Trailing Indian the very whitest of characters. It was as honest as Harebell Farm, he said, and honester.

"That's enough, Black—I don't want to go further into it," concluded Geoffry. "My warning is a friendly one. If needed, you will do wisely to act upon it; if unneeded—why there's no harm done."

"It's a shame that people should try to take away my character behind my back!" exclaimed the landlord in a deeply injured tone. "There's not a ounce of bacca or a gill o'brandy comes into the Trailing Indian, but what has been through his Majesty's Customs."

"As to smuggling, the popular belief is that the whole country smuggles when it gets the chance—from a duchess downwards," carelessly remarked Geoffry. "But," he added, dropping his voice, "to harbour stolen goods, or those who deal with them, is a very different thing, Black. Don't let the Trailing Indian be suspected of *that*. Good afternoon."

He vaulted over the stile at a run, leaving Black looking as dark as his name. Geach came sauntering forth from the inn door, behind which he had been peeping all the while.

"What's up, Randy? You look fit to eat your grandmother."

"If this is not the work of that confounded rat, call me false for ever!" cried Black, stamping with passion.

"What work? What rat?" naturally asked Geach.

"Robert Owen."

CHAPTER VIII.

JONATHAN DREW'S MIDNIGHT RIDE.

A FROSTY night in December. The roads were hard; the moon, bright as silver, was riding in the sky. Mr. Jonathan Drew, Sir Dene's bailiff, who had been a day's journey on horseback, and was returning home across country wearied and tired, turned off the turnpike road into Harebell Lane at its upper end; as if he were a traveller going to demand hospitality of the Trailing Indian.

He was well buttoned up from the cold; and had tied a handkerchief over his ears, which was surmounted by his high-crowned hat. The horse, weary as his master, sought the soft grass by the side of the lane, rather than the harder middle, on which some stones had recently been laid. Drew was feeling very cross. He had told his niece, who had kept his house and did for him, to have his supper ready by nine o'clock; but his business had detained him longer than he had anticipated, and it was now past midnight. A very late hour, that, for a rural district; no travellers were supposed to be abroad at so unearthly a time.

The vague reports, none of them too good, connected with the Trailing Indian, caused Jonathan Drew to turn his eyes over his right shoulder on that hostelrie as he was passing it. It lay on the opposite side of the lane to the one he was riding on. Closely shut up, it looked to be: the moon played on the casements, behind which the curtains were drawn; its inmates no doubt being abed and asleep.

"As I ought to be," growled Mr. Drew. "Get on, Dobbin. What ails ye?—ye bain't at home yet."

For the horse, finding his tired hoofs on the soft grass, had begun to take it easily, slackening his pace to a walk. Drew was about to urge him on with the spur, when a bright light, as if from a door suddenly opened at the side of the house, fell on the inn-yard. Drew let Dobbin's nose seek the ground then, and sat still. He had halted close to the stile that led into Mr. Owen's grounds—the same stile that Geoffry Clanwaring had leaped over when he went to speak that word of warning to the landlord of the Trailing Indian. The branches of the trees, thick there, were bare enough at this season, but the holly hedge was high; it encompassed man and horse within its shade, and he could look across at leisure into Mr. Black's yard, on which the moonbeams shone freely, without fear of being observed.

Just for a short while, Drew, in spite of the moon's light and the other light, was slow in making out what there was to see. His sight was excellent still, except for close print; it was not that: but there seemed to be some large, dark object, of indistinct form, drawn right across the yard. And when at length he slowly made out that, and other things, Jonathan Drew's head seemed to turn the wrong way upwards, and his life-blood to curdle within him.

It was a hearse. A black hearse with four plumes at its corners. The end of it was drawn up to the side-door, whence the light issued; and there seemed to be some figures moving. Four or five men: and they were bringing something out of the house; something that the bailiff at length made out to be a coffin.

"Who can have died there?" softly ejaculated Drew in his bewilderment. "When I was at the place yesterday, I see Black, and the ostler, and—no, I didn't see *her*."

It flashed into his mind with the last words, that Black's wife had been very ill recently; Mr. Priar had been attending on her. Low fever, or something of that.

"It must be her that's in the coffin. Why didn't Black say yesterday she was dead?—And what on earth are they burying her for at this witching hour?"

But, as reason gradually replaced the first confused surprise, Drew remembered that they could not be taking out Mrs. Black at this hour to be buried, unless they were going to do it without "bell, book, and candle;" ay, and without priest also. Recalling Black's character, recalling the fact that he was popularly supposed not to stick at any dark deed, Jonathan Drew felt some ugly doubts creep over him: and he asked himself why they should be carrying away Mrs. Black's body in this surreptitious manner, unless it was to conceal her death. And, if Black did want to conceal it— what was the reason?

A sudden loud neigh from one of the two black horses harnessed to the hearse, caused Drew to start, and Dobbin to turn his head. Close upon that, the door of the vehicle was shut on what had been placed within it, and it began at once to make its way out of the yard.

Still as a statue, sat Drew: hoping, nay, almost praying, that no piercing eye might discern him, watching there. If— as he firmly believed—some ill deed was being enacted, it might not be safe for these desperate men to discover him. In the fear lest they should, he almost resolved to ride across boldly, ask whether Mrs. Black had died, offer his condolences in an unsuspicious manner; and then ride off at a gallop. But prudence told him it might be best to remain still. Concealed under the shade of the thick holly hedge, the chances were that he would not be seen.

On, the hearse came, slowly and quietly. One man sat beside the driver; both of them wearing black cloaks and hatbands. Turning out of the yard to the left, it thus traversed the short distance to the end of the lane: there it set off quickly along the high road, just in the direction that Mr. Drew had come. A high road that led, as may be said, all over the world, London included.

Drew, watching in utter stillness, heaved a sigh of relief. They had not seen him. Somebody—the ostler he thought, by the gait—came and shut the gate of the yard: after that, the side-door was shut, and all was quiet. For any signs that remained of what had passed, a spectator might have thought it a dream.

Drew walked his horse quietly on the grass until he came to the corner of the lane, near Harebell Pond; and then he rode away as if the deuce had been behind him. He could not get Black's wife and the coffin out of his mind. Drew was neither a timorous nor a superstitious man; but the solitary lane struck him as being unpleasantly solitary to-night, and he was glad to get out of it.

Be very sure that he would take the near way home:

the fine new road, Dene Hollow. If ever Drew felt special cause to congratulate himself on Sir Dene's having made that road, he did now. Turning off by the front gates of Beechhurst Dene, he gained it. A fine, smooth, beautiful road, lying white and cold in the moonlight. So bright was it, that the ghastly branches of the bare trees cast their shadows on it in places here and there as clearly as they did in the sunshine of day.

"Now I hope that wench, Pris, has kept my supper warm," muttered Drew, as his sure-footed horse began to descend. "She's a regular sawney, though, in some things. Shouldn't wonder but she——"

A start, a bound, a spring: and Jonathan Drew was thrown violently to the ground. The horse had started, as if in some great terror; had leaped from one side of the road to the other, across the footpath, against the bank. It was like one who flies from some mortal enemy. Very nearly, if not quite in the same spot, it was where the accident had occurred to Sir Dene Clanwaring; and the sudden spring of the horse had been the spring made by Sir Dene's horses.

How long Jonathan Drew might have lain there undiscovered, but for one fortunate circumstance, it was impossible to say; most probably until broad daylight. Mr. Priar came down the road, and found him. He, the surgeon, was returning home from a late visit to Harebell Farm. George Arde, his wife, and the baby had come there to spend a week or two and stay over Christmas: the child had been taken with convulsions in the afternoon; and Mr. Priar had considered it in so much danger that he went up again to the farm the last thing before bedtime, and remained till past midnight.

Drew lay insensible. The spurs on his boots and the riding-whip at his side disclosed to the doctor the fact that he must have been thrown from his horse. He tried to rouse him, but could not; and feared there might be concussion of the brain. Getting assistance from the mill lower down—a rather difficult matter of accomplishment at that hour of the night—Drew was conveyed to his home.

It was not concussion of the brain; at least, to any serious extent; for Drew recovered his senses by the time he was at home, and his intellect seemed uninjured. What Mr. Priar began to fear now was concussion of the spine. Drew seemed powerless to move or stand; but he *said* he was not hurt, and talked away. Priscilla, his niece, said Dobbin had come galloping home with his coat in a sweat, all in a mortal fright.

"I cant think what ailed the brute," observed Drew to the doctor when they were alone. "He never served me such a trick afore."

"Dobbin was always so steady and sure-footed," rejoined Mr. Priar.

"He's sure-footed enough; 'twarn't that," said Drew, fractiously. "The fool took fright."

"What at?"

"Why, at *nothing*," returned Drew. "Nothing that I could see. He wants a good hiding, and he'll get it to-morrow."

Mr. Priar privately thought Dobbin's master would not be so soon abroad to give him one. He let it pass, however.

"If the horse started, it must have been at something, Drew," observed the surgeon. "Perhaps a hare scudded across his path."

"There warn't no hare and there warn't no rabbit," retorted Drew; whose temper was certainly not improved by his mishap. "I tell ye, doctor, there warn't nothing. All around was just as still as still could be; and the road was as bright as day."

Mr. Priar did not contradict again. He finished his examination of Drew, found that no bones were broken, and was imparting that cheering news, when the patient ungratefully interrupted him.

"Bother bones! As if mine was young and brittle, that they should snap at a shoot off a horse. I say, Dr. Priar, what was the matter with Black's wife, up at the Trailing Indian?"

"She has had low fever."

"When did she die?"

"Die!" repeated the doctor in surprise. "Mrs. Black's not dead. She is better."

"Is she, though!" complacently returned Drew, as if it afforded him pleasure to contradict for contradiction's sake— as in fact it did. "When did you see her last, sir?"

"Two or three days ago," was the answer. "She is tolerably well now, and I took my leave of her."

"Well then, I can tell you, doctor, that she is *dead*."

Looking up into Mr. Priar's face from the mattrass on which he was lying, Drew related what he had seen that night. It sounded so strangely mysterious altogether, that

Mr. Priar at first thought his patient must be wandering. But Drew repeated the story minutely, and the notion passed away.

"Surely it cannot be Mrs. Black who has died?" exclaimed the doctor, feeling, himself, a disagreeable thrill.

"It can't be nobody else," disputed Drew. "When I was up there yesterday, they'd got no strangers in the house at all: Black was a-grumbling that not a soul had put up there for a week or two."

"No," said Mr. Priar mechanically, his thoughts very deep just then; "the house has been empty of guests lately."

"Well, then—you can add up, doctor, can't you? Black was there, and the ostler was there; I saw 'em both: Mrs. Black I didn't see nor hear. Now, Mr. Priar, what I'd like to ask is this—whether there was anything wrong about the woman's death. Else why should Black conceal it, and smuggle her out o' the place at midnight?"

"I don't like the look of it," said Mr. Priar, after a pause. "The woman was in no danger of death when I took my leave of her. Even if she had had a relapse—which I don't think was at all likely to happen—it could not have killed her so soon as this."

"I think it ought to be looked into," said Drew. "Black has the credit of being capable of acts as black as his name. There was that talk o' the travelling pedlar, you know—seen to go into the inn, but never seen to come out on't again—that has never been cleared up."

"I shall look into this," replied Mr. Priar with decision. "If the woman is dead, Black must render an account of how she died. I'll go up there in the morning."

Drew laid his hand on Mr. Priar's arm. "Doctor, don't you bring in my name to Black; don't say 'twas me that watched 'em," he urged, some instinct prompting him to ask it. "Randy Black shan't be coming here to abuse me while I be helpless: he'd have it all his own way. Let me get about again, and I'll soon tell him what I saw—and ask the reason on't."

Mr. Priar nodded an unhesitating acquiescence to the request. Not only to oblige Drew, but also in the sanitary interests of that gentleman. He strongly suspected that poor Drew would soon be in a condition to render "abuse" from Black, or any one else, dangerously excitable. He was just as unpleasantly impressed with this strange account of the midnight doings at the Trailing Indian as Drew had been; and took his leave.

In the course of the following morning Mr. Priar went up to the inn. He saw his patients first; including Drew and Mrs. Arde's baby. Drew appeared to be in just the same state, there was no material alteration; the child was very much better. Indeed it seemed well—after the elastic habits of babies. From Harebell Farm, the doctor went straight to the Trailing Indian, taking the near cut through the fields. As he crossed the stile between the high holly hedge, he thought of what Drew had said—that it was close by that spot where he and Dobbin had halted the previous night. When Black, peering forth from within his stable door, saw the doctor cross it, he knew that he had come from Harebell Farm. The fact that he had been summoned the previous day to George Arde's little child was no news to him.

The Trailing Indian presented its customary still and silent features. Nobody was about that the doctor could see. He went over, his mind full of the dead woman. Stepping in at the front door—which would make a show of keeping itself open for a few hours in the daytime—Mr. Priar passed on to the kitchen: and the first object his eyes alighted on was Black's wife. Black's wife, with a bucket in her hand. No wonder, considering what his thoughts had been running on, that the sudden apparition startled him more than if he had seen her dead.

"Bless my heart!" he exclaimed, in the fulness of his astonishment. "Why, Mrs. Black, I—I—had reason to fear that something had happened to you."

"I'm getting a good deal better and stronger, thank you, sir," she said, lodging the bucket of water on the edge of a small tub. "What did you fear had happened to me, sir?"

"Why I thought that you—had died, in fact; or something of the sort. Who is it that has died here?"

"That has died here!" gasped Mrs. Black, suddenly struck into timidity—but her manner was timid at the bravest of times. "No one has died here, sir."

"Oh, yes, they have," said the doctor, thinking it best to speak out, now he was in for it. "And was taken away in a coffin and hearse last night at midnight."

Mrs. Black's answer to this—if answer it might be called—was to let fall the water and bucket into the tub, and to sink, herself, down on the nearest chair. The doctor had rarely in his life seen a picture of fear such as this. She shook from head to foot; her face and lips turned ghastly, sad to look upon. Mr. Priar began to feel sorry to have entered on the subject to her: but in truth it had escaped him in his utter astonishment.

"What's all this row?"

The interruption came from Black; who—to judge by his badly-suppressed savage aspect and white looks, nearly as white as his wife's—must have heard. The woman started from her chair and escaped, leaving him to deal with it.

Through thick and thin Black swore that nothing of the kind, as described by Mr. Priar, had taken place. That the only foundation for it lay in this:—About ten o'clock the previous night, just as he and his wife were going up to bed, a hearse drove into the yard: the two men accompanying it wanted to bait their horses and to take some refreshment themselves. At twelve o'clock, both men and horses being refreshed, they drove away again. Black was ready to take his oath to this before any justice of the peace; as being all he knew about the matter. He had asked the men, he said, who it was they had got, and they answered that it was a lady who had died away from her home and was being taken to it across the country for burial.

Now perhaps Mr. Priar might have believed this; might have concluded that Jonathan Drew's eyesight had not seen so much as it had fancied, but for the consciousness and terror displayed by Mrs. Black. What the mystery was, what the crime, he did not attempt to guess at; but it must be something.

"Do you mean to say, Black, that the coffin was not taken out of your house at this very side-door, opposite to me as I sit, and put into the hearse?"

"That it never was," foamed Black.

"Look here, Black. I don't pretend to fathom the mystery of this. My information is correct, I believe: the person who witnessed this has good eyesight. He saw the yard-door open, he saw the coffin brought out of it by three or four men at least, and put into the hearse. It was as light as day. You say the coffin was not taken out of the hearse at all, or I could have understood that it was merely being put back again."

Black's positive oath, taken in the first heat—that the coffin had never been removed from the hearse—began to burn his lips. He thought what a fool he had been.

"They didn't take it out that I saw," he growled. "Why should they? Where was the man standing—that you say watched all this mummery?"

"Over the way; by the stile."

Black threw back his head as if he had expected the answer. "Who was it, Mr. Priar?"

"I am not at liberty to tell you. It is of no consequence who it was."

Black laughed an evil laugh. He thought he knew better than Mr. Priar could tell him. Who was likely to be about at that time of night, and at that spot, the stile, but Robert Owen? With his own eyes, he had seen Owen leaning over it at night, as if watching his house, more times than one.

"He is a cursed sneak, whoever it was, to come out to spy at a neighbour's castle in the dark, Mr. Priar."

"He did not come out to do anything of the kind. What he saw he saw accidentally."

"Saw accidentally!" retorted Black, curling his lip in scornful disbelief.

"I assure you, Black, it was so. He happened to be passing. But that has nothing to do with the point in question. I must tell you candidly I think there is more in this matter than you would like me to believe."

"Any way, that's all I know about it," was Black's stolid answer. "If your friend wants better information, Mr. Priar, he must go after the hearse, and seek it out for himself. Where was it now the men said they were bound to?—Somersetshire, I think. Here Joe; come in," he called out, as the ostler passed the side-door. And the man came.

"Tell the doctor all about that there hearse that was at the inn last night," continued Black. "He has come up with a confounded story that the Trailing Indian sent away a coffin in it."

Joe, a short, powerfully-built man, with ragged flaxen hair and a swinging gait, as if he might sometime have been a sailor, looked stolidly from one to the other.

"I dun' know nothing o' the hearse, save that it stopped here to bait," said he.

"What time did it come?—and what time did it go away? and who was with it?—why don't you speak?" cried his master, stamping his foot impatiently.

"It come in about ten—as near as I can tell; and it stopped a good two hours. The horses had a feed o' corn; and the two men had some'at to eat and drink in here; I dun' know what; the missus do; she served 'em. They'd got a lady in the hearse, the driver telled me, and was carrying her off to her own family's place for bur'al."

Either the master and man were telling truth, or else they had conned their tale by heart. Which of the two it was, Mr. Priar could not quite decide, in spite of his suspicions. But, as Mrs. Black had assuredly not been carried away in the hearse, and it might have been simply as Black stated, the doctor did not consider that he was called upon to investigate the matter further. Intimating as much to Black, who did not appear to receive it with any gratitude, he took his departure.

"What did all that there mean?—and why was I called upon to speak?" demanded the ostler then, of his master.

"Well, we got watched last night, Joe; that's all. The load was seen to come out o' here, and watched into the hearse."

Joe said a word he might have been fined for. And another; and another.

"*Watched!* Who by, master?"

Randy Black extended his hand and pointed in the direction of the stile over the way. And Mr. Joe broke out into several ugly words in succession, joining them with the name of Robert Owen.

Could Mr. Priar but have known the ill he unconsciously worked that day to the innocent master of Harebell Farm!

One of the first visitors to Mr. Jonathan Drew's bedside was Mary Barber. Going down to Hurst Leet for some yeast the morning after the accident, she heard the news: Drew had been thrown from his horse in the night, and was supposed to be seriously injured. "I'll call in and see him," thought she. "He served mother that ill trick—pretending to know nought o' the paper gave by Squire Honeythorn—but we be kind o' relations, after all; and I'll go in." Accordingly, just about the time that Mr. Priar was at the Trailing Indian, Mary Barber was with the injured bailiff.

"Where be you hurt, Drew?" she asked, setting down her jug.

"I can't say where I be hurt," retorted Drew, who was in a fractious humour. "I don't feel to be hurt nowhere much—but I've got no more power to stand nor a child. Drat it all;

I ought to ha' been at Leigh-Sinton to-day, about some stock. Drat that beast of a Dobbin!"

"How came the beast to throw you?" was Mary Barber's next question.

Drew told her, just as he had told others, that he did not know how it was, or why it was. He described the sudden start and spring, the evident terror that had assailed the horse, all for no apparent cause. Mary Barber listened in silence, her mind busy.

"Drew," said she, "it must have been the shadow that frightened him."

"You are a fool," returned Drew.

"You called me that before, Drew, when I told you what mother said about the shadow on The Hollow."

"The old woman was dreaming when she said it," returned Drew.

"She was dying; not dreaming. And, Drew, them dying people sometimes get a curiously clear insight into things. What the shadow she saw might be I don't know no more than you. But I be sure she did see it: and I think it stands to reason it was that, and nought else, that startled Sir Dene's horses. I should say the same thing startled Dobbin's."

"Why don't you say as pigs fly?" roared Drew.

"Because pigs don't fly," was the matter-of-fact answer. "Anyway, Drew, putting what mother said out of the question, Dene Hollow don't seem to be a lucky road. If it never should be, one ought not to wonder. It was cut out of oppression; it was formed out of a poor old woman's sobs and cries; it broke her heart, and took her life away afore its time. And God's blessing, perhaps, 'll not lie upon such work as that."

"Granny Barber was a'most eighty. There warn't no reason in a mummy, got to that age, a standing in the light of other folks."

"Come, you be civil, Drew, toward a body that's dead," advised Mary Barber. "Being come to that age, there was all the more reason why Sir Dene and you should have let her alone. She couldn't be expected, in the nature o' things, to live much longer. I told Sir Dene so. If she'd been only a middle-aged woman, it might ha' been right to ask her to go out. Or, let's say, not so cruel."

"It's a fine, grand, level road; there ain't a better in the county," shrieked Drew, going beside the question. "I dun' know what ye would have"

"Anyway, it don't seem to carry travellers over it in safety," retorted Mary Barber, who never failed to try for the last word. And Drew, recalled to the thought of his own mishap and present bed-ridden condition, turned his eyes away with a resentful grunt.

"I don't wish to speak a word to hurt you, Drew, now that you be lying here, but I can't help saying that if you had honestly told Sir Dene mother had that paper from Mr. Honeythorn—for you knowed it just as well as she did—the road might never have been made, and this might not have happened."

"You are a great stupe!" raved Drew.

"Well, I must be going," she said, catching up the jug from the floor, where she had put it to stand, "for they be waiting at home for this barm. And I wish ye well through, Jonathan; and I'll look in again upon ye."

Hurrying away, jug in hand, amidst the trees by which the house was surrounded, she encountered Squire Arde, who was coming to ask particulars of Drew's mishap. Mary Barber stayed to give them to him, winding up the narration with Priscilla's account of the horse "tearing home in a lather o' foam."

"Drew says he don't know what frightened the horse; Sir Dene didn't know what frightened his horses; and perhaps it don't much matter what it was," she resumed. "But I'm afeard o' one thing, sir—that that new road is not going to be a lucky road. I've just said so to Drew."

"Seems not to ha' been over lucky yet, Mary, girl," returned Squire Arde.

Mary *girl!* This hard-looking, middle-aged woman seemed but as a girl to the old man. He had had her on his knee when she was an infant.

"Drew, he goes on about its being a beautiful fine road: and so it is," said Mary Barber. "But, ye see, Squire, 'twas made out o' my poor mother's sobs and tears: and that's not a good legacy."

"I never liked that business," remarked Squire Arde, shaking his head. "'Twas no concern o' mine; but I'd not ha' done it had I been Sir Dene. 'Taint well to remove your neighbour's landmark."

"It's a odd thing, sir, come to think on't, that them two should fall to ill on the road: Sir Dene and Drew."

"Ay," said the Squire, absently. "How's that baby, up at your place?"

"It's all right again now, sir. 'Twas her teeth. Many babies gets a fit o' convulsions in cutting their teeth. A fine little child, it is; as pretty as its mother."

"So 'tis. How's she?"

"She? Well, I'd not like to be a croaker, Squire Arde, but I'm afraid we sha'n't have her long among us. Mr. George, he sees it, too, I think. She seems to be wasting away as poor young Tom wasted."

"Tom! Who's Tom?" asked Squire Arde.

"Tom Owen. He was the youngest of 'em, sir; a beautiful young lad, as well looking as his father. He died in the old place, at Hallow, afore we come to live here."

"Well, it's a nice baby; 'twould be a pity for it to be left motherless," concluded the Squire, as he went on to Drew's house.

CHAPTER IX.

SIR DENE'S PERPLEXITY.

SIR DENE CLANWARING sat in his bow-windowed parlour at Beechhurst Dene. He seemed very busy and very restless. The table was strewed with papers and parchments; the upright secrétaire—or, as Sir Dene called it, secretary—standing against the wall opposite the window, was open. It seemed that Sir Dene did nothing but make pilgrimages from the papers on the table to the papers pushing out of the drawers and pigeon-holes of this piece of furniture. Altogether, the papers appeared to be somewhat confused: but, in truth, they were not half as much so as was Sir Dene himself.

The days had gone on; Christmas was turned; from a fortnight to three weeks had elapsed since the accident to Jonathan Drew. And Mr. Drew's injuries had turned out to be of a very serious character. After the first day or two of uncertainty, fresh advice was called in from Worcester: and it was decided that the spine was permanently injured. Drew was removed to Worcester, to the house of his widowed daughter: so as to have good nursing and advice. His furniture followed him, and the lodge where he had lived was left empty—for it was known that he would never be of use again. In one sense this was less of a misfortune to Drew than it would have been to many, for he had saved money, and was comfortably off.

But the state of perplexity it threw Sir Dene Clanwaring into was untellable. Drew had united the offices of bailiff and steward: he had not only been manager of the estate out of doors, but kept the accounts connected with it. Many of these papers on the table had been brought up from his house. Drew was too ill now to be consulted, or to be asked even a single question; and Sir Dene felt helpless as a child.

He knew absolutely nothing about the deeds and other matters. A schoolboy, bade to sit down amidst a shoal of books, and prepare himself in one day for passing a civil service examination, could not have been more hopelessly at fault than was the master of Beechhurst Dene. One person alone, of all the world, could have helped him out of his dilemma: and that was his discarded son, Geoffry.

Opening this parchment, shutting that, glancing at one receipt, throwing aside another, fuming and fretting! While Sir Dene was thinking himself worse off than the babes in the wood, Gander entered.

"Farmer Hill has got me to come in and ask whether you'll be likely to keep him much longer, Sir Dene. He says he has a sight o' things to see about this morning.

Sir Dene groaned. He was no nearer finding the papers necessary to the business on which Mr. Hill had come up than he was an hour before.

"I don't know an iota about it, Gander; that's the fact; and I can find nothing. Tell Mr. Hill to call again to-morrow morning: I'm sorry to have kept him waiting. And—here, Gander. Is Mr. Clanwaring in?"

"Mr. Clanwaring's lying on the sofa in the library, Sir Dene."

"Ask him to step here."

John Clanwaring appeared, a book in his hand. It was one of the volumes of a favourite work of the day. Sir Dene, in his helpless perplexity, appealed to his son.

"You are younger than I am, John, and your brain's clear. Mine's clear enough too, in one sense; but I've never been used to this kind of thing. Do you think you could help me?"

"In what way?" asked Mr. Clanwaring—who had unwillingly dragged himself from London to spend Christmas at Beechhurst Dene, and intended to get away from it the moment he decently could.

"Well, in—in looking into things. Getting some of these

papers straight, for instance: and—and mastering the various matters connected with the estate."

John Clanwaring quite believed he had not heard aright. "I, sir. I could not possibly undertake anything of the kind."

"There's nobody else so fit," rather sharply spoke Sir Dene. "It will be your own proper business sometime."

"I expect when that time comes—which I hope will not be yet awhile, father," he broke off to say in a fit of duty—"that I shall mostly leave it to a steward, as you have done."

"It is an awful trouble for Drew to have fallen out of things in this sudden way! Look at all these papers, John! —I can't make head or tail of them. And there's twice as many more down at his house."

John Clanwaring looked from the papers on the table to those standing out of the secrétaire. He would as soon have meddled with the Augean stables.

"And things are going on out of doors nearly as bad as they are within," resumed Sir Dene. "The men—when they work at all—do it all the wrong way. They plough up meadows, and leave—for goodness sake don't mix the papers, John! I've had work enough to sort them."

For Mr. Clanwaring, seeking for a place on which to deposit his book, had been pushing some of the papers one upon another.

"You won't try what you can do, then, John?"

"As I should be sure to make no hand at it, sir, I had better not."

"At least you might ride about a bit, and direct out of doors."

"I should only mislead: knowing nothing about it myself, or what your wishes are. Besides, father, I shall be gone again in a day or two now. My chief home is London, you know, sir."

"What will you do when you come into the place after me? Whoever holds Beechhurst Dene should live on it."

"As, of course, I shall. It will be different then."

Sir Dene sat looking straight out before him. Some solution must be found to his present perplexity. His son spoke.

"If I were you, sir, I should engage a new bailiff forthwith. Some competent man of experience, who can grasp these matters at once, in Drew's place."

"Should you!" retorted Sir Dene. "He'd be more of a stranger to it than I am: and who is there to put him in the right way, I'd like to know? There's only one man able to grasp them: and that's your brother Geoffry."

Mr. Clanwaring drew in his thin lips, and superciliously took up his book. He considered it an insult to the rest of the family for Geoffry to be so much as named in their hearing.

"If I put down a few heads of questions upon paper, John, would you mind riding over to Malvern, and getting the answers to them from Geoffry?"

"I should mind it very much indeed, sir. Nothing would induce me to go on a mission to *him*. If absolutely necessary that some one should see him, send Gander."

Sir Dene, vexed with John, vexed with everybody, said no more: and Mr. Clanwaring seized on the opportunity to return to his sofa and his novel. The baronet had missed Geoffry all along; but never so much as now, at the close of the year.

After the first burst of indignation had blown over, consequent on the discovery of the marriage, Sir Dene had calmed down wonderfully. John went away again, Miss Clewer betook herself off: there was only Sir Dene at home, and he felt very lonely. Not an hour of the day but he thought of Geoffry, who had never before given him an undutiful look or word, who had been his constant companion of late years; he would often catch himself wishing that he could see Geoffry riding up the path. The applying to Geoffry to help him out of this dilemma, resulting from the incapacity of Drew, seemed therefore more easy of accomplishment to Sir Dene than if his feelings had retained their full bitterness against his son.

An hour longer he sat over these confusing papers, never touching them; attempting no further to reduce them to order. Had he seen any other way out of the trouble, had any one living person, save Geoffry, been able to help him, he would not have sought out his discarded son. But there was no one else; and so Sir Dene could not well help himself. He waited, shilly-shallying, until the afternoon was passing; and then, saying nothing to John of his intention, ordered his horse and rode away in the direction of Malvern. In his heart of hearts, Sir Dene was glad of the opportunity of once more seeing Geoffry.

"*He* never turned a deaf ear to any request of mine, as

John does," thought the baronet bitterly. He would often feel a little bitter with his eldest son.

At this time Great Malvern was a very different place from what it is now: the houses did not much outnumber the hills. The cottage to whose lodgings Geoffry had taken his wife was a small abode nestled near the foot of the hill on the road leading to St. Ann's Well. They had been married nearly two months now, and were in it still.

It would have been dull for the young wife, the Christmas in these confined lodgings, but for the intense love she bore her husband. If hallowed by his presence, all places were alike to her—a paradise. An African desert would not have been a desert with him. They were invited to spend Christmas Day at Harebell Farm: Geoffry Clanwaring accepted it, because it would give pleasure to his wife. However, the day before Christmas Eve a deep snow set in, rendering the roads bad for travelling; and so they stayed at home. A delusive dream of hope had lain on Geoffry—that his father might relent in the blessed Christmas-tide, and summons him and his young wife to Beechhurst Dene.

This was the last day of the old year; and it was Geoffry's birthday. Twenty-six to-day. He had suddenly remembered it as they were seated at their one o'clock dinner, and proclaimed it to his wife.

"Oh, Geoffry!—never to have told me! Never to have let me wish you many happy returns of it when you woke this morning?"

"I forgot all about it. You can wish it now, love."

She got up, and put her arms about his neck, whispering softly; the tears filling her eyes with the intensity of her emotion. Geoffry held her to him while he thanked her and kissed her. Kissed her as fondly as he had on their wedding-day.

"We ought to have made a festival of it, Geoffry," she said, going back to her place; "to have had a plum-pudding at the very least. And there is only this cold beef for you!"

"Cold beef is as good as hot, Maria."

"I shall make a feast for tea."

He laughed a little. "What will it be? Roast peacock?"

"Jam; and pikelets; and Malvern cakes."

"You extravagant girl!"

"But it won't be your birthday again until next year."

When dinner was over, and Geoffry sat thinking of things, it occurred to him to wonder whether his birthday was being remembered at Beechhurst Dene, and whether a letter of repentance, written to his father on that day, might produce any softening towards him. It would be necessary to try to induce Sir Dene to relent if possible; for his little stock of hoarded money would not last for ever. He and Maria were practising plain economy: but times were hard at that period, provisions very dear.

"A letter will do no harm if it does no good," decided Geoffry. "And in any case I should like to wish my father a happy New Year." So he drew his chair to the table and wrote.

The snow had disappeared some days now, and this day was very fine: but early in the afternoon that dense mist came on, well known to the dwellers under the Malvern Hills. It used to be worse than it ever is now: perhaps the mist cannot fight against the large town the place has grown into—the number of houses, their warmth, their lights, and the heat of the fires and gas. At half-past three o'clock, when Geoffry folded his letter, he could hardly see to write the address.

Sitting down by the fire, he stirred it into a blaze, and drew his wife to him. She was putting up her work, for it was too dark to continue it.

"Just look at the mist, Geoffry!"

"Ay. You cannot go out now, young lady, for your Malvern cakes. I sha'n't let you."

She had been saying that she would go with him when he went to post his letter. Maria looked out at the mist a little wistfully.

"You will bring the cakes in for me instead, won't you, Geoffry? And the pikelets."

"I dare say!"

"And we will have tea early, and shut out the mist—say, half-past four. Oh, Geoffry, it will be a happy evening!"

"You little syren!"

He sat on, talking with her of the letter, of the probable effect it might have on Sir Dene; and the minutes slipped on. When the clock struck four, Geffory rose to go on his errand.

"How many pikelets, and how many cakes?"

"Three pikelets," she answered; "two for you and one for me. And three twopenny cakes." "Malvern cakes," it should be said, had in those days a world-wide fame.

"And the jam you talked of? I'm sure the shops will take me for a porter."

"Jam! Oh, I have plenty of that. Mamma gave me some

jars of several sorts, packed in a basket, when we were last there. Don't you remember, Geoffry?— We brought it home in the gig."

Geoffry Clanwaring went into the bedroom for some silver, and departed. Maria called the landlady, asked her to bring in the best tea-things, and said there would be pikelets to toast. That worthy person immediately turned crusty— which she had a habit of doing. The best tea-things she made no objection to: but the pikelets were pronounced "impossible. She had just raked up her kitchen fire, leaving only a spark o' blaze to bile the kettle, for she was a-going out later to watch-in the New Year with a friend. Pikelets couldn't be toasted nohow at the black bars."

"Never mind, Mrs. Brown; I'll toast them here," said Maria cheerfully—who, young and timid, was entirely under Mrs. Brown's dominion. "Bring in the butter, please, and the toasting-fork." And Mrs. Brown bestirred herself.

"I shall dress in my best frock for this evening," thought Maria, as she watched the woman lay the table. "I will go now, while Geoffry's away, and surprise him. And then I shall be ready to do the pikelets."

The first thing Maria saw when she entered the bedroom was the letter lying on the dressing-table. Geoffry must have laid it down, and forgotten it. She made ready, all but her dress; then carried the letter to the other room, and waited, knowing he would be coming back for it.

Presently he appeared, with the paper of pikelets, the cakes, and a beautiful pink camellia, that he had picked up somewhere, for Maria. She strenuously declared that it ought to be in his own coat, as it was his fête day. Geoffry laughed well at that, and put it in her dress-body, saying that a dandelion would be more in place for him.

"Do you know that you left Sir Dene's letter at home, Geoffry?"

"I know it now. The hunt I had in all my pockets when I went to put it into the box, amused the village boys amazingly."

He took the letter, went out again, and Maria hastened to attire herself in the gala robes. It was her wedding-dress that she put on; the beautiful sprigged India muslin she was married in. No opportunity had offered of wearing it since; and perhaps it was rather light in texture for this evening, what with the cold season and what with the mist. Maria deemed it the most appropriate dress in the world—for was it not her husband's birthday.

With her beautiful hair falling; with no ornament in the delicate robe, save the pink camellia; with her pretty white neck and arms bare, after the fashion of the day, Maria Clanwaring returned to the parlour as charming a picture as man's eyes ever rested on. The candles were lighted on the table; and—if she stole a glance of admiration at herself in the chimney-glass, vanity itself would forgive the sin.

"Geoffry will not know me," she softly said, as she knelt down to toast the pikelets. "Why!—how soon he is back!"

For the front door had been knocked at, and answered. Steps approached the room; the door was flung wide, just as Geoffry flung it.

"You'll not know me, Geoffry," she called out.

"Is Geoffry Clanwaring here?"

The voice was a strange voice, proud and stern. Maria started up, nearly dropping the pikelet off the toasting-fork into the ashes. She felt ready to drop too when she saw Sir Dene. They stood, gazing at each other: Maria in trembling dismay; Sir Dene in involuntary admiration.

Never in all his life had he seen so lovely a picture. She looked, in this white dress, little more than a child, with her smooth falling curls, her blushing cheeks, and her delicate face. Gently putting down the fork—it was at least a yard and a half long—she moved a little nearer, in all shrinking modesty, to receive him.

"You are my son's wife, I suppose, young lady?"

"Yes, sir."

"And one to make any son forget his allegiance for," muttered Sir Dene to himself. "Hanged if I can be sure I should not have done as Geoff did!"

"Will you please to take a seat, sir?" she ventured to ask.

"I'll shake hands with you first, my dear," he said. And, taking her hand, he stooped and kissed her.

The tears rushed into Maria Clanwaring's eyes at the unexpected kindness. Sir Dene saw them, and kissed her a second time.

"There's nothing to cry for, my dear."

"Oh, sir, it is your kindness! I think Geoffry, when he knows it, will be nearly ready to cry too."

"Where is Geoffry?" asked the baronet, sitting down.

"He has gone out to put a letter in the post: it is for you, sir. He will not be long."

"And you were toasting pikelets for tea," said Sir Dene, observing the good things on the table.

"The landlady had let her fire go low, sir, and could not do them. But it is Geoffry's birthday."

"His birthday!" cried Sir Dene. "I forgot it."

"That is why we are having a nice tea," she continued, half in apology, deeming some kind of explanation necessary.

"And why you are dressed up?" added Sir Dene smiling, as he glanced at the set out table.

"Yes, sir. It is my best white frock. I"—was married in it, she had been about to add, but remembered in time to change the words—"had just put it on. Geoffry brought me home this beautiful flower."

A beautiful flower, no doubt: but a sweeter flower she. A simple, guileless, pure girl: *that* was self-evident. Sir Dene had been in the room but two or three minutes, and he felt that he nearly loved her. The next entrance was that of Geoffry: who stood in unmitigated astonishment. Between his father's presence and his wife's dress, he thought he must be looking at a vision.

Sir Dene did not shake hands with his son. An idea struck him that it might be a compromise of dignity to do that all at once. He told Geoffry, speaking distantly, of the difficulty he was placed in through the accident to Drew, and that he should require his assistance to disentangle affairs from the confusion that, to him, they appeared to be in. Geoffry at once replied that he would do anything and everything in his power. Seeing them thus engaged, Maria, almost by stealth, resumed her toasting. Geoffry came up, and would have taken the fork from her.

"I'll do this, my dear—if it has to be done here? What's Mrs. Brown about?"

"She has let her fire out. *Please*, Geoffry, let me do it," she whispered. "Indeed, indeed, I would rather! Stay you with Sir Dene."

She was in real earnest, her trembling voice and her eyes alike pleading anxiously. So Geoffry relinquished the fork to her and returned to his father. When the pikelets were buttered and the tea made, she waited by the fire in silence. Geoffry looked at the table and looked at his father.

"Would you take some tea with us, sir," he asked with much deprecation.

"I don't care if I have a cup," said Sir Dene. "The mist has got into my throat."

So they all sat down together; Maria's hand shaking visibly when she handed him his cup. "A good, modest, gentle girl, and every inch a lady—as poor Geoff said," again thought Sir Dene. "She's worth a dozen of John's grand London wenches, with their powdered and patched faces."

Sir Dene partook of the good things with much relish; the pikelets, the cakes, the strawberry jam; and he drank three cups of tea. He said he must go, unless he would be entirely benighted. He did not kiss Maria when he went away: but he shook hands cordially, and called her "my dear." It was arranged that Geoffry should meet Sir Dene at Drew's house, as early as he could get there after breakfast in the morning. Geoffry walked down with his father to the small inn—the Unicorn—where he had left his horse; and saw him mount. Sir Dene gave him his hand.

"Thank you father, for coming over," said Geoffry in a low tone that was full of feeling. "Thank you doubly for speaking kindly to my wife."

"Well, you see, Geoffry, she's very nice and pretty."

"She is more than that, father. Good night, sir."

Standing over the fire with his wife when he got back, his arm round her waist, her head leaning against him, Geoffry Clanwaring spoke of the hopeful turn that affairs seemed to have taken. He had been feeling the estrangement from his father and his home far more deeply than he had ever cared to tell his wife.

"Sir Dene may not take us into full favour quite at once, Maria; it is not to be expected; but I think the way is being paved for it."

"He kissed me, Geoffry," she whispered, her eyes shining through their glad tears.

"Kissed you!"

"He kissed me twice; he did indeed. It was when he first came in."

"Thank God!" thought Geoffry. But he said nothing. Only held his wife the closer.

CHAPTER X.

THE BAILIFF'S LODGE.

BE you very sure Geoffry Clanwaring did not let the grass grow under his horse's feet in riding over to Hurst Leet the following morning, New Year's day. Break of day had seen him in the saddle. At Drew's house he found Simmonds the gamekeeper, who had been placed in it to take care of things upon the bailiff's departure.

It was a very pretty place, this dwelling, commonly called the bailiff's lodge. Mr. Honeythorn used to say it was too good for Jonathan Drew. Had a gentleman been the inhabitant, it would have been a cottage ornée. Sheltered amidst trees and shrubs, with some of the same kind of yellow jasmine on its walls that had been on the Widow Barber's, it was as rural a lodgment as any in the district. There were two sitting-rooms: one, used as a bureau, or office, by Drew, contained the papers and things relating to the estate; the other had not been used at all; for Mr. Drew had found the kitchen good enough for his meals and evenings. The chambers above were three: two large, one small.

Geoffry Clanwaring sat down at once to the papers; and when Sir Dene arrived, they were all in nice order for the explanation to him. For a good half hour Sir Dene did his best to master them; and found it a failure.

"I'll tell you what it is, Geoffry," said he. "I shall make nothing of these things myself: my capacity does not lie in this bent, I think; and John won't attempt — though he ought. You will have to come back again."

"I should desire nothing better than to be allowed to come back," spoke Geoffry with candour.

"Not to Beechhurst Dene," hastily rejoined the baronet, fearing he might be misunderstood. "That could not be. I should have your brothers up in arms: John especially. Reginald is at a safe distance, thank goodness. He can write sharp letters, though."

"I did not think of coming back to Beechhurst Dene, sir," said Geoffry quietly.

"That's well. Look here, Geoffry: I must speak out plainly, and then we shall understand each other," continued Sir Dene. "You were guilty of an act, marrying as you did, entirely unjustifiable: it involved, to me, both disobedience and ingratitude. Had your wife been—been—different from what she is; had she been vulgar or upstart, for instance, I could never have forgiven you. Never. As it is—well, I must partly forgive you. Though I cannot receive you on a familiar footing as one of my sons, or welcome you to Beechhurst Dene, I will extend to you my countenance in a degree. If you are not above taking the management of things in Drew's place, why I will make it worth your while."

"I am not above it, I assure you, sir," said Geoffrey; "but would accept the post, and thank you very truly. After all, I shall only be doing what I have done ever since you bought the property. More responsibility will lie on me; somewhat more work: that is the only difference, sir."

"You would have to live on the spot, you know."

"Of course. Why could I not have this house, sir?"

Sir Dene coughed. With all his vexation, with all Geoffry's misdoings, he had not liked to *propose* that a son of his should succeed to the bailiff's cottage.

"It would be the best and most convenient thing. But I thought you might not like it, Geoffry."

Geoffry Clanwaring smiled. "After our two rooms at Malvern, sir, I fear I and Maria shall be fancying ourselves in a palace here."

"Then that's all settled, Geoffry," concluded Sir Dene, gladly, as if he experienced a kind of relief. "I'll have some furniture put into it, and you had better move over without delay. Or, stay. Do you get the furniture, Geoffry," added Sir Dene on second thoughts: "you know best what will please you and your wife. Pay for it out of the funds: you'll have plenty in hand now."

"Thank you very much, father."

"And now come up to Beechhurst," said Sir Dene. "The papers there are in a fine mess: and Hill no doubt is in a passion at being kept waiting two mornings running. He was already there when I came away."

They walked up the new road, Dene Hollow. It was only natural that the spot should bring back the remembrance of Drew's accident. Geoffry, who had not heard much of the particulars, inquired how Dobbin, known to be sure-footed, came to throw his rider.

"Noboby seems to be able to tell," replied Sir Dene. "Drew says he can't. It made me think of our accident,

Geoffry: we never could imagine what possessed the horses, you know. 'Twas just in the same spot, too."

"It seems odd," said Geoffry.

"Our mishap was odd—and to me always will be—but I don't say as much for Drew's. Many a horse, brave as a lion by day, will start at shadows cast by the moonlight. Besides——"

"Besides what, sir?" asked Geoffry, For Sir Dene had made a sudden pause.

"Well, Geoff—though I'd not mention it to anyone but you," broke off Sir Dene, confidentially—"I cannot help thinking that Drew must have had a drop more than was good for him at the time. He had had a long and tedious journey, and the night was cold. If a man's seat is not steady, a slight thing will unhorse him; the very fact of Dobbin's galloping down the hill might do it."

"I have never once seen Drew the worse for drink," was Geoffry's reply to this.

"Neither have I—don't think I would asperse the man causelessly," returned Sir Dene. "Priar, too, says he was sober. But still there's a lurking doubt in my mind that he was not himself: and I don't say it without a reason."

"What is the reason, sir?" naturally questioned Geoffry.

Upon that, Sir Dene told the tale—calling it a cock-and-bull story—that had been told to him: of what Drew saw, or thought he saw, at the Trailing Indian. Sir Dene entirely disbelieved it. The surgeon had informed him what Black's version was; and Sir Dene, judging by common sense, believed that to be the true version. Geoffry listened in silence.

"Now what I think is this, Geoff: that no man could go the length of fancying he saw what Drew fancied, unless his imagination and eyesight were both a little helped by drink. If it was so, this would account for the accident. Drew confesses that he was going down here at a tolerable pace."

Sir Dene turned his eyes on the road as he spoke. They were just abreast of the spot.

"Did Drew hold to his story afterwards?" asked Geoffry.

"In the most positive manner. He says he was never in his life more sure of anything than he is that the coffin came out of the inn. Of course, having fancied he saw it, it became impressed upon his imagination."

"For my own part, I should not be disposed to trust to a

word asserted by Black," remarked Geoffry. "I'd rather believe Drew."

"Nonsense," said Sir Dene. "Drew's story carries improbability on the face of it; whereas Black's has been confirmed. There was nobody ill at the Trailing Indian: nobody was stopping there: so how could anybody die?"

"In what way was Black's account confirmed?" asked Geoffry.

"He said that the hearse merely called at the inn to bait the horses. About ten o'clock, he told Priar, it drove in. Now it happened that some man Priar knows saw a hearse turn off the turnpike road at that hour and drive in to the inn yard. So far, Black was confirmed."

"Yes," acquiesced Geoffry. But it crossed his mind that the hearse must equally have driven in sometime, had its errand been to fetch the dead away.

"Have you seen Black, sir, and questioned him upon the subject?"

"Not I," said Sir Dene. "Why should I? He would probably tell me to my face that hearses are just as much at liberty to demand refreshment at his house as carriages. In short, I hold no doubt whatever that the whole explanation, both of that and the subsequent accident, lies in the fact that Drew had taken a glass too much."

"It may have been so, sir. But I have a bad opinion of Black. I don't think he would stick at much."

"It is just this, Geoff, as I believe; that Black's case is an illustration of the old saying, 'Give a dog a bad name, and hang him.' He is not a white sheep by any means: but I dare say report makes him out to be a great deal worse than he is in reality. Come along."

In going up the slight ascent, Sir Dene, quite unconsciously, took Geoffry's arm. Forgetting the escapade of which his son had been guilty, quite forgetting the late estrangement, he put his arm within Geoffry's as he used to do. A gentleman, who happened to be walking amidst the trees on the high bank above them that skirted the side of the road, approached the edge and cautiously leaned over to look down. It was the heir, John Clanwaring. He had recognised his father's voice, and wondered who it was that he was with.

And if Mr. Clanwaring had seen Sir Dene familiarly walking with a long-armed baboon, he could not have felt more utterly astonished. With Geoffry!—arm in arm! John

Clanwaring closed his eyes for a moment and opened them again, thinking perhaps some mist obscured his sight. But no. It was Geoffry. Geoffry the renegade! The heir stood holding on by the firm tree-trunk, watching them up, and wondering whether his father had gone clean mad.

He watched them in at the gates of Beechhurst Dene: he saw the woman at the lodge run out to drop a curtsey to her master. She dropped two—two!—to Geoffry. Mr. Clanwaring came to the conclusion that not only Sir Dene must be mad, but a great part of the world beside him.

Little suspecting that condemning eyes were following them, Sir Dene and Geoffry continued their way to the house, turning off to the side entrance. Mr. Clanwaring went on slowly to the front, gained the library, and rang an imperious peal on the bell for Gander.

"Did Sir Dene come in a few minutes ago?"

"Yes, sir," was the man's reply. "He's come in with Mr. Geoffry. They be hard at work amid the papers in Sir Dene's parlour. Hill at the Lea Farm is gone in to 'em now."

From Gander's long service in the family, and the confidential terms he was on with the boys when they were young, they said anything to him, never caring to be reticent.

"I wonder Sir Dene did not kick him out, rather than hand him into his parlour," quoth Mr. Clanwaring, standing before the fire with his coat-tails under his arm, and speaking deliberately.

"Mr. Geoffry have come by appointment, sir," said Gander, who liked the younger brother ten times better than he did the elder. "Leastways, I take it to be so."

"And why do you 'take it' to be so?" scornfully asked the heir.

"Because Sir Dene says to me last night, says he, 'Mind you get a good fire early in my parlour, Gander: I'm expecting Mr. Geoffry on business.' That's why, sir."

"Mr. Geoffry must have the impudence of Satan to write and proffer a visit *here*," cried John Clanwaring, assuming such to have been the fact.

"Well, Mr. Clanwaring, it strikes me that Sir Dene went and fetched him," returned Gander, confidentially, secretly rejoicing that he had it to say. "When Sir Dene got home last night, he told the groom that him and his horse had a'most got lost in the mist, coming down the Link. So we took it that he must have been to Malvern."

Worse and worse. John Clanwaring signed impatiently for Gander to go, and then indulged his wrath alone. Let us give him his due: except on the score of the marriage, he had no ill-feeling against Geoffry; but in his proud and haughty temper, he considered that act had brought a stain on the family not to be redeemed.

The morning wore on. Sir Dene and Geoffry remained in the parlour, very busy. At luncheon time Gande went to tell his master that it was ready.

Sir Dene rose; and sat down again. How could he go to his luncheon and not ask Geoffry? And yet—to invite him to partake of a meal in the house would look as if his offence were entirely condoned. And (here lay the obstacle) what would John say?

"Oh, bother John—I can't help it," mentally spoke Sir Dene in his perplexity. "Will you come and have some lunch, Geoffry? You must be peckish after your early ride."

"Thank you, sir," said Geoffry. And rose to follow him.

In the dining-room stood the heir. When he saw Geoffry come in with his father, quite as it used to be, to sit down at the same table, one of the family, he felt that it was a little more than he could stand. Geoffry went up to him, his kindly eyes looking straight into his brother's, as he held out his hand, hesitatingly.

"You would not shake my hand the last time we parted, John: your anger was fresh against me then. Will you now?"

"No," said John Clanwaring, in a voice low from concentrated passion. He was never loud, this young man; but all the more firm and bitter.

"And yet, my father has—in a degree—forgiven me!"

"But that I see—what I see—with my own eyes, I had not believed that Sir Dene would have lent his countenance to disgrace."

"Oh hang it, John!" interposed Sir Dene, testily, not feeling over comfortable, and half ashamed of his own leniency. "Geoffry is the only one who can help me out of the confusion caused by Drew's departure. You would not try, you know. Come, sit down."

"No, Sir Dene. Not with him."

"He is your brother, John."

"Unfortunately—yes. But I can never again regard him as one."

Mr. Clanwaring stalked deliberately out of the room, vouchsafing no further notice; ordering Gander, as he brushed by the man, to bring him a plate of something to the library.

"You see the difficulties I have to contend with, Geoffry," quietly remarked Sir Dene, when they sat down. "I can't do quite as I would."

"Yes, sir, I see," was the answer. "Be assured I will not intrude upon you here unnecessarily, to increase them."

And so, Geoffry Clanwaring and his wife took up their abode in the bailiff's lodge. And the months went on.

CHAPTER XI.

IN THE SAME SPOT.

Mr. AND Mrs. Owen sat at supper in the ordinary living room at Harebell Farm. They were taking it later than usual. It was Saturday, and Easter Eve. The Farmer had been over to Worcester market: after his business was transacted, he had gone to stay the evening with his daughter Mary and her husband and invite them to spend Easter Day at the farm. Which made him late in reaching home.

"How does she look, Robert?" questioned Mrs. Owen, upon his saying that the invitation was declined.

"Polly? she is—I don't see that she looks much better," was the cautious answer. Glancing at his wife from under his handsome eyelids, Robert Owen decided that she was too poorly just now to be troubled unnecessarily. The impulsive reply he had been about to utter was, "She is worse, and weaker."

"And the baby?"

"Oh, that's peart enough. It's a pretty little thing: can almost talk."

Mrs. Owen laughed slightly. "Almost talk! Why, she is but nine months old yet."

"Any way, she tries to. Girls are never backward with their tongues. The child had got its sleeves looped up with a row of pink coral beads, gold clasps," continued Mr. Owen. "Squire Arde took them there this week. He said they had belonged to his own child when she was a baby."

"That is a curious thing for Squire Arde to do!" exclaimed Mrs. Owen, after a pause of consideration. "One would think he must have taken a fancy to the child."

"Oh, I don't know," said the less imaginative farmer. "He might have thought 'twas as well to put the beads to use—lying by and doing nothing. Polly was saying that Geoffry Clanwaring and Maria have promised to go over for a day next week."

Supper over, Mary Barber came in to take the tray away. Joan, the hard-working household servant, was never kept up later than ten, except on an emergency. It was nearly eleven now, and she had been in bed an hour. The farmer began looking about for his cap.

"Have you to go out again to-night, Robert?" asked Mrs. Owen.

"As far as the two-acre meadow: I must take a look at Lightfoot."

"Bugle is sure to have gone round there the last thing," she rejoined, slightly in remonstrance.

"Not so sure, Betsy," was the dissenting answer. "He has been growing lazy lately—or careless. Was Cole up to-day, do you know?"

"Yes," Joan said she saw him in the yard with Bugle. "I am sure you must be tired, Robert. I don't see that you need go."

"I shall go," persisted the farmer, rather obstinately. "You had better get to bed, as it's late."

"Then you'll read now," said Mrs. Owen. For the day was always finished up at Harebell Farm with a chapter from the Bible. As Robert Owen took the book, his wife opened the parlour door.

"Mary, will you come into the reading?"

"I be busy, missis," was the reply given back to her from the kitchen.

"It will not hinder you more than two or three minutes," said Mrs. Owen.

"It'll hinder me more time than I can spare, with all these here late supper things to clear up: and I'm sure I'm not a-going to leave 'em till morning," returned independent Mary Barber. "The master can read without me to-night, missis." And Mrs. Owen shut the door again.

He was going regularly through the Gospels, and read the chapter at which he had left off the previous night—the eighth of St. Mark. Then he put on his great coat; took his hat—not readily finding the cap he kept for night use—and went out.

It was a night late in March, almost April, but different from the one twelve months before, when the two men in smock-frocks had gone stealing up Harebell Lane. That night was bright and windy; this, still and misty. The moon ought to have been out to-night, but was not. Lightfoot, a favourite cow, was lying ill in the shed off the two-acre paddock; and Robert Owen had latterly had cause to doubt the attention of Bugle, his herdsman: hence his personal visit. He reached the shed: found all tolerably right there, and turned his steps homewards again.

Ever since he came out, his thoughts had been glancing back to the chapter he had read: now that his mind was at rest as to Lightfoot, he let them dwell entirely upon it.

"Ay, true," ran his reflections: " what shall it profit— though a man gain the whole world, if he lose his own soul? 'Tis but a short life here at best: and there's all the never-ending ages of Eternity to succeed it. Why don't we, throughout our poor brief lives, take better note of the lessons God has written for us?"

Why it was that Robert Owen should have taken "better note" latterly, he could not tell. The fact was so. Without any apparent will of his, he had found his thoughts turned absolutely on serious things, and on the life that must come after this life. Three months ago, at the new year, he had quite electrified his wife (and astonished the parson) by staying at church to take the sacrament. For Robert Owen, like too many more householders of the district—and of other districts too, for that matter—had not been in the habit of doing such a thing. They were content to leave this practical part of religion to the women and to a future time. Perhaps it was the thought of his dying daughter—for that Mary Arde was dying, dying gradually, lay on him with a conviction firm and sure—that brought these reflections home to him, especially to-night. They had never been more vivid.

"Poor young Tom gone on, and Polly going: William and Maria left. Two in that world: two in this. Somehow, I feel as if I'd as soon go as stay. If Betsy—halloa! Who's abroad at this hour?"

The sound of footsteps and suppressed voices had struck upon his ear. He was in that narrow pathway, between the grove of trees and the fence, just above Harebell Pond. As it had been that past night twelve months before, so it was this. The two self-same men—or two that looked precisely like them—came stealing up the lane; nothing was in their hands: but by daylight their smock-frocks might have looked rather bulky. Just as Robert Owen had been in that spot and watched them pass that other night, here he was, this. It was a singular coincidence: he had never seen men since in that particular spot.

He stood his ground, leaning sideways against the fence and looking at them as they came on. It was sufficiently light for them to see him there, but they passed on without speaking; apparently without looking.

"More underhand work at the Trailing Indian," thought Robert Owen, as he pursued his way homewards. "I wish that affair of what Drew saw was cleared up! I don't like it —and so I told Priar; in spite of Mr. Randy Black's glib explanation. However, it is no business of mine."

The men were the same that had gone up the former night —Michael Geach and Robson. They arrived at the Trailing Indian in a state of fury. Even Geach, generally so careless and easy, had changed his tone of late, and become quite as savage as Robson in regard to what they thought was the espionage of the master of Harebell Farm.

"It's true, as I'm a living man, Black!" he foamed, when they were disencumbering themselves in the private room of sundry articles that had been stuffed about them. "In that old spy place, just above the pond, there he was, the devil!"

Black answered by some of his bad language.

"I'll tell ye what it is, mates," spoke up Robson, waking from a sudden reverie, and bringing his closed hand down with passionate force upon the table—"that there man must have some means o' getting at our movements. It's as sure as eggs is eggs."

"I have thought so some months past, be shot if I've not," acquiesced the landlord.

Geach, never prone to be very suspicious, glanced questioningly from one to the other. He did not readily understand. "What d'ye mean?" he asked.

"What do us mean?" retorted Robson. "Why, what should us mean? Owen has got spies at work, and lays hisself out to watch us according to the information they bring him in. Don't ye be a fool, Geach."

"I'm no more a fool than somebody else is. How could Owen have spies at work?"

"I dun' know how he could: he *has*," retorted Robson.

"Send me dumb, if it ain't so. Warn't he stuck in that there place to-night, awaiting and awatching for us? But for expecting of us to come, would he ha' been out at this hour, perched *there?* No: it don't stand to reason as he 'ould. There be none of his ewes i' th' mead now."

"Robson's right," spoke Black. "I've been a'most sure of it since the night he watched the load away in the hearse. How could he ha' knowed anything was to be took away that there particular night, but for being informed of it? Would he have stopped out at that there stile a watching our place till past midnight for nothing? You must be a fool, Geach, if you think he'd ha' posted himself there on spec."

A silence ensued, the three men looking at each other. If this really were so—that Mr. Owen had spies at work—it affected their interests in a very grave manner. Geach began to come round to their way of thinking.

"What possesses the man?—what does he do it for?" he asked, scarcely above his breath.

"Ah, what does he do it for!" repeated Black, sneeringly. "Why, to get me out o' the Trailing Indian. Now that that girl of hisn's married to Sir Dene's son, of course Owen's got the young man's ear—'twas only him that set the young fellow on me at the time you know of: pretty broad hints, too, them he gave about the doings here! Owen is a-plotting to get us out o' the place: nothing more nor nothing less."

Robson rubbed the moisture from his startled face. "They might be down upon ye at any time, Black. He might ha' come over that there night, folks helping him, and looked into the coffin. My patience! What on *earth* should we ha' done?"

"Have ye heard much about that since, Randy?" resumed Geach. "Had more questions asked?"

"Never one—though I've waited for 'em," replied Black. "Neither from Priar nor nobody else. They've got hold of the tale round the place, though, and call it Randy Black's coffin. The mischief was, getting it away of a light night, you see; but 'twas in a hurry: and who was to fear eyes would be in this lonely place at midnight? I wish Owen had been dead, I do, afore he had seen it!"

"But what's to be *done* with the man?" demanded Geach, his eyes ablaze with excitement. "We can't submit to be watched in this way; 'twould be destruction: and we shall want the hearse again soon."

"Hang him," said Robson, quietly, by way of answer. "'Twouldn't be no sin," he defiantly added. "Hanging's the nat'ral punishment o' spies. And he's a spy, out and out."

Again the men looked at each other, very meaningly. Black broke the silence.

"He'd only got his deserts. Trust me for one thing, both of you: Owen shall be out of Harebell Farm afore he gets me out o' the Trailing Indian."

Jonathan Drew's sight had not deceived him; neither had he taken anything to obscure it. The hearse had brought the coffin to the inn, deposited it inside the house, empty, and received it again, filled, two hours afterwards. This hearse was in the habit of making periodical visits to the Trailing Indian, always at the ghostly hours of night. But—to relieve the reader's feelings—it may as well be stated that it never took away a human occupant, alive or dead. Had the coffin been charged and opened by Mr. Jonathan Drew that moonlight night, it would have been found to contain nothing worse than closely packed layers of valuable lace, with some costly articles of jewellery wedged in between them.

It was a sure and safe way of transporting articles to London or elsewhere, which might not be sent in the broad light of day. Who would dream of suspecting a hearse, whether travelling along the high way by moonlight or sunlight; or of searching the coffin inside it? Not even a Bow Street runner.

CHAPTER XII.

THE MORNING DREAM.

THE bells of Hurst Leet church wafted their melodious sound up to Harebell Farm in the stillness of the Sabbath morning. When the wind set this way, their chimes could be heard distinctly. The thick mist of the previous night—when Mr. Owen had walked to the two-acre meadow and seen the men stealing up Harebell Lane on their way to the Trailing Indian—had given place to a clear atmosphere. The air was bright, the sun shone, the skies were blue. Generally speaking, Hurst Leet bells only gave out a brief ding-dong, to show the world that it was Sunday; to-day they were ringing. It was the custom of Hurst Leet church at that period to administer the Sacrament four times in the year: at Christmas and Easter; at Midsummer and Michaelmas. On those occasions the bells rang cheerily for a few minutes at early morning. This was Easter Sunday.

Mary Barber was laying the cloth for breakfast when the bells broke out; the sound caught her ear through the open window. She turned sharply round to look at the cuckoo clock against the wall. It wanted ten minutes to eight.

"I was sure it was behind," she exclaimed to herself testily. "That clock's always getting itself slow now."

Robert Owen came down the stairs, before the words had well left her lips, and entered the room. Never was the man's singular beauty more remarkable than on a Sunday morning, when he was always dressed as a gentleman. He looked rather surprised not to see the breakfast laid: for the farm was punctual in its habits, and sat down precisely at eight on a Sunday; on week-days at seven.

"You be down to the minute, master," was her greeting. "And I be late."

It was so very unusual a thing for Mary Barber to be "late," that Mr. Owen slightly lifted his eyebrows at the acknowledgment. "Your mistress is late, too," he observed, "and will not be down for some minutes. She has had a bad night."

"What *I* did was to drop asleep just as I ought to have been a-getting up," said Mary Barber. "I have had a bad night too—in one sense, and —I've a great mind to tell you, master, *why*."

Her manner, as she said it, was very peculiar. Mr. Owen, who had gone to the open window and was listening to the bells, turned and looked at her.

"I have had an ugly dream, master. Two dreams in one, as may be said; for I woke between 'em; and then went to sleep, and dreamed it on again. 'Twas about you."

Mary Barber was superstitious in the matter of dreams. She did not have them often. Very rarely. It must be confessed that two or three times in her life her dreams had appeared to foreshadow coming events—events that afterwards happened. When young, she had dreamed of the death of her father, and told the dream: some few days subsequently, his death, which was quite unexpected, took place.

Robert Owen smiled. He was one of the least superstitious men living: would as soon have put faith in a ghost as a dream.

"Yes, sir," she said, the smile somewhat nettling her, "I

know how you'll ridicule all I say. But I think I'd better say it, for all that. There's some ill in store for you, master; so take care of yourself."

"Is the ill ghostly or bodily?" he rejoined. And Mary Barber did not like the evident mockery, goodnatured though it was.

"Bodily, I should imagine," was the half-defiant answer, as the tea-spoons were rattled into the saucers. "Listen to me while I tell you, master," she added; "it will be off my conscience."

"You had better be quick about it, then, or you will have your mistress down," he said, in resignation. "It may be as well not to tell dreams to her, if they are ugly ones."

She finished putting the things in their places on the cloth, and then stood in front of the table, facing him. Mr. Owen was at the open window still, listening to the bells.

"Master, I thought in my sleep that it was to-day dawning; this very same Easter Sunday that is. All of us here seemed to be in a peck o' trouble; in great distress: and it was about you. You had to go somewhere: I don't know why or wherefore. It seemed to us that if you did go, some awful ill would come of it: ill to you; we knew that it would; and yet there seemed no help for it; never a thought crossed any of us to say, Don't go. It seemed just one o' them things that *must be*, that's as sure as night or day; there was no question of passing it. We were in frightful distress: it was worse than any we can ever feel in this world; sharper and more real. Dreams are vivid; I often think they picture things a bit like what they'll be in heaven; that is, when we shall no longer see through a glass darkly. There was never such distress in this house, master, as we seemed to be in then, and because you had to go: it was just a keen anguish. The whole lot of us were crying bitterly."

"What do you call the 'whole lot?'" questioned Robert Owen, as he paused.

"I don't know. I think my missis and the young lasses were here; I know it was home; this farm, these rooms; and several of us stood about. The only face I clearly remember was Joan's: she was sitting down on the wooden chair by the ironing-board in the kitchen, her hands clasped on her linsey apron, and her eyes hot and red with tears. Nobody but you seemed to be unconcerned, master."

"Oh, I did, did I?"

"You were moving about among us; I saw you more than once. But you seemed not to notice us, and not to feel any of the trouble that we felt—not to know of it. 'When's the master going?' I said to Joan; and I woke before she had time to answer."

"Is that all?" cried the master, far more absorbed by the bells, whose sound he loved, than by the tale.

"No, master; it's not all. I woke up with the distress, as it seemed: and I thought to myself what a strange dream. I wondered what the time o' night was, and got up and looked from the window. Dawn was just a glimmering, and I saw the mist had cleared. I got into bed, dropped asleep, and was in the dream again. The same dream, master; it seemed to go on just as if I'd never woke. Joan was standing by the same chair, not sitting then, and she was cleaned now, and had got her best things on. But you were gone, master: and I saw, as plainly as I could ever see awake, her red and swollen eyes. The house seemed to be in the same awful distress as before—it couldn't be worse—and we never could feel it like that in life. We all set off to look for you, a great lot of us, it was; but we knew in our hearts that, look as we would, you would never again come back to us: we knew it as certainly as we can know anything in this world. All the same, we ran, crying sadly; some went up the lane, and some went over the fields, and some hadn't got beyond the fold-yard: but all of us bearing off for the same point, as it were: and all a-looking for you."

"Which point? The moon?"

"The Trailing Indian," she answered, too much wrapt in her tale to resent the words. "At least, it was towards that direction that we all seemed to be making for. I was one o' them in the lane, and I awoke with the running. This clock was striking half after five, master; and I sat up on end in bed, and asked myself what the strange dream could mean. The tears stood in my eyes, and the sweat was on my brow, with the sorrow and the running. I've never hardly had such a life-like dream as that."

Mr. Owen made no answer.

"I lay a thinking what it could mean. Then I went and called Joan, for 'twas time; and, after that, I lay thinking again. Just as I ought to have got up, I dropped asleep: and that has made us late, master."

Mr. Owen bent his ear to catch the last chime of the bells. To him they were of the sweetest melody.

"And, master, I'm not able to tell what it means, though it has never been for a minute out o' my thoughts since I got up. But, as sure as can be, it forebodes some ill for you."

"The bells have finished," said Mr. Owen, as the vibration of their sound was dying slowly away. "Mary, woman, I'd not let a foolish dream disturb me, if I were you."

"I know that it makes just as much impression upon you, sir, as if I said I had read it in the newspaper," returned Mary Barber tartly. "But I've told it you; and my conscience is, so far, at ease: and I'd say further, take what care you can o' yourself. That's all, master."

She whisked out of the room, brought in a dish of ham, and set it on the table with a dash. Mr. Owen had his prayer-book in his hand, looking out the proper psalms for the Easter service.

"Master, what ails Mr. George Arde and his wife, that they can't come over to-day for their Easter dinner?" resumed Mary Barber in a different tone, for she had done with the other subject for good. "Our chiscakes 'll be good enough for gentlefolks, I'll answer for't."

"Cheesecakes!—it is not a question of cheesecakes," he answered, with a sigh. "Polly is not strong enough to come. Unless I am mistaken, this is the last Easter she'll see in this world."

"Perhaps if she'd make an effort, master, she might ha' got here," suggested Mary Barber in a softer tone—for the answer somewhat appeased the resentment she was feeling against things generally, and especially against herself for having dropped asleep when she ought to have got up. "Our chiscakes is beautiful, this Easter: and Miss Polly always was fond of 'em. The baby might ha' pecked abit, too. Miss Maria never cared for 'em as Miss Polly did."

"We must send her some, Mary Barber."

"Ay, master, that us will. I don't like to hear of her getting worse. At Christmas she looked like nothing but a drooping snow-drop. Tom was enough to go, without——"

"Hush!—here's your mistress," was the warning interruption.

Mrs. Owen entered; and not a word more was spoken on either of the two subjects that master and maid had just then at heart: she, the dream; he, his daughter's failing strength. Mrs. Owen was in too delicate health herself to be troubled unnecessarily.

Again Robert Owen stayed to partake of the Sacrament after morning service; and again Mrs. Owen (she was in the habit of staying), and the parson equally wondered. Geoffry Clanwaring and his wife also stayed—for the first time together. Sir Dene was in his pew as usual; but afforded himself no opportunity of speaking to Geoffry and Maria. He always came out of church when the congregation, including his son and daughter-in-law, had departed.

Things were going on quietly between Sir Dene and Geoffry. They met frequently on business matters, and Sir Dene seemed cordial; now and then he would say, "How's your wife, Geoff?" But Geoffry had not been invited to take a meal at Beechhurst since that luncheon, already told of: his visits there were confined to business ones in Sir Dene's parlour. If any rare necessity brought Sir Dene to the Bailiff's lodge, he would shake hands with Maria, and speak very kindly.

Sir Dene was alone this Easter. John Clanwaring had sent a wordy excuse for not quitting London. The heir was engaged to be married now, and his ladye-love had claims on his time. Geoffry, knowing all this, had wondered whether Sir Dene might open his heart and invite him and his wife to partake of dinner at Beechhurst. But nothing of the kind took place.

So Geoffry and his wife went up to dine at Harebell Farm, and stayed there the rest of the day. Maria was grievously disappointed not to meet her sister.

"Is Polly so much worse that she could not come, mamma?"

"I don't think it is exactly that," said Mrs. Owen. "She is very weak and delicate, you know, Maria; but I suppose she could have come. George Arde has a bad cold, your father says; nearly laid up with it. They have a fresh nurse-girl, too. Polly had to send away the other."

Yes, Mr. Owen, to his wife, had put the non-coming for the Easter dinner upon any trivial excuse, rather than the true one—Mary Arde's fading life. And so the cheesecakes were eaten without her, and the day passed.

The night was bright, quite different from the previous one; it was almost as light as day. When Geoffry Clanwaring and his wife were departing after supper, Mr. Owen put on his cap to walk part of the way with them.

"I should think that cap of yours will never wear out, papa," saucily observed Maria.

"It does not get fresher," returned Mr. Owen; "but it is good for a cold night, lass."

This cap had been a standing joke with Robert Owen's daughters. It was of seal-skin, originally bought for travelling; was expensive, and considered very handsome, in accordance with the taste of the day. A year or two ago, when it was growing worn and shabby, Mr. Owen had taken it into night use: one evening, in standing over the candle to read a letter, the front of it had got wofully singed; burnt, in fact. Mary Barber, who never would see anything wasted that could possibly be used, edged it round with some white fleecy fur. It rendered it more comfortable than before: but certainly not more ornamental; for it made one think of a magpie.

"Robert, won't you put your great coat on?" asked Mrs Owen, as she followed them to the outer door.

"I think I will," he answered, turning back to take it from the peg. "The air is frosty."

She stood a minute at the door watching them along the path that led round to the side of the house, Maria arm-in-arm with her husband; Mr. Owen buttoning his coat, his favourite stick in his hand. A chill seemed to take her and run right through her frame; she hastily shut the door and returned to the fire.

"What be you shivering at, missis?" questioned Mary Barber.

"It is cold at that open door," answered Mrs. Owen, beginning to stir the fire. "I have felt a little shivery all the evening. This best parlour is not half as warm as the other."

It was then ten o'clock. Mary Barber, busy in the kitchen, helping Joan to put things straight there, did not come in again for nearly an hour. Mrs. Owen had dropped into a doze over the fire, and woke up with a start.

"Dear me! I was asleep. What's the time, Mary?"

"Hard upon eleven, missis."

"Hard upon eleven!" echoed Mrs. Owen. "Why, where can the master be? He must have gone all the way with them."

"It's a rare fine night," responded Mary Barber—as if tacitly implying that the fact might have tempted her master on.

Mrs. Owen put the Bible on the table against her husband

should come in. Mary Barber sat down on the other side of the fire; and they waited on, talking of various things. Joan wanted a whole afternoon's holiday on the morrow— and a "whole" afternoon dated in Joan's vocabulary from one o'clock in the day. Mary Barber did not approve of Mrs. Owen's having consented to Joan's taking it; and said so. The cuckoo clock struck half-past eleven.

"Why, where *can* he be?" exclaimed Mrs. Owen.

Wondering did not bring an answer. The time went on to twelve. Mrs. Owen was in a state of great surprise then, somewhat of alarm.

"Mary, do you think he can be staying all this while at Maria's?"

"Not unless him and Mr. Geoffry Clanwaring have got smoking a pipe together, missis. And that's not over likely."

"But, even if they had, the master would not stay all this while."

The house was very still: nothing to be heard but the ticking of the cuckoo clock, that came faintly through the open door of the other parlour. Joan was in bed and asleep, recruiting herself against the morrow's pleasure; Parkes, the man who slept in-doors, was also in bed. The clock ticked on for another half-hour: and with every minute Mrs. Owen's uneasiness grew greater.

"Mary, it will soon be one," she said in excitement. "It is not *possible* but that something must have happened to him! Perhaps he has fallen down somewhere and hurt himself."

"The best thing, missis, for you to do, is to go to bed."

"Go to bed! Nonsense, Mary. I could not sleep if I did. You must call Parkes; and let him go out and look for his master."

"It'll take more time and trouble to waken Parkes than to go myself," was Mary Barber's answer. "Once that man gets asleep, there's no rousing him till worktime i' the morning. *I'll* go, missis."

If a thought crossed Mrs. Owen that she should feel very lonely all alone, she suppressed it. Mary Barber was even then putting on her bonnet and warm cloak. Her mistress flung a shawl over her shoulders, and went with her to the corner of the house where she could see the fold-yard. They both listened for a minute, hoping to hear footsteps: but not a sound broke the night's stillness.

"Take the open road down Dene Hollow, Mary. That's the way he'd come up: perhaps you may meet him."

Now it is a positive fact, and one often spoken to by Mary Barber afterwards, that with the relating of the dream to her master in the morning, it had gone out of her memory. What with the preparation of the good cheer (deemed necessary for Easter Sunday and for the visit of Mr. Geoffry Clanwaring and his wife), and with the scuffle it was to get out to afternoon service herself, and to let Joan get out; in short, what with the bustle of the day altogether, Mary Barber's mind had been fully occupied, and she had not once remembered the dream. Never at all. As she passed through the footgate into Harebell Lane, some night bird flew, with a cry, across the trees higher up, its wings making a great rush and whirr.

"That's a owl," thought Mary Barber, turning her face full towards the sound. "I hate them owls."

All at once, in that moment, as she stood gazing up the lane, the dream came flashing into her memory. Just as it had been in the dream, so it was now in reality—Mr. Owen was missing and being looked after. Only, in the dream there had been a good many of them looking, and here it was but herself. So intensely did the fact—nay, the fear—come home to Mary Barber, that her arms dropped by her side as if a weight had pulled them.

With a feeling of certainty, that no persuasion could have shaken,—with a dread terror that seemed to catch her heart and hold it,—with a shivering sensation that perhaps she had never in her life, save once, experienced, the conviction crossed her that it was in that upward direction she ought to search, not the other. And Mary Barber had all but started up the lane at the top of her speed.

But, even with the most superstitious and fanciful, common sense must, and does, in a degree exert its sway. It told Mary Barber that there would be no *reason* in looking for her master in the opposite direction to that he had been bound upon. There was nothing, absolutely nothing, likely to have taken him up Harebell Lane, especially when he had been going the other way. But, had she started as impulse led her, it would have been the very exemplification of her dream —when she and others had been flying along the lane; for what particular point she knew not, only that it was in the direction of the Trailing Indian.

"It's very odd," she said to herself with a sigh, as she turned about the other way—and her heart felt like a lump of lead. "How was it I forgot the dream all day long?—and why should it ha' come rushing over me as I looked up the lane at the cry of that bird? Was it the sight o' the lane brought it back, I wonder? But what's odder than all the rest, is the fact that master should be missing as he was in the dream; and that I should ha' come out after him."

Very quickly she went on now; not exactly with a run, but at a sharp walking trot. Under the park wall of Beechhurst Dene went she, turning off opposite its front gates, down the smooth road of Dene Hollow, so cold and white in the frosty moonlight. A few minutes brought her to the bailiff's lodge, Geoffry Clanwaring's humble residence now.

That Mr. Owen was not lingering there, appeared pretty evident; the house was closely shut up, its upper curtains drawn. By dint of knocking for a few minutes, Mary Barber succeeded in arousing Geoffry Clanwaring. He opened his chamber window, and looked out.

"Is the master here, sir?" asked Mary, standing back against the shrubs to look up.

"What's it you, Mary Barber?" he exclaimed. "Your master? No, he is not here. Why did you think he was?"

"Didn't he come here, sir, with you and Miss Maria?"

"No. He came as far as the new road; and then turned back. He said he was going to look at a sick cow: Lightfoot, I think he called it."

Maria's head appeared beside her husband's shoulder. A thought had struck her.

"Is mamma taken ill, Mary Barber?"

"Not she," replied Mary Barber. "Why should you think that, Miss Maria?" For Mary rarely gave the young lady her new matronly title; the other was more familiar.

"Then why should you have come after papa? What is it that's the matter?"

"There's nothing the matter, except that he has not come home."

"Oh, is that all?" returned Maria, carelessly: and neither she nor her husband appeared to have an idea that it was so late. Suddenly aroused from sleep, they were naturally confused. "Then why need you have come?" repeated Mrs. Clanwaring.

Mary Barber possessed a large share of prudent reticence. It occurred to her that she need not further alarm this young girl—who was not altogether in strong health—by saying what she feared. "We got a-wondering where the master could be stopping, Miss Maria—and your mamma wanted to go to bed," she said. "That's why I come."

"Well, I hope you have liked your walk—and you've given me a fright besides. Good-night, Mary; I wish you a pleasant ramble back again."

"Mr. Owen is sure to have been with Lightfoot," added Geoffry. "You will find him at home when you get back. Good-night."

He closed the window; and Mary Barber turned slowly away, the weight at her heart ten times greater. Had Lightfoot been dead or dying, he would not have stayed with the animal all that while. An awful prevision lay on Mary Barber—that he was dead. He, her master.

It had been calm and still as she went down, but now a breeze had arisen; stirring gently the branches of the trees, passing through them with a slight moan. The shadows played on the white road up Dene Hollow: Mary Barber thought of that other shadow that her mother professed to have seen, and shivered a little as she passed the spot. What with the remembrances attaching to the road, and this present midnight dread, things looked to her a little ghastly.

A quick, firm step on the upper path. Mary Barber heard it, and her heart leaped with hope. But it proved not to be her master. It was Mr. Priar. They met at the corner opposite Sir Dene's lodge. The surgeon looked thunderstruck at seeing her.

"Why, Mary Barber! What brings you abroad here at this hour?"

A brief, mutual explanation ensued. Mr. Priar was on his way from the Trailing Indian, to which inn he had been summoned in desperate haste some few hours before.

"What on earth for?" demanded Mary Barber. "Who's ill?"

He told her who—at least, as well as his knowledge of facts allowed him. That afternoon a comely young woman, footsore and tired with walking, made her unexpected appearance at the inn door, in search of Mr. Michael Geach, whose wife she announced herself to be. Geach went into a towering passion, abused her for coming after him, and ordered her away again. She refused to go; and a general quarrel ensued. What with the fatigue, and the excitement of the quarrel upon it, the young woman was taken ill. Her symptoms grew serious; Mr. Priar was sent for, and arrived in time to usher an infant into the world.

"Well, I'm sure!" cried Mary Barber, when she had listened to the story. "Geach?—Geach? I've heard that name afore now."

"He is an acquaintance of Black's," said Mr. Priar. "Some loose fellow, who appears by fits and starts at the Trailing Indian."

"Is the young woman his wife?"

Mr. Priar gave his mouth a twist, clearly distinguishable in the moonlight. "If required to produce her marriage 'lines,' I fancy she might have some difficulty in doing it," said he. "Black turned virtuous over it, I hear: he is annoyed that she should be laid up there. She is very ill, poor thing."

"Did you see my master at the Trailing Indian?" resumed Mary Barber. "Or in the lane as you came along it?"

"No. I should hardly be likely to see him at the Trailing Indian. As to the lane, it seemed more lonely than ever to-night, as if not a soul had been in it for ages."

He was making a movement to pass on, naturally wanting to get home to rest. Mary Barber put her hand on his arm and detained him.

"James Priar"—she had called him so before in solemn moments: and this seemed to be one of the most solemn she had ever passed—"there's a feeling upon me that some great ill has happened to the master. I think he is dead."

"Dead! Mr. Owen?"

With the moon shining right upon her face, Mary Barber disclosed her reason for saying this, and related her dream, regardless of the wondering stare that Mr. Priar fixed upon her. As she went on, speaking very earnestly, the incredulous surprise on his countenance gave place to a kind of concerned perplexity. Perhaps he was somewhat superstitious himself.

"*That's* why I asked you, James Priar, whether you had seen him up there. Because in the dream we seemed to know it was the right place to search for him in—somewhere toward the Trailing Indian."

"I've neither seen sign of him, nor heard news of him," was the answer. "If Geoffry Clanwaring tells you he was going to see the sick cow, no doubt that's where he went to."

"But he'd not stay in the cowshed all this while."

"You don't know. Possibly, he found the animal worse, and may have gone after Cole the farrier. It's not unlikely, Mary."

This idea had not struck Mary Barber. It was certainly possible.

"Yes, yes!" said the surgeon hastily. "For goodness' sake don't let your mind run on those other dismal thoughts. You'll find him all right when you get home."

She slowly shook her head, in spite of the faint hope that arose within her; and they parted. "I might think it," she said, "but for my morning dream. And them morning dreams come true."

CHAPTER XIII.

AT THE TRAILING INDIAN.

"Is he come home?" was Mary Barber's first question, as she burst into the farm. And Mrs. Owen caught hold of her as if it were pleasant to find herself again in companionship. The past hour had been worse than solitary.

Robert Owen had not come home. There were no tidings of him within, any more than without. Mary Barber mentioned the suggestion offered by Mr. Priar.

"There's nothing in it, missis, as I believe," she said. "But I'll rouse up Parkes, and make him go with me to the shed. If we see nothing o' the master, we'll come back and go down the hill to Cole's."

After a considerable amount of shaking and thumping, Mr. Parkes, a thick-headed rustic of twenty, was aroused, and he and Mary Barber started off across the fields. The night was so light that they could distinguish every feature of the way clearly; almost every blade of the sprouting grass.

"I see the master to-night a-going on to the shed," suddenly cried Parkes: who had a round crop of red hair, and kept a few steps behind Mary Barber.

She turned her face and her tongue short upon him. "You see the master going on to the shed!" she repeated in a tone of dispute. "What do you mean by that, Parkes?"

"So I did," said Parkes. And he proceeded to explain

how it had happened. Parkes had spent the afternoon at his mother's—who lived two or three miles away, on the highroad that crossed the upper end of the lane near the Trailing Indian—and came back later than he ought to have come. Jumping over the stile opposite the inn, he crossed the first field to the two-acre meadow. There he suddenly saw his master come round the narrow path between the fence and the grove, just above Harebell Pond. Not caring to be seen —for the rule was that he should be at home earlier—Parkes sheltered himself under the hedge, saw the master strike across the field towards the cowshed, and then made onwards as fast as his legs would carry him.

"What time was this?" questioned Mary Barber, when she had heard the confession.

"Blest if I can tell a'zactly," replied the young man. "I know 'twere a sight a'ter ten."

Therefore it appeared certain, from this testimony, that Mr. Owen, after parting with Geoffry Clanwaring and Maria, had gone straight on to the cowshed, through his fields. "But you must have been a fool, not to show yourself and bear him company, as you were there, Parkes," cried Mary Barber, who liked nothing better in life than keeping the youth in order.

They passed round the narrow path, so often mentioned, between the grove and the fence— Mr. Parkes taking a temporary recreation by catching up a clod of earth and dropping it over into Harebell Pond. It was the nearest way into the two-acre meadow, cutting off the width of a wide field.

The shed was there, and the cow was there, all right and comfortable; but Robert Owen was not. No sign, even, was seen to tell that he had been: but of course such sign was not to be expected.

"Let's go and have just a look at the Trailing Indian," cried Mary Barber.

Parkes tramped off after her, over the stile, and across the field to the other stile, opposite the Trailing Indian. All still and quiet lay the house in the moonbeams; closely shut up; there was not so much as a light visible to indicate the chamber of the sick woman told of by Mr. Priar.

"We'll take the way o' the lane back," said Mary Barber, "and go on straight to Cole's."

It was just possible her master might have fallen somewhere, she thought; might be lying still, and so escape the eyes of Mr. Priar, who said the lane was empty. She kept her own wide open, looking well to the banks on either side: and looking fruitlessly. Parkes flung another clod into the pond as he passed it, bestirring its green and slimy waters. It took more time to knock-up the farrier than it had Geoffry Clanwaring. But the man had not seen Mr. Owen.

A more miserable morn than that dawning on Harebell Farm could not well be imagined. Do what she would, bring any confuting argument to bear against the impression, any amount of sober reasoning, Mary Barber was unable to divest herself of the conviction that some untoward fate had overtaken her master, or of the notion that the Trailing Indian and its inmates had something to do with his disappearance. She started off for the inn as early as she thought it would be astir, her footsteps brushing the dew from the grass. The side door of the house was open; she entered without knocking, and penetrated to the kitchen. The kettle was singing away on the sway over the fire; and Mrs. Black, kneeling down before the hearth, was raking the dust from the cinders into the purgatory. A teapot and caddy stood on the table.

"Where's my master?" sharply demanded Mary Barber.

Mrs. Black started up as though she had been shot. By the white hue her face changed to, certainly telling of terror, Mary thought the woman must be taking her for an apparition. There was a minute's silence.

"Who did you ask for, please?" then questioned Mrs. Black in her close, meek way.

"I asked for my master: Mr. Owen, of Harebell Farm. That's what I've come for."

"But I don't know anything of him," returned the woman, after a pause, and in what appeared to be very genuine surprise. "He is not here."

"Didn't he come here last night—say at half after ten, or so;" pursued Mary Barber, hazarding the question.

"Not that I saw; not that I know of. I think the house was shut up afore that."

"He went to the two-acre meadow about that time, to see a sick cow. We be a-thinking that he may ha' come on here: perhaps for something or other that he wanted."

The landlady gave her head a shake, as if hardly understanding. "I'll ask the ostler, if you like," she said. "I wasn't about here last night myself: we've got a sick woman up-stairs."

"I feel as sure in my heart that the master come on here as though I'd seen him come, Mrs. Black."

"Well, he might, in course," admitted Mrs. Black, after a pause given to the consideration of the matter. "I can't say: but Joe'll be here in a minute or two."

Mary Barber sat down without being asked. Mrs. Black finished her cinder job, and pushed the fender into its place.

"Where's Black?" was Mary Barber's next curt question.

"He's not up yet," replied the landlady. "As for me, I've not been to bed."

Mary understood the reason—that she had sat up with the sick woman. "I heard ou't," she said. "How is the person?"

"Well, she's bad enough."

A short silence ensued. Mary Barber seemed impatient; the landlady stood waiting for the kettle to boil, and took occasional glances at her morning visitor.

"But I don't understand why it is you've come asking about this," she suddenly observed, the point striking her. "Did Mr. Owen get home tipsy last night?"

"He get home tipsy!" was the indignant rejoinder. "That was never a failing of his."

"Then why should you think he come to the inn?"

"We don't know what to think. He never come home at all."

Mrs. Black lifted her eyes in much surprise.

"Since the time when he went to that there cowshed last night, he has never been seen or heard of. My belief is that he has been made away with."

The woman was in the act of putting a spoonful of tea into the tea-pot, as Mary Barber said this. The words seemed to strike her with a shock. Her hands shook so that she spilled the tea; her face again turned ghastly.

"Why, what do you mean?" escaped from her trembling lips.

"What I say," sturdily replied Mary Barber. "We have been abroad all night looking for the master, and he's not to be found above ground. I fear he has been murdered."

"Mercy upon us!" cried the woman aghast.

It was evident that if the Trailing Indian (according to Mary Barber's theory) knew anything of Robert Owen's disappearance, its mistress did not. Gathering up the bits of tea from the table and putting them into the pot with her trembling fingers, she was in the act of lifting the boiling kettle off the sway, when the ostler appeared, carrying two buckets of water from the well.

"This good lady's come round to know if Mr. Owen at the farm called in here last night," she meekly said, speaking in a sort of hurry. And the man gazed out at her with some questioning surprise in his eyes—perhaps at her white lips.

"Owen o' the farm don't never come here," he briefly replied.

"I think he must ha' come last night," interposed Mary Barber, rising to address the ostler. "We've not heard nor seen him since; he never come home."

"He never come here," said the man, stooping to pour the water from one of the buckets into a sort of portable cistern that stood away near a sink. "What time was't?"

"Nigh upon half-after ten. May be quite that."

"And we was shut up afore ten struck."

"That you warn't," retorted Mary Barber. "Dr. Priar never went away till one o'clock i' the morning."

"The house was shut up afore ten; that I'll swear to," asserted the man. "When Dr. Priar was ready to leave, I unlocked this here yard door and let him out myself."

"I told the good lady I thought so—that we was shut up early," spoke the hostess, who had kept her back turned, doing something at the fire.

"We had no callers o' no sort i' the place last night," resumed the ostler, taking up the other bucket. "As to Owen at Harebell Farm, he warn't in the habit of coming at all. If he'd been here last night, I should ha' seen him."

"Be you sure o' that?" asked Mary Barber.

"I be. I'll take my oath he was not anigh the place."

Mary Barber paused. "Was Black abroad last night?"

"No," replied the ostler, "he never went out at all. He was abed afore we shut up."

Apparently there was nothing to stay for. Mary Barber said good morning and went away, feeling that her errand had been a useless one.

Before the sun was high in the heavens, the news had spread far and wide: Robert Owen of Harebell Farm had mysteriously disappeared. Hurst Leet put itself into a commotion. The mere fact of his disappearance might not have excited a tenth part of the interest, but for the persistent assertion of Mary Barber, that he had been, in some way, "made away with."

The testimony of Parkes, as to having seen his master on the previous night was confirmed, at least in a negative degree, by two individuals. Joan said that when Parkes got in "late and all out o' breath," he told her he had nearly been "dropped upon" by the master in the two-acre meadow. The other was Gander, Sir Dene's butler. Gander, returning home soon after ten from taking a cup of ale with Cole the farrier, overtook Mr. Owen at the entrance to Harebell Lane, gave him the good night, and saw him turn in to his own gate. Therefore, no doubt whatever could rest on any mind that the farmer had proceeded, as was assumed, direct to the shed, on quitting his daughter and her husband. The question now was what had become of him afterwards.

Harebell Farm that day, was like a fair. So many sympathising friends and neighbours were flocking up to it. George Arde, who had come over from Worcester on other matters, found it in this commotion. Geoffry Clanwaring was there; also old Squire Arde. Mary Barber got these three to herself in the best parlour, and there related her dream. The once keen eyes of Squire Arde, watery now, twinkled with merriment as he listened. To use Mary's words, when commenting on it later, he "stared and grinned in her face."

"Mary, woman, I'd not set myself up for a laughing-stock if I was in your place; the parish might be taking me for a nat'ral. Dreams, indeed!"

But in spite of the old man's ridicule, Mary Barber never wavered an iota in her asserted belief. Her master was *dead*, she said: she knew it by her dream. Dead, or else in some sore plight that would prevent his ever coming back again; she was certain he had seen his home for the last time.

Though not given to be superstitious, her steady assertion and its persistent earnestness made an impression upon the two listeners who may be said to have held the largest interest in the matter, as they were Mr. Owen's sons-in-law: George Arde and Geoffry Clanwaring. They grew to think that he really might be dead. And then they asked themselves and each other, how—if this were so—his death had been accomplished. By accident, or by assault from without?

"See here," said Squire Arde, looking up from the chair where he sat—"a'most as many accidents happened on a moonlight night as a dark un. People's eyes get deceived by the shadows. I should have the ponds dragged."

"What ponds, sir?" said George.

"Eh? What ponds? Why, any pond that lay in his way. There's the one by the fold-yard here, the duck-pond; and there's the pond in the lane. Have 'em emptied—or dragged."

"Should you think he could have fallen in, sir?" returned George Arde, in what he would have made a tone of mocking incredulity, but that he was speaking to the Squire.

"I think he might have walked in," was the answer. "Yes, you young men with your young eyes may stare to hear me say it; but if you live to Robert Owen's age, you may find 'em cheat you, Did ye ever hear o' one Squire Honeythorn, as lived at Beech Dene?" he quaintly asked. And they smiled at the question.

"Well, one night, moonlight it was too, Honeythorn, in walking home down Harebell Lane, walked right into the pond. He hadn't had a single sup o' drink; don't you two go a thinking that; but he was getting in years and the shadows deceived his sight. I know a lady, too, as walked right into the Worcester-and-Birmingham canal, and thought it was part o' the towing-path. Hardly saved, she was, either; some boatmen heard her cries as she was sinking. It might have gone hard with Honeythorn, only a man on horseback happened to ride down the lane at the time. And that was me."

"If Mr. Owen walked into a pond, it must be the duck pond here," said George Arde. "He did not go into Harebell Lane."

"How do you know he didn't go?" retorted the Squire.

"We don't *know*, sir, any of us; but we may judge by probabilities."

"I'd recommend you not to speak so positively, young man. 'Probabilities' have let in older folks than you, afore now."

"Well, sir, do you see any likelihood, yourself, of his having gone into the lane?"

"No, I don't," candidly spoke Squire Arde. "I only say he might ha' gone. But there: let Harebell pond be. Try this un."

"I do not fear the ponds," interposed Geoffry Clanwaring, who had been in a deep reverie. "Knowing the ground as Mr. Owen knew it, a bright night besides, it seems next door to an impossibility that any harm of that sort should come to him."

"Master ud no more walk into a pond, whether by daylight

or by moonlight, than I should walk into the middle o' that fire," cried Mary Barber, with a fling of her hand towards the grate. "Squire Arde, it's not *there* we must look for him."

"Where then,?" asked the Squire, noting the significance of the tone.

"I think—I think," she slowly rejoined, as if not quite sure, herself—"that it's up at the Trailing Indian. There has been a deal of ill-feeling on Black's part to the master ever since we came to this farm: and I say that if harm has been done to him, it's by the people *there*."

That Black had accused Robert Owen of spying upon him, they were all aware. The neighbourhood knew so much as that. Also that Mr. Owen had emphatically denied any intentional spying on his own part. He had not looked out for the ill-doings of the Trailing Indian : only, when they, or a suspicion of them, had come under his notice incidentally, he had not shut his eyes. That was all.

Squire Arde administered a reproof. "Mary Barber, there might ha' been ill-feeling on Randy Black's part to your master; it's like enough. But you shouldn't go and say the man has murdered him."

"I didn't say it, Squire. I didn't go as far in speech, whatever I might ha' done in thought. Truth is, I don't know what to think," she continued, after a pause, "my brain's all in a muddle o'er it. If no harm has come to the master, where *is* he? I should like to ask Black whether he's alive or dead. When I was up at the Trailing Indian this morning, I couldn't get to see him.

Every little item connected with the past night bore its own individual interest. Geoffry Clanwaring mentioned that as he and his wife were walking home, Mr. Owen told them he had seen two suspicious-looking men stealing up Harebell Lane on the Saturday night, no doubt on their way to the Trailing Indian. Geoffry could have added, had George Arde not been present, that Mr. Owen changed the subject to speak of his daughter Mary—saying he did not think she would be long in this world.

"'Twould do no harm if some of us went up and had a talk with Black," said Squire Arde. "There has been a sight o' trampers and such-like ill-looking folk about lately. If any of 'em set upon Farmer Owen last night in the two-acre meadow, sounds of it might have been heard at the Trailing Indian. They've got a habit, them tramps, of creeping into sheds to sleep: may be, Owen found some in his. Let's go."

Nothing loth were the two young men to accompany him to the inn, and they took their hats at once. In the fold-yard of the farm stood Gander. Geoffry Clanwaring stopped to accost him.

"You saw Mr. Owen last night, I heard, Gander?"

"Yes, sir; I overtook him i' the lane yonder, as he was turning in at the gate here."

"What passed?"

"Nothing to speak of," was Gander's answer. "I said 'Good-night, sir,' to him: 'Good-night, butler,' he answered back again. That was all, Mr. Geoffry."

"You did not hear anything of him afterwards?" Geoffry stayed to ask.

"No, sir; nothing."

"Or see any strange men about?"

"Not a soul, sir."

Black stood in his yard, rubbing up the metal of some harness, when they reached the inn. It may as well be mentioned here what was gathered, partly by the man's own admissions, partly by the corroboration of others, of the doings on the Sunday at the Trailing Indian.

In the course of the morning, while people were in church, the man named Robson took his departure from the inn, he and Geach having lodged there on the Saturday night. Dinner was served at two o'clock: Black and Geach sitting down to it, Mrs. Black waiting on them. The meal was just finished, when a young woman arrived; a foot-traveller, who asked for Michael Geach, and announced herself as his wife. Geach, astounded at the sight, met her with abuse and passion; while Black, who had not before known there was a Mrs. Geach, abused Geach for letting her come: or, rather, for letting it be known, by her or anybody else, that he might be found at the Trailing Indian. Both the men had partaken plentifully of strong ale at dinner; it tended to inflame their tempers, and they quarrelled with each other. Quarrelling is thirsty work; and the men found it so. They quitted the ale for spirits, and soon got into a state of intoxication. The ostler, in describing it, said they were only "half gone;" that is, they were not totally unable to talk or walk. During this time, Mrs. Geach fell ill, and was unable to depart, as ordered. What with that fresh annoyance, with the quarrel and the drink, Geach's fury reached its climax. He betook himself off in a passion, mounted a public conveyance that happened to be passing along the highway, and left Mrs. Geach to her fate and the hospitality of the Trailing Indian. That was about five o'clock. Black, after swearing a little at things in general, sat down in the settle before the fire in what was called the parlour, and fell into a heavy sleep. He said that he never awoke from the sleep until Joe, the ostler, was shutting up the inn for the night, just before ten; and then he went straight up to bed. The ostler said this also; Mrs. Black said it. Before this, the sick woman grew so ill that Mrs. Black became alarmed, and about eight o'clock despatched the ostler for Mr. Priar. All agreed in these two important points—that Robert Owen had not been to the inn; or, so far as they saw, near it: and that none of the inmates of the inn had gone forth from it at all that evening, save the ostler on his errand. He, the ostler, returned to it with Mr. Priar, and did not quit it again. If this statement could be positively verified, it was quite certain that Black could have had nothing to do with the disappearance.

He nodded to the three gentlemen civilly enough when they entered the yard, but kept on rubbing his harness. Frightfully ill he looked, his complexion a kind of sallow whiteness, the effects probably of intemperance. It was not often Black yielded to the failing; when he did, it was sure to pay him off the next day in a racking sick head-ache.

"Well, Black," began Squire Arde, "we've come up to have a word or two with you. Do you know anything of Mr. Owen?"

Black grew suddenly whiter; with an accession of sickness or of anger. He let the strap fall from his hand, and its buckle clicked against the stable door.

"What *I'd* like to know, sir, is, why I should be asked it. I'm free to put that question, I suppose," he added, his voice shaking with what seemed concentrated passion. "Here's been folks coming up every hour o' the day since morning light, asking me what I've done with Robert Owen. That woman of their'n was here afore' the house doors was undone. Why should I be bothered about Owen, more nor others?"

"For one thing, you are his nearest neighbour, Black," was the Squire's answer. "For another, the last seen or known of Owen was in the two-acre mead over there, within a stone's throw of you."

"There might be two hundred Owens over in that there mead, and me never know it," contended Black.

"Mr. Owen was there—it has just been ascertained—at about a quarter past ten last night, or from that to half-past," rather sternly interposed Geoffry Clanwaring. "He has not been seen since. Do you know anything of him, Black?"

"No, I don't, sir," replied Black, speaking with tolerable civility to his landlord's son. "Long afore that time I was abed. Fact was, I got a drop too much inside me yesterday afternoon—and my head's fit to split, through it, to-day," he added, as if in apology for his sickly face. "I fell asleep in the parlour and never woke nor stirred till bedtime. Joe disturbed me, shutting-to the shutters, and I went straight up to bed."

"What time was that?"

What time?" repeated Black. "Joe knows more sure nor I do," he added. "'Twasn't ten."

"It wanted ten minutes o' ten," interposed Joe, who was splashing away at the horse-trough close by, cleaning it out. "We don't often shut up till ten have struck; but there warn't no customers i' the house, nor none likely to come, and I thought I'd close. The master swore at me, saying it warn't time; he was cross at bein' woke up."

"And you swore at him again, I suppose," remarked Squire Arde.

"No I didn't," replied the ostler, in his stolid way. "When a man's in his cups, he's best let alone. He didn't give no opportunity for't, neither; he stumped right off to bed."

"What strikes me's this, Black," said the Squire—who appeared quite to have forgotten the notion of any suspicion against Black. "There's a sight of ill-doing tramps about; always is after a hard winter; if any of 'em had crept into the cowshed, and Owen found 'em there, he and they might have a row together."

"I've never knowed so many o' them tramps about as now," returned Black, hastily and eagerly. "Two bad uns was at the door on Sunday morning, frightening my missis, and begging for scraps o' bread. They'd got just the look o' cut-throats."

"Ay," nodded the Squire. "Who knows but them same two laid up somewhere about here till night, and set on Robert Owen? You might have heard the noise over here Black."

"I warn't likely to hear nothing," answered Black. "I fell asleep the minute after I got into bed: and when I'm in that stupid state my sleep's heavier nor a top."

At this juncture Mr. Priar appeared at the side-door, having come downstairs from paying a visit to the sick woman. They remained a few minutes longer talking, Black steadily persisting in his denial of having heard or seen anything of Mr. Owen; and then they all turned to depart, including the doctor.

There's an old and good saying—Let well alone. Black did not allow it to govern him just then. Like many another zealous self-defender; he thought the more words he used, the better his cause might be served.

"I've not had a answer to my question, gentlefolk," he began, arresting them as they were going out. "What I'd like to know is, if there's any cause for *my* being singled out to be badgered about Owen—what's become of him, or what's not?"

Upon that, George Arde, who had been silent hitherto, contenting himself with looking and listening, turned to face the man, and told him of the bitter ill-feeling he was known to have cherished towards Mr. Owen. He spoke with open, and rather stinging plainness, of the suspected private ways of the Trailing Indian: not particularising their nature (perhaps he could not), but alluding to them in a general manner, as "ill-doings."

It put up Black's temper. He was under no obligation to Mr. George Arde, or to his relative at his side, the Squire; and he retorted warmly.

"Well, and he had had cause to feel bitter again Owen: though he had never molested him—nor thought of doing on't—nor never had done it. He had got his own proper feelings, he hoped, though he was but an inn-keeper, and the farmer 'd never let him alone. Didn't Owen watch him continually?—warn't he a spy upon him—didn't he talk about him at Hurst Leet? *No!* says the gentlemen afore him. *No?* One on 'em, at least, knew better nor that. Look at them lies about the hearse what stopped to bait at his house that night in the winter. Father Owen had set it about that it had come to take away a corpse, and had sent Dr. Priar up to accuse him on't. If——"

Mr. Priar lifted his arresting hand to command silence. "Don't be so fast, Black. Who told you Mr. Owen sent me?"

"Why, you did," retorted Black—while the ostler stopped his splashing in the trough to listen. "Didn't you confess that the man stood o' purpose at that stile, over there, and watched the hearse away? You know you did, sir."

"I did not," said Mr. Priar. "I told you, Black, that the person was not watching purposely, but saw it incidentally in passing; I impressed this upon you as plainly as tongue can speak. And I most certainly never told you that the person was Mr. Owen."

"I know *that* without you telling me, Dr. Priar. There warn't no need to mention names—oh, dear, no."

"But it was not Mr. Owen."

"Not Mr. Owen! It's all very well for you to try to make me believe that now, sir," added Black, with a sneer.

"I tell you the truth, Black: it was *not* Mr. Owen. The person who saw you was Jonathan Drew—lying disabled now, poor man. In riding past, he saw the hearse at the open door here, and drew up Dobbin by the stile to watch what came of it."

"I can speak to it's being Drew," interrupted Squire Arde, "for he gave me the history of it the next day from his bed. About the hearse he talked, and all what he had seen brought out o' the yard door here, and shut into it. Don't give your betters the lie to their faces, Randy Black."

Randy Black did not speak. He looked from the curious old man to the doctor, silently asking whether this were really true. So, at least, Mr. Priar interpreted it.

"You need not doubt, Black," said the surgeon. "It was in galloping away from the sight, down Dene Hollow, that Drew's horse threw him—and I wondered at the time that your own common sense did not show you it could have been no one but Drew, knowing, as you did, that he must have just rode past here. The first thing Drew did when I got him home that night was to tell me what he had seen. He concluded it was your wife that was put into the hearse: so did I. And that's what brought me up on the following morning."

Black's lips parted to speak, and then closed again. In some way or other the narrative was evidently making some great impression on him.

"Drew was mistaken," he burst forth at length. "He never saw it; he couldn't ha' seen what was ne'er there to see. The hearse only stopped to bait; 'twas never opened.'

"It is of no consequence now, one way or the other; the thing's past and done with," coolly rejoined Mr. Priar. "Only don't continue to fancy it was Mr. Owen: he saw no more of the matter than I did. As it happens, I am in a position to testify that Mr. Owen never went out of his house that night. I was up there, you remember: and we were all in distress about the little child. Mr. George Arde, here, can bear out what I say: he was at the farm, too."

George Arde nodded in confirmation.

"Ay, ay," wound up the Squire. "Don't you be fond of laying hold o' wrong notions, Black, and then sticking to 'em i' the teeth o' people."

They turned without further speech to quit the yard. Black drew a long breath as he looked after them. "You can finish the harness, Joe," he said to the ostler, and went indoors.

As they crossed the lane and the opposite stile, Mr. Priar spoke to what had come under his own cognisance the previous evening. It was past eight o'clock, he said, when the ostler, Joe, came to fetch him; they both went back together to the Trailing Indian, reaching it about nine. Black was fast asleep at the corner of the settle: and Joe remarked that his master was "sleeping off some drink." About a quarter before ten Mr. Priar went downstairs for something he wanted: Black was then still asleep in the same place and position, and Joe was sitting by the kitchen fire. In a minute or two Mr. Priar went up again, and did not see Black again. It was quite possible that the man might have gone up to bed before ten, as he asserted; Mr. Priar could not say one way or the other, for he was shut up with Mrs. Black in the sick woman's chamber. He did not think the ostler went out again: they had occasion to call two or three times for hot water and other things, and the man was always at hand to bring them up. When Mr. Priar came down to leave, an hour after midnight, the ostler was waiting up in the kitchen to let him out. Mr. Priar took half a glass of hot brandy and water before going out, which Joe mixed. He stood by the kitchen fire and talked to Joe while he drank it: and he remembered that the man incidentally mentioned that his master had gone to bed before ten.

All this tended to corroborate Black's own statement: it certainly did appear that he could not have harmed, or helped to harm, Robert Owen. In passing the shed, they turned into it; for curiosity's sake, more than in expectation of making any discovery. Lightfoot, recovering fast, was there, and turned her head to welcome them: but there was no sign that any struggle had taken place in it. In fact, the undisturbed litter spoke to the contrary.

"Whatever happened, must have happened *after* he had paid his visit here, there's no doubt of it," remarked Geoffry Clanwaring, as they went out. "Parkes saw him making straight for the shed: had he been molested before reaching it, the man could not well fail to have heard the cries. The door was found fastened too, just as Mr. Owen would leave it. Now then—let us see. He would naturally go straight back home again, knowing Mrs. Owen was waiting up. That would be across here"—stretching out his hand to the two-acre meadow, which lay green and smooth before them as they walked—"round the narrow strip of path, and so across the fields home. It's a pity the sheep are on the other side the farm this year," he added: "had they been here, the shepherd might have been about."

Crossing the stile over to the narrow pathway, they traversed it slowly. It was very narrow: not possible for two to walk on it abreast; the fence, a low one, lay on their right; as they walked their left shoulders brushed the trees. In length it might have been twenty yards; not more. In the middle of it Squire Arde stopped and looked over at the pond in the lane underneath.

"Ah," said he, "if Owen had been a going through the lane i'stead o' up here, I should say he had mistook his way amid them rushes, and walked into the pond."

"But don't you think, sir, even had such a thing happened, that he would have been able to get out of it again?" spoke Mr. Clanwaring.

"Like enough: some might and others mightn't," answered the old man. "What's this?"

He had his back against the fence now, glancing at the brushwood that grew amidst the tree-trunks immediately in front of where he stood. It appeared to be a little torn.

"One might a'most fancy that somebody has made a dash through it just here. What d'ye think?"

The three others, glancing to where the old man pointed, did not appear to think much about it. "Some animal, perhaps," one of them carelessly answered.

"I suppose we must give up all suspicion of Black," remarked Geoffry Clanwaring, as they went on over the open field. "The account he gives seems fair enough. Likely to be true."

"Ay: I don't doubt him in this, for my part," acquiesced the Squire.

"Neither do I," said Mr. Priar.

"I don't altogether doubt him; but I don't altogether trust him," dissented George Arde. "Look here: while you were talking to him, I was watching him: taking observations, as may be said. There was one thing I did not like—his enlarging on the state he was in yesterday. It is not considered a great crime to get drunk in these drinking days; nevertheless, most men in Black's position would rather hide the fact from their betters than gratuitously proclaim it. I wondered whether he had any motive for wishing us fully to believe that he *was* drunk. Another thing: he never while he spoke, looked one of us in the face throughout the whole interview."

Squire Arde, deep in his own thoughts, had not been listening. "Who didn't?" he sharply asked, waking up.

"Who, sir!" returned George Arde, slightly surprised. "I was speaking of Randy Black."

CHAPTER XIV.

HAREBELL POND.

THE singular disappearance of Robert Owen excited more speculation and comment than anything that had occurred in the neighbourhood of late years. The turning out of doors and razing the home of the widow Barber, the stolen marriage of Sir Dene's son, both of note at the time of their occurrence, did not excite the prolonged commotion that this disappearance caused. As the days went on and brought no tidings, the painful interest increased. He was not a man likely to have gone away of his own accord; and yet he could not be heard of above ground. Mary Barber's opinion, that he had been put under it, spread silently.

The duck-pond near the fold-yard was searched; it yielded in recompense nothing but mud. In returning home from his visit to the shed (if he did return), Mr. Owen might pass the brink of this pond. The probability was that he would; though he could have gone round on the other side the barn. Harebell pond was let alone: it was universally assumed that nothing would be likely to take Mr. Owen into the lane. To have returned home that way, after leaving the shed, he must have traversed the outer field, crossed the stile opposite the Trailing Indian, and thence through the whole of the lane—a regular round for nothing. So Harebell pond was not meddled with.

The feeling against the Trailing Indian died away. Mary Barber avowed *her* doubts of it openly enough, and this at first raised somewhat of doubts in the minds of others: but as there was absolutely nothing to corroborate these doubts— nay, as the Trailing Indian seemed, for that one evening at least, to be beyond the pale of suspicion, the thought of connecting Black with the disappearance faded away, so far as regarded the public. Mary Barber, however, do as she would, could not get rid of her fear so easily; it clung to her in spite of herself, and perhaps influenced in a degree some of those about her.

Sir Dene Clauwaring, waiving prejudices for the time being, made a call at Harebell Farm. Never, since his son's marriage with Maria, had he exchanged a word with Robert Owen, or condescended to notice him by so much as a nod in passing. He did not accuse the farmer of having in any way helped on the marriage, or of being privy to it; but his wounded pride would not brook the slightest approach to intercourse. In his interest now; his curiosity, and perhaps also in a better feeling—that of compassion for Mrs. Owen— he considered it his duty as landlord to call. Mrs. Owen, however, was keeping her room, too ill to receive him; but he saw the son, who had been summoned home in the distress. William Owen was the eldest of the family; a slight, quiet young man of three-and-twenty, very much like his mother. He was with a farmer in Wiltshire, gaining experience, and earning a small salary. Harebell Farm had been no larger than Mr. Owen could himself well manage; and the son was waiting until his father could spare the funds to take a small farm for him. Sir Dene was a little taken with the young man, whose manners were very gentle and pleasing. Sir Dene questioned Mary Barber what her grounds had been for doubting Black—of which doubt he had heard from his son Geoffry: and Mary Barber, nothing loth, regaled Sir Dene's ears with her singular dream. Sir Dene did not attempt to dispute the dream, or to cast ridicule upon it: he simply asked, when the relation was over, *what* there was in that dream to cause her to suspect Black. She replied that the only part of the dream which could have had reference to Black, was the concluding part of it—when they were searching for Mr. Owen in their distress, and were all making, as if by instinct, towards the direction of the Trailing Indian—and that it was *not* the dream which led her mind to doubt Black, but the ill-feeling which the man, as was well known, had long entertained towards her master. Sir Dene nodded acquiescence to this, and took his leave courteously. Since the finding of the paper given by Squire Honeythorn, he had been very civil to Mary Barber when by chance they met: as if he would tacitly apologise for having doubted her mother's word.

The weather in England is capricious; as we too well know. Before the Easter week was quite out, the lovely spring sunshine had given place to a heavy fall of snow. One day in the next week, when the ground was white, Sir Dene and his son Geoffry were returning home on foot through Harebell Lane from a visit to some outlying land on the estate, and caught the sound of some young voices in dispute, as they approached the pond. Suddenly a man's tones drowned the others.

"What's the matter there, I wonder?" carelessly remarked Sir Dene to his son. "That's Black's voice."

The matter was this. Two little ploughboys, not quite so hard-worked as usual by reason of the snow, had met in Harebell Lane, and went in for a game of snow-balling. It ended in roughness. There was a personal tussle on the edge of the pond, and both fell amid the snow and rushes. Fell on something that hurt the under one. It proved to be a thick, nobbly, walking-stick, polished to the brightness of mahogany. Both lads seized upon it, each claiming it for his own booty. While they were fighting for possession, Randy Black came up the lane, pounced upon the combatants, like the hawk in the fable, and took the stick. As Sir Dene came in sight he was holding it above his head, beyond the reach of the howling and indignant boys, who were vainly jumping up to try and get it back. Black had his back turned, and did not see that anyone was near.

"What stick's that?"

The stern, authoritative interruption was Geoffry Clanwaring's. It arrested the boys' noise; it startled Black. As the man turned sharply to see who spoke it, he flung the stick into the Pond—and Geoffry, springing forward, was too late to save it.

"What did you do that for, Black?" demanded Geoffry.

"It's the best place for it, Mr. Clanwaring," was Black's answer, as he made a show of touching his hat to Sir Dene. "These here young devils 'ud a fought to their skins for't else."

"It is *not* the best place for it," returned Geoffry, with some emotion. "Wait an instant, sir, please," he added to his father, who was walking on. "Whence did you get that stick, Black?"

Something seemed to be the matter with Black. He had turned so deadly white.

"What stick was't?" questioned Black of the boys, moving to face them. "These here young hounds had got a fighting over it when I come up."

"'Twere 'mong the rushes," sobbed one. "'Twere me as it hurted, a falling on't; 'twere me as had it first."

"Why do you inquire, Geoffry?" asked his father. "Is the stick anything to you?"

"Yes, sir. The stick was Mr. Owen's. It was the one he had with him that night."

"Nonsense!" cried Sir Dene in his surprise. "Mr. Owen's!"

"I am sure of it. As Black held it up, I saw it distinctly, and recognized it. What was your motive for throwing it into the pond?" he asked, turning on Black.

"Motive! I'd got no motive, sir—but to pay out these here two varmints," was Black's ready answer. "Why don't ye tell about the stick, and where ye got it?" he savagely added to the two young culprits, boxing one, and kicking the other. "Not as I should think 'twas any stick of Owen's. 'Taint likely."

"I tell you it *was*," said Geoffry, with a touch of his elder brother's hauteur. "How dare you dispute my word?"

"If you think 'twas, sir, I'm sure I be sorry to have pitched it in," said Black, humbly. "I never thought it was any stick o' consequence; and I don't think it now. As to you two young beasts, I hope you'll come to be hung, for getting me into this row.

He touched his hat again and went on towards the Trailing Indian. Geoffry Clanwaring looked after him.

"Father, I do believe that man knows more about the past

than he ought. He pitched in that stick in sheer terror—to conceal the stick. So it seemed to me."

"Owen's stick!" cried Sir Dene, unable to realize the fact. "What is to be done, Geoffry?"

"We must have the pond searched, sir. If the stick was really lying amid the rushes on its brink, the probability is that he is lying within it."

Sir Dene recognized the necessity for action; and no time was lost. In the presence of quite half the population of Hurst Leet, who flocked up to see the sight, Harebell pond was searched. The stick was first of all fished up, and then its master.

Just as he had gone out of his home that night; in his great coat, his magpie cap tied on over his ears, apparently untouched, not a fold of his garments ruffled, so he was found. At first it was supposed that it was a simple case of accidental drowning. But soon the discovery was made that he had been injured—apparently by a blow—in the back of his head. Was that blow accidental?—or wilful?

Squire Arde, making one of the throng, and whose opinion from his age and position had long held sway in the place, thought Robert Owen had fallen into the pond from above.

"When he left the cowshed that night, he might have halted at the fence to look up and down the lane, have leaned too far over it and overbalanced himself; his head struck again some sharp substance i' the pond, which stunned him, and so he lay and was drowned. As to the stick, it fell amid the rushes, and was hid. Or else," added Squire Arde, "some villain struck at him from behind as he was standing above there, stunned him, and hurled him over. 'Twas one or t'other, I think. D'ye mind what I said t'other day, Mr. Geoffry Clanwaring—about the brushwood being disturbed up there?"

The public took up the notion from that hour. Robert Owen, either by accident or assault, fell over the fence into the water, and lay there quietly to drown. There was no proof at all: only supposition. The coroner's inquest was assembled, and brought in an open verdict: Found drowned in Harebell pond.

And that was the ending of Robert Owen in this world. The ill-fated man was buried in the churchyard at Hurst Leet, a crowd of spectators attending the funeral.

One piece of impudence must be mentioned. On the day

following the interment, Randy Black presented himself at Beechhurst Dene, and craved an audience of its master. He had come to ask for the lease of Harebell Farm, and offered (as an inducement) to pay the first year's rent in advance. Sir Dene thought it the coolest piece of impudence he had ever met with; and very nearly (in wish at any rate) kicked Mr. Randy out of the house. Harebell Farm, he said, was not in the market.

That was true. It had been arranged that William Owen should manage the farm in his late father's place; and Sir Dene had already accepted him as tenant.

A week or two went slowly on. The inclement snow, the biting winds again gave place, in accordance with their capricious fashion, to genial spring weather and bright sunshine. But, long ere a month had elapsed, a very startling and disagreeable rumour arose in the neighbourhood—it was not quite certain whence or how. The substance of it was that Robert Owen could not rest in his grave, but came back again to haunt the earth. It was said that he had been seen more than once hovering about Harebell Lane.

After the rumour had been whispered well about, the first person to see the apparition—or to fancy he saw it—was Sir Dene's butler, Gander. One moonlight night, towards the end of April, just about four weeks after that other moonlight time which had witnessed the disappearance of Robert Owen, Gander went up on an errand to the Trailing Indian, sent thither by his master. Sir Dene happened to be out of tobacco: none, for miles round, was to be had so good as that kept at the Trailing Indian, and even Sir Dene did not disdain to avail himself of that ill-reputed house's goods. "Get a pound of it, Gander," said he: "and as much more as Black will spare."

Gander got the tobacco, paid for it, and accepted a glass of ale, hospitably proffered by Black. Like his master, he could forget the doubtful reputation of inn and host, when his interest was concerned—and Gander knew what good ale was as well as anybody. "To drink it up at a gulp and bolt, 'ud be fine manners," thought the butler. So he sat down and sipped it, and had a chat with Black.

"How's that young woman as was ill here?" he asked.

"She's not about yet," answered Black, angrily, for the matter had annoyed him from the first. "Got a bad leg, or something."

After sitting about a quarter of an hour, Gander started for home at a quick pace, the paper of tobacco in his hand. "That's a rare good tap up at Black's," he said to himself, as he went along the lane. "Wish Sir Dene 'ud keep as good a one for us!"

In approaching the pond, he got thinking of him who had not so long ago been found there; which was but natural; and the association of ideas caused him to glance up at the fence above. And if ever a man felt that he was struck into stone, Gander did then.

For there, leaning over the fence and staring at him—just as he might have leaned the night of his death—was the well-known form of Robert Owen.

"Mercy be good to me!" gasped the butler.

Dropping the paper of tobacco, never stopping to pick it up, Gander sprung off with a yell that might have been heard at the Trailing Indian, and never drew breath or step till he burst into the servants' hall at Beechhurst Dene.

CHAPTER XV.

ONLY SADNESS.

This chapter will be a sad one. I am sorry, but there's no help for it. The reader will say, attributing the story to the imagination of the writer's brain, Why make these people, in whom we have got interested, *die?* The answer is,—Because they *did* die. For this tale is not a tale of fiction, but a real record of the past: of people that lived, and of the events that happened to them. When an author is trammelled by reality, and would be a faithful narrator, he cannot put sunshine where darkness lay, or make dark that which was light.

Some months have elapsed since the death of Robert Owen, and they have brought at least one grave and grievous misfortune in their train. Geoffrey Clanwaring, out one day with a party shooting small birds, had received a gun-shot wound in his side. There was little damage outwardly, and of that he soon recovered; but the doctors had a suspicion of some grave inward injury: and if their fear proved correct, poor Geoffry would not be long for this world. His father, Sir Dene, did not know of this fear—indeed, it was confined pretty much to Mr. Priar and the other surgeon—a skilled man from Worcester—who had attended him in the accident.

Not being absolutely sure themselves, they did not talk of it. The relations between Sir Dene and Geoffry remained the same: cordial, but not intimate: and Geoffry and his wife had not been admitted as guests within the gates of Beechhurst Dene.

No new light had been thrown upon the death of Robert Owen. The singular report—that his ghost might be sometimes seen in and about Harebell Lane—did not subside. While some scouted it as utterly absurd, and old Squire Arde laughed over it till his eyes ran tears, the greater portion of the community lent ear to the story. Gander—as related—had been frightened nearly out of his senses by the sight. He was not the only one: and Harebell Lane was more than ever shunned at night. Mrs. Owen remained at Harebell Farm with her son William, and things went on there in their old groove.

There were great doings at Beechhurst Dene the first fortnight in September. John Clanwaring, the heir, brought down his newly-married wife on a visit: and a party was invited to meet them. She was very pretty, and a great heiress: altogether an irreproachable match—as John Clanwaring, with his caution and his pride, was sure to make. It served, by contrast, to make darker the marriage contracted by Geoffry: and if by ill-luck Mr. Clanwaring met his brother, he would pass him as scornfully as he might have passed some despicable character—say Randy Black, for instance—his head in the air. At the fortnight's end, the company quitted Beechhurst Dene again: all, save John Clanwaring and his wife. They remained on for another week or two; but their established home was in London.

A few days before their departure, the brothers again met. It was a lovely September day: the sun-light lay on the plains, the woods were beginning to assume their beautiful autumn tints. Mr. Clanwaring, his wife on his arm, was about to cross a stile in the Dene woods, when Geoffry appeared at it on the other side. He (Geoffry) was at it first; but, in courtesy to the lady, drew back to wait. John Clanwaring got over, handed over his wife, and walked on with her. Save that he snatched his coat round him that it should not touch his brother's in passing, he took no notice whatever. It galled Geoffry: he thought John might have first introduced his wife to him when they thus met, face to face.

"I wonder whether he would have done it did he know

there's a chance that I shall soon be lying low?" thought Geoffry. "And that chance exists. I cannot well mistake my own feelings: and Priar, unless I am mistaken, knows it better than I do."

Geoffry was on his road home to the bailiff's lodge. Busy with Sir Dene's affairs that morning, out of doors as well as in, he had been letting the time slip away past the dinner hour. He could not ride about as he used to before his accident. Maria would be waiting for him, he knew; so he put his best foot foremost. Not the fleet foot it once was: for quick walking hurt him nearly as much as riding.

The first person he saw on entering his cottage home was Mr. Priar. Geoffry mentally leaped to the truth at once: his wife must be ill. Even so. Her illness had been waited for for some days now: Geoffry was expecting a little heir! Heir! It was a slip of the pen. Heir to what?—his misfortunes? What contrasts exist! When John's wife should present him with a son, it would be the future inheritor of a title and of the rich lands of Beechhurst Dene; Geoffry's child would be be but a humble dependent. Could poor Geoffry have foreseen how humble, how dependent, how despised and put upon, he might have wished to take the child with him when he himself should die.

"Is all going well?" was Geoffry's first question to the surgeon.

"I—hope it will," answered Mr. Priar—and the slight want of assurance in his tone at once struck Geoffry. "We have been sending after you to Beechhurst Dene, Mr. Geoffry Clanwaring: the messenger brought back word that you were not there."

"I left Beechhurst Dene two hours ago. I had things to attend to up at Simmonds's Is my wife very ill?"

"Not very; not particularly so. You can see her."

Mrs. Geoffry Clanwaring was quite alone in her sickness. Her mother, Mrs. Owen, was confined to her bed with illness, just then: her sister, Mrs. Arde, growing gradually but surely weaker, was not able to come. Maria herself had been in more delicate health all the summer than she need have been: her father's death and the sad manner of it had shaken her greatly.

But if Mr. Priar had entertained any doubt of the result, it would seem to have been needless. The baby made its appearance, and was a fine boy. When Geoffry first took the little curiosity in his arms, he felt prouder of him than if he had been born with a silver spoon in his mouth.

"How light its hair is, Maria!"

"Yes: it is like yours," she answered with a happy smile. "I can trace a likeness to you and to Sir Dene."

"He'll be a fine little shaver if he's like my father. We shall have to choose a name for him, love."

Just a day or two of these fond hopes, this delusive security, and then a change came. Dangerous symptoms set in for Maria Clanwaring; and a horseman went galloping to Worcester for one of the best surgeons the city afforded. He came and saw her: in conjunction with the dismayed Mr. Priar: and they no doubt did their best, if there was anything, best or worst, that could be done. It was all in vain: the life, fleeting away, could not be arrested. The baby also began to droop: it almost seemed as if it would go with its mother. The truth had to be told to Geoffry.

Evening came on. The bustle of the going and coming of the medical men, of the awful shock, was past, and over the household reigned a solemn stillness. She lay on her bed, pale, quiet, exhausted, resigned: far more resigned than poor stunned Geoffry. He sat by the fire, more like one in a dream than a living man; but for disturbing her, he would have taken the pale, sweet face from the pillow to his breast, and cried aloud to heaven over it in his despairing anguish.

"Perfect quiet, mind, Mr. Geoffry Clanwaring," had been the doctors' urgent warning to him. "Once excite her to emotion, and all will be over."

So there he sat, controlling his bitter grief he knew not how; his golden hair damp with the struggle, his blue eyes o'erladen with misery.

The clergyman came; and Geoffry and his dying wife partook of Christ's last sacrament together. Next, the baby was brought forward for baptism: Maria wished it done. Geoffry leaned over his wife to ask her wishes about the name.

"Call him Tom," she feebly said. "It was my dear little brother's name who died: and it is one of yours, Geoffry."

"Tom," said Geoffry, returning to the clergyman.

"Tom?" echoed the minister questioningly, his fingers already in the water.

"Tom," repeated Geoffry.

And so "Tom" the child was christened.

So bewildered and confused with trouble was Geoffry Clanwaring, that he never remembered until too late that the name ought to have been Thomas. It was a mistake: but a mistake that did not cost him a regretful thought. Under the shadow of real calamities, trifling ones go for nothing.

Almost before they were alone again, the last moments approached for Maria. Geoffry might give way as much as he pleased then; nothing of emotion could harm her more in this world. He held her to him mid his sobs of anguish, his hot tears falling on her face.

"Not for very long, my darling; the separation won't be for long. But a little while, a few weeks, or months at most, and I shall have followed you."

She looked at him as if scarcely understanding.

"Ay, it is so. I have kept it from you, Maria: I meant to let this illness of yours be well over before I spoke. And, oh my wife, my dear one, I know not how I should have told you —or how have borne to leave you here behind me. I am dying of that gunshot wound, Maria; there was some fatal inward injury. I have suspected it all along: and to-day when the doctors were here, I got them to acknowledge that they suspect it too. You will not have long to wait for me on the other side."

She was past speaking much, but a glad light shone in her dim eyes. Geoffry's sobs made the room sound again. Let us leave them together for the last hour.

It had all been so rapid that there was no time to apprise the world of the danger that had suddenly set in. But the news was spreading now, and some people were arriving in hot consternation.

Mary Barber was the first. She had been staying at Worcester for some days with Mrs. Arde; had only come back to Harebell Farm that afternoon. Geoffry Clanwaring's modest household consisted but of one servant, Susan Cole, eldest daughter of Cole the farrier; a good-natured, talkative girl of eighteen, with frizzly-looking hair the colour of old rope, and a fixed colour in her face. She was in the kitchen with the nurse when Mary Barber arrived. And when Mary Barber heard that—instead of the danger she had come to inquire into—life was all but over, she after giving a minute or two to digest the shock, nearly shook Susan Cole.

"You heartless, wicked huzzy! You couldn't come up to say so?"

"I didn't know it till just now," returned Susan, who was crying silently in grief for her pretty young mistress. "It have come on us as sudden as a blow. As to master, he's like a man dazed. I don't believe he have been able to recollect nothing. But he *did* send to the farm."

Mary Barber, standing upright in the small kitchen, thought over the past two or three hours. Upon her return from Worcester, Joan had said a messenger had been up to say there was a change in young Mrs. Clanwaring: and Mary Barber set off, but not at once, for she had never thought of *this* change.

"Where's the baby?" she asked, under her breath. For, now that the first shock to her feelings had been relieved by blaming somebody, the extent of the calamity subdued her.

"He's sleeping in his cradle," said the nurse. "He seems a bit better to-night than he did earlier in the day."

"Whatever will be done about bringing him up?"

"Oh, as to that," returned the nurse, "children 'll sometimes thrive as well without their mothers as with 'em."

A movement overhead, and a call from Geoffry, sent the nurse and Mary Barber upstairs, the latter flinging off her cloak and bonnet as she went. The last moment was at hand: the fleeting spirit and the earthly body were fighting in their separation.

"My poor lamb!" wailed Mary Barber, leaning over the pale face, quiet again now. "Oh wasn't it enough that your poor father should have went—that your sister should be fast going—but that the Lord must take you! We'd say that it was cruelly hard—only that His ways are not as our ways."

There was a gentle flutter on the face, and Maria turned her head upon the pillow, looking away to a distant part of the room.

"Yes," she said in a distinct, cheerful voice, as if answering a call.

Geoffry was hastening round, but Mary Barber lifted her finger for silence. *She* knew the sign—and what it meant.

"Hush, Mr. Geoffry. She's passing now. It was her answer to the summons!"

And the spirit did pass, even as the woman said it. Passed with a deep, long sigh. Mary Barber caught up her breath with another.

"I know that death was coming to the family, Mr. Geoffry:

but I thought it was for Mrs. Arde. I knew it by my dreams."

As Geoffry quitted the room, leaving the two women in it, quitting it like one who gropes his blind way in the dark, so stunned were all his faculties, he became dimly conscious of a loud, sharp knocking somewhere. It was in reality at the panel of his house-door—but it seemed to him miles off; or perhaps only in some distant region of his brain. Susan Cole opened the door, and the voice of Sir Dene was heard. That aroused him to passing events, and he went downstairs. Sir Dene was standing in the parlour; their one sitting room, that Maria had made so pretty. Vases of bright flowers stood about, fresh yet: she had put them there on the morning of the day she was taken ill.

"Geoffry, what's this I hear? That your wife is in imminent danger," began Sir Dene. "Coming out just now for a stroll after dinner, I met young Harry Cole, and he mentioned it."

"My wife is dead, father."

Sir Dene looked at his son, as if he quite believed his mind must be wandering.

"Yes, she's dead," was repeated by Geoffry's quivering lips. "Only just now: not three minutes since."

"Lord bless me!" broke from Sir Dene.

He backed against the upright bookcase, and stood staring, waiting for his senses to come to him.

"Why!—you told me yourself this morning, Geoffry, that she was going on all right!"

"And so she was father. A change took place an hour or two after midday. Priar came, and Dr. Woodyat was fetched. They could not save her."

"It is awfully sudden," cried the dismayed Sir Dene. "Poor thing! Poor young thing!"

Geoffry, come to the end of his equanimity, put his head down on the table, and sobbed aloud. Great bursting sobs that shook him. Sir Dene wondered whether there was any brandy in the house, or other kind of cordial, and where he could find it. Self-reproach was stinging Sir Dene keenly. When those whom we have injured or not sufficiently regarded in life are dead, it is then that repentance touches us. He had not been as kind as he might to this poor young girl, now gone from them all for ever. True he had been pleasant and courteous to her when they met; but he had never invited her inside his gates, he had not treated her as a daughter-in-law: and he wished now that he had done it, in spite of the prejudices of his eldest son and heir.

"Don't give way, Geoff, my boy. Don't! Bless my heart, but this is a dreadful blow, and I'm—I'm truly sorry for it. Poor young girl! but little more than a child! Can I find a drop of brandy for you, Geoff?"

Geoffry did not want any brandy: he could not have touched it. Drying away his tears, swallowing down his bitter sobs, striving manfully with his emotion, he there and then disclosed to his father the fact that he himself (as he truly believed) should not live long after his wife; that the same grave might almost be kept open for him. It would have been a greater shock to Sir Dene than the other, only he did not put faith in it.

"Dying of that gun-shot wound!" he repeated. "Geoffry, my poor fellow, things are wearing their gloomiest hue to you just now; 'tis but natural. If there is anything wrong inwardly, we'll soon have you set to rights."

"Father, I don't think there'll be any more setting to rights for me; I don't, indeed. You can ask Priar or Woodyat about it: they know, I fancy. It's only within a week or so that I have felt sure of it myself."

"Nonsense, Geoffry. It was not much of a hurt at the worst. You shall be doctored up."

Geoffry said no more. But a sure and certain prevision lay upon him this evening, that his own end was not far off. It might come upon them almost as suddenly at the last, he thought, as his wife's had come upon him.

"Geoffry, I'd like to see her," said Sir Dene, when he rose to depart.

They went up the narrow staircase with hushed footsteps. The house was like one of death, in its utter stillness. The infant slept in another room; Sir Dene never once thought about him at all.

They had already dressed her for the grave. The sweet, calm, pale face looked almost like that of an angel. Sir Dene felt pain, regret, grief—nearly as he had when his own wife died.

"Poor darling!—poor innocent child!" he murmured, touching her brow. "May the good Lord have taken her to His happy Rest!"

"She was kind and good and pure as one of Heaven's angels, father." And Geoffry's sobs broke forth again.

M

As Sir Dene was walking up the Hollow on his way home, the death-bell suddenly struck out from Hurst Leet Church. Mary Barber had sent Susan Cole flying to tell the sexton. Sir Dene stopped and listened: it seemed to bring more forcibly than ever the event before him. Three times two: and then the sharp quick strokes to denote that the soul was passing.

"I wonder who's gone now?"

The irreverent words, for their careless tone made them so, absolutely startled Sir Dene. Standing to listen, his back turned to his gates, his face towards the village, he had not observed that any one was near. Tempted by the beauty of the evening—a warm, still moonlight night—Mr. Clanwaring had come out for a stroll just as his father had previously done. It was he who spoke.

"What did you say?" asked Sir Dene, sharply turning upon him.

"I thought you were listening to the passing bell, sir. Some village woman, I suppose, has dropped off."

"They'd not trouble themselves to ring the passing-bell at this time of night for a 'village woman,' I expect," said Sir Dene sternly, for the words grated harshly on his present frame of mind. In truth, he had not been feeling very genially towards his heir as he walked up. But for him and his prejudices, Sir Dene would have relented to Geoffry and his poor young wife: he saw things clearly now, and knew it.

John Clanwaring wondered at the tone. "Do you know who it's for, then sir?" he asked.

"It is for your brother's wife."

"*Who?*" cried John Clanwaring, forgetting his grammar in his surprise.

"For your brother's wife. Don't I speak plain enough? Geoffry's sweet, pretty young wife: poor Owen's daughter. She's dead.

"I'm sure I'm sorry to hear it, for her sake," said Mr. Clanwaring, somewhat taken aback. "It's very sudden, is it not, sir?"

"It is sudden. You were harshly contemptuous to her, John, in your judgment: she is gone where neither harshness nor contempt can reach her. She looks like an angel, lying there, with her pale, innocent face."

"It is a sad fate for her, poor thing: I really pity her, sir," admitted John Clanwaring. And there was a pause.

"I am not sure but Geoffry will be the one to go next,

John," resumed Sir Dene. "We shall wish then, perhaps, that we had been a bit kinder to them."

"Is he likely to die of grief?" asked John.

"Grief's a complaint *you'll* never die of; you've not got feeling enough," retorted Sir Dene. "Geoffry talks of that shot he got a while ago; he fears it left some fatal injury behind it. For my part, I think it must be only fancy."

"Of course it is only fancy," returned John Clanwaring, in a tone of assertion. "Were there any permanent injury, Geoffry could not go about as he does."

They fell into silence. The quick strokes of the bell were dying away to give place to its slow and monotonous toll. It had a weird, solemn sound, breaking out at intervals in the stillness of the autumn night.

CHAPTER XVI.

SEEN BY MOONLIGHT.

"You had better come back to Beechhurst Dene, Geoffry."

The speaker was Sir Dene. They had just returned from the funeral, and Sir Dene had entered Geoffry's home with him, leaving the other mourners—John Clanwaring, George Arde, and William Owen—to disperse. Mr. Clanwaring had condescended to attend the funeral. Sir Dene put it to him strongly—that he *ought* to do it. So he delayed yet his departure for town, and waited. It probably went against the grain to stand side by side with William Owen, mourners at the same grave: but John, cool and impassive, made no sign. He had condescended to shake hands with Geoffry, and say he sympathised with him in his loss. Sir Dene went in with Geoffry afterwards. The little dwelling seemed strangely still and solitary; and the baronet felt it as a chill.

"You had better come back to Beechhurst Dene, and be taken care of," he repeated. "Now that the poor young thing's gone, there's nobody to do anything for you here; nothing to keep you in the place. Geoff, my boy, *I* never disliked her."

"No, father, I don't think you did."

"I shall never forget that time I saw her at Malvern toastnig a pikelet at the fire. Pretty creature! standing there to face me, so sweet and modest and humble, in her white India muslin frock and the blue ribbons in her hair. I know real India muslin when I see it: nobody better. She couldn't put the toasting-fork down at first, Geoff, for timidity, but kept it in her hand. 'Twas as pretty a picture as a man ever saw."

Geoffry, who was beginning to look sadly worn and thin, made no answer. His heart was brim-full.

"Then you'll come back home, Geoff?"

"Yes, father, thank you; I think I had better. If John does not object."

"John object!—John be—be shot!" exploded the baronet, pulling up the word he had been about to speak when he remembered where he had just been. "It's not John's house yet, that he should rule it. He and his wife are going posting off again, I'm glad to say: somehow things are never so pleasant when he is at home. Come to-morrow: to-night, if you will. You must never think of running away from me again, Geoff."

Geoffry smiled faintly. "Not in the same manner that I did before, father; I'll promise you that."

"Nor in any other, I hope," was Sir Dene's quiet rejoinder. "We'll nurse you into strength at the Dene."

Accordingly on the following day, in the forenoon, Geoffry Clanwaring walked up to his old home, just as though he were going to make a call, or to do an hour's work in the business parlour, as usual. He carried in his arms his not yet fortnight old baby, wrapped in a red shawl. As he was about to enter the front gates, there came thundering down the avenue a close carriage-and-four, the post-boys spurring their horses to make the exit in proper style, after the fashion of the day. The carriage bore the arms of John Clanwaring, the heir: he sat in it with his wife; an attendant man and maid in the rumble behind. Geoffry stood aside to let it pass. No one saw him but the valet, who touched his hat—and wondered, no doubt, what Mr. Geoffry Clanwaring had got in the red bundle. They were commencing their journey to London. Mrs. Clanwaring, he saw, had no mourning on.

"And yet Maria was every whit as good as she; ay, and better," thought Geoffry: and as he went on up the avenue, he could not see the ground for his blinding tears.

Not tears for the lack of black on Mrs. Clanwaring. No. But this coming home with the little helpless burthen, brought all too painfully to his mind what he had lost.

"Goodness me!" exclaimed Sir Dene, as Geoffry sat down in the library, and undid the shawl. "Why—that's your baby, Geoffry."

"Yes, father. I couldn't leave him behind."

"Bless the child! I declare I forgot all about him. Well, the women shall take care of him. There's plenty of them to do it. What's his name?"

"His name's Tom," replied Geoffry. "She was anxious about it before she died, and I had it done. The child drooped and ailed that day, just as though it knew its mother was leaving it. It seems all right now."

"You mean Thomas, I suppose."

"No: Tom. The mistake was mine. I was confused with grief, and said 'Tom' twice over to the parson, never recollecting that it should have been Thomas. It will not matter, father: Tom is as good a name for him as any other."

"No, it won't matter," replied Sir Dene. "What does he live upon, Geoff? Sop?"

"He lives upon barley-water mixed with milk," said Geoffry. "He won't cost much. Susan Cole is bringing some up: she can show the maids here how to feed him."

The child, who had slept through this, awoke now, opening his eyes. Sir Dene advanced to look at him—such a little face it was, peeping out of the shawl. Geoffry took off the cambric cap, and showed his bits of fair hair.

"He has got just the look that you had at his age, Geoffry. I remember it well. The first of you born, John, had a black head, like his mother; you were fair, like me. It's a pretty baby: it will be just like you."

"So poor Maria said. Like me and like you, she thought."

"Ay: at your age I was much what you are, Geoffry. Poor little motherless lambkin!" added Sir Dene pityingly, as he stroked the baby's face.

"Soon to be fatherless also," spoke Geoffry.

"No, no, my boy; I trust not," said Sir Dene.

But Geoffry shook his head: he knew better.

"Father, you'll give him a bite and a sup here when I am gone, and a pillow in some odd corner, won't you?"—and the words seemed to come from the very depths of an aching heart. "He'll be in nobody's way, poor little waif."

"I will, Geoff," heartily answered Sir Dene, his eyes dimmed by some earnest tears, that rose and were checked. "I promise it you. The child shall be as welcome to his bit and his sup as you were. There's my hand upon it."

People rarely give themselves more trouble than they can help. None of the maids showed themselves too ready to undertake the (at best) onerous charge of an infant, as proposed by Sir Dene: and when Susan Cole arrived with the barley-water and milk for its food, and sundry of its clothes, tied up in a large silk handkerchief, the servants, who did pretty much as they liked, told her she had better remain for a day or two, and see to the child. The day or two grew into a month or two, and that into a period indefinite, Susan Cole taking the entire charge; Sir Dene falling in with the arrangement as if it was a matter of course, without a word either way. He was very fond of the child, would often nurse and toss it: and when he saw its sleeves tied up with black ribbons and a black sash round its waist, that Susan Cole put on the day poor Geoffry died, Sir Dene held the little face to his own for some minutes, as if that black made a fonder link between them.

So the baby grew, and thrived, and got its teeth, and learnt to walk and talk, just as other healthy and happy children do: and Sir Dene loved the boy; and Susan Cole was proud of him; and Gander admired him more than he had admired anything since poor Geoffry himself was young; and the other servants alternately indulged and snubbed him. With it all—in spite of his being Sir Dene's grandson and that he had his home at Beechhurst Dene—he was not altogether considered by the servants as a child of the house; he did not get the deference that a son of, for instance, John Clanwaring would have received.

The boy, as he grew older and stronger, incurred the danger of being allowed to run wild. Sir Dene had about as much notion of the proper way of bringing up a child as he had of a young tiger; and nobody else interfered to suggest. There was no day nursery. As long as the child was in arms, Susan Cole sat where she pleased with him—mostly in the kitchen or servants' hall; when he could run, he roamed where he would about the house at will. Sir Dene would pick him up and talk to him, and put him by his side at table, and call for a plate and a spoon for the child. If Tom ran out to see Sir Dene mount his horse, Sir Dene would lift him on to the saddle, bare headed and bare armed, and ride off with him, perhaps for miles, in the summer weather. When not with Sir Dene he would be left very much to his own devices, for Susan Cole was a frightful gossip, and regarded social intercourse with anybody that would talk to her, as the sweetest thing in life. There were times also when Sir Dene was away from Beechhurst, and during these seasons Tom got very little attention at all. Gander, who was regarded by Sir Dene as head of the servants, and in a degree ruled them, would be with his master, and at home it would be high life below stairs. To save trouble, little Tom's plate and fork would be set at the kitchen table: he would be looked for and brought into meals: and that was about all the care. He was one of those quiet, happy children who amuse themselves: would sit for hours on the library floor, looking at a picture-book, or in some remote room amidst the animals out of his Noah's ark. The servants knew the child was safe, and that sufficed. Cole, the farrier, had a journeyman; he was Susan's sweetheart;—consequently she passed a great deal more time in her father's forge than in looking after Tom. In fact, save the odd moments of tenderness bestowed upon him by Sir Dene, the little child was very much what his poor father had called him the day he brought him up in the red shawl—a waif. He was a wonderfully pretty and engaging child, with the sweet temper and gentle manners of his mother, and the kindly blue eyes and fair curls of his father. A child to be loved and cherished: a child that with proper training would make a good and noble man: a child to whom God had been generous, in implanting in his heart a full portion of most excellent seed.

Sir Dene was often away. He had taken permanent rooms in London, and could go there at will. John Clanwaring never came down now to Beechhurst Dene. His wife's health had been very delicate since the birth of her child, a girl; John said she was not strong enough to move about, and therefore he did not. At any rate, it was a good excuse for his remaining in the place he liked best and never cared to be out of—London. Perhaps this took Sir Dene there. John was not his favourite son—*he* was gone—but John was better than none: and the baronet found it very lonely at Beechhurst Dene. So, he and Gander away for weeks together, the servants took their own ease and Tom his own way. No wonder the neglected child grew fond of going to Mrs. Owen's: once or twice he had run off thither alone. He also went to Squire Arde's.

No longer the old Squire: the little man who was so odd and quaint; but a new one. Changes were everywhere The strange little old man was dead, and George Arde reigned at the Hall, and was called Squire in his turn. The will he left was nearly as odd as he had been: so at least thought the public. It was certainly unexpected. A notion—gathered from observation of the old Squire's character, and perhaps from occasional words let fall by him during his later life—had become fixed in men's minds: that he would never leave a shilling of his money to any relative: but all of it to charities, and especially to those charities connected with the insane. "Droitwich 'll be the better for his savings," quoth the neighbours to one another—alluding to the well-known asylum at that place—when the news went forth that Squire Arde was dead. "He'll direct the Hall and all its belongings, inside and out, to be sold; and Droitwich mad-house 'll get the whole on't."

The neighbours were mistaken. Squire Arde's will did not give a shilling to any charity: Droitwich asylum (or, as it was universally put then, "madhouse") was not as much as mentioned in it. The Hall, with all that pertained to it and the income attaching to it, was left to George Arde, to his own intense surprise.

George Arde's wife was not then dead. In her very delicate state she had lived on much longer than any one could have supposed, fluttering always, as may be said, between life and death. Now and then the old Squire would call when he was at Worcester, and see the child, little Mary, to whom he seemed to have taken a fancy. Necklaces, and trifles of that description that had belonged to his own dead child, the other Mary, he would bring it. "I should not be much surprised at his leaving her a thousand pounds," said George Arde one day to his wife, when the Squire had been, and brought a *new* coral with silver bells.

Not one thousand did he leave the child, but twenty. The will bequeathed a certain sum of money to "Mary, daughter of my third cousin, George Arde." Which sum, already out at safe and good interest, would represent twenty thousand pounds on the day Mary Arde should be eighteen: and it was to be her's then unconditionally. So little Mary, granddaughter of the late unfortunate Robert Owen, and cousin of young Tom Clanwaring, turned out to be an heiress.

Before George Arde took up his abode at the Hall, his wife died. She had been in so weak a state, and it had become so evident that her death was near, that the trouble of removing was spared her. She died in the small house where they had lived, and was buried in the same mouldy old church that had witnessed poor Maria Owen's stolen marriage—St.

Peter's. George Arde and his little daughter went to the Hall then.

This removal occurred when Tom was about a year old. Two years have already gone by since. The boy was fond of going to the Hall. Susan Cole enjoyed the society of the servants: Tom that of the little girl. George Arde welcomed the lad freely, whenever he was at home: but he had taken to visit about a good deal. Rumours of his second marriage were abroad: George Arde, owner of Arde Hall and Squire of the parish, young still, and an agreeable man, was no undesirable match, and was courted in the county accordingly.

Would the little girl, the heiress, live to come into her wealth? The question was arising. Symptoms of delicacy (she was her mother's child all over) were beginning to manifest themselves, and it was feared she might *not*. George Arde was intensely fond of her: and perhaps the first thing that put a second marriage into his head was the wish to have some kind and gentle lady in his house who would watch over the child carefully, and stand to it in the light of a mother. Once having made up his mind to this, Mr. Arde was not long about it. He chose his second wife from one of the first and proudest families in the county. It was rather singular that the day of the marriage should be little Tom's birthday: he was three years old.

On that self-same night occurred an incident which must be mentioned. Robert Owen appeared again. The miserable rumours—that his spirit came back to trouble the earth—had never died away. From whatever source arising, whether delusion, superstitious fancy, or actual (if unaccountable) fact, they but gained ground and spread. No sooner had one report of the appearance had time to subside and people began to forget it, than another fright would come. Now it would be a belated labourer, going home at a tardy hour up Harebell Lane; now a carter's boy; now some traveller on his way to the Trailing Indian. On this night that we are now speaking of, two people saw it, one of whom was Black.

Black had been down to Hurst Leet on an errand. Coming home again about nine o'clock through a flood of moonlight, he burst into the Trailing Indian in a fearful state: his breath gone, the sweat pouring off him, his hair on end. More abject terror could not well be seen. Mr. Priar happened to be there —for Mrs. Black's sickly state required him to pay her an occasional visit, and he would go up at any odd moment when leisure allowed him; two or three men were also drinking in the kitchen; when, in burst the landlord in the extraordinary state described. That his fear had no sham in it could not be mistaken: though how it was possible for a hardened man like Black to feel afraid of any earthly or ghostly thing, Mr. Priar, for one, could not imagine. Mixing some brandy and water, the doctor made him drink it. Black's teeth chattered as he told what he had seen—Robert Owen standing at that part above Harebell Lane, where he was supposed to have fallen from, and gazing down at the pond. Question after question was poured into Black's ear, especially from the startled men: but he could tell no more than he had told. Coming up the Lane by the pond pretty quickly, he happened to turn his eyes up to the fence above the water; and there, leaning over it, was the figure of Robert Owen, his face as white as it had been when he lay dead, his beard as silvery as it was in life. Black did not stay to give a second look, but came off as fast as his shaking legs would carry him: and the strangest thing of all was, that he should sit there in his kitchen and confess to it. But fear takes pride, and reticence too, out of the most hardy men.

Before Black had at all recovered his equanimity, or had done trembling, a choice friend of his came in—Michael Geach, who had arrived that evening on one of his unexpected visits to the Trailing Indian. One might have expected ridicule of the tale at least from Geach; but, on the contrary, it seemed to make him rather uncomfortable.

"I never was a coward," he observed; "but it's no light thing would persuade me into Harebell Lane of a night now. Hanged if I'd not rather come slap upon a body whitening in chains on the gibbet, than see Owen's ghost. Cheer up, Randy, and don't shake so; you are all blue."

"When did *you* come here?" asked Black, in no pleasant tones.

"Me! I've been here this hour, and more; a waiting for you to come in."

"Why couldn't you ha' sent word you was——Drat it altogether! *You* needn't shake."

The concluding observations were made to Black's wife. His eyes happened to fall on her as he was addressing Geach, and he left his sentence to that worthy gentleman unfinished. Poor Robert Owen might be a ghost, but he could not look like once more than Mrs. Black did. Her face was livid: her disabled hands entwined themselves one within the other in a nervous dread, that Mr. Priar rarely saw equalled. Black, forgetting his own symptoms, told her she was a fool, and drove her from the room.

Well, Randy Black was not the only one to see the ghost that night. And if the reader despises me for repeating these stories of superstition, I can plead but one apology—that I am relating only what absolutely passed, the events of this really true tale. The other one to see it was William Owen.

The flying reports, that Robert Owen's spirit could not rest, had annoyed greatly the inmates of Harebell Farm. As was only natural. Even superstitious Mary Barber, burying her private convictions in regard for the honour of the family, protested far and wide that it could not be true. None of them had seen anything to warrant it, up to this time: not even William, who was often abroad at night on his land. But not on that part of it that lay towards the Trailing Indian. The very fact that the ghost was said to haunt those fields, and especially the two-acre meadow, caused him not to put sheep there. The shepherd absolutely refused to go near the spot at night.

On this evening William Owen had gone on foot to a farmhouse, a mile or two beyond the Trailing Indian. Mary Barber had a nice bit of hot supper ready for him, and when nine o'clock struck she wondered how much longer he meant to be. Soon afterwards she heard his footsteps, and opened the back door to admit him.

Could it be the moonlight that made his face look so white? He took no notice of her, but walked straight into the best kitchen, where his supper was laid.

"What's the matter now?" cried Mary Barber, following him, and gazing in surprise at his strange countenance. "Be you took sick, Mr. William?"

His face was whiter than death: he was wiping the moisture from it with a trembling hand. Mary Barber saw that no light matter was stirring him.

"What is it?" she said, sinking her voice to a whisper, that seemed to partake of his own dread emotion.

"I have seen my father," was his low answer.

"No!" she exclaimed.

"Mary, as true as that you and I are here, living, I saw him. There's no mistake about it. He looked exactly as I've seen him look a hundred times in life: his old cap on, and his white beard flowing."

"Heaven be good to us!" cried Mary. "Where was this?"

"I crossed the stile opposite the Trailing Indian, to come home straight over the fields," said William Owen. "Just past the narrow path between the grove of trees and the fence above the pond, I chanced to look back: and there, standing with his back against the trees, looking after me as it seemed, I saw my father. I stood like one turned to stone, Mary, not knowing, I believe, whether to go for'ard or back'ard, or where to run to; and there *it* stood, the two of us staring at one another. The next moment the thing was gone; vanished into air, as it seemed to me; and I came away, leaping hedges and ditches."

Mary Barber caught up her breath with a gasp; her young master bent his head on the face of the old-fashioned mantelpiece. Presently he spoke again.

"I have been thinking whether there was anything to cause me to look back; any sound, or that. It could hardly have been chance."

"Nay, 'twas no chance, Mr. William, I—wonder—what—it can want?" she slowly added.

William Owen could not say what, any more than she could. All he knew was, that he would give half of his future life not to have been subjected to the terror—to the distress—to the calamity altogether.

"You should have gone up and asked it, Mr. William."

William Owen looked at her, a strange horror in his eyes. "I'd not have done it for that tureen full of sovereigns," he said, pointing to the large soup tureen on the dresser. "Were I ever to see it again, Mary, I could not stay on the Farm."

"It's an awful thing."

"Take care that you keep it from my mother, Mary."

"From all other folks, as well as her," was Mary Barber's answer.

However, the story got wind. At least, a suspicion of it. Added to the more public account of what had befallen Randy Black, it was enough to frighten a timid neighbourhood: and people grew to have a mortal dread of Harebell Lane after the dark had fallen.

CHAPTER XVII.

VERY MUCH OF A WAIF.

"Grandma!"

Mrs. Owen, who had dropped into a doze in her easy chair, did not hear the call. The handle of the door (rather a difficult one to open) was twisted this way and that by little fingers, and the appeal came again.

"Grandma! Won't you let me in, grandma?"

"Is it my dear little Baby Tom?" cried Mrs. Owen, rising to admit the intruder.

Baby Tom it was, poor Geoffry's orphan boy. Mrs. Owen tottered back to her seat, the child in her hand. She was always weak and ill, as her most delicate and gentle face betrayed. Never strong, the calamitous death of her husband, and the subsequent death of her daughter, had been nearly fatal to her. She certainly lived on: but it was as a woman who has nearly done with this world, whose whole thoughts are in the next.

She took off the child's straw hat—a broad-brimmed hat, with a bit of yellow ribbon tied round the crown. Lifting him on her knee, she pushed back the golden hair from his open forehead, and gazed into his earnest, dark blue eyes. He was little for his age; three years old on the previous day—for this was the morning following the events related in the last chapter—he might have been taken for not much more than two; but, as is sometimes the case with these small bodies, the mind was unusally advanced. But for his exceedingly retiring disposition, the shy, modest sensitiveness of his nature, with its invariably accompanying quality, reticence, he might have been that most undesirable thing, a precocious child. His gentle manners saved him from it.

As if divining somewhat of the peace of Mrs. Owen's inward life, the boy when with her was ever more gentle than at other times, strangely thoughtful, quiet, and tractable. It has been said that this story is not one of ideal fiction; and people were wont to remark to one another during this, the latter portion of Mrs. Owen's years, that her life lay in heaven. While she was looking at those wonderful eyes—and the child really had such, they were so beautiful—he began to cry.

"Why, Tom, what is it?"

"Grand-papa rode away without me. Susan wouldn't make haste with my things, and he did not wait. When I cried, she said I wanted a shaking."

"Did Susan bring you here?"

"No. I came."

Mrs. Owen need scarcely have asked the question. The child had come off without superfluous ceremony, in his brown holland pinafore and old straw hat. Susan would have dressed him first.

"Will you read me a Bible story, grandma?"

"Ay," said Mrs. Owen. "Run and fetch the book."

There were Bible stories for children in those days just as there are in these; but they did not get read so much. Mrs. Owen took care that Tom should hear them. He could just reach the little book from the side-table, and brought it to her. He was so fond of hearing one of the stories in particular, that the book opened of itself at the place—Christ forgiving the thief on the Cross. His little tongue, its language imperfect as yet, was never tired of asking questions: sometimes Mrs. Owen's ingenuity was puzzled to answer.

But it was not only that she read to him: that was the least part. The story over, she would close the book, and talk to him, as on this day, in a loving, winning, gentle voice. Talk to him of heaven and the glorious happiness of those who shall attain to it: of what he must do in this world, or rather try to do, if *he* would be one of them: of patience in long suffering; of loving kindness to others; of self-sacrifice for their benefit; of truth and honour, and generosity: all in language suited to his years, but quite clear and forcible. She would impress upon him the great fact that God was ever near him, watching, guiding, hearing, seeing him: and she contrived so to imbue him with the belief in God's loving care, that the child trusted to it beyond any earthly thing. When a stranger, spending the day with Sir Dene, once asked the child what he most wished for (expecting he would say some choice toy—a sword, a wheelbarrow, or a live rabbit), the answer was that he might be good and go to heaven. Sir Dene laughed and kissed him: the stranger thought what an odd little boy. Oh, but these early lessons did him good service in after years; without them he might never have borne the indignities cast on him.

"Grandma, I'll never be naughty. Never."

Mrs. Owen knew too well what the corruptions of the human

heart are, and what the temptations of the world. She only smiled sadly in answer.

"Was mamma ever naughty?"

"Oh yes."

"And papa?"

"Yes."

"But they went to heaven!"

"Ay, dear. They went very near together, too. The thief on the Cross had been very, very naughty; but the moment he asked Jesus to forgive him, Jesus did, you see."

"I'll ask, if ever I am naughty," said the child, after a thoughtful pause. "Grandpa Owen went too. And you'll go, grandma. And I'll go."

"But you must first grow up to be a man and do a great, great deal of work in this world, and a great deal of good," said Mrs. Owen. "God sent us here to work."

"Shall we work in heaven?"

"I don't know. If we do, it will be pleasant work, happy work, angels' work. Yes, we shall."

"Have you had to do a great, great deal of work here, grandma?"

"Yes, a great deal. And I have had to bear a very great deal of sorrow: sorrow and sickness, and heart-break. But for God's loving help, Tom, I don't think I could have got through it."

"Shall I have a great deal of sorrow?"

"You will be sure to have it sooner or later. Don't forget what I have told you, Tom—that God often sends the most to those he loves the best. You must be very brave in all things."

"Yes, I'll be brave," answered unconscious Tom.

The sitting was over. He jumped down, and ran to find Mary Barber. Mary Barber, preserving damsons in the back kitchen, and also sadly disturbed by William Owen's communication of the previous night, was too busy to have much leisure for Tom. Spreading some of the hot jam upon a slice of bread, she told him to run into the garden and eat it.

Tom was making for the garden in all dutiful obedience—never a more implicitly obedient child than he. But William Owen's dog Sharp came barking up to him in play. It would go into a fit of delight at the sight of the child. The dog ran, and Tom after it, neglecting to eat his jam, until they reached the gates at Harebell Lane. Sharp bounded over the small one, and knocked down a little girl in a pink cotton bonnet and tattered frock. Tom, with inherent gallantry, ran to pull her up.

It was that child, mentioned a few chapters ago, who had been born at the Trailing Indian the night of Robert Owen's disappearance. She was called Emma Geach. Before the mother was strong enough to leave the inn, Mrs. Black fell ill with rheumatic fever. The woman undertook to nurse her, and to do the work. The illness was a long one, some months in duration, and Mrs. Geach stayed on. After that, she would go away and come again by fits and starts: but did not take her child. The child had never been away from the inn yet: for all that could be seen to the contrary, it seemed likely to be her permanent home. Mrs. Black liked the child, and would have kept her always. Black did not like her. He was almost savagely angry at her being left there: but gossip said, he did not dare to turn her out or insist too strongly on her removal, lest Mrs. Geach in revenge should betray some of the secret doings of the Trailing Indian.

"Don't cry; don't cry," said Tom. "I'll give you some bread and jam."

The child stood up at the tempting offer, and ceased roaring. Born six months before Tom, she looked at least a twelvemonth older: a tall child, with hair that looked like threads of fine-spun yellow grass, chubby red cheeks, and eyes of so remarkably light a shade that they might have been called white, rather than blue. Tom tore asunder his piece of bread and jam, and gave her the largest half.

Whether Miss Geach was starved at the Trailing Indian, or that damson jam was amidst luxuries unknown to her, certain it was that she gobbled up the piece in a wonderful fashion. It disappeared before Tom had finished his first mouthful.

"I want some more," she said, fixing her greedy little eyes on the rest. So Tom, never hesitating, broke it again, but not so deftly as before: the soft and the jam fell to one part, the dry crust, unjammed, to the other. He handed the best to the child, and nibbled away at the dry crust.

"What's your name?" asked Tom.

"Emma. What's yours?"

"Tom. Where d'you live?"

"Up there," she answered, pointing along the lane. "I've got a whistle at home: 'll you come and see him?"

Whistles are charmingly tempting things, and Tom yielded without question. The two children ran up the lane comparing notes of possessions : Tom's Noah's ark and picture book, and a whip with a green handle; against Miss Geach's whistle. The dog, sharing the crust with Tom, leaped beside them. Randy Black met them close to the inn.

"Holloa!—who have ye got here, you little wretch?" cried he to the girl. And she, who seemed to have plenty of assurance for her years (or, as the inmates of the Trailing Indian were wont to put it, "stock") answered boldly without sign of fear.

"I'm going to show him my whistle."

Black had spoken before he well gave a look to the boy; immediately he knew him for the little grandson of Sir Dene Clanwaring, and of the dead master of Harebell Farm. He had seen him abroad often enough since his babyhood, with Susan Cole or Sir Dene.

"This here baint no place for little gentlefolk, master; you'd best run home again. As to you, you young pig," he added to the girl, "if you bring stray children here, I'll souse your ears in the horse-trough."

"Mayn't I see the whistle?" asked Tom, who had not understood a word in ten.

"Wait, will yer," cried independent Miss Emma to Tom. "I'll bring him out."

Black did not interfere to prevent it. He was gazing down at the boy, and whistling softly.

"You're the very cut o' your father," said he. "Same eyes, same hair, same face. He'd ha' made a second Sir Dene in looks : so'll you. Not bad uns, them eyes of yourn."

All the little boy's answer to this was to look up at the man with these self-same eyes. Even Black, the hardened, could but note, you see, their kindly nature, so full of sweetness.

"What be your name?" he went on, less roughly than he was given to speak.

"Tom."

"Bain't it Dene? Nor Geoffry?"

"It's Tom," repeated the boy.

"Where's your hat?"

"I left it at grandma's."

The ostler appeared in the yard, and called out some question to his master about corn. As Black went away to give the answer, Emma ran out with the whistle, whistling shrilly with all her might. Black bade her "hush her noise," and gave her a box on the ears, which sent her staggering and threw down the whistle. Perhaps she was used to be boxed, for she did not cry or complain: only waited till he was a few paces from her, and then picked up the whistle. A rough wooden toy, with streaks of paint across it, that Mrs. Black had bought of a man at the door for a halfpenny.

Had it been of ivory, mounted in gold, it could not have seemed more precious to little Tom. He whistled, and she whistled, the two taking it by turns, long discordant shrieks enough to frighten the cows, grazing over the way in William Owen's field. Mrs. Black came to the door to see what the cause of the noise might be. A poor, pale woman, more shrunken and meek than ever, since her long bout of rheumatic fever—which had left her fingers contracted. Young though the girl was, she was already of use in the house: and perhaps that was one of the reasons why Black did not insist upon her removal. Mrs. Black could not have done the entire work now, and a child was a safer inmate than an older person might be.

"Emma, what boy's that?" demanded Mrs. Black—just as Black had done.

The whistle was too absorbing for Emma to answer immediately. At about the fifth repetition of the question she turned round.

"His name's Tom."

Mrs. Black came slowly out. Her feet were affected as well as her fingers: in short, she was not now much better than a cripple. She had begun to talk to the children pleasantly enough when Black came back and sent the group flying: Mrs. Black and the girl indoors; Tom off, down the lane.

"And don't you get fond o' prowling up this way, youngster; or maybe the kidnappers 'll lay hold on ye," was his parting injunction to Tom. "There's lots on 'em at this here house sometimes."

Tom ran along the lane with all the speed of his little legs. He was constitutionally brave; and by the time he turned the corner, the kidnappers were forgotten. On either side the lane blackberries grew in abundance, and Tom helped himself at will: scratching his hands, and staining his face and pinafore crimson. What with the marks left by the jam and the running juice of the blackberries, Tom might have had his portrait taken as something to be stared at. In this condition he was pounced upon by Susan Cole.

Susan at once administered a couple of shakings. The one for going off on the loose; it was her own expression; the other for the crimson state he had put himself into. Tom, full of contrition, looked down at his hands and pinafore: and then offered Susan some choice berries squeezed up in his fingers. Susan, instead of accepting the treat with gratitude, flung up his hand and sent the blackberries flying.

"You oudacious, naughty child! Where's your hat?"

"It's on the table at grandma's."

Pulling him along by the hand to the Farm, Susan Cole dashed into the back kitchen, where Joan happened to be washing, and lathered his face and hands well with soap-suds. Then she got his hat and took him off again.

"Now look you here, Master Tom," she said, as they crossed the lane and entered the back gates—"if you take to go off by yourself, nobody knows where, a frightening me into fiddlestrings and getting yourself into this shocking pickle, I'll run away and leave you. I won't stay at the Dene no longer to serve an ongrateful little boy."

Tom was very quiet during the afternoon, playing with Noah's ark and the animals, and giving no trouble to anybody. The servants were busy that day, for company was coming to the Dene. Lady Lydia Clanwaring, the wife of Captain Clanwaring, Sir Dene's youngest son, had just landed from India, with her three children, and her arrival at the Dene might happen at any hour: to-day, to-morrow, the next day. Sir Dene expected her to make a long visit, and looked forward with pleasure to an event that would break the monotony of his home.

Sir Dene reached home for dinner: kept it waiting in fact. Tom's quick ears, on the alert for the sound, heard the horses' hoofs; he ran out, and met them halfway down the avenue. The groom behind dismounted; lifted the child up in front of his master; and Tom was conveyed back in triumph.

"Master Tom will dine with me," said Sir Dene to Gander, as he led him indoors.

So the child sat beside the baronet; chattering, however, more than eating, for he had just had tea. No longer the young vagabond all blackberry stains, scouring the lanes at will, bare-headed and bare-armed: but a beautiful little prince in crimson velvet, with a falling plaited frill of snow-white cambric on his neck, and his bright curls hanging down in a shower of gold. Susan Cole took care to dress him always towards evening, in case Sir Dene should ask for him.

"Emma's got a whistle, grandpa," said Tom, when they were left alone at dessert.

"A whistle, has she?" replied the baronet, not in the least knowing, or caring, whom "Emma" might be.

"A nice big whistle all green and blue, grandpa. I wish I had one."

"Tell Susan to go to Hurst Leet to-morrow and buy you one," was the answer of Sir Dene.

"I'm afraid she won't. She's angry with me."

"Oh, indeed! Have you been a naughty boy?"

"Yes. I made my hands and face dirty with the blackberries, and spoilt my pinafore."

Sir Dene laughed: a very venial offence, this. "There's another walnut for you, Tom. Peel it well, you rascal."

Tom eat away at his walnut, peeling it first. "Some more water, please grandpa."

Sir Dene poured out some water. He was sensible enough to know that wine and children were best apart.

"Mary Barber gave me some bread and jam, grandpa. Sharp knocked Emma down, and I——"

A commotion outside stopped the history. A chaise-and-four (the sound was easily distinguished from that of a chaise-and-pair) had clattered up to the front entrance. Dogs barked; servants ran; Gander rushed into the dining-room.

"Sir Dene," said he, "I'll lay anything as it's my Lady Lydia come." And Sir Dene went into the hall.

It was Lady Lydia Clanwaring. A tall, meagre woman, two or three years past thirty, with a pale, discontented face, sharp features, keen, restless black eyes, and thin compressed lips. Her children followed her, black-eyed and black-haired; the oldest, a girl, seven years old, two boys, six and five. As if fatigued with the journey—they had posted up from Portsmouth—Lady Lydia sunk on a chair as soon as she entered the dining-room. The children ran to the table, and stood eyeing eagerly the good things on it.

"They'd like some dessert, Gander," spoke Sir Dene. "Bring plates."

Hats and bonnets were thrown on the floor. The children dragged chairs to the table, and seated themselves without further ceremony. Tom, who had shyly retreated to the background at the large influx, remained unseen.

"Take care that everything is brought in, Dovet," screamed out Lady Lydia to her maid, in the same hard, shrill voice that had used rather to grate on Sir Dene's ears in India—for he liked that most excellent thing, a sweet voice in a woman. "We must have had twenty small packages at least inside, of one sort or another."

When the bustle had somewhat subsided Sir Dene inquired after his son Reginald, who remained in India.

"Captain Clanwaring was very well when we left him, but as cross as a bear," replied Lady Lydia. It was a peculiarity of hers that she always called her husband "Captain Clanwaring." "It is a wearing life out there: and last season was a frightfully hot one. No, Jarvis, you *can't* have more wine; you are going to have supper. Good gracious, Louisa, don't crack that walnut with your teeth! Jarvis, crack it for your sister."

"Crack it for her, Otto," said Master Jarvis imperiously, to his brother. And the younger one cracked the walnut.

"Captain Clanwaring says there's no chance of his getting leave. None. Just now——"

The words died away on Lady Lydia's tongue. She had turned from her children to face Sir Dene again; and stopped in utter astonishment. A beautiful child, habited in crimson velvet, with blue eyes and golden hair, was leaning familiarly against Sir Dene; had stolen his little hand within his. What child could it be?

"Who is that?" demanded Lady Lydia.

"It is my little grandson," said Sir Dene.

Little grandson! That John Clanwaring the heir had now an infant son in long clothes, Lady Lydia knew. There could be no other grandson. She thought she had heard, as the French express it, à tort et à travers.

"*What* grandson? Who is he, Sir Dene?"

Sir Dene answered by taking the child on his knee. "Tell the lady what your name is, and who you are."

"It's Tom," said the child.

"What else?" continued Sir Dene.

"Tom Clanwaring."

"Well—now tell who you are."

"I'm grandpapa's little boy."

Sir Dene, pleased with the words, kissed him fondly. Lady Lydia knitted her brows and sent forth some keen glances from her black and restless eyes.

"He is the son of my dear boy, Geoffry, who's dead and gone, Lady Lydia. Poor Geoff left him to me as a legacy."

It took Lady Lydia a minute or two to digest the words—and she did not fully comprehend, even then. That Geoffry Clanwaring had made some low marriage before his death, and so brought disgrace on himself and the Clanwaring family, she knew. John the heir had sent out a version of the calamity to India: Captain Clanwaring had been quite as indignant as John, and at once wrote back his opinion of matters to Sir Dene. But to see this fair, aristocratic child, aristocratic in dress as in looks, sitting on Sir Dene's knee, fondled by him, and evidently at home at Beechhurst Dene, was something so entirely opposite to the ideas Lady Lydia had formed upon the affair, that she did not quite at once recover her equanimity.

"Does he—live here?" she asked in condemning amazement.

"Oh dear, yes. He has no other home."

"Where's his mother, pray?"

"Tell where," said Sir Dene, to the intelligent listening boy.

"Mamma's dead," said Tom. "She and papa went to heaven."

"Ay. They went within three months of each other; the same grave, hardly closed, received them both, Lady Lydia."

And to her ladyship's infinite astonishment, she saw that Sir Dene's eyes, bent on the little boy's head as he spoke, had filled with tears.

CHAPTER XVIII.

GUESTS AT BEECHHURST DENE.

THE handsomest guest-chamber that Beechhurst Dene afforded, with a small cheerful sitting-room opening from it, had been assigned by the servants to Lady Lydia Clanwaring. The title sounded imposing in their ears. The heir's wife was really of better family, and an heiress to boot; but she was only plain Mrs. Clanwaring: Lady Lydia was Lady Lydia, and received homage accordingly.

The Lady Lydia Clanwaring was the daughter of a poor and obscure Irish peer; she had absolutely not a shilling of her own in the world. Her father, Mr. Riley, had succeeded to the title suddenly. Perhaps it was the long fight with poverty previously to that that had rendered her so sharp in worldly interests, so mean in petty details, so grasping in everything where money was concerned. Mr. Riley had never expected to come in to the title: when he did so his daughters were grown up: until then, they had all led a scrambling sort of life, their time passed in one long scuffle, trying to make both ends meet; sometimes in a remote corner of Ireland, sometimes in a cheap Continental town. After his succession, the Earl was not much better off, for the estate, never worth much, had been impoverished until the income derived from it was of almost nominal value. One of Lydia Riley's sisters had married an officer in an Indian regiment. Lady Lydia went out to stay with them, and there met Sir Dene's son, Lieutenant Clanwaring. Stationed in a quiet place where there was but little society, they were thrown much together, and one day Lieutenant Clanwaring made her an offer: or at least, what she chose to consider one; and in point of fact, he said more than he could in honour retract from. Be you very sure she did not let him retract. He would have laughed it off, but found he could not. He had never meant it, he said to himself: it had been said in thoughtlessness, in the incaution of the moment: but he had to abide by it. How very many more men are there, who have been caught in a like manner! Mr. Clanwaring submitted to his fate with a good grace, and made no sign. Save for a word he let drop in Gander's hearing one night that he came to his father's rather shaky from the mess dinner, he never let it be known that the Lady Lydia was not his best choice. He was but a boy, barely of age: she was three or four years older in years, and half a century in depth. So they were married; and until now had lived together in India. Lady Lydia had had time to get heartily sick and tired of an Indian life, and of making the best of a narrow income. Sir Dene did not allow much to his youngest son: at the same age he, himself, had been obliged to make his pay suffice; and he thought it no hardship for his son to do it. Weary of it altogether, Lady Lydia determined to have a change. She told her husband that the time had come when it was necessary the children should go home, both for their health's sake and that their education should be entered upon. Captain Clanwaring agreed. He was tired of it, too: tired of his wife's fractiousness, and of the troublesome and noisy children. He wrote to his father, asking him to receive them for a time, until suitable schools should be fixed on: and Sir Dene acquiesced with pleasure. On this, the first night of their arrival, Lady Lydia told Sir Dene she should remain about a year in Europe visiting different friends in England and Ireland; and then return to her husband. In her private heart she cherished a very different plan—never to go back at all, but to establish her footing and her home at Beechhurst Dene. And if there was one woman more capable than most other women of carrying out her scheme persistently and bringing it to bear, that woman was the Lady Lydia Clanwaring.

All the way home, amidst the many months' discomfort of the sailing ship—there were no fleet steamers in those days—had she been nursing her eggs and reckoning her chickens. "Sir Dene has neither kith nor kin; he has no grandchild to make much of," she would repeat to herself, "for John Clanwaring and his wife do not go near Beechhurst Dene. The field lies open and clear for me. I will be the place's mistress: my children will be their grandfather's indulged pets and playthings."

But Lady Lydia, to her intense astonishment, found that Sir Dene *had* a grandchild near him, located in his home, allowed to climb his knee at will, altogether made as much of as she had intended her own children should be. More especially had she cherished this intention for her elder son. He was beloved by her in that inordinate degree that mothers do sometimes love their children. It is said that like clings to like. Certain it was, this young Jarvis Clanwaring was remarkably like his mother, in person as in temper. He had the same pale, sharp face, the keen, restless black eyes, with the sly look in them; in disposition he had the same crafty depth, and the secretive, unpleasant temper. The younger one, Otto, was a dull plodding boy, worth ten of his brother—who put upon him always. From the moment Lady Lydia Clanwaring saw the child, Tom, on Sir Dene's knee, she resolved that he should lose his footing in the house if clever manœuvring could accomplish it.

She stood at the window of her bedroom the following morning, looking out on the early sun. Lady Lydia was by far too restless natured a woman to lie in bed late, even on the day following a tiring journey; she liked to be up and doing. She had just wound her coal-black hair in coils round her head, and was dressed all but her gown. The fine panorama of scenery lay beyond, with its green fields, its woods, its gleams of water, and its sprinkling of dwellings; Hurst Leet, the little village, was near, the fair city of Worcester more distant: all pleasant things to look upon under the blue sky of the autumn morning. But to Lady Lydia they were as nothing. *She* looked with covetous eyes at the park beneath; at the lodge at the end of the avenue; at whatsoever pertained to Beechhurst Dene. "A grand old place," she repeated to herself, "and I'll reign here, its mistress."

The door opened, and she turned sharply round. It was Dovet, the maid: she had reddish hair, and eyes of a fine green, and wore a buff gingham gown with white frills, and was just as crafty as her mistress. Lady Lydia had lost no time. On the previous evening when she went upstairs to take off her things before supper, the vision of the fair child in his crimson velvet dress clouding her mind, she called Dovet, and charged her to find out all particulars concerning the boy—how he came to be there at all, and why. Dovet liked nothing better than to ferret out secrets for herself or her mistress: to do her justice, she was in that respect a faithful servant.

"Well, Dovet," began Lady Lydia, "have you got at any of the circumstances?"

"I flatter myself that I have obtained a few, my lady," minced Dovet, who was as full of conceit and affectation as any fine dame of the day could be. "It was quite a error of judgment to have allowed the child to have come here at all."

"The mother was a frightfully low person, I know."

"Oh, frightful low, my lady. They live at a farm near; quite working people; an inferior set altogether. The girl was pretty, and Mr. Geoffry was drawn in to marry her one day when Sir Dene was safe away in London. A fine uproar there was over it. Sir Dene posted down from London with Mr. Clanwaring, and a aunt posted over in her carriage from somewhere nearer. They turned Mr. Geoffry out of the house; kicked him out, I believe, my lady; and he went off to lodgings with the girl. Sir Dene relented a little later, and let him live in a cottage on the estate and made him his servant as bailiff. The girl died when the child was born, and the day after she was interred, Mr. Geoffry came home here again (like his impudence, it seems to me, my lady) and brought the infant with him wrapped up in an old shawl. And here the infant have been ever since."

Dovet had got her tale tolerably correct, you see. Fortune favoured her. An under-housemaid, Patty, who was under orders to leave—through a quarrel with Susan Cole, in which Susan's part had been taken, and hers not, and in consequence of which Susan was just now worse to her than poison—had fallen in Dovet's way. In the woman's sore feeling she had put the worst colouring on the past, as connected with Geoffry Clanwaring and his wife, simply because Susan had been their servant. Revenge makes the best of us unjust.

"The girl's people live near, do they?" remarked Lady Lydia, when she had listened to what Dovet had to say.

"Quite close, my lady. It's a old farmhouse, right opposite the back gates here, just across the lane. The little child is running there continual."

"Then why is it that the child cannot be with them altogether?" was Lady Lydia's indignant rejoinder.

"Why indeed, my lady!"

Lady Lydia said nothing further. Perhaps she thought all the more. That this low-born child, this interloper, should certainly lose its footing at Beechhurst Dene and be got out of it, she fully resolved. But she knew that she must proceed to work cautiously: feel her way, as it were. Very smooth and smiling was her face as she went down to breakfast.

"Will you allow me to preside, Sir Dene?" she asked, when her children were seated.

"I'm sure I wish you would—if you don't mind taking the trouble," heartily replied Sir Dene—who, averse to exertion himself, as many who have lived long in India are, had been about to tell Gander to stop and pour out the coffee. So Lady Lydia took her place at the table's head—and kept it for the future.

In came Susan Cole. "Is Master Tom to take his breakfast here this morning, Sir Dene?"

"What d'ye say?" cried Sir Dene, who had not caught the words, as he turned his head to the speaker.

"Master Tom is wanting to have his breakfast with you, Sir Dene. He knows, you see, sir, that the other children are here."

"To be sure: let him come by all means," was Sir Dene's answer. And the lady, busy with the coffee cups, did not like the glad and ready voice it was spoken in.

So Tom came. In a cotton frock this morning, with his clean round brown holland blouse over it. Susan placed his chair at Sir Dene's elbow, and put down his basin of bread-and-milk.

"Go and say good morning to your cousins, my pretty one," said Sir Dene; and my lady coughed a harsh and resentful cough at the word "cousins." Tom held out his little hand to them in succession: and each shook it in silence, staring at the boy as if he were a wild Indian. The children had not brought much manners with them. Then Susan lifted him into his seat; and Sir Dene kissed him, and stroked his pretty hair.

It happened that Sir Dene had to go to Worcester that morning, to attend a public meeting. His phaeton came to the door at eleven o'clock. Lady Lydia stepped out to admire the fine horses.

"I want to go, ma," said Jarvis. "I *shall* go."

Lady Lydia appealed to Sir Dene with a sweet smile. "You will take him, will you not, Sir Dene?"

"Can't to-day," replied Sir Dene. "Should not know what to do with him in Worcester."

The lady's face clouded—threatening signs of one of her ugly passions. "Oh, do indulge him this once, Sir Dene," pleaded the mother. "All is strange to him here as yet, poor dear little fellow."

But Sir Dene was not one to do a thing against his will. On the whole he was not fond of children—Tom excepted—and very much disliked to be put to any personal trouble with them.

"Very sorry, Lady Lydia, but I am going in on business. The meeting may last for hours: it would hardly do for—what's the lad's name—Jarvey—to be left in the streets. The coachman can drive them all out to-morrow."

Sir Dene got in, taking the reins, the groom stepped up beside him, and away they went. Master Jarvey's first move was to fling himself on his back on the gravel and kick and howl as if the deuce had got inside him. The words, please, are Gander's, who was looking on. His next move was to spring on his feet, furiously tear up a handful of gravel and fling it after the carriage.

"*That's* nice bringings up," cried Susan Cole critically in Gander's ear.

"*Her* bringings up!" retorted Gander, with a side nod in

the direction of Lady Lydia. "Don't think she knows much about that. One can't expect nothing from a pig but to grunt."

"You don't like her," remarked Susan. "No more don't I." "I didn't like her in India, nor nobody else did: young Mr. Clanwaring in course excepted," added Gander, with a curious twist of the mouth. "And I don't like Dovet neither—birds of a feather, they be. Dovet had got her fox's nose inside my pantry this morning, whispering with Patty: I'd like to know the reason why."

Lady Lydia, smarting under the rebuff Sir Dene had given her boy, who was idolized by her as no other human being ever could or would be in this world, retired to her rooms in dudgeon, where Dovet proceeded to unpack, with Susan Cole to help. By-and-by Lady Lydia put on her bonnet and shawl, and strolled out to the back entrance to look about her. Not a corner of the passages but she took it in with her observant eye; not a bush of shrubs outside, but she noted. Gander, coming to the door to shake a table-cloth, saw her with her nose flattened against the glass doors of Sir Dene's parlour, peering in. With independent ease, Gander did not seem in a hurry to retreat again; he leisurely stood and shook, and shook and stood.

"This seems to be quite a business room, Gander," she remarked, stepping back. "What a quantity of papers lie about!"

"It is Sir Dene's business parlour, my lady."

"His business parlour! What has Sir Dene Clanwaring to do with business?"

"With a big estate like this, there's a host of business to be transacted; a sight o' matters to be done. I know this much, my lady: it pretty nigh drives the master at times off his head. Dell, the bailiff—it's one he took on after poor Mr. Geoffry died—ain't o' much good as it seems to me, for folks come up here all the same a-pestering Sir Dene.—Where do them two paths lead to, you ask, my lady: why the one straight afore us goes direct to Harebell Lane: t'other on our right, the privet walk, 'll take you round to the front o' the house."

Lady Lydia, avoiding the privet walk, chose the straight one before her, and arrived at the gates opening to Harebell Lane. Remembering Dovet's words, she looked out for the Farm: but the opposite hedge was high, and hid it. She took her way up the lane on an exploring tour, and reached in time the Trailing Indian.

Two children—dirty little ragamuffins upon whom the Lady Lydia did not vouchsafe to cast a second glance—stood near, blowing alternately at a whistle. The one ran up to show it to her in his sociable nature.

"Isn't it nice? It's Emma's."

To Lady Lydia's unbounded astonishment, she recognised Tom. But Tom in unmitigated grief, so far as his clothes were concerned. In the busy state of the Dene that morning, and of Susan Cole, Tom neglected and looked askance at by the Indian children, took the opportunity to run off, as usual, to Mrs. Owen's. In the lane, he was waylaid by Emma Geach, and that young lady seduced him to stay and play with her. Companionship is sweet. Having tasted of it once, she was no doubt longing for it again, and had come off surreptitiously to find Tom. It is always the women, we are assured, who seduce the men. Running up to the Trailing Indian in search of the whistle, which she had not brought out, Tom fell down by the pond, and plastered himself with green mud. Emma, by way of consoling him, fed him with blackberries, and—there he was, face, hands, hair, and pinafore, a picturesque compound of red, and green, and muddy disreputability. Lady Lydia turned her outraged eyes on the other child. An unmistakable ragamuffin, she, of the lowest type: clothes coarse, shabby, torn; toes out of shoes, socks down at heel.

"Is that your sister?" demanded Lady Lydia, her ideas somewhat confused.

"It's Emma," repeated Tom. "Grandpapa said Susan was to buy me a whistle like this, but Susan has not got time to-day."

Every nerve within her revolted at the word "grandpapa," as used by this child, of Sir Dene. "Where does 'Emma' live?" she asked.

"I lives there," burst forth the girl, with all her native "stock," as she pointed to the Trailing Indian.

Lady Lydia cast her eyes on the inn, picked up her skirts, and walked on. "Low-lived little beast!" she exclaimed of Tom, not caring whether the roadside inn bore much relationship to him, or none. "And it is *this* child of disgraceful connections who has been allowed to get a footing at Beechhurst Dene!"

The high road, running crossways just beyond the Trailing Indian, did not seem to promise much of interest for Lady Lydia, and she turned back. The girl, Emma, had been called into the inn then, whistle and all, and the door shut. Tom, left alone, ran along by the side of Lady Lydia, unconscious that he was doing wrong: did she not belong to the Dene?

"What do you mean by following me?" she stopped to ask. "Why don't you go home?"

"I'm going to grandma's," said Tom. "It's down here. Mary Barber will wash me."

He spoke timidly. The angry face had a look in it that frightened him. Children have keen instincts, and Tom drew behind. At the turning of the lane he suddenly darted before her, and into the arms of a young man who was advancing. A gentle-faced, pleasant young man, who wore working clothes. It was William Owen.

"Oh, Tom! what a mess you are in!" he cried—and then took off his hat to Lady Lydia as she passed.

Tom repeated that he was going to ask Mary Barber to "wash" him. Mr. Owen put him down, and told him to make haste about it.

"Who was that?" Lady Lydia condescended to question of Tom, when he came on.

"It was Uncle William," said the child. "He gave me a little boat one day."

Lady Lydia tossed her disdainful head. Uncle William! —a common working clodhopper! and this objectionable child, with the low connections and the low tastes and companionships, was allowed to call Sir Dene Clanwaring his grandfather, and to have his home at Beechhurst Dene!

The child—the offences of the morning condoned by Susan—appeared at dessert again in his costly velvet dress—only this time it was blue velvet instead of crimson. Susan Cole, in conjunction with Miss Reynolds, the noted mantua-maker on the parade at Worcester, had been allowed to order attire for him after the pride of her own heart, unchecked by her master. It was with difficulty Lady Lydia kept her temper down to a decent show of tranquillity. She had assumed the head of the table, as she had at breakfast, sitting at the opposite end to Sir Dene; or, rather the foot, for Sir Dene always took the head. But the temper, bubbling up within her with strange fierceness, betrayed her into an incaution she was not often guilty of—that of speaking at the wrong time.

After the children were gone to bed, and she had been in the great drawing-room a long while alone, Sir Dene came in from the dinner-table. It was the custom in those days for gentlemen to drink a great deal of wine: Sir Dene did not exceed as some did; but he liked a generous glass. To-day, however, the reason of his tardy sitting was, that, fatigued with his tiresome meeting in the city, he had dropped asleep at the table. Lady Lydia, nursing her rage all that while at the prospect of what she was pleased to term her children's wrongs in having found a supplanter in Sir Dene's affections, was just in prime order, and entered at once upon the battle. Very quietly, softly, craftily, and tenderly—just as though she were a sweet angel of consideration, and had no interests in the world at heart, save Sir Dene's and Tom's.

Tom's sad connections were hinted at; Tom's over-low predilections; Tom's vagabond state out of doors—as witness how and with whom she had found him that day. For such a child Beechhurst Dene was not a suitable home, she gently pointed out: and —would it not be better to send him to his grandmother Owen's?

"Send him to his grandmother Owen's?" repeated Sir Dene, when he had gathered what all this was driving at— and he spoke a little explosively, as it seemed to his wary listener. "Why what do you mean, my lady?"

"Even at the cost of having to pay a slight yearly sum for his maintenance. Dear Sir Dene, I only suggest it in the child's best interests."

"His interests can be taken better care of at Beechhurst Dene than they would be with his mother's family," returned the baronet. "You must be dreaming, Lady Lydia."

"I fear, unfortunately, that I am rather wider awake in regard to this matter than you can be, Sir Dene," she said, with the sweetest smile her face could put on. "Were the child to remain here, he would grow up with notions ridiculously unsuited to his future position."

"And what do you fancy his future position will be?" retorted Sir Dene, his temper getting up. "The child is my grandson, Lady Lydia: you don't suppose I shall turn him out into the world to follow the plough's tail, do you?"

"Oh, Sir Dene! the plough's tail!" she simpered.

"Well, Lady Lydia, what is it that you mean?" he asked.

And then, vexed in her turn, she said openly that the child ought never to have been at the Dene—ought to be sent from it without loss of time.

"Never, while I live and am master here, Lady Lydia," was the firm answer. "I gave my hand on it to my dear son, Geoffry."

"It is scarcely behaving fairly to your other sons, Sir Dene. To Mr. Clanwaring's well-born wife; to me. The young woman was so very obscure and low a person."

"She was one of the best and loveliest ladies the world ever saw—I can tell you that, my lady," returned Sir Dene, in choler.

"But so very low, I say. Were her friends not able or willing to receive the child, he should have been sent to the parish. It is really not *becoming* to have him here—and to make much of him, as though he were a son of the house. Pardon me, dear Sir Dene, I am only speaking in all our interests, his included."

"Very likely you are, my lady: but as your notions and mine don't agree in this, the subject may be dropped. Geoffry was my favourite son: and this little son of his has taken his place in my home."

Sir Dene rang the bell as he spoke—a loud peal that startled Gander. Susan Cole was wanted.

"What is this I hear?" thundered Sir Dene, when she appeared. "That you suffer Master Clanwaring to run wild in the lanes and play with any vagabond child he may pick up! Take you better care of him in future, Susan Cole: or else you may cut your service short at the Dene."

And the Lady Lydia, smoothing her fingers over her cambric handkerchief at the fire, found she had spoken somewhat too soon. Her rebellious heart rose up within her, and had to be forcibly controlled to silence. "Master Clanwaring!"

CHAPTER XIX.

FRIGHTENING THE PONY.

The June roses were in bloom, shedding their perfume on the air, and the hot midsummer sun lay on the smooth highways, on the plains sweet with the drying hay, on the ripening corn.

On never a smoother and fairer road to look at than the

one you have so often heard of, Dene Hollow. The lad on his pony going down it, Otto Clanwaring, must have expected a pleasant ride on its white and level surface. Running after the pony, as it turned out of the gates of Beechhurst Dene, came Jarvis Clanwaring. And, standing with his back against the fence, was Tom. Time has grown older, and the boys have grown with it. Tom is nearly seven now, Otty nine, Jarvis ten.

There is not, except for this, much change in them. Jarvis is thin and wiry as ever, with the same dark, sly eyes; Otto is rather fat, dark, and stolid; Tom has the same golden hair, the frank face, the kindly, thoughtful, rich blue eyes. The three boys are at school, but not at the same one; for Lady Lydia Clanwaring (putting it upon the score of difference in years) had successfully contrived that Tom should not contaminate the same establishment that her boys honoured. They have come home for the midsummer holidays; and are tired with the long morning spent in the hay-field. But that Jarvis is excessively tired, and has besides some appointment connected with ferrets, he would have taken the pony for himself. It is one Sir Dene keeps for the boys' use when they are at home, and is called Whitestar, from a white star on its forehead.

Tom is standing perfectly still against the fence, somewhere about the exact spot on which had once stood the dwelling of the Widow Barber. His elbows are pushed back on the lower rail, and he is in a brown study, watching the approach of the pony and its rider. Gander had told him he might go out on the pony that afternoon: but, just as he was about to mount, the two elder ones ordered him away, and took it themselves. Tom feels no resentment; only a little disappointment: it does not occur to him that he is ill-used, for he has become accustomed to give up to his cousins in all things, just as a servant yields to his masters.

Otto put the pony into a gentle canter, and came on; Jarvis was following slowly on the pathway. As the pony passed Tom, it swerved violently, as if startled, dashed off at a gallop and threw its rider. Jarvis rushed up in a fury.

"You young hound!" he cried, seizing on Tom's head and beginning to pummel it, "what did you frighten him for?"

"I didn't frighten him," said Tom.

"You did, you varmint! I saw you."

"I didn't, Jarvis; indeed I didn't," cried Tom.

Otto came back, rubbing his head and looking ruefully. His clothes and face and hair were all dust; his temple was grazed.

"Was it him did it, Jarvis?"

"Of course it was him, nasty little devil! He's always up to some mean trick."

"Otto, I didn't," persisted Tom. "I didn't do anything."

"I heard him give a hiss, and I saw him kick his leg out and pitch a stone; and it frightened Whitestar."

Now this barefaced assertion of Master Jarvis's was neither more nor less than a deliberate lie. He had all his mother's ingenuity of invention, and was never happier than when exercising it to the detriment of the scapegoat Tom. A scapegoat in every sense of the term; and destined to be one, poor fellow! As you will find when you read on.

Otto looked from one to the other—on his brother's thrust-out face with its evil black eyes; on Tom's piteous one, with its running tears. Otto had this good quality—that if he knew a lie to be a lie he would never uphold it; no, not even for Jarvey. But Otto was by no means goodnatured, he was too selfish to trouble himself to be so; and moreover, he was being reared to despise Tom and put upon him.

"I never stirred my leg or hissed, and I didn't heave a stone," pleaded the lad earnestly. "It wasn't me, Otto."

Jarvis kicked, and pummelled, and pushed, and so drowned the words in pain. A man who had caught Whitestar, was leading him up. Thus the damaged party entered the Dene gates. Lady Lydia, seeing it from her window, came flying out to learn what the matter might be, and heard of Tom's iniquities. Poor Tom's voice was like a little piping reed amidst the fierce ones of his accusers: even in self-defence he scarcely dared to lift it in the presence of Lady Lydia. She had long ago inspired him with an awe that he trembled at, but did not attempt to subdue or resist.

They had it out in the hall: Dovet and some of the inferior servants looking on. Gander was not in the way, neither was Sir Dene. Lady Lydia was in a silent passion of rage: she, to do her justice, believed, in this instance, that Tom was guilty. When did she *not* believe him guilty of anything he might be accused of? Had Jarvis brought to her a story that Tom had drunk the Severn dry she would have given ear to it.

Baby though he was, or but little removed from one, she hated him with a bitter hatred. The fear of Sir Dene had not let her entirely crush him; but she was doing her best towards it in a quiet way, always working on for it safely and silently.

"Wicked, crafty reptile!" cried Lady Lydia, her eyes ablaze with a flashing light. "Poor dear Otto, poor inoffensive boy, riding by without thought of treachery, must have his pony startled and his life put in danger by *you!* Take him, Dovet, and whip him. Whip him well."

Dovet seized on Tom by the hand to bear him off to punishment. It came pretty often, this chastisement, and Tom neither might nor dared resist. On trying to resist once, the whipping had been redoubled: in Dovet's hands, a strong woman, Tom was not only powerless, but conscious that he was. He submitted so quietly in a general way, that Dovet was quite astounded at his breaking from her now.

It was only to run back to Otto. A sweeter disposition than heaven had implanted in this little orphan of Geoffry Clanwaring's never was possessed by son of man. He could not bear, literally could not *bear*, that another should suffer through him. Lady Lydia had reiterated to him that he might have killed Otto: and the words struck sorely on the child.

"Otto, I'm going to Dovet to be whipped," he said, the tears streaming down his face, "but I didn't do it. Please don't think it was me, Otto."

There had been no latent thought in his mind that this further denial would prevent his punishment. Without a moment's hesitation he turned to Dovet's capturing hand and was caught by it, his little legs running to keep up with her strides, his tears flowing.

"Mamma," said deliberate Otto, after giving a minute or two to ponder matters in his mind, "I'm not sure that it was him. He doesn't tell stories often."

Tom never told them. One of the chief characteristics of the boy was simple, innate truthfulness. He had learnt to be silent and take as his due unmerited correction, but an untruth he had never told in his life. No one at the Dene believed this: even its master almost doubted. The fact was, Jarvis and Tom were so very often in opposite tales, the one's word against the other's—and Jarvis was both keen and crafty, with his mother to back him, and moreover had the advantage over Tom by three years, and generally contrived to make his own assertion appear good—that Tom was beginning to be looked upon by some of them as an audacious little story-teller.

"I say it mightn't have been him, mamma," repeated Otto, a second time, finding that he received no notice. "Shall I go and tell Dovet not to whip him."

"No," sharply returned Lady Lydia. "He does not get whipped often enough, low-born brat!"

"But if he *didn't* frighten Whitestar?" persisted Otto: who was not without a sense of justice.

"Not frighten Whitestar? Did you not hear Master Clanwaring say he saw him! Hold your tongue, Otto."

Just as she had called her husband Captain Clanwaring,—and Major Clanwaring now, for he had got his promotion—so did she generally speak of her oldest son as "Master Clanwaring," even to his brother and sister. Otto to the servants was "Master Otto;" Tom simply "Tom" when she condescended to name him at all; she generally spoke of him as "that boy."

Tom took his punishment with tears and sobs; not loud but deep: if he had made much noise Dovet would have treated him to a double portion. She kept an old thin leather slipper for the purpose, and whipped him soundly with that: Dovet's expression was, "warmed him," and she did it kindly.

Lady Lydia Clanwaring's resolve to remain and rule at Beechhurst Dene had been admirably carried out. Very soon after her arrival, trouble sprang up with the servants. She, assuming full control and management of the household affairs by Sir Dene's will, introduced certain new rules and regulations, which the old servants rebelled against. Warfare waged hotly. Blame lay on both sides. Lady Lydia was arbitrary and haughty; they, long accustomed to their own will, were disobedient and insolent. The result was, they left in a body; Lady Lydia dismissed them. All went, including the housekeeper and Susan Cole. My lady had tried in a cautious manner to get Gander out also, and failed: Gander was perhaps a firmer fixture at Beechhurst Dene than she was. A new set of servants came in, engaged by my lady, and things went on peaceably. She made Dovet housekeeper under herself; but Lady Lydia was the real manager. That she was a very good one could not be denied: with fewer servants there was a vast deal more of quiet order and less of outlay. Sir Dene felt the benefit of her rule: his pockets

Frightening the Pony.

were saved, he had greater comfort; he was grateful accordingly, and learned to put trust in the Lady Lydia. As to her quitting the Dene, such a thing was never named. Sir Dene was glad to have her there, the house had wanted the controlling law of a mistress, and it left him at liberty to be absent as much as he chose, knowing that all was going on in due order at home. He was away more than ever, for he had grown to like a London life.

Of course, these frequent absences of Sir Dene put absolute power into the hands of Lady Lydia. She ruled with despotic will. She was rather nearer in housekeeping matters at these times than the servants liked: they whispered, one to another, that of the liberal sum allowed by Sir Dene, a good portion went into her own pocket. Which was true. Little Tom had hard times of it at these intervals. If it happened that Sir Dene was away during the Christmas or Midsummer holidays, Tom felt the loss severely. Scarcely ever was he allowed to dine at the same table as his cousins, but was banished to Dovet's room, and took his meals there. The children, taking their cue naturally from their mother, had wholly despised him from the very day of their arrival, they did not look upon him as one of the same order as themselves, but as an inferior and dependent; and the feeling grew and grew. Even in the matter of dress he was not as they were: the old clothes of Jarvis and Otto were mended up for him: what few new things had to be bought were of a coarse and poor description. Sir Dene failed to see it, or to detect the miserable influence at work. If he noticed that Tom looked less well-dressed than the others, Lady Lydia would say, Yes, because he spoils his things so. In truth, Tom's clothes often came to grief; but it was chiefly through Jarvis. Jarvis did not spare him: he boxed Tom, he tore his clothes, he sent him up trees and into ponds. Somehow or other Tom was always in trouble, and the house in a commotion on account of his misdoings. Continual dropping will wear away a stone; and the complaints of Tom's sins were so continual, that Sir Dene, sick and tired of it, grew hard upon the boy himself. Where's Tom? sometimes the baronet would say, missing him for the rest: and then Jarvis or his mother would tell some bad tale of Tom, and my lady say she had banished him for punishment. Which meant either that he was consigned to Dovet's society, or to his bed in the garret, or shut out of the house to run abroad anywhere.

She got to say that Tom's bad example would contaminate her children: she assured Sir Dene that he was the "greatest little liar" under the sun. Poor Tom, cowed, timid, sensitive, intensely generous, did not often defend himself: how could he when his words, truth though they bore, were flung back in his teeth by others? And so Sir Dene got to think less well of the boy, and to suffer the slighting treatment cast on him—not that he saw or suspected the one-half of the oppression. But he loved Tom still in his heart—far better than he would ever love Jarvis or Otto.

Tom's punishment with the slipper over, he was put to stand by Dovet in the corner of the room, his face to the wall. Leaning his head against it, he cried away the smarting pain, and finally cried himself to sleep. Gander came in and saw him crouched down on the floor, his poor little face, the tears still wet on it, upturned.

"What's been the row this time?" familiarly demanded the butler.

"He has almost killed Master Otto!" was the comprehensive answer of Dovet, who was dashing away at some cream with a whisk.

"A'most killed Master Otto?" repeated the startled Gander. "How on earth did he do that?"

"Master Otto was on the pony. He kicked out and shouted and started it on, malicious little wretch—and poor Master Otto was thrown."

"Why—what made him do it?"

"What makes him do other wicked things?" retorted Dovet.

"Did he do it?" said Gander.

"Did he? Don't I tell you he did?"

"Well—look here, Mrs. Dovet. There's always something or other being brought against the child—and I don't believe he is in fault one time out o' ten. Now don't you fly out like that: keep your tongue for others. One o' these days I shall be telling the master how the child's put upon. As to malicious, that he never was."

"Suppose you mind your own business, and let other folks' alone," suggested Dovet with composure.

"He's Mr. Geoffry again all over, that child is. He had got no maliciousness about him, he hadn't."

Dovet whisked away.

"The very moral of his father, he is," went on Gander,

"save that he's a sight more timid and quiet—Mr. Geoffry never was that. The child has got that from his mother. And a good thing too: else you'd ha' broke his spirit, afore this, among you."

The voice and step of Sir Dene in the passage outside, stopped Gander. The baronet had come in by the back entrance, and was walking straight to the housekeeper's room, a bunch of water-lilies in his hand.

"Put them into water, Dovet. Lady Lydia—"

He caught sight of Tom at that moment, and stopped. The noise aroused the boy, and he stood up. Sir Dene saw something was wrong.

"He has nearly killed Master Otto, Sir Dene," spoke Dovet, in explanation. "Leastways 'twas not his fault that he didn't. Little, mean, disreputable boy he is, I'm sure!"

At that moment Tom did look tolerably disreputable. His face dirty with the rubbing and crying, his pretty hair rumpled into a tangled mass, his clothes dusty and untidy. Jarvis and Otto, hearing the entrance of Sir Dene, came trooping in, followed by Lady Lydia. And Sir Dene was made acquainted with Tom's iniquity.

"How came you to do such a thing?" demanded Sir Dene, sternly. "You naughty, mischievous boy! Suppose you had killed him?"

"I didn't do it, grandpapa," replied the child, his blue eyes raised to Sir Dene's through their blinding tears. And those eyes, Geoffry's over again, never failed to make their own way with Sir Dene.

"You did not do it?" he said, more gently.

"Indeed, indeed I did not. I was by the fence, and I never stirred."

Jarvis fiercely interposed. He had *seen* it all, he said: seen the kick-out and the stone flung after Whitestar, and heard the hiss. As usual, it was word against word; Tom's feeble and tearful, Jarvey's bold and self-asserting. But for those earnest blue eyes that so brought back his dear son Geoffry, Sir Dene had not hesitated. He looked from the one boy to the other —as Otto had done in Dene Hollow—and wavered. Sir Dene had his private reasons for thinking Jarvey might be mistaken. Mistaken, you understand; not wilfully false. The Lady Lydia did her best always in confidential moments to persuade Sir Dene that his eldest grandson (eldest in years) was an upright little gentleman, next door to an angel.

"What have *you* to say about it, Otto?" asked the baronet. "Did Tom do this thing, or did he not?"

"I couldn't see, grandpapa. I had my head turned the bank way: Tom was against the fence."

"Did you hear him hiss?"

"No, I was whistling."

"Or feel the stone?"

"No, and I didn't feel the stone. I think he must have flung the stone, else why should Whitestar have started? He'd not take fright for nothing."

Sir Dene did not feel so sure of that—remembering the particular spot it occurred in.

"You might have heard the hiss he gave down at Hurst Leet," protested Jarvis. "You might have seen him fling the stone a mile off."

And then the talking nearly overpowered Sir Dene, and quite bewildered him. Lady Lydia said there *could* not be a doubt about it—Master Clanwaring had seen all this with his own eyes; and she furthermore said that Tom had done it in revenge, because Otto had taken the pony when he wanted it for himself. To have listened to her, Sir Dene might have thought that there never existed so wicked a little lad on earth, as this waif of his favourite son's. Nevertheless, he believed that the charge might have arisen from misapprehension, the pony not having been wilfully started. He knew also that boys, at the best, are carelessly mischievous, doing ill sometimes in very thoughtlessness.

"If I thought you had done this thing maliciously, Tom, I should flog you myself—and that I have never done yet," he said. "I can but believe that some action of yours, perhaps unintentional on your part, startled the pony. You beg Otto's pardon directly, sir; and tell him you will be more careful for the future."

Never daring to maintain that he was wholly innocent, Tom, his eyes streaming, did what he was told, and begged Otto's pardon. The very fact of his doing it without any demur, convinced some of them that he was guilty. In a degree it did Sir Dene.

But, seated alone in the solitude of his own bay-windowed parlour, the baronet, weighing the matter in his mind, believed that the pony might have started of its own accord. For he had grown, even he, Sir Dene Clanwaring, had grown to dislike that spot for horses.

Accident after accident had continued to take place upon it. The series, inaugurated by Sir Dene's own horses—the reader may remember the day he was being driven down the road by poor Geoffry—had culminated only a month or two ago in a very singular mishap indeed. How many there had been between the two does not matter: several; but not one fatal. Drew the bailiff had recovered partially of his: he could go about in a hand-chair, and talk and laugh and eat his meals at will: and his had been the worst case.

Dene Hollow, smooth and level and well-kept road though it was, was getting a bad name. People talked about the "shadow" on it a great deal more than Sir Dene liked. Not that any shadow was ever seen there by human eyes; but the popular belief was, that there did in some way exist at times that shadow, and that horses were startled at it. Sir Dene thought it was the most ridiculously absurd notion a sane parish had ever picked up: and no doubt the reader is thinking the same. The fact, however, was indisputable—and I am recording nothing but the truth—that horse after horse had been startled there in a mysterious manner: mysterious because there was apparently nothing to startle them. Twice over Sir Dene had had the road examined by officers connected with what was called the post-horse duty, lest any imperceptible roughness or ridge might be found to lie on it—but nothing of the kind could be discovered. Whenever Sir Dene drove or rode up or down it now, he held his horses very carefully in hand; for though he utterly scouted the superstitious gossip around, he could not scout the fact that horses did come to grief there, frequently and unaccountably.

The last mishap is one to be recorded. A gentleman named Dickereen, living in Hurst Leet, died; and his remains were to be taken to a small village church, lying out beyond the Trailing Indian. The funeral was proceeding up Dene Hollow at the usual decorous pace, Hurst Leet bell tolling solemnly, and Hurst Leet having turned out to watch the progress. A funeral of the better class, involving a hearse and mourning coaches from Worcester, with a black chariot in front for the parson in his surplice, and sticks and mutes and feathers, was not an every-day sight in the rural district. As the hearse approached the ill-omened spot (the parson's chariot having passed on soberly), the four horses, with one accord, as it seemed, attempted to turn suddenly round. The driver, scandalized at their behaviour, stopped it, of course, and whipped them up. But no: the horses would not go on. And what precisely happened then, nobody could afterwards tell, for all was over in a moment. There was a noise, a bustle, confusion: undertakers' men on foot ran, drivers shouted: in the midst of it the hearse seemed to spring up on the bank with a violent jerk, which sent the door open and the coffin out endways.

Only think of the scandal to a sober funeral! Hurst Leet remembers it to this day. What could have possessed the fat, steady, slow-going horses, hardly ever moving beyond a foot's pace—that they should have danced up the bank as if they were dancing a jig, and shown signs of fear until their coats ran wet again? It was never accounted for. It was, in truth, unaccountable. The funeral was going up-hill, you understand; not down. The astounded mourners got out of their coaches; the horses were soothed to quietness; and the attendants shut up the coffin in the hearse again.

Now this happened. It was talked of far and wide. Hurst Leet would tell you of it to this day. Even Sir Dene Clanwaring could no more explain it than he could deny it. And since then a hazy sort of impression had floated in his mind that there must be something at the spot that did frighten horses, though man could not see it. Hence he believed that Otto's pony might have started without any help from little Tom or anybody else.

These thoughts in his mind, Sir Dene, sitting in his room, sent for the child. He held Tom before his knee while he talked to him. First of all, he gave him a lecture about telling untruths, saying that his papa (Geoffry) had never told any, and would be sure to have whipped Tom for doing it, if he were living. "And I'm sure *I* cannot continue to love you," concluded Sir Dene.

With his little heart nearly breaking at the sense of the injustice that all seemed to deal out to him,—with the tears welling up in his blue eyes,—with the bitter sobs impeding his utterance, Tom said again what he had said before: that he did not do anything to frighten the pony, or think of doing it. Sir Dene saw how earnestly the child spoke; he noted the confiding look of the honest blue eyes that shone upon him through their tears. Never had he felt inclined to believe Tom more than now: especially with those accidents to other horses filling his thoughts.

"I could believe you from my heart, Tom, and understand

it into the bargain, but for Jarvey. He says he *saw* you purposely frighten Whitestar.'"

Between his extreme sensitiveness for others' feelings, his large generosity, and his innate timidity—which was increased ten-fold by the thraldom he was kept in, the slights he received—Tom was literally unable to say to Sir Dene that Jarvis told falsehoods. This was only one instance out of many where Jarvey had accused him without any manner of reason, and he had never said to Sir Dene, " It is Jarvis who tells the stories, not I." Another thing may have helped to deter him—the certainty that he should not be believed. Jarvis would make his own case good, and Lady Lydia turn the tables on him with a vengeance.

"I didn't do it, grandpa," was all he repeated, catching up his breath in pain.

"But you know you do tell stories, Tom."

"No I don't, grandpa," sobbed the child. "I should be afraid for God to hear me."

"Then Jarvey must have seen double—sees so often, too," cried the baronet explosively—for somehow the answer carried truth with it. "Anyway, I believe you now. And there's a shilling for you, Tom."

But, as a rule, Sir Dene did not question the boy in private, and Jarvis got all the credit, he none. The wondering whether the pony had really been startled accountably—or unaccountably, after the fashion of the other horses—had caused Sir Dene to question now. It was the exception.

And it sometimes happened in the accusations brought against Tom, the tales told of him, that he would be partially in fault. In the escapades that all three of the children shared—and the girl Louisa with them—Tom alone would be made out to have been to blame; he was always the scapegoat. If all were throwing stones and a window got broken—Tom was said to have done it; if the pigs were let out of the sty or the chickens out of their pens, it was Tom who had opened the door: when the miller's little boy was pushed into the stream and nearly drowned, Tom was the culprit. Tom knew that he had, himself, done nothing of all this; but he had been with those who had, and no defence existed for him.

> " A lie that is all a lie can be met with and fought outright,
> But a lie that is part of a truth is a harder matter to fight."

CHAPTER XX.

MISS MAY.

A FIELD whose perfume was redolent of new-mown hay, and whose prolific cocks told of a good crop, lay open to the sun on the fair June morning. The day was yet early: the hay-makers sang at their work. Attended by her nurse, Susan Cole, came a pretty little lady of some three years old, with a round, lovely, childish face, and rich brown eyes that looked out frankly from their long brown lashes, curling upwards. She wore a large white sun-bonnet, after the fashion of the children of the district, and was doing her best to scatter the hay about that the hay-makers had just raked up. Doing it quite in defiance of Susan Cole: for she was a very saucy and independent young lady indeed, continually in hot water with the ruling powers.

"Miss May, don't I tell you that them big cocks is *not* to be disturbed to-day—giving double trouble! I never see such a naughty little child as you be in all my life."

Miss May's answer to this was to climb up one of the mounds and pitch-pole down on the other side, bringing all the top of the cock with her. There she sat, quite still, for a wonder. And stillness was so unusual an element in Miss May Arde, that Susan Cole stepped round to see what other mischief she might be in.

"Oh! Well, I'm sure! Oh! You ondacious little girl!—a-pulling off your shoes and socks afore all the hay-makers!"

For the young lady had been quietly divesting herself of these articles of social attire, that she might dance in the hay barefoot. Eluding Susan's grasp with a ringing laugh, she flew off screaming, and flung herself into the arms of little Tom Clanwaring, who happened to be running up. *Little* Tom, in point of fact, but big Tom in the young damsel's eyes: his seven years, compared to her three, seemed to constitute a whole age.

Tom clasped the truant in his arms, and kissed her: they were the best of friends. Susan, bearing the socks and little shoes of bronze, took forcible possession now; and sat down on the field with the child on her lap. But the process of re-socking and re-shoeing was a difficult job. Laughing, rebellious, kicking out arms and legs, struggling and fighting with Susan, was Miss May. Tom helped—by tossing the socks over Susan's head.

"Now, Master Tom, I'll tell *you* what it is. If you be to encourage her in her naughty tricks, I'll ask my missis not to let you come in here at all. T'ain't your field. She's the tiresom'st little worrit to-day that ever was. You be old enough to tell her better, you be. I never had half the trouble with you. Miss May, if you take your socks off as fast as I put 'em on, where'll be the end on't?"

Miss May managed to get one sock in her fingers, and sent it up on the next hay-cock. Tom was ordered to fetch it down.

At length, by dint of dexterous sleight-of-hand, Susan got on the socks and one shoe. While she was putting on the other, the young rebel tore off that one—and tore off the strap that fastened it round the ankle. Susan saw the mishap with dismay.

"There! Now you have done it, Miss May! Your shoe won't keep on without the strap—and how the sense be I to get you home in your sock? Of all ondacious little plagues, you be the worst."

The "little plague"—Susan's attention being momentarily absorbed by the damaged shoe—got away, seized two armfuls of hay, and flung it over Tom. The children rolled on the ground together.

"A'most as good as a new pair, they was," lamented Susan. "And the kid be all tore right out o' the back so as it can't never be mended. My missis 'll blame me; she'll say I might ha' took better care. Tiresome monkey! I must go home for another shoe for her now. Master Tom, 'll you take care o' Miss May while I run to the Hall and back?"

Tom, feeling excessively proud at the request, turned to Susan, chivalrous earnestness sparkling from his deep blue eyes.

"I'll be sure to take care of her, Susan; she shan't hurt herself, or run away."

And Susan, knowing that in point of fact both the children would be safe under the protection of the haymakers, men and women, busy close by, and all familiar peasants of the district, departed on her errand.

You may be wondering who this girl of three years old is —whose second name, Mary, generally got shortened into May. She was the child of George Arde and his present wife: the only child of the Hall. That frail blossom, the first Mary, the child of George Arde and Mary Owen, the little one to whom the old squire used to carry presents, coral beads and else, and to whom he left the fortune, was no more. The delicate little creature, who had inherited her mother's beauty and no doubt her mother's frailty of constitution, had pined away and died. The second Mrs. Arde did her best to nurse and cherish her into health; but it was not to be: God called her to Himself. Before this other child was born (destined to be the second Mrs. Arde's only one), the elder was lying by her mother's side in St. Peter's churchyard at Worcester. Mary happened to be the second Mrs. Arde's name also, so it was one of the names given to her infant: "Millicent Mary." They had got into the habit (especially Mr. Arde and Susan Cole) of calling that departed little one the first "Mary." For this second Mary no fears were entertained on the score of health: she was hearty and strong. Susan was wont to say at reproachful moments that if she had only as little mischievousness in her as she had tendency to sickness, she'd do.

Susan Cole's life had undergone a blight—she had been crossed in love. At least, that's what she said of herself when wishing to be confidential. But where the blight had fallen and how it had affected her, was not so clear; certainly it had touched neither her tongue nor her cheerful temper. That false journeyman at her father's forge had married another. At the very time (as may be said) that he was whispering love vows in Susan's ear, he was courting another at Worcester: and one fine morning he went off and married her—a great ugly malkin, as Susan expressed it. Cole the farrier told Susan she was well out of it; for the man (he had previously had to discharge him) had grown so drunken and idle that he was hardly worth his salt at the trade, and would not be likely to get a living for any wife. Perhaps Susan, in her heart, thought the same. At least she wasted no superfluous time in grief. It occurred just as she and the other servants were being turned out of the Dene through Lady Lydia: the nurse at Arde Hall was leaving, and Susan stepped into the post.

Little Tom Clanwaring had been allowed to run in and out the Hall since its new mistress came to it as freely as he did before. Mrs. Arde liked the boy, with his golden curls and his wonderful eyes of blue that gazed so straightly and fearlessly into her own: she liked his gentle manners, and his curiously strange (at that early age) consideration for others. No one had wept more bitterly for the little girl's death than

Miss May. 207

Tom. It had pleased the child to have Tom very much with her: Mrs. Arde allowed it: and perhaps the scenes of sickness, the distressing grief evinced by Mr. Arde, had made an impression on Tom that he would never lose.

That she had gone straight up to be an angel in Heaven, no earthly power could have reasoned him out of. For days and weeks after her death, he would fancy he saw her robed in white, with a little harp of gold in her hand, and a crown amid her hair, looking down at him from the skies. Tom—then between three and four years old—was taken to the funeral at St. Peter's by Squire Arde: and Sir Dene had him put into mourning for his cousin. Lady Lydia, supremely indignant, would have pitched the black things out of the window had she dared. "Spending money to put *that* beggar's brat in mourning!" she mockingly remarked to Dovet.

A month onwards, and the other little girl came to the Hall to replace the one lost. Tom had never seen anything so wonderful as this new baby. The reverence with which he would regard the infant, when allowed to hold her for a minute in his arms (seated safely flat on the carpet), was great and real. The baby called forth the first true-love of his heart: in his own mind he acquired a kind of proprietorship in her: and he would far rather have died himself than suffered harm to come to the little one.

So that when, on this day, Susan told him to take care of her while she went home for another shoe, Tom was in the seventh region of gratification. The field belonged to Squire Arde, and was within a stone's throw of the Hall.

"May," began Tom, as Susan's footsteps faded on their ears, "I've got a new picture-book that Grandma Owen bought for me. "I've got it in my pocket."

May, with all her wild fun, was intensely fond of "picture-books." Down sat the children together at the foot of a haycock, their feet stretched out (one of Miss May's shoeless) and the book held between them.

Like all books bought by Mrs. Owen for Tom, it had a religious tendency. That is, while the story in itself was beautiful, and calculated entirely to rivet the interest of a child, it insensibly led its young readers to higher and better thoughts. Such books, when they are well and suitably written, are the very best that can be put into the hands of a child. There has been a singular dearth of them in these latter years. There they sat, the two: May's little tongue asking questions about the "pictures," and Tom explaining to the best of his ability. Which explanations might have sent a grown person into fits of laughter.

"Me wis me tould read!" exclaimed May, when, the pictures exhausted—the book only containing three—they had to fall back upon the reading.

"I'll read it to you, May," said Tom.

With their backs against the haycock, and their heads bent over the book, the little lady's cheek touching his, Tom began. The progress was not satisfactory; since at the end of every two lines, or so, Tom was called upon to say why this was, and why that was. Suddenly a shadow fell upon the book and upon them. Up went their heads, and nearly a whole haycock was flung in their faces. Not lightly, either; for the flinger was Jarvis Clanwaring. Absorbed in the book, and with each other, neither had seen him approach. May burst into a loud cry of pain: the hay had struck her in the eye. Down went the book, and up jumped Tom.

"What did you do that for, Jarvis? You've hurt her.

"What did I do it for, you insolent young rat! How dare *you* ask me what I did it for? Because I chose. There! Squalling little cat! She's not hurt."

May, who hated Jarvis at all times, because she was afraid of him, began kicking out with all her little might as she sat, the tears falling from her smarting eyes.

"Make him go away, Tom! make him go away. Me tell mamma."

"You are to go away, please," said Tom, standing up bravely to shelter May. "You've no right to hurt her, Jarvis."

"She's not hurt—nasty little toad."

Tom, his eyes flashing fire (as his sweet-natured father's had flashed once or twice in his brief life), clenched his impotent small fist, and struck straight out and upwards at Mr. Jarvis's face, catching him between the eyes. The blow could not hurt very much; but it was a bit of a smart, and it smarted all the more because it was not expected. Jarvis, in a frantic passion, pummelled Tom's face back again, and an unequal fight ensued. May screamed as if she was going mad with terror; and one of the women and Susan Cole rushed up together. Tom's nose was streaming with blood; Jarvis was not apparently injured. But in that culminating moment he contrived to damage himself. Turning shortly upon his heel to confront the indignant Susan, he stumbled over a rake handle, that the woman had let fall, and cut his upper lip with the rake's teeth. More blood: and May screamed worse than ever from sheer terror. Susan caught up the child and hid her face upon her protecting shoulder.

"How *dare* you get fighting, Master Tom—and when I left you to take care of Miss May!" demanded Susan, not caring to attack Jarvis in his present state of fury: for once, when she had interfered with him, he had kicked her in a rather serious manner. "Well, I'm sure! We shall have a baby in arms, I suppose, standing up to fight next!"

"He called May names," said Tom, who could not restrain his tears between pain and excitement. "He hurt her in the eye."

"You confounded little blackguard!" cried Jarvis, trying to dodge up to Tom again with outstretched hand. "Do you suppose I shall ask your leave whether I call names or not? She is a toad. There!"

"She's not a toad, and you sha'n't call her one," retorted Tom. "You are a coward."

Further demonstration on Jarvis's part was stopped by his swallowing a tooth. A first tooth, nearly ready to fall out before, and which the blow on the rake must have quite done for. Tom Clanwaring's instinct was sure and true: Jarvis *was* a coward. Not only in the matter of bullying little girls and fighting boys less than himself, but in other matters. This swallowing of the tooth sent him into a state of mortal terror: he had heard a tale at school of some boy who had swallowed a tooth and died after it. Jarvis, suddenly remembering this, turned tail and rushed off the hayfield the colour of chalk.

"You come on to the Hall, Master Tom, that your nose may be seen to," said Susan. "A sweet pickle it's in! Enough to frighten the crows."

"A brave little gentleman, wi' all his pretty manners, that born son o' poor Master Geoffry's," was the comment of the woman to the other haymakers when the fray was over. "As to the big un, he's more of a Tartar nor his mother."

Arde Hall was not much to look at. A rather long, red-brick building, two storeys high, with narrow windows and a slated roof, its front looking towards the village. The old-fashioned portico in the middle of the house opened upon a lawn that was intersected with flower-beds; on which bees and butterflies were sporting that sunny June day. Mrs. Arde—a nice-looking, but somewhat reserved and stately woman—fond of gardening, was tending her flowers in a sun-bonnet and pair of old gloves, talking the while to her husband, who sat at one of the open windows. Naturally they felt some surprise at the entrance of the procession: Susan carrying May, who sobbed aloud still: Tom with a damaged face and bleeding nose. Susan opened at once upon his delinquencies—that he "up with his fist" and struck Master Clanwaring, and they had a fight.

"He called May names," said Tom, with fresh tears, but looking up fearlessly. "I couldn't help hitting him."

Squire Arde burst out laughing. "A very knight-errant," said he; "taking up the cudgels for damsels in distress!"

"But what ails May?" said Mrs. Arde, as she took the sobbing child.

"Oh, *she's* only frightened, ma'am," was Susan's slighting answer. "And enough to frighten her, to see the blood on this here face of his'n," concluded the girl, as she walked Tom off to the pump.

The lavatory process over, Tom came back to kiss the little girl—then seated on the grass—and whisper that Jarvis should never frighten or hurt her again, or call her names, if *he* could help it. Then he ran off home.

Where the discomfited and frightened Jarvis had previously arrived. At this time, Mrs. Clanwaring, the wife of John the heir, was on a visit to Beechhurst Dene, with her daughter, Margaret, her eldest boy, and two little twin sons, younger: so that just now the Dene seemed full of children. She was a goodnatured and very pretty woman—her own large fortune enabling her to indulge in show and luxuries that might not even be dreamed of by Lady Lydia. For instance, she had arrived with a lady's maid and three nurses, and one male servant who was called her own footman, the party having posted from town in two carriages and four. These things were looked upon as necessaries by Mrs. Clanwaring, because she had been reared to them: but she was, herself, entirely unpretentious, of quite simple tastes and manners. The two ladies were sitting together in that attractive room, the library, when Jarvis burst in upon them like a panting ghost—if ghosts ever display cut lips, and chins dripping human gore. The boy was literally terror-stricken: his features were swollen with his insane endeavours to cough up the tooth coming along, his eyes rolled, his face was whiter than any ghost's ever seen yet. A deplorable figure altogether. Up jumped the Lady Lydia, uttering scream upon scream; she quite believed her darling boy was either mad or killed, and began to hug him. Pretty Mrs, Clanwaring, in defiance of her good manners, laughed a little.

The tale that Master Jarvis told was as good as a play: no dramatic author ever drew more on his inventive powers. Tom was represented as a very monster of iniquity, who had attacked Jarvis with a rake, "on the sly," cut off his lip and knocked all his teeth down his throat.

But that the teeth were in his head still, plainly to be seen beneath the swollen upper lip *not* cut off, Lady Lydia. in her dismay, might have sent off for the nearest stomach-pump. The whole house was aroused to commotion. Basins of hot water were ordered in succession; Lady Lydia, Dovet, and a dozen others bathing with soft sponges, and without intermission, the injured lip. Under the assurances of my lady and Mrs. Clanwaring, that a solitary tooth, going down by accident, never killed people, but on the contrary was rather good for digestion, the gentleman was soothed into calmness. The disturbance had brought forth Sir Dene from his bay-parlour, where he was engaged with accounts : he stayed long enough to hear the woful account of Tom's savage attack, and then went back again.

When Tom got home, shortly afterwards, Jarvis was lying on the sofa, his mouth tied up with a white handkerchief, and some delicious apricot jam by his side. Dovet met Tom in the Hall.

"*You* have done a nice thing," cried she, nearly jerking his arm out of its socket. "You've almost killed Master Clanwaring."

Almost killed Master Clanwaring ! Full of consternation, the words striking no end of remorse on his little heart, Tom opened the library door and went in timidly. He did not present any grand appearance himself, for, in running home, his nose had burst out bleeding again. The moment Jarvis saw him, he leaped off the sofa and gave him an ugly kick. Mrs. Clanwaring ran to the rescue and pushed Jarvis off: but the vicious malice that blazed in his eyes, she did not forget for years.

" Not in my presence, Jarvey. How can you attack a little fellow who is no match for you ? It is perfectly wicked to kick any one in that savage way. I am afraid you are a coward."

"Why did he attack me in the hay-field?" retorted Jarvey. "I'll kill him if I can."

But Lady Lydia pounced on Tom and whirled him off with her. What with the sight of him, and what with Mrs. Clanwaring's words, her fury at least equalled that of Jarvis. On the mahogany slab in the passage, leading to the side entrance and Sir Dene's parlour, lay the boy's riding whip. Seizing hold of it, she struck Tom: not perceiving, perhaps not caring, that a young man not belonging to the house, was at that moment turning out of the bay-parlour. Struck him anywhere: on his shoulders, on his unprotected face, on his bare hands. Gander, propping his back against his pantry door, stood looking on. As did the stranger, who was no other than William Owen, of Harebell Farm. The cuts were sharp and quick: Tom shrieked with pain, and it brought out Sir Dene. My lady ceased then: and the baronet pushed by William Owen.

"Wait!" cried Sir Dene in a voice of thunder, as she was making off with the child. "Wait, I say!" But Lady Lydia left the boy, threw down the whip, and disappeared. Sir Dene caused Tom to stand and confront him. His poor little face had a livid weal across it.

"Now, sir, tell me the truth. Did you strike Jarvis before he struck you?"

Up went the honest eyes, through their tears with fearless truth, straight into Sir Dene's.

"Yes, grandpa. 'Twas me hit him first."

"Did you cut his mouth? And knock his tooth down his throat?"

"I suppose so. I didn't know."

"And what on earth tempted you to be so ferocious a child as to do all this?"

"He called May wicked names, grandpapa; he hurt her in the eye and frightened her. Susan had told me to take care of her while she went for another shoe."

Sir Dene bit his lips to prevent a smile. The same thought occurred to him that had come to George Arde—and amused him—this little lad, rising seven, doing battle for a lady attacked! But he was frightfully annoyed at my Lady Lydia.

"Who hurt your nose?—and made it swell like that?"

"Jarvis did: he made it bleed. He hit me worse than I hit him."

"No doubt on't," commented Gander, from the kitchen door.

"Well, you must have been a naughty boy altogether, Tom; very naughty; and Lady Lydia has punished you for it. Try and be good for the future—if you can."

Sir Dene turned into his parlour again; William Owen, although his interview was over, followed him in after a moment's hesitation and shut the door. Gander retreated into his pantry.

All sobbing and wounded as he was, Tom ran out at the side-door and down the straight path, to take shelter at Harebell Farm. His heart was cruelly sore as he went up the stairs—for Mrs. Owen was keeping her chamber. Not sore at thought of his weals and wounds, but at the injustice dealt out to him. Jarvis had been more of an offender than he, and was petted up with jam; *he* was taunted and whipped. Tom had been *inured* to this unjust treatment, but it did strike him with pain to-day. Mary Barber, coming out of her mistress's chamber all in a bustle, on her way to make some dumplings for dinner, was quite struck at the sight of Tom.

"Mercy upon us!" cried she. "Why, what in the name o' goodness is the matter?"

Sobbing, choking, Tom told his tale, leaning for protection —and it seemed to the child that he needed it—against Mrs. Owen. She had some warm water brought up, and bathed his poor face and hands, and spoke gently to him, and soothed his spirit: the tears falling from her own eyes, as she thought it might have been better had the poor little waif died with its mother.

"But that I think I shall not be long here, and that William seems bent upon not staying in the place afterwards, I hardly know why, I would beg and pray of Sir Dene to let me have the child entirely," ran Mrs. Owen's thoughts.

As they had run, at odd times, for a long while now. Ever since the arrival of Lady Lydia, Mrs. Owen had clearly seen what the child's treatment was at the Dene, and the contempt he was held in. It was bad enough during these, his young years, when he could neither feel it very keenly nor attempt to rebel against it: what the result might be in later years, what complications and misfortunes it might bring about for the friendless child, she dreaded to think of. That Sir Dene would not be wilfully unjust to Geoffry's son, she believed; but Sir Dene was a man who loved peace and quietness, ease also; he was given to credit implicitly what he was told, never searching beneath the surface of things, and he was already nearly completely in the hands of his designing daughter-in-law.

His face in less of a smart, his grief over, save for a catching sob that took his breath at intervals (and Mary Barber gone down to bake a little cake for him), room was made for Tom on Mrs. Owen's sofa. He sat nestling against her, her arm round him, her pale face, so sweet and delicate, and telling of sorrow and suffering, bending towards his. Never did Mrs. Owen fail to improve these occasions in the manner she thought it right and best to do. In place of standing out for vengeance on Jarvis or others, as some might have counselled, she whispered of endurance, of forbearance, of persevering on in the path of patience and truth, however much he might be tried, and of the ensuing of calm and holy peace. Trouble was certainly trying the child early; but she strove to show him, and to think, that it must be for the best. On some children these lessons might have been lost, might have borne no fruit: but Tom's natural disposition was so admirably adapted to receive them, that they did on his. There's no doubt—however the reader may feel inclined to dispute and perhaps to ridicule this small portion of the tale—that these inculcated lessons had a strangely good effect on Tom. They helped him to bear now; they tended to form his character for after years. But for them, he would have been utterly miserable, might have sunk into a broken-spirited child, and, perhaps, become a veritable abandoned young Arab. Day after day did Mrs. Owen patiently labour at her work—for never a day passed but Tom was driven out of the Dene by some oppression or other, active or passive—and she would send him back with all the sweetness of his disposition renewed, ready to bear again.

"Was it wrong to hit Jarvis, when he called May those wicked words, grandma?"

Now here was a puzzle. Mrs. Owen privately rejoiced at Tom's spirit: but it was hardly consistent with the peaceful lessons she was inculcating to say so.

"Well, Tom, I—don't think in this case it was very wrong."

"I wish he'd let me alone! I wish he'd not get grandpa to

believe bad things of me. Oh grandma! you don't know how cruel it all is at home!"

A sobbing sigh, proving how sore his little heart was, followed on the words. Mrs. Owen pressed him closer in her clasp, and spoke in a whisper.

"My darling, I do know it. I know how cruel it is, and how hard it is to endure. God sees it all, Tom, never lose thought of that, no, not in the worst moment. You bear on fearlessly in truth and honour, my boy; always striving to return good for evil, even to Jarvis, in sweet-tempered, patient, generous forbearance: and trust all things to God. He will be sure to take care of you, and bring you to comfort in the end."

Tom nodded with ready cheerfulness, as he had many and many a time before. There was resolution in his little face, cast up just then to the summer sky.

"I will, grandma, I will; I'll never forget. And, grandma, papa is looking down to take care of me too, and mamma is; and they are with God's angels."

"Even so, my darling. Your best friends are in that better world where God is. I shall soon be there: and you will come to us in time. All these sufferings and trials are but making you ready for it."

And the tractable little fellow, gazing up at the blue sky, and picturing all kinds of radiant things beyond it, quite forgot present pain.

"Now then, Master Tom!" called out the sharp voice of Mary Barber from the foot of the stairs, "come down for your lard-cake. It have come out o' the oven beautiful."

CHAPTER XXI.

DRIVEN FROM HAREBELL FARM.

"CAN you see anybody, Sir Dene?"

"Who is it?" asked Sir Dene, turning round from his desk, that was drawn before the window of his bay-parlour. And he spoke in rather an impatient tone, for he was busy writing letters, and did not care to be interrupted. As Gander knew.

"It's young Mr. Owen, of Harebell Farm," replied Gander.

"What does he want?" questioned Sir Dene. "Is it particular?"

"Don't know, sir," returned Gander. "He came to the

door, and he asked could he be let see Sir Dene: I told him I'd come and ask."

"Show him in," said Sir Dene.

This colloquy occurred just about the time that Master Jarvis had been soothed to tranquillity on the sofa with some apricot jam at his elbow, as already described, and that the unlucky Tom was on the run towards home from Arde Hall. For the day is not yet over, and we must go back an hour or so in it: it is not practicable for the cleverest author living to describe two series of events at once, although they may have taken place at one and the same moment of time.

William Owen appeared, shown in by Gander: and the baronet shook hands with him without rising, and motioned him to a chair. He always shook hands with his better class of tenants. As to any other recognition, or symptom of cordiality, William Owen did not get it, and did not in the least presume to wish for or expect it. Sir Dene had practically forgotten that there was any link whatever between them, save that of landlord and tenant: the past connection might have absolutely faded out of his thoughts ere this, but for the existence of Geoffry and Maria's child.

The business that William Owen had come upon surprised Sir Dene: and he stared at the young man—seated before him in the opposite chair, his hat held across his knees—while he listened to it. William Owen wished to transfer the lease of Harebell Farm to another tenant, if Sir Dene would permit. Not at present: perhaps not for a long while to come: but he wished to do it as soon as the time when he *could* do it should arrive.

"As long as my mother lives, sir, I must stay where I am, for she would not like to go out of the house; neither would I disturb her by asking it. But when she shall have left us— and she thinks herself it may not be over long first now—then I shall be glad to give it up, and leave the place altogether."

"What fault have you to find with the farm, Mr. Owen?" distantly queried Sir Dene.

"None, sir. It's as good land as ever I'd wish to cultivate. That's not the reason."

"What is the reason, then?"

William Owen seemed at fault for a reply. Sir Dene noticed that a look of pain sat on his refined and pleasant face.

"You must have some reason, Mr. Owen, for wishing to quit a productive farm."

"True, Sir Dene: I have. But it is one that is quite private to myself. I can't speak of it even to you, sir."

Sir Dene looked at him. The same contraction of pain was in the face; the same tone of distress lay in the voice. He greatly wondered what could be the matter. William Owen saw the puzzled surprise: and just for a moment, the thought crossed him that he would speak out fully to Sir Dene. But the impulse faded again in a feeling that lay between shame and sensitiveness. Perhaps had Sir Dene been simply his landlord as he was of other tenants, and no more, the disclosure might have been made: but that past connection caused William Owen to be always retiring and reticent. In his sensitive nature, he would not have pushed himself forward for the world, or presumed in the slightest degree.

"I have no fault to find with the farm or the house or the land, sir; but I must leave it, for all that. I can't stay in it. And I'd be glad to know beforehand that you will allow me to do this, so as to have my mind at rest. As long as my mother is there, there I must be: but when she's gone, I shall go elsewhere."

"Do I understand that you will leave the neighbourhood entirely?"

"Yes, Sir Dene. And get as many miles from it as I can."

"What has it done to you?"

William Owen stroked the nap of his white beaver hat with his gloved forefinger: for he had dressed himself as a gentleman to hold this interview with Sir Dene—and he looked like one, too. He seemed to be considering what answer he could make to the question.

"It is just that—what it has done to me—that I am unable to tell, sir," he at length replied. "It is an unfortunate and painful affair altogether; and I cannot talk of it."

"Suppose I do not release you from the farm?" said Sir Dene. "What then?"

"But I hope you will do it, sir. As to what then, I'm sure I don't know what I could do. Perhaps you'd let me underlet it."

"Are you going out of the farming business?"

"Not at all, Sir Dene. I like it: add to that, I don't know any other. I shall meet with a farm elsewhere: perhaps in Dorsetshire."

"You'll not get a better than this. If it's small, it's good."

"And I don't expect to, Sir Dene. If this becomes vacant,,

there'll be plenty of good tenants glad to snap it up. Were it known that I thought of leaving it, they'd be here to-morrow. But I'd rather there was no stir made at all about it, sir: I'd like, when the time comes, to be away and gone before it was as much as known abroad that I was leaving. That's why I am asking you to promise to let it be ceded to Philip Tillet, when this time shall come: to let me go out and him go in. The farm could not have a better tenant, Sir Dene, than he."

Sir Dene knew that much. A better tenant than William Owen himself: insomuch as that he was a man of larger capital. Philip Tillett was a thoroughly good farmer.

"It seems to me that he will have to wait an indefinite time," remarked Sir Dene. "Mrs. Owen may get better."

"He is quite content to wait, sir, whether it's for weeks or whether it's for years. The farm he is in belongs to his uncle, and he can go out of it at any time. He likes his present one very well; but he'd like Harebell Farm better."

"Does he know why you are leaving?"

"Yes, sir, I told him. No one else knows; not even my mother."

There ensued a short silence. Sir Dene was thinking this a curious kind of application. As in truth it was. William Owen, who held a long lease of Harebell Farm, was asking to be allowed to cede it provisionally to Mr. Philip Tillett. Provisionally on the death of his invalid mother. When she should die—and he acknowledged that it might be weeks or months, or it might be years first, for that's what the doctors said—then he wished to walk out of it, leaving Mr. Tillett to walk in.

"Would Tillett take to the stock?" abruptly questioned Sir Dene, when he had arrived at this point in his mental summary of events.

"To all things as they stand, sir; household furniture included," replied William Owen. "He knows about what the value of everything is as well as well as I do, and he is a just man. We shouldn't quarrel over that."

There was something in the young man's refined features, in his gentle manners, that put Sir Dene in mind of poor Maria, as he had seen her that New's Year's Eve when he broke in without ceremony on the Malvern lodgings. Had he wished to refuse this thing, he could not, with that remembrance upon him.

"Well," he said, rising, in intimation that the sitting was

over, "I will give my consent to this, Mr. Owen. You have my word. Though I wish you had freely told me your motive for leaving. Stay! Have you got into any trouble? Is it that?"

"None whatever, I assure you, Sir Dene," was William Owen's reply, his sensitive face slightly flushing. "Circumstances over which I have no control, and could not have any, are driving me away. I wish it had been otherwise."

"Then, until there shall be the last change in your mother, things go on as they are, and you remain my tenant?"

"If you please, sir. I thank you truly for your kindness to me, Sir Dene."

Sir Dene shook hands, and William Owen let himself out at the room door. He was just in time, as the reader has heard, to see Lady Lydia horsewhip Tom. Hearing the cries, Sir Dene walked out also. And when the affair was over, and he went back to the room, he found that the young man followed him. Sir Dene was surprised: and William Owen shut the door.

"I crave your pardon, Sir Dene, for presuming to interfere. But I would like to ask another favour. Let the poor little boy come home to *us*. I'll bring him up and do for him as if he were my own."

Sir Dene's face flushed angrily. The request seemed to reflect on the hospitality of Beechhurst Dene.

"Come home to you!" he exclaimed. "The boy's home is here, Mr. Owen."

"Yes, sir, I know. I know that Beechhurst Dene is a very different home from any I could hope to give him. But at least he'd have kind treatment with us, Sir Dene."

"What is it you would imply?" asked Sir Dene haughtily.

"I don't presume to imply anything, sir; but what I know, I know. Hardly a day passes, but the child is insulted and put upon, very often beaten. Not by you, sir: not, I feel sure, within your knowledge; but by those about you. The best is being done that can be done to break his heart and his spirit."

In the gentlest and most respectful tone possible William Owen was saying this. Somehow Sir Dene felt mollified. The child was Geoffry's child, and he did not like to hear of his heart or his spirit being on the road to breakage.

"He has been very naughty at times of late, very; and when he is so he must be corrected. The boy seems quite changed. Spare the rod, and spoil the child, you know."

"Sir Dene, I believe the child to be one of the very best children that ever lived: he is good and truthful as the day——"

"They say he has taken to tell stories," interrupted Sir Dene. "I can't credit it, though."

"No, Sir Dene, believe me, he never does tell stories. What I fear is, that others tell them and lay it upon him—though of course it is not my place to say as much. He is regarded as an unwelcome interloper here, and treated accordingly. There's not a servant in your house, Sir Dene, but could bear testimony to this if you questioned them—though they might not like to confess it. He is a truthful, honourable, upright little lad: I don't think he could tell a lie if bribed to it. Witness just now how he spoke up Yes, when asked if he was the first to hit Master Clanwaring. The boy has no chance here. I wish you would let me have him, sir."

"It is out of the question," sharply replied Sir Dene, feeling vexed and annoyed at more things than one. And William Owen took the answer, and departed by the back entrance.

It has been said that close upon this door the trees and shrubs grew thick, almost like a wilderness. Branching off from hence on the right, a path called the privet walk (a high privet hedge running along on either side it) led round to the front; while the straight path that led direct to Harebell Lane bore somewhat to the left. William Owen was taking this latter way, when he saw Squire Arde coming along the shady privet walk. Mr. Arde made a sign, and William turned to meet him.

"Is Mrs. Owen worse?" was the question put. "I saw Priar hastening up your way just now."

"My mother? No; not worse than usual," was the answer. "He was not coming to our house, that I am aware of."

"Oh, well, I'm glad of that. I am afraid, though, that on the whole she is very ill."

"Yes, sir, there's no doubt of that."

Never presuming, never self-asserting, William Owen, generally called Squire Arde "sir." They were, or had been, brothers-in-law; but he did not attempt to ignore the social distance between them. George Arde in the old days had been above his sister; he was a great man now in local estimation, on a level with Sir Dene Clanwaring and such as he. Neither did Mr. Arde forget their distance: something in his manner betrayed that: nevertheless, they liked each other very well, and were on intimate, not to say confidential, terms whenever they met. Standing there together in the narrow privet walk, the young man told Mr. Arde what his errand had been at Sir Dene's—the remarks on his mother's state of health perhaps inducing it.

"Tillett to take to the farm as it stands as soon as anything happens to her, and you to go out of it and quit the place altogether!" repeated the Squire in amazement. "Well, now, why is this, William Owen?"

And William Owen told him—told him what he had not chosen to disclose to Sir Dene. And however the reader may feel inclined to cast ridicule on the cause, he may not disbelieve the fact: for no other reason did William Owen quit Harebell farm. Speaking in a whisper, his pale face wearing again its marks of pain, he breathed it into Mr. Arde's ear. The troubled spirit of his father, haunting the precincts of the farm, was driving him away from it.

"He has been dead now seven years and some months, Squire Arde: and people talked of its walking for more than three of those years before I ever saw it, or believed it. Altogether I've seen it three times: the last was on Sunday night. News was brought to the farm that a poor houseless woman had crept into that shed on the two-acre meadow to die. I went off to see about it; and there, hovering in and around the grove, was the spirit, in the same place where I had seen it twice before. I saw it clearly: 'twas a very light night."

Squire Arde remembered what a bright moon had shone on Sunday night. He was not a superstitious man, but nothing could be further from his thoughts than to meet this communication with contempt: others, worthy of credibility, had said just the same as William Owen.

"I can't make it out, William," he said. "Are you *sure* that your eyesight was not deceived by some tree or other?"

The young man shook his head. "What I saw was undoubtedly the very figure and image of my father, looking as he used to look in life. He seemed to have a coat buttoned up round him—about that I can't be sure: it was indistinct—but he wore that same queer magpie cap he was drowned in; and his silver beard was never plainer. I was thinking of nothing but the woman in the shed, and what could be done with her at that time o' night; and there, as I went along towards the grove, the figure stood facing me, right in the moonbeams."

"It is strangely singular!" exclaimed the Squire. "The queerest thing I've met with in all my experience."

"Stay on the place I cannot," said William Owen. "It unnerves me for everything—though I should feel ashamed to acknowledge it to most people. The very moment my poor mother sets me at liberty by leaving me alone in the world, I shall get away. But for her sake, I'd go to-morrow."

He had turned to walk towards Harebell Lane, Mr. Arde strolling by his side. William Owen changed the subject to that of the child: mentioning the cruel chastisement he had witnessed, and what he had subsequently said to Sir Dene.

"When I shall be gone from the place, perhaps you'll give the poor lad a kind word now and then, sir. He'll have nobody else to do it. I'd have liked to take him home to Harebell Farm: Sir Dene was very much offended at me for asking it."

"Lady Lydia and her children put upon him and thrust him into the background," remarked Mr. Arde. "She has got a nasty temper of her own."

They parted. William Owen pursuing his way home, where he found Mary Barber making a miniature lard-cake for Tom: Mr. Arde entering the bay-parlour at Beechhurst Dene. Sir Dene Clanwaring was in one of his testy humours, and said a few fractious words about "Things going cross in the house."

"Young Owen has been taking upon himself to tell me that the child—my boy Geoffry's son—is not well treated here!" he cried, in an explosive tone. "Fancy his assurance, Arde!"

"Then I'll take up the word for him, Sir Dene, at the risk of your attributing assurance to me," spoke up Mr. Arde, half laughing. "In this instance, at any rate, the child did not deserve chastisement—though I fancy somebody else may. If that ill-natured young Jarvey came home with a false tale—as I conclude he did—it is he who ought to have got the whipping."

"What do you know about it, Arde?"

Mr. Arde related the truth of the day's fray—as he had heard it but now from his haymakers, in coming through the field; and, as he remarked, they were unbiassed witnesses. He spoke out far more freely than William Owen had ventured to do, telling a few home-truths about Tom and Jarvey, and the Dene in general, including the baronet himself. Sir Dene's blue eyes opened (in more senses than one), and his lips took a haughty curve as he listened.

"A false, ill-conditioned young rascal!" spoke he of Jarvey.

"It's the first time I ever knew a Clanwaring could concoct a deliberate lie."

"His mother is not a Clanwaring," observed Squire Arde drily. And the baronet gave a kind of assenting sniff.

"No, *he* has nothing of the Clanwaring about him at present," pursued the Squire. "Little Tom's one to the backbone: he is his father over again. They look upon the child as being in the way here, you see: don't let them quite break his spirit. There, that's all, Sir Dene. Good morning."

Break his spirit! The same words that William Owen had used. Had Jarvey been there at the moment, Sir Dene might have three-parts killed him. With the red flush dyeing his face, he strode forth to the presence of Lady Lydia. She was in the drawing-room.

Sir Dene controlled his temper, and spoke quietly. Quietly, but very peremptorily. He touched slightly upon the treatment of Tom by her and her children generally—the scandal he found it excited in the neighbourhood, the discomfort it brought to the Dene. And he said that for the future she had better take lodgings at Worcester during holiday time, and have her children there with her.

Lady Lydia's blood turned cold: was it *possible* that her footing at the Dene was being imperilled? In her mind's confusion, in her angry passion, she did the worst thing she could have done—began to cast slurs on Tom and his birth.

Were *her* darling children to be discarded for that low-born brat, whose mother——

"Why, what the devil do you mean, madam?" interrupted Sir Dene, too much put out altogether to weigh his words. "Low-born! You are speaking of my own grandson, Tom Clanwaring."

"He is not fit company for my boys, Sir Dene."

"If what I am told be true, they are not fit company for him—one of them, at any rate," retorted Sir Dene. "You can take them out of it as soon as you please, my lady."

Her very lips turned white. Before this, she had believed she had acquired firm hold on Sir Dene. He looked like one not to be trifled with just now. An angry man, there, pacing the carpet.

"You—would—turn my children out for *him?*" she resumed, in a subdued gasping tone, partly put on, partly the result of the low-lying fear. "Oh, Sir Dene!"

"My lady, it is this. The home is my grandson Tom's: it

was his home before any of you came to it; it shall be his home as long as it remains mine. I was willing to let it be your children's also: but it seems the plan does not answer. It is my pleasure that Tom Clanwaring shall be honoured in this house, aye, and be loved too, at least as much as anybody else is. Your children will not do this: they have taken up a prejudice against him: therefore there is only one alternative—they must spend their summer and winter holidays elsewhere."

No mistake now. He was in real earnest. My lady, smoothing her black hair from her pale face damp with emotion, changed her tactics on the instant. She would inquire into it, she meekly said: if Jarvis had been knowingly unkind to the child or told fibs of him, he should be punished. For her own part, she had always thought Tom a sweet little angel. Children would fight, though; boys would be boys. But the little child should be her best and special charge for the future, now that she understood Sir Dene's wishes.

My lady gathered her three children in her room that same evening to a private interview, and treated them to sundry tutorings. Dovet also received some hints. The result was, that Tom found a change: there was no more open ill-treatment, no further complaints of him carried to Sir Dene. And, on Sir Dene's part, nothing else was said about the exodus.

But the lady's resolution—*to put Tom down*—had not changed: she only altered her tactics. As the time passed on, this little episode was forgotten by Sir Dene. Easy and good natured to a fault was he; Lady Lydia's sway over him when he was at Beechhurst Dene increased: during his frequent absences she reigned absolutely. And Tom Clanwaring was taught and trained to look upon himself as a poor dependent, kept at the place out of charity; an interloper, but not a son. Tom insensibly fell into these views of himself in all belief, and learnt humility. More specious than deceit itself was the Lady Lydia Clanwaring.

END OF PART THE FIRST.

Part the Second.

CHAPTER XXII.

AFTER THE LAPSE OF YEARS.

This, as you perceive, is the second part of the story. Years have elapsed since the conclusion of the first: and those children, boys and girls, told of then, have grown into men and women.

There is not very much to relate of the interval. Time has wrought some changes—as time invariably does. They may be briefly summed up in a few lines. And it may be as well to state that, in spite of the lapse of time, we are still writing of a period very many years back.

Sir Dene Clanwaring has lost both his sons: John the heir and Reginald the major. The one died of neglected cold; the other fell in battle. Pretty Mrs. Clanwaring, John's widow, is married again, and lives chiefly at her husband's estate in Scotland. Her two sons, Dene and Charles, nice, pleasant young fellows with plenty of money in prospect, and her only children living, are very often staying with their grandfather, Sir Dene; the older of the two, Dene, being his heir. Their sister, Margaret, had died at Beechhurst Dene only two years ago, under circumstances of a painful nature: Sir Dene, who was very fond of her, has not been quite the same man since.

Lady Lydia Clanwaring is at Beechhurst Dene still. She has never, in fact, been away from it since that autumn night when she arrived to take up her abode. Up to the time the husband died, she was always "going back to India shortly." After his death, she had no home even to talk of going to, and no means of setting up one—everybody knows what is the pension of a major's widow. So she remained at Beechhurst Dene without question as to her leaving it; and her children looked upon it as their home just as surely as though they had a legal right to it. Lady Lydia had really grown useful to Sir Dene: and her tact (she never forgot it again) was such that he valued her, and quite believed the household could not get on without her. Her daughter, Louisa, had married early; Jarvis was in the army; Otto was a barrister in Lincoln's Inn.

Tom Clanwaring had not been got out of the Dene. The fact is worthy of being recorded, considering Lady Lydia's private machinations to accomplish it. Never again had she tried for it openly since that one last great explosion, when Sir Dene had suggested that she and her children should go, rather than Tom. Indeed she soon gave up hoping for it, and let the fact alone. But she had successfully managed to put Tom in the background, and keep him there. He was reared as an inferior-born dependent, who must never presume to confound himself with the genuine Clanwaring family. Sir Dene insensibly fell into the snare; habit is strong; the neighbourhood fell into it; Tom himself fell into it. During his boyhood he was kept away at school as much as possible: in the holidays he met with cold neglect; was made to estrange himself from the drawing-room, and to herd with the servants. It taught him humility. Sir Dene honoured and regarded him as his grandson just as much as he did the other boys; in his heart he loved Tom best of all; but, nevertheless, he tacitly sanctioned Tom's being put in the background. Habit, I say, is strong; and this had grown into the habit at the Dene.

When Tom Clanwaring grew to manhood, his occupation rendered this isolation from the rest, or semi-isolation, easy of accomplishment. Tom was to the estate very much what his father had been—overlooker. When the lad was driven to seek sources out of doors by the home neglect, he had found them on the land. With Dell the bailiff, riding or walking round; watching for poachers with Simmons the gamekeeper; following the plough to have a chat with the ploughman; sitting in a corner of the barn, eating his bread-and-cheese dinner, while the men threshed the wheat; helping to load the waggon with barley: going to the corn-market at Worcester with Dell: in all places and at all work, Tom was at home. Nothing teaches like practical experience: and there were few better farmers in the county than was Tom Clanwaring. It had not pleased Sir Dene to give him any profession: perhaps he had all along intended (seeing his aptitude for it) to make him useful on the estate: or perhaps he did not care to send Tom away from him. When Tom left school, Dell was in failing health; and the lad at once took upon himself a portion of his duties, helping him all he could. It was only natural that on the bailiff's death two or three years afterwards, Tom should slip into the place. There had been no regular appointment of him by Sir Dene—as had been the case with his father, Geoffry; but Tom was the bailiff to all intents and purposes.

The Lady Lydia, though not cordially approving this, did not actively oppose it. There was no longer any motive for wishing to banish Tom Clanwaring. He had been effectually *put down* in the house, and was too insignificant to trouble her: but the idea did dimly cross her mind, she could not tell why or wherefore, that it might be as well for him not to be the overseer of the land. Perhaps she thought it might give him power—a hold on the place. Therefore she advised Sir Dene not to keep Tom at home, but rather give him some calling, profession, or occupation, out in the world. For once Sir Dene did not listen to her. There was nobody so fit to be on the estate as Tom, he said: look how he had been robbed and imposed upon, especially since Dell had been less able to attend to his business: Tom was, so to say, a born farmer as poor Geoff had been; he had got his head on his shoulders the right way, as Geoff had, and would take care of things as he did: who else was there, he finally put it to my lady, that was capable of looking after his interests in this way, save Tom?

Who else was there? She put it to herself, and the answer came—none. And yet, instinct did seem to foretell danger in Tom's becoming this permanent fixture. In vain she appealed to her two sons; pointing out that it might be better worth while for one of them to take this post than to toil upwards in their respective professions. Jarvis was simply astonished, somewhat as John the heir had been on a similar appeal once before. Jarvis stroked his black moustache in supercilious incredulity. *He* an overlooker! *he* taking upon himself the office of bailiff! He asked his mother whether she had lost her senses. Reginald civilly replied that he knew nothing about land and its management—which was true —and that his tastes and wishes lay in quite a different line of life. So Lady Lydia dropped the point, and Tom went on with his duties unmolested. He had nothing to do with the accounts; Sir Dene had kept those himself for many years.

Thus, with all his business lying out of doors, it will readily be understood how easy it was for Tom's estrangement from the family circle to be taken as a matter of course by Sir Dene. It was often one of convenience or necessity: and he would hastily eat what he wanted in the housekeeper's room and be off again. Except on Sundays, Tom did not much trouble the family: if by chance he dressed himself and went in, he got cold looks and contemptuous silence for his welcome. His business with Sir Dene was transacted in the bay-parlour: and the latter would sometimes say, "Can't you manage to be a bit more with 'em, Tom?" Tom never said why he did not. If Lady Lydia or her oldest son met Tom out on the land, they passed him with the indifference they would have accorded to any of the men. As to Tom himself, he had grown up to be just what his childhood promised. Truthful, honourable, upright, generous: of singularly modest and pleasing manners, patient-natured, sweet-tempered, altogether of sterling worth and goodness. Mrs. Owen had lived long enough to do her work efficiently, and to see the excellent seed she had sown strike firm root in his mind and heart.

Harebell Farm had had another master for some years now. Mrs. Owen lay by her husband in Hurst Leet churchyard (though, if popular gossip might be believed, *he* did not lie quietly, even yet), and William Owen had migrated into Dorsetshire. Philip Tillett occupied Harebell Farm. It was well known that Randy Black's vexation was excessive when he found the farm had been ceded privately to Mr. Tillett. Some friend of Black's, with a good amount of money and apparently respectable character, had been looking out for it —for the fact that Owen entertained thoughts of leaving had oozed out—and Black openly said it was a mean trick Sir Dene had served the public. However, the "trick" was one that nobody had power to undo. Mr. Tillett went into the farm, and told Black to his face that if he saw Robert Owen's ghost every night of his life, it would not drive him off it again. Nevertheless, in spite of his brave assertion, it was observed that Mr. Tillett did not put himself much in the way of the grove of trees by the two-acre meadow after dark, which that supernatural figure with the silver beard was wont to haunt in the moonlight. Not that there was any authentic or recorded history of its having been seen for some few years past now. And that is enough of retrospection.

It was a green Christmas: bright, lovely, almost as warm as spring: and as the congregation turned out of Hurst Leet church, they congratulated each other on the fine weather as much as on the festive day. Everybody had walked to church: there was no necessity to bring out carriages on such a day as this.

Everybody, except one: Sir Dene Clanwaring. Hale as of old, though his years had long passed those allotted as the age of man, he had a weakness in his limbs that rendered much walking, or exertion of any kind, difficult. As he stepped from his pew, allowing most of the congregation to depart first, Lady Lydia held out her arm, and he took it. She counted more than fifty years now: but she was tall and meagre as ever, looking the scarecrow she always did, her face worn and sharp, her small black eyes grievously restless. But that it was very much the natural expression of her face, one might have said some inward torment troubled her. Sir Dene's pew had been full that day, for all his grandchildren had come to the Dene for Christmas. They might be seen, most of them, wending their way homewards beyond the churchyard.

Close by the waiting pony-carriage, stood a young, slender, gentlemanly man. His fair, fresh Saxon face, with its fine frank features and good-natured, deep blue eyes, was something strangely pleasant. Those who were old enough to remember Geoffry Clanwaring could never need to ask who it was, the likeness was so great. He had waited, he so tall and strong, to assist his grandfather into the carriage and drive him home—as he had driven him in coming. But Lady Lydia turned about impatiently, looking for some one else to do it.

"Take care, Tom, the other leg up."

"Shall I drive you, sir?" asked Tom, when he had carefully placed him in: for reared in the habits of complete submission, he never presumed to put himself forward even to do a service, without first asking leave.

"Ay, do: my hands are cold."

Lady Lydia interposed. She pushed Tom aside: not rudely, but with cool, indifferent hauteur, and stepped in herself. He did not appear in the least resentful; he had been used to nothing but this contemptuous indifference always; and he arranged her petticoats under the warm rug with as much assiduous attention to her comfort as he had evinced for that of Sir Dene.

"I was not aware you intended to go with Sir Dene yourself, Lady Lydia," he remarked, his tone one of courteous apology.

"There, that will do," she said, cutting him short. "Give me the reins."

"No," spoke Sir Dene: who retained all his old detestation of being driven by a woman; and who would rather have had his grandson by his side than her. "Give them to me, Tom. I shall drive, myself, Lydia."

With a flourish of the whip, and a cheery bow to the few villagers and peasantry who had stayed to watch the departure, Sir Dene drove on, Tom lifting his hat to Lady Lydia with as happy a smile as ever sat on man's face yet. Do not mistake him, or think this courtesy to her put on—as in truth it well might have been, considering all things: but the frank sweetness of Tom Clanwaring's nature was such, that he had genuinely kind looks even for her. Sir Dene's progress was not a quick one: many acquaintances were waiting for a word or a handshake, and the pony was pulled up continually. Tom's long legs soon got ahead of it: and he overtook two ladies; mother and daughter, as might be seen by the likeness: nice-looking women with pretty features and complexions of delicate bloom: but the young lady's face was pleasanter than her mother's.

"Mrs. Arde, I wish you a merry Christmas."

Mrs. Arde turned at the greeting. "Is it you, Tom Clanwaring? Thank you. I wish you the same."

Her tone was not a cordial one. The best that could be said of it was that it was coldly civil. Liking Tom in her heart as much as ever, a certain thought had startled her lately, and caused her to treat him very distantly: it might have been supposed that she was taking a lesson out of the Lady Lydia Clanwaring's book. Miss Arde did not speak to Tom at all: but as she glanced up shyly, there shone a smile of welcome in her rich brown eyes, and the rose-bloom deepened to carnation on her dimpled cheeks.

Tom just touched her hand. "And a very merry Christmas to *you*, May," he said in a low tone.

The little carriage came rattling up. "What has taken

Arde that he was not at Church to-day?" called out Sir Dene, as he checked the pony.

Mrs. Arde went round to the baronet's side. "Oh, Sir Dene, I am sorry to say that he is ill. It is one of his bilious attacks. We left him in bed."

"In bed!" echoed Sir Dene. "That won't do at all, you know, Mrs. Arde. We dine at five sharp. He must not fail us."

"I hope not. He expects to be better by that time."

Lady Lydia's keen glances were taking in everything—as they had a habit of doing. Tom Clanwaring was talking to Miss Arde: and she noted that the young lady's eyes were cast down as she listened, that her face was flushed to a beautiful crimson. My lady drew in her thin lips: she did not like the signs any more than did Mrs. Arde. But at this moment there came up one from the opposite direction, one who could always dispel the gloom on Lady Lydia's face—her eldest and best beloved son.

Two peas never were more alike than Jarvis Clanwaring and his mother: not a bit of the Clanwaring was there about him in looks. Tall, lean, dark, he had the same thin compressed lips as hers, the shifty black eyes. His black moustache was fierce, even for a soldier, very fierce indeed for those days when such an adornment was uncommon, and he had altogether a worn, dissipated air. But Captain Clanwaring was popular with his friends and the world. A serious attack of illness had entailed a long leave of absence to recruit health, and he passed his time agreeably between London and Beechhurst Dene.

"Jarvis," began Sir Dene, the tone a peremptory one, "why were you not at church to-day?"

"I overslept myself, sir."

"Overslept yourself! Well, I don't know. I asked after you half an hour before I came out, and Gander told me you were up, and letter-writing in your room. I choose that everybody about me shall attend church on Christmas Day. I thought you knew that."

Jarvis Clanwaring slowly raised his hat in response, by way of cutting short the discussion. A keen observer—which Sir Dene was not, and never had been—might have detected some covert scorn in the action. With a hearty adieu to the ladies, and telling them not to be late for dinner, Sir Dene drove on.

One little incident may be mentioned of the drive home. At

the turning to the road, Dene Hollow, Sir Dene drew the right rein, and kept the pony on the straight road—the old, long round. "Oh pray don't go that way, Sir Dene!" interposed Lady Lydia with fractious haste, "I want to get home. Take Dene Hollow." A shade of annoyance crossed Sir Dene's face; but he complied, and let the pony take the way he had wished to avoid. Slowly he drove now, at a snail's walk: gentle though the ascent was, Sir Dene Clanwaring had grown to *dread* Dene Hollow.

Meanwhile Jarvis and Tom Clanwaring continued to walk along with Mrs. and Miss Arde. In a line at first; but as they turned off to the narrow path, the nearest way to Arde Hall, they had to separate: Mrs. Arde in front with Captain Clanwaring, Tom and May behind. The Lady Lydia, bowling on in the direction of Beechhurst Dene, mentally saw the position as surely as Mrs. Arde saw it. It did not continue long: at the entrance to the enclosed grove belonging to the Hall, the ladies wished the young men good morning, and the latter went on.

Walking in silence. Captain Clanwaring never wasted superfluous words on Tom the scapegoat: Jarvis was twenty-seven now, Tom twenty-four. Tom's intelligent eye was noting all points as they walked, with the quiet air of one who knows every inch of the land. The officer looked out straight before him, seeing nothing: buried in thought was he, and not pleasant thought. Thus they came in view of the rural lodge where Tom was born, and Maria, his pretty mother, had died. Simmons the gamekeeper lived in it now. Jarvis pointed to it with a wave of his hand.

"Go across and tell Simmons I shall want him to go out with me betimes to-morrow morning. And to mind that he brings my own gun this time."

There was supercilious command in every tone of the voice, in every gesture of the raised hand. Tom Clanwaring turned off with the obedience of a child: he had been *made* to know that Jarvis and Otto were as his masters. Half-way through the trunks of the bare trees, a thought caused him to halt.

"*To-morrow* morning, Jarvis?"

"I said to-morrow morning. Can't you hear?"

"But to-morrow will be Sunday!"

"Well?"

"Sir Dene would not like it. Only think if he heard the guns!"

"I want none of your remarks, Tom Clanwaring. Do as you are told!"

And Tom went to do it.

Lady Lydia Clanwaring, her bonnet and shawl thrown off, met her son in the hall when he entered. Clutching at his arm, as one who is in anger or pain, she drew him to the fire —a large bright fire of wood playing in the hearth of the hall. Standing there, ostensibly warming her hands before going in to luncheon, she spoke to him eagerly and impressingly; but so quietly that Gander, who happened to pass, never saw that her lips moved.

"Every hour of your existence you vex me, Jarvis! Why are you not more cautious? You fly in the face of Sir Dene's prejudices in the most foolish, reckless manner possible. To think that you should have stayed away from church!"

"A man, worried as I am, has no fancy for church or for anything else," returned Captain Clanwaring in a half-indifferent, half-sullen tone. "As to studying the old man's prejudices—whether I study them or whether I don't, it seems to come to the same thing: no money. Have you asked him again?"

"It's not likely. Were I to enter upon business matters to-day, he would only stop me. Jarvis, indeed I don't think I shall be able to get it. I have had so much money from him for you that I am driven to my very wits' end to invent excuses for its use. I can't say it's for Louisa this time, because she's here, and he might question her himself: neither can I say it is for Otto, for the same reason. In these scarce visits that Otto pays us, I am kept in a state of chronic terror, lest the old man should speak to him and discover that he knows nothing of the sums of money he is supposed to have drawn. Otto was always so inconveniently truthful, you know."

"He is a close, steady-going muff. I know that."

"Try Dene again."

"No good, mother. He told me yesterday I had bled him once too often: and meant it too. The goose is killed in that quarter."

"Well, Jarvis, I only speak the truth when I tell you that I believe it will not be possible for me to get you this money that you want. Sir Dene suspects, I think. He is not so cordial with you as he used to be—and you do nothing to conciliate him. Why were you not at hand to drive him to church and back?"

"Because I didn't go myself," was the cool rejoinder. "I *must* have the money; I cannot do without it. It would bring ruin and double ruin."

There was a pause. Captain Clanwaring lifted his shapely boot—in dress he was one of the greatest dandies going—and pushed a falling log on to the blazing hearth. His mother thought what a handsome leg and foot it was.

"Why don't you make better play with Mary Arde, Jarvis?"

"*Why* don't I! You must ask that question of herself, my lady. She is a vast deal more inclined to make play with the goat than she is with me. I suspected it when I was down here last."

"Ridiculous!" replied Lady Lydia, her tone one of passionate irritation. "That is perfectly absurd, Jarvis; and you know it. *He* mate with Mary Arde! The very idea is an outrage on social decency."

"I know that she likes him. And that she does not like me."

"Don't talk so loud. I tell you you might as well accuse her of a liking for her father's bailiff as for Tom Clanwaring. What else is he but a bailiff? You——what do you say, Jones?" broke off Lady Lydia, as a servant came out of the dining-room, and spoke.

"Luncheon is waiting, my lady; and Sir Dene is asking for you."

Lady Lydia gave a final rub to her hands over the blaze, and went into the dining-room. But when the man said "Luncheon is waiting," he used a figure of speech. Sir Dene never waited luncheon for anybody, and he had nearly finished now. It was only simple fare: they had breakfasted at nine, and would dine at five. The table appeared to be crowded, but Lady Lydia's place at its head was left vacant. Dene the heir sat at it and his brother Charles, pleasant-looking slight young fellows, hardly out of their teens. Otto was there; a dark, short man of twenty-six, steady looking enough to have had his barrister's wig on his head out of court as well as in it. Louisa, the wife of Colonel Letsom, and her three little ones, Sir Dene's great grand-children, completed the party. Captain Clanwaring looked out for a seat.

"You young ones must sit closer together," remarked Lady Lydia in rather a cross tone, for she could not bear that her favourite son should be put out in the very smallest degree.

"They might have taken their luncheon upstairs, Louisa: they are going to dine with us. Make room for your uncle Jarvis."

"You can have my seat, Jarvis," interposed Sir Dene, rising and catching up his stick to leave the room. As Jarvis sat down, ill-humoured as usual, he said something about hoping the dinner-table would not be as crowded, for it was possible one or two of *his* friends might be dropping in.

"The dinner-table is always large enough when we know how many are to be at it," said Lady Lydia. "Of course it will be full to-day. In case of an unexpected guest arriving late, Tom Clanwaring must eat his dinner below."

"I'll be shot if he shall!" exclaimed young Dene, with all the authority of the baronet's heir. "It is Christmas Day, Aunt Lydia, and Tom shall have his place at table for once, as well as the rest of us. It's not often he gets it."

Lady Lydia, cutting a piece of cake, cut it so sharply that the plate nearly came in two. Dene began again: he and Charles both liked Tom.

"No. If Tom's place at table is filled up to-day, he shall have mine. It would never do for *him* to be absent. What would Mary Arde say?"

Dene threw out this little shaft mischievously: he had his suspicions of many things, and privately hoped that Tom would in some magical manner get May, rather than cross-grained Varges. My Lady's green cheek turned a shade greener: and it is a positive fact that in moments of annoyance her pale, putty complexion, took a tinge of green. At this juncture, in came Tom.

Nobody moved, nobody made room for him. Dene began ordering the children to sit closer, "two of you on a chair," but Tom settled the matter by lifting one of them, taking the chair himself, and putting the child on his knee. Social, cordial, ever sweet-tempered, it was impossible for children to help loving Tom Clanwaring: and the little thing laughed in glee, and put her fat hand up to stroke the smiling Saxon face.

"Did you see Simmons—and give him my message?" demanded Captain Clanwaring of Tom, without the superfluous courtesy of looking at him.

"Yes."

"What did he say?"

"I'll tell you by-and-by, Jarvis."

CHAPTER XXIII.

SIR DENE'S REPENTANCE.

Sir Dene Clanwaring passed a good deal of his time now in his chamber, or in the small sitting-room next it. He was a different man from what he used to be: since he had been unable to take long walks in the open air, but was confined much of necessity to his chair or sofa, there was less of open, easy indifference in his manner, more of silent care. Advancing years and infirmities brought serious thought in their train: and events had helped it on.

Strange though it may seem to have to say it, stranger still to believe it, but it is nevertheless true, a great remorse, repentance, grief—call it what you will—had seized on Sir Dene Clanwaring. And for what? For having made the road, Dene Hollow. In the lapse of years that we have skipped, and of which no record has been taken, accidents had continued to occur occasionally: and cautious people preferred to go the old round way, rather than use it. But in all the mishaps that had taken place there, only one had been fatal: and that was to the granddaughter Sir Dene so fondly loved —Margaret Clanwaring. A conviction seized hold upon him that the death of this fair young girl was nothing more than a retribution on himself, sent direct from Heaven.

Sir Dene had surely sent the Widow Barber to her grave earlier than she would have gone: he had grown to see the fact clearly, and it came home to him in these later years with a great remorse. He never spoke of it: but the shadow of it lay on his mind always—just as the other Shadow was said to lie at times on the unlucky road. The poor widow was more often in his mental eye than he would have liked to confess: not as he had first known her, the hale red-cheeked little woman stirring actively am'dst her milk-pails with her more than seventy years on her back; but as he had happened to meet her a few days before she died: hollow of face, sad of eyes, wasted to a shadow. Sir Dene remembered that he had turned to look after her in some doubt, debating whether that worn woman *could* be Mrs. Barber.

Bending forward from his arm-chair in the room above, on this Christmas afternoon, his hands clasped on the top of his stick, his blue coat off and a loose one on, sat Sir Dene, thinking of this; and of some other things that annoyed him, but in a less degree. Lady Lydia came in to disturb him. Lady Lydia was wont to boast in a quiet way of her influence over Sir Dene—that she could "turn him round her little finger." In truth he yielded very much to her sway, for he hated contention, and loved to be at ease more than ever. The wish to get Tom Clanwaring away from the Dene, which had lain in abeyance for so many years, had sprung up anew of late in my lady's heart: the interests of her dear son, Jarvis, were rendering Tom's absence from the place, as she believed, imperatively necessary. Jarvis must secure May Arde and her twenty thousand pounds to get him out of his terrible embarrassments: it would never do for Tom to stand in the way. There was no fear of Tom's *marrying* Miss Arde: their relative positions forbade that: but Tom was a remarkably good-looking young fellow (though it went against the grain for my lady to acknowledge, even mentally, that fact), and he and the young lady seemed to be on the best of terms. If she got a fancy into her head that she liked Tom, she might —why yes she might—reject Jarvis. To guard against this, Tom must quit the neighbourhood; and not continue to see more of May while he stayed in it than could be helped. Turning these things about in her mind, Lady Lydia quite determined, as a preliminary, that Tom should not sit down to the Christmas dinner-table that evening when May would be present. At least, if any clever scheming of her own could prevent it.

Stirring Sir Dene's fire into a blaze, she took a chair opposite him, and began talking of a subject that was sure to excite Sir Dene's ire—poaching and poachers. There had been more trouble from that cause on the estate this winter than was ever known before. Night after night these marauders came about in the most audacious manner; and with impunity, for they had never once been caught. Randy Black was suspected to be the ring-leader; and Sir Dene had gone the length of causing the Trailing Indian to be searched: but no game was found. In talking of it now, Sir Dene, as usual, grew excited, and said this should be done, and the other should be done; my lady agreeing in all, and suggesting measures on her own score. Thus the afternoon wore away.

After luncheon, Captain Clanwaring had gone out somewhere, returning home about half-past four o'clock. Tom Clanwaring was standing by the hall fire when he came in, and took the opportunity of telling him that Simmons refused to attend him on the morrow.

"What the devil do you mean?—or does he mean?" demanded the captain.

"What he said to me was this: that he'd not go out shooting on a Sunday for anybody, neither would Sir Dene allow him. You cannot expect the man to do it, Jarvis," added Tom in a tone of reason. "Putting other considerations aside, it would never do for the guns to be heard in our woods on a Sunday."

Jarvis swore a little—at Tom for his gratuitous opinion, and at things in general. Saying that he would soon teach Simmons what it was to disobey *him*, he strode off with a furious step: and just then, down came my Lady Lydia from Sir Dene's room. Advancing to Tom, she told him it was Sir Dene's pleasure that he and the gamekeeper should be on the watch that night in the oak coppice.

Tom Clanwaring verily thought she must be saying it for a joke. Gander had not lighted up; and as he scanned her face by the light of the fire, he enquired whether she was not mistaken.

"Not in the least," she decisively replied. "Something has come to Sir Dene's knowledge about the poachers having laid fresh gins and snares in the oak coppice: it has put him out worse than anything yet. This evening, when all the world are supposed to be indoors, making merry, will be their opportunity, he says; and you and Simmons are to go at once on the watch. With the best haste you can make, starting now, you and he will not get to the oak coppice too early. There's not a minute to be lost."

"But Sir Dene does not wish me to go now?—before dinner?" cried Tom, wondering more and more. For Sir Dene was a man who not only liked to enjoy his Christmas dinner heartily himself, but chose that all about him should enjoy it.

"Sir Dene wishes you and expects you to go at once," was the emphatic rejoinder. "It has not come to the pass yet, I hope, of your disobeying *him*."

"I have never disobeyed him yet, Lady Lydia, or wished to do it," was the young man's answer, as he turned to the staircase. "I am ready to obey his wishes now and always."

My lady stopped him with a peremptory question.

"What do you want upstairs?"

"To change my coat."

She glanced at Tom's clothes, that sat so well on his

graceful figure: and mentally allowed with a grunt that they were not quite the things to go a watching in.

"Take care that you don't disturb Sir Dene," she crossly said. "He is trying to get a little nap before dinner."

Tom nodded and ran lightly up. But just as he was passing his grandfather's door, the baronet opened it and saw him.

"Is that you, Tom? What's the time?"

"It wants about twenty minutes to five, sir."

"Is it so late as that? Come in and help me to get my coat on. We shall have Arde here. I begin to think sometimes, Tom," added the old man as they crossed the sitting-room to his bed-chamber, "that I shall be reduced to the effeminacy of taking a valet in my old age. My legs and arms won't serve me much longer."

"Make a valet of me, sir. You might let me help you more than I do."

"I don't like to give in, Tom; that's it; I have waited on myself all my life. Sit down at the fire while I wash my hands: you can put the water out for me. You are ready yourself I see."

"Ready for what, sir?" asked the young man, not quite understanding.

"Ready for what? Why, for dinner."

"But I—I can't dine to-day, sir," said Tom impulsively.

Sir Dene took his hands out of the water, and turned round to stare at Tom.

"Why can't you dine?"

"There's no time, sir. I am going on the watch with Simmons at once."

"What for? Where to?"

"The oak coppice. As you desire."

"Going on the watch with Simmons!" repeated the baronet, a great wonder on his fine old face. "On the watch on a Christmas night! No, no, my boy; nobody belonging to me does that. What put such a thing in your head?"

"Lady Lydia has just told me———" Tom Clanwaring stopped. He was a true gentleman at heart; ay, and a true Christian, too, though some in the world, reading this, may laugh at it. Not even in this case, barefaced though he at once saw it was, would he take his own part at the expense of others. But Sir Dene was looking at him, and he resumed.

"That is, I understood Lady Lydia to say you wished me to go with Simmons this evening. Perhaps she misunderstood."

"You must have misunderstood between you. Send my

people on the watch on a Christmas night!" reiterated Sir Dene. "I'm not a heathen."

"Lady Lydia talks of fresh gins in the oak coppice. What have you heard, sir?"

"What I've heard will keep, Tom. She ought not to have begun about it to-day; she knows it is a subject that worries me. *She* heard it; I didn't. Jarvis picked it up somewhere out of doors, she says. Any way, it must be left till Monday. There: let it drop. See if you can give my hair a brush. I must have got a touch of rheumatism in this arm, Tom; it's painful since morning. The driving home from church did me no good. Priar talks of strained muscles—but I fancy it's rheumatism."

Tom had brushed the white hair and helped on the coat, when there came a smart knock at the door, and Lady Lydia entered. Sir Dene at once began about the misunderstanding, telling her she ought to have known better than to suppose he should allow any of his people, whether grandchildren or retainers, to go out on the cold watch on a Christmas night.

Tom Clanwaring quitted the room: of no use now to wait to assist his grandfather downstairs: my lady took care that Tom should never assist him in any way, when she could help it. Scarcely had he gained the hall when he heard himself called to. My lady was following him; her face white with anger, her restless eyes ablaze with pride.

"How *dare* you carry tales to Sir Dene?" she hissed—and really her harsh voice was often very like a hiss. "You! a dependent, a serpent—for that's what you are—*you* presume to interfere and try to set aside my orders—and Sir Dene's!"

"You are mistaken, Lady Lydia. I did not intentionally———"

"Be silent, sir; I will hear no lying excuses from you. As you are afraid of a little night cold for yourself and Simmons, you may go and share his hearth with him this evening. You don't dine in my presence. One of us must be absent from the table; you or I."

"Very well, Lady Lydia. I will not intrude upon you."

He went straight out at the front door. Really with no purposed intention, but in the minute's vexation. Generous-tempered though he was, patiently submissive as he had been trained to be, he could feel anger at times when the oppression or injustice was unusually great. And Mary Arde would be at the table that he was thrust from!

Would she! A few paces from the door he encountered a footman. Tom recognised him in the evening's darkness for one of the servants at the Hall.

"What is it, Mark?"

"My mistress has sent me up with this note, sir. The Squire's quite unable to come out this evening. They are very sorry it should have happened so."

"Are none of them coming? Not Mrs. or Miss Arde?"

"No, sir; they intend to dine quietly at home," was the man's reply, as he went on with the note.

"I'll go and ask them to give me some dinner," quoth Tom to himself, his blue eyes brightening with an amused smile, his heart giving a great leap in its happiness. "All happens for the best."

Whether the love that existed between Tom Clanwaring and May Arde—for it's of no use to disguise this ill-omened fact any longer—would have sprung up had they been always on the original terms of intimacy, cannot be told. Perhaps not: the liking for each other might have continued to be more like that of fond brother and sister. Not that Miss May had ever pretended to be fond of Tom: she had teased him and tortured him at will, like the capricious little damsel that she was. When May was growing up, Mrs. Arde had a serious illness, and the doctors ordered her abroad. She went with her husband and daughter, and they were away nearly three years. Three years will make great changes, you know, in people's looks as well as in other things. Tom was three-and-twenty when they met again as strangers; May turned nineteen: she saw a most attractive man, tall and strong and noble; he saw a sedate, modest young lady, with a shy and sweet face. That first interview sealed their fate: from that time they were as passionately in love with each other, as ever man and woman can be in this world—and that's saying something. Never a word of it had been spoken by either: Tom Clanwaring, remembering his position, was of too honourable a nature for that: but each knew quite well how it was with the other. There was about as much chance that Tom, poor and prospectless, would be allowed to win her, as there was that he might win the moon. Each was contented to leave the future to itself: as long as they met daily, or almost daily, the present had bliss enough.

And so, this last year, since May's return, things had gone on quietly and happily. That they would not continue so to

R

go on much longer, certain signs were telling. Matters seemed to be approaching a crisis in more ways than one. Captain Jarvis Clanwaring was getting into deep water—was in it, indeed—and there appeared to be no way of extricating him but by some grand coup-de-main; such as espousing a wealthy heiress. The heiress was at hand, and a very charming and lovable heiress too; and Captain Clanwaring made no end of visits to Beechhurst Dene on her account. But there was one curious fact—he did not seem to make much way with her. To Lady Lydia this had been utterly unaccountable until quite recently—when the horrible fear had suddenly suggested itself that May loved the scapegoat—the name he had gone by amidst them for years—the miserable, despised dependent, Tom Clanwaring. Somehow Mrs. Arde was catching up the same fear: possibly it had been craftily awakened by Lady Lydia, for we rarely see these things for ourselves. Mrs. Arde was not at all sure about it. She thought it next door to impossible that Mary could be so much of an idiot.

Tom, laughing outright at the turn affairs had taken that evening, walked on to the Hall. He knew quite well, if nobody else did, that my lady's motive for banishing him from the dinner-table was because Miss Arde was to be at it. But, for once in a rare way, Tom had won and my lady lost. Tom knew that the persecution, renewed of late, the under current of effort that was at work again to drive him entirely from Beechhurst Dene, arose from my lady's fear that he was standing in the way of Jarvis. He could afford to laugh, he thought: whatever the result might be as to himself, he felt assured that May would never have anything on that head to say to Jarvis Clanwaring.

When Mr. Arde had found in the afternoon that he grew no better, a dinner was hastily prepared at home: his wife and daughter declining to leave him. He had these bilious attacks often, and would look as sallow as a guinea while they lasted, which was sometimes three days. Mrs. Arde wrote the note to Beechhurst Dene, and sent to ask the Miss Dickercens to come in and dine at the Hall: two middle-aged neighbours, cheerful and talkative; who were made all the more of because they had lost the greater part of their fortune. The party was in the act of sitting down to this dinner, Mr. Arde included, when Tom walked in. Every one looked surprised to see him: May blushed scarlet.

"Will you give me some dinner, sir?"

"If you want it," returned the Squire. "And welcome. Anything the matter at the Dene?"

"I have offended Lady Lydia—no unusual thing, you know, sir—and she forbids me to sit down with them. I thought—as it was Christmas Day—perhaps you and Mrs. Arde would take me in."

He spoke in a half-jesting, half-serious tone. The servant put a chair for him next May: the Miss Dickereens sitting opposite, in the warmth of the fire. The Squire's spirits went up: Tom's good-looking face and kindly nature seemed to impart a new element of cheerfulness to them all. George Arde had always liked him from the time he held the little unconscious infant in his arms by the bed where its mother was lying cold and dead, and poor Geoffry sat in a chair against the wall sobbing. The Squire, who had only come into the dining-room to carve, protesting he could not touch a bit, ventured on a morsel of turkey. It tasted so good that he took a larger piece, and then another, and another. His aching head seemed to grow better as if by magic, and he soon felt as well as ever he had in his life. These impromptu meetings are often more gay than premeditated ones. Have you ever observed this? It was the case here. You remember the remark of the good old Vicar of Wakefield in reference to their last-recorded merry meeting: "I don't know whether we had more wit amongst us than usual, but we had certainly more laughter." The laughter at the Squire's table that night might have been heard half way to Hurst Leet. Every countenance was happy, every heart at rest: even Mrs. Arde forgot her semi-doubts, and yielded to the genial and happy influence of the moment. It was one of the merriest Christmases spent that day within the three kingdoms: an evening to be recalled with a thrill; an hour that would stand in the memory as one of unalloyed pleasure, amid the stern realities, the dull cares of later years.

"What was the matter at home this time?" asked Mary of Tom confidentially, when they had a moment to themselves at the end of the drawing-room. "Did my lady really forbid your sitting down to table?"

"She said that either she or I must be away from it. Of course it left me no choice, May."

"But why?"

"Well, the ostensible reason was that I had carried tales to my grandfather—which of course I had not. The real reason was, that she did not want me to be at dinner."

"But why?" again questioned Mary.

"Well, she—she had her own reasons, I conclude," was Tom's not very satisfactory answer, a smile playing about his mouth.

Did Mary guess at the reason? Faintly, perhaps. Her face wore a blush.

"Tom," she softly said, glancing up through the shade of the long brown eye-lashes, "I can't bear Lady Lydia."

"Now, May, that's what I call ingratitude," was his laughing answer. "She says she *adores* you."

"Does she! But, Tom, if I were you I'd not really quarrel with her. She might send you away. I know she's trying for it."

"I know it myself. Sometimes I think she'll do it."

"Would you like to go?"

"Well—no. I'd rather stay where I am. On account of my good old grandfather."

Had it been to save his life, he could not have helped the expression that momentarily escaped his blue eyes meeting hers. It quite plainly said that there was some one else also he would like to stay for. Mary's heart fluttered fifty ways in its sense of happiness.

"What are you thinking of, child?" asked Mr. Arde of his daughter, when their guests had departed, and he was lighting his bed candles.

For Mary seemed buried in a profound reverie. She woke out of it with a start at the question.

"Papa, I was thinking how very happy we have been to-night. I was wondering if anything could ever look cloudy again."

Meanwhile the dinner and evening had progressed at Beechhurst Dene. Not so merrily. Sir Dene was out of sorts: the children were troublesome, allowed to take up nearly all the attention—a very mistaken and unpleasant thing at all times to everybody except themselves and their unwise mother. The friends Captain Clanwaring had said might drop in, did so: two of them getting over from Worcester in a gig. Both were, as Jones, helping Gander to wait at table, expressed it, "millingtary." The one, Major Fife, was at least fifty years of age: and there was something about his height and uprightness, in his clearly-cut features, ay, and more than all, in the long, flowing silver beard he wore, that put Sir

Dene strongly in mind of Robert Owen, dead nearly five-and-twenty years before. Gander was so struck with the likeness as to be excessively discomposed, for it brought to the man's remembrance that long-past night of his great terror in Harebell Lane. The resemblance was certainly remarkable; but the expression of the two faces wholly different: for while Robert Owen's had been good and winning, Major Fife's was that of a roué, bad altogether. Sir Dene had heard of him as a hard drinker and hard player; in short, as bearing not too reputable a character in any way, especially since he quitted the army. The other, Lieutenant Paget, seemed an inoffensive and rather a simple young man. But Sir Dene was not pleased that Jarvis should have taken upon himself to introduce these men to his table that evening; he did not care that entire strangers should join the family dinner on Christmas Day. The baronet was of course civilly courteous to them, as in duty bound to be; but his manner had no cordiality in it, and he was very silent. That, or the absence of the Ardes, or something else, undoubtedly threw a gloom on the meeting. They were half through dinner before Sir Dene noticed the absence of his favourite grandson. Ay, and in his heart he *was* the favourite, little as my lady or any one else might suspect it.

"Where's Tom?" he exclaimed.

No one answered. He repeated the question loudly and sharply. Lady Lydia could no longer affect not to hear.

"Oh, Tom? He has gone over to Simmons's, I believe," she carelessly said.

Sir Dene laid down his knife and fork. "To Simmons's!" he repeated, every feature of his still fine countenance hardening to stern expression. "What has taken him there on Christmas night?"

"His low tastes, I conclude," was her hardy reply. "He has that kind of taste for such company, you know, Sir Dene."

"If he has, my lady, it is thanks to you, for it was you who first drove him out to frequent it," was Sir Dene's retort. But nevertheless he felt bitterly vexed at Tom, for absenting himself from dinner on Christmas Day.

Nothing more was said then. In the drawing-room Lady Lydia took occasion to speak a few words in Sir Dene's ear. She intimated that it was *Tom* who had wanted to go and watch in the oak coppice; that he was disappointed at not spending the hours with Simmons, whose company he preferred, and so had gone off to do it at his home. Sir Dene, angry and vexed, went to bed in the belief. He was not feeling well that evening, and disappeared even before the children.

A slight incident occurred to Tom Clanwaring as he came home, which may as well be mentioned. Hurst Leet clock was striking eleven when he turned in at the Dene gates: the air was clear, though not cold enough for what is called seasonable Christmas weather, and the sound of the strokes came up distinctly to Tom's ear. Rather to his surprise, as he neared the house, he saw a gig standing before the front door. One of their own grooms was in it, apparently asleep.

"What's this gig here for, James?" he asked of the man.

"It belongs to two gents as come over from Ooster* to dinner, sir," replied the groom, waking up. "Friends o' the Captain's, Gander says. And don't I wish they'd come out," he added partly to himself. "Stuck in this gig for an hour or two's spell, bain't the work for a Christmas night."

"When all the rest are making themselves comfortable," said Tom, with good-humour.

"That's it, sir," returned the groom, intensely aggravated. "There they be, a roomful of 'em; men and maids, a-drinking hot punch round the fire; and Gander a-telling of 'em stories about Injee."

The picture of comfort was so vivid that Tom would not disturb it. Intensely considerate of others, both by nature and because he had been trained to be, was Tom Clanwaring. Instead of ringing a peal on the hall bell, that must have brought forth Gander or one of the others, he turned to go round to the back door, which was never fastened until the last thing. He was just emerging from the privet-walk, the door in view, when a tall young person, showing a profusion of light curls under her bonnet, came in his way. It was Miss Emma Geach,—whom we have not met since she was a child.

"Why, Emma!" exclaimed Tom. "Is it you? Do you want anything?"

"Hush, please!" she said, sinking her voice to a whisper. "I was only waiting to—to speak to one o' the servants, Mr. Tom."

"Which of them is it?" he asked, insensibly dropping his voice to assimilate with her tones. "Shall I call—"

---

* Worcestershire patois for Worcester.

"No, I don't want you to call nobody," she quickly interrupted, as if the proposition startled her. "Go on your way and take no notice on me please, Mr. Tom. If he comes out, I shall see him: if he don't, I shall just run back home wi'out it."

The sound of the whispering penetrated to the grove of trees (bare now) at a few paces distance: and Dene Clanwaring and his cousin Otto strolling about to smoke, looked out to see who might be thus covertly talking. Emma Geach drew back behind the privet hedge to hide herself: Tom went on to the drawing-room.

Jarvis, his two friends, and Lady Lydia were at whist when Tom entered, looking—they could but notice it—rather particularly radiant.

"Hope you have enjoyed your evening with Simmons!" sarcastically spoke Mrs. Letsom. Like Sir Dene, she had thought it very bad taste, even of Tom, to abandon the home party.

"With Simmons!" cried Tom in surprise. "I have not been with Simmons, Mrs. Letsom."

"No! Well, I thought it curious that you should go there on a Christmas night," she rejoined. "Where have you been, then, Tom?"

"Dining at the Hall."

"Where? What?" sharply asked Lady Lydia, in a kind of shrill scream.

"I have been dining with the Ardes, Lady Lydia. A right merry evening we've had. The Miss Dickereens were there."

Grave as a judge was his face as he told it: never a ghost of a smile did it wear, to betray that he knew what the announcement must be to her. She made no answer; only bit her quivering lips. The captain threw down his cards, as if something stung him, and his eyes wore an evil look as he turned them full on Tom Clanwaring.

CHAPTER XXIV.

SENT TO THE TRAILING INDIAN.

MONDAY morning. The week seemed to be inaugurating itself rather gloomily for some of the inmates of Beechhurst Dene. At least, if the countenances of my Lady Lydia and

Captain Clanwaring might be any criterion. Gloomy enough was the aspect of each, in all conscience; cross too. My lady was sitting a little back from the library window, in the shade of the delicate green brocade curtain. The room was as charming as it used to be: renovated from time to time, the prevailing features and colours of its furniture were always retained.

Gazing on outer things as one who sees them not, was Captain Clanwaring. A suspicion of frost lay on the grass of the park, the trees looked bare and bleak. He had been telling Lady Lydia once again that he *must* have money, and immediately; and she had returned him the same answer as on Christmas Day—that she did not see how it would be possible. In truth he had more need of it than even his mother knew—for he did not tell her of various little items that were pressing him amidst greater ones. They were passing through his own mind as he stood. Major Fife's visit on Christmas Day, independent of partaking of a good Christmas dinner, was to press Jarvis for a certain debt of honour, lost to him in London. The major had made the journey from London to Worcester to get it: and was staying there at a great cost at the Hop Pole. Jarvis was owing some money up at Black's at the Trailing Indian, and *that* was pressing. Miss Emma Geach's appearance in the privet-walk on Christmas night was, in point of fact, owing to this: she was waiting in the hope of seeing Captain Clanwaring—in spite of her plausible excuse to Tom. About these two items of debt he said nothing to my lady: but rather enlarged on certain claims he owed in town, and the terrible embarrassment *they* brought him. Which was only too true.

Jarvis Clanwaring was one of those men who cannot, or will not, keep out of debt. His tastes and pursuits were of a nature that must inevitably bring debt in their train to a poor man—ay, and to a rich one. As to curbing his inclinations—his expensive horses, his fine clothes, his dinners, his betting, his gambling—such a course never entered his mind. Where was the good of having a baronet for a grandfather, who must possess pots of money laid by, unless he was of use to you, the Captain was in the habit of arguing with his friends. There was only he who wanted help. Young Dene and Charley had money enough of their own. Otto made what he earned at his profession do for him, did not spend a fraction more, and troubled nobody. Jarvis's private opinion was, that Otto must live upon five shillings a day. Perhaps he did. Close, prudent, hard-working Otto Clanwaring was the one to make both ends meet, however small the means might be. Jarvis had once got twenty pounds out of him. Driving down to Old Square one day in a friend's curricle, Jarvis had told a tale of some temporary need for twenty pounds; and Otto let him have the sum, relying on his promise of honour to bring it back on that day week. "Sly dog, that Otto; he's putting by already," was Jarvis's comment—and he had never repaid the money from that day to this. Otto had left off asking him for it. Jarvis had money from young Dene more than once; "bled him," he called it. Dene had grown wary now, and refused to lend another stiver: he was not yet of age, and only had his allowance. In short, all sources seemed closed to Jarvis, except Sir Dene's. Sir Dene had helped him so much in response to open applications, that he would lend no more. In point of fact, he had helped him far more than he had any suspicion of, through the contrivances of Lady Lydia. That lady would get money from Sir Dene—ostensibly for herself, for Otto, for Louisa Letsom. It was always for one or the other, as she told Sir Dene: whereas, in point of fact, every coin went into the yawning pocket of Jarvis. There seemed to be no end to it, Sir Dene had recently told her—and added that he strongly suspected she must be assisting her elder son in secret. So my lady might well assure the captain that for the present she was unable to do more. It was not at all a bright state of affairs, and each one tacitly acknowledged it to the other, on that wintry morning.

"Jarvis, it is as I have told you," spoke Lady Lydia. "You must make play with Mary Arde."

"And don't I do it—and mean to do it?" fractiously retorted Jarvis: who was just as undutiful to his mother in manner and speech, as it is the pleasure of some of these idolized and indulged sons to be. "I shall go in for her now in earnest."

"Of the twenty thousand pounds that will be hers on her wedding-day, ten of it will be settled on her; ten will go to her husband, if he be a man they like—Mrs. Arde told me so much. Some of that loose ten thousand will set you straight."

Set him straight! Ay. Jarvis Clanwaring drew a deep

breath, and his face took a bright look as he thought of it. The mines of Golconda could hardly have seemed to him fairer and richer.

"Twenty thousand pounds on her wedding-day, and a large provision for life besides," continued Lady Lydia. "Of course Mary will come in for the Hall as well, and for the whole of her father's fortune. A prize worth striving for, Jarvis."

Yes. Jarvis felt it to his heart's core. And he liked Mary for herself besides. A prize worth any strife, any sacrifice.

"I shall not let her slip, you may rest assured," he said aloud. "But, don't you see that I must contrive to go on smoothly until that time comes? Were my embarrassments to leak out, old Arde might fight shy of me."

She did see it. Looking up at Jarvis, she told him she saw it.

"Well, then, for that reason, if for no other, I must have money."

"It is all very well to say 'must,' Jarvis. But how?"

He turned from the window in some agitation, lifting his hand to give emphasis to his words.

"Mother! as surely as that you and I are talking here together,—as surely as that we shall eat our dinner to-day,—as surely as that we shall some time *die*, what I say is truth: if I do not get money between now and this day week, some inconvenient things will come out to the world. I cannot put it more forcibly."

"What things?"

"What things! Why, obligations that I owe. Liabilities. Debts."

"You have been frightfully imprudent, Jarvis."

"A man of the world is obliged to be," carelessly remarked the captain. "But a steady-going dromedary like old Arde might not allow for that. I think he'd not. Once let him get an inkling of the state of my exchequer, and I fancy he would cut up rough."

"He and Mrs. Arde both like you, Jarvis. She especially does."

"And to retain their liking, I must keep my name clear. Don't you see it?"

Oh yes again, she did see it; she saw it in all its truth and force. Sitting on in silence, she bit her compressed lips.

"There's no excuse I can invent that would weigh with Sir Dene, Jarvis. It is not a fortnight since I had money from him ostensibly for myself: and I cannot say it is for Louisa or Otto while they are both here. There's no other way. He has taken to settle the house-keeping bills himself —through Gander."

"Gander be smothered!" said the captain gloomily, straying a little beside the mark. "You will have to say it is for me."

"It would not avail," she quickly answered. "At least— I don't think it would. He told me to my face that he believed the last money was for you, and it was high time your extravagance was checked. Jarvis, I think this—if you don't mind, he will be warning Squire Arde himself."

"No!" uttered Jarvis, aghast at the suggestion.

"Well, I fear he might. It is just an idea of mine. I must have time to think this over, Jarvis."

Captain Clanwaring, stretching himself, strolled away, leaving her to do it. Half way across the room he turned to say something.

"There's the second trouble—that cursed scapegoat. He must be got away somehow or other. Dining at the Hall on Christmas Day; drinking tea there yesterday—it won't do, you know. He and May were coolly pacing the beech avenue together for an hour in the afternoon. The idea of there being anything between them is preposterous; too contemptible to speak of: he would never dare to lift his eyes to her, nor would she stoop to him: nevertheless, he will be better out of the way than in it." Jarvis reasoned exactly as my lady reasoned, you see: their instincts were the same.

"Leave that to me," was the careless and yet assured answer of Lady Lydia. "I've got it in hand."

And well in hand, too.

Jarvis, cramming his pipe with tobacco, lighted it, kept it in his mouth unheld, by some habit of dexterity, and strolled out at the side door, his hands in his pockets. A more miserable mood than his could not well be. It was absolutely necessary that he should have money, to avoid—well, he hardly knew *what*. Exposure, for one thing. If my lady failed in getting this money for him, he would be reduced to the necessity of selling his commission.

Brooding over these troubles, he had got as far as the gate opening to Harebell Lane, and was leaning his arms upon it, puffing away, when Tom Clanwaring came up the lane with a quick step. The contrast presented by the two was remarkable; Jarvis, an idle, lounging, smoking, pale, dissipated dandy; Tom, fresh, active, upright, striding along in his worn velveteen coat and splashed top-boots, as if he had all the work of the parish upon him, his fair Saxon face bright and beautiful to look upon. The one was a worker, the other something worse than a dreamer.

"I'm not sure but we shall have snow, Jarvis," spoke Tom cordially, as he went by.

"Snow—ah!" responded Jarvis indifferently. "Do you happen to be going past the Trailing Indian?"

"No. Why?" continued Tom, halting.

"I wanted a note left there. For Black."

"A note—for Black!" echoed Tom, in surprise: wondering what Randy Black and the fastidious captain could have in common.

"About tobacco," Jarvis condescended curtly to explain. "Can you take it for me?"

"Yes, if you like: it won't be much out of my way," responded Tom, with his usual cheerful good-nature. Jarvis handed him the note from his pocket, and Tom went on.

Sir Dene had kept his bed all day on the Sunday, with the rheumatism in his shoulder, and Mr. Priar came up to see him. Tom went in twice, and was received coldly: Sir Dene, who had not been enlightened as to the truth, retained his anger at Tom's having gone (as he thought) to Simmons's instead of staying at home to dine. He was too angry to reproach him: for one thing, his shoulder was in great pain, and my lady had been flinging in a little edged shaft or two against Tom.

To-day, Monday, Tom was very busy out of doors. His post as overlooker was the great barrier Lady Lydia had to contend with in her newly taken-up resolution to drive him off the estate. Remembering the instinct that had hazily warned her against his thus remaining, she thought how true it had been. The arrangement had worked well hitherto, separating in a wide degree the poor scapegoat from his kith and kin: and but for this awakened fear in connection with Squire Arde's daughter, Tom Clanwaring might have stayed as he was, unmolested, till Doomsday.

"Don't make quite so much noise, Emma. Please don't, there's a good girl!"

"If thee kicks up that there clatter, I'll shy this blessed brush at th' yead. D'ye hear, wench?"

The pleading appeal came from Mrs. Black; the rough one from her husband, who caught up a short hearth-brush that happened to lie inside the fender, as he spoke. They were sitting on either side of the kitchen fire, objects to look upon. Poor Mrs. Black, a helpless cripple now,—indeed, the extraordinary wonder was that she had lived so long,—looked a shadow, not a woman; her small, meek face, with its perpetual glance of terror, was weary, shrunken, piteous. In point of condition, Black did not look much better than his wife: he was worn almost to a shadow too: though he had not been fat at the best of times. His countenance had acquired an anxious, uneasy expression, and his eyes a restlessness, as if he were always waiting for some unpleasant surprise. People accounted for it curiously: they said Black lived in perpetual fear of seeing Robert Owen; that the fear of it tormented him. Just now Black was really ill: a week ago he had taken a violent inflammation on his chest, necessitating Mr. Priar's attendance, and was in some danger. The danger had passed: he could sit up: but he was more ill-spoken and irritable than when in his usual health. And that need not have been!

The reputation of the Trailing Indian and of its landlord, had not materially improved with the course of years. The mysterious trade in smuggled and stolen goods, midnight hearses, and the like, had dwindled away; but there was more of poaching carried on than ever. Somewhat perhaps of smuggling still; for nowhere could there be found such brandy and tobacco as Black's. The men who had helped in the other work had died off one by one; Michael Geach, the last of them, some five or six years ago. As to Mrs. Geach, she disappeared entirely from English society at a remote period, and was supposed to be in Australia. And Miss Emma had remained, a permanent legacy, at the Trailing Indian: Mrs. Black kind to her, Black generally swearing at her.

Emma Geach had grown up just what she promised to do: a tall, fine, very good-looking girl, as impudent as she was high. Her fair face and profusion of light hair, which was really beautiful, gained for her much outspoken admiration from the frequenters of the Trailing Indian, which was sometimes conveyed in broad language. Emma Geach took the admiration as her natural due, and for the rest, she responded in kind. Never backward was she at retort; no matter what its nature, she was equal to it. A bold girl, undoubtedly, by instinct as well as from circumstances, and the neighbourhood did not speak too well of her. Not that any absolute charge had been brought against her until quite recently, when gossip had begun to say that there was palpable cause for scandal, and respectability picked up its skirts against contact with hers in the road. A laughing, bustling, capable young woman as to household matters, was she, quite the right hand of the Trailing Indian, and getting through more work in an hour than poor Mrs. Black had ever accomplished in a day.

But she was always noisy with it. This morning—washing up the Sunday plates and dishes—which she had chosen to leave over till the Monday—she made clatter enough for ten: one might have supposed the crockeryware was being broken continually. Standing at the sink at the end of the kitchen, a small tub of hot water and bucket of cold before her, she rubbed the grease off the plates with a dish-cloth in the hot water, plunged them for a moment into the cold, and put them, wet, in the rack above.

"I shall ha' done soon," was all the notice she took of the remonstrances given her: and went on with as little regard to peace as ever. Her cotton gown was pinned up round her under the coarse apron, her arms were bare, her shoes were down at heel in a slatternly fashion; but her very light eyes glistened with almost unnatural brightness, and her hair, as just said, was profuse and beautiful. Miss Emma was proud of it; and if she did not always keep her shoes in tidiness, she kept *that* so.

"Have Priar sent up that there dratted physic?" demanded Black, after a fit of coughing.

"Not as I've seen," replied Emma.

"Then you'll go off down and fetch it."

"As soon as I've got these here things i' the rack," said Emma, with ready acquiescence—for she liked going out better than any recreation in the world.

At this moment in came Tom Clanwaring, bringing the note to Black. Tom was, so to say, quite at home with the inmates of the Trailing Indian: he would often run in to say a kind word to poor, miserable, suffering Mrs. Black, or have a chat with Emma. The acquaintanceship, begun in the old days over the whistle, had never ceased. Tom the child, taught to look upon himself as an irredeemable vagabond by my lady and her children, saw not so much difference between himself and the other vagabond, Emma Geach. He of course learnt better later, but he was by far too good-hearted to entirely "cut" Miss Emma. Tom liked the girl very well, and on occasion had done her many a good turn in shielding her from Black's furious passions. Emma liked him too; what's more, she respected him—and that's saying a vast deal for impudent Emma Geach. Black on his side, from some cause or other, had been always tolerably civil to Tom, and was rarely surly with him as he would be with other people.

"Don't break the plates, Emma," said Tom in his open, off-hand manner, as he went into the midst of the noise.

"Thank you for telling of me, sir," returned she—her answer always ready.

Tom laughed. "I've brought you a note, Black," he said. "Captain Clanwaring asked me if I'd leave it with you."

Black's hungry fingers grasped the note as if it were something good to eat: and Emma Geach glanced at him sideways, a sharp, inquiring look in her light eyes. Tom sat down on the table to speak to Mrs. Black.

"Wait till he comes down from Lunnon again!—not if I knows it," broke forth Black, when he had torn open the note and read the few lines it contained. "It's the money I wants, and the money as I'll have. Promises 'on't do: folks knows what *his* be, and I knows it. Mr. Tom Clanwaring, you——"

"Does Captain Clanwaring owe you anything for tobacco?" interrupted Tom, wondering at the man's excitement.

"Well—yes, he do owe it me; it is for 'bacca," rejoined Black, after a pause, and a hard stare full in Tom's face. "He comes in here when he's down at the Dene, a saying he can't get 'bacca like mine nowhere not all over Lunnun, and runs up a heavy bill for 't—and 'stead o' handing o'er the money, sends me excuses and these here notes."

"I thought the note had been to order some," returned Tom. "He said something about getting no tobacco like yours, when he gave it me."

"The note is to say as he can't pay me the money he promised to bring up here o' Christmas Eve," said Black, deliberately and savagely. "You tell him, Mr. Tom Clanwaring, as I says——"

"I cannot carry back any message concerning it," interrupted Tom, not choosing to interfere in Jarvis's debts. "Captain Clanwaring saw me coming up this way, and asked if I'd leave the note: but you must send your answer to him yourself, Black."

Black growled some indistinct words under his breath—a wheezy and short breath to-day. "When's the Captain a going back to Lunnun?" he asked aloud.

"Not yet, I fancy. In two or three weeks, perhaps."

"And in two or three days I hope to be on my out-o'-door legs again, and I'll be on to him. Captain Clanwaring hain't a going to play with Randy Black. He needn't think for to——"

Black's menace was cut short by the entrance of some customers demanding ale. A shooting party, sporting in the neighbourhood, who had become thirsty over their work. They came trooping into the kitchen with their guns: Otto Clanwaring and his cousin Dene the foremost of them, Simmons the hindmost. Tom laughed, jumped off the table, exchanged a few words with his relatives, and then went off on his morning's business.

"Be thee a going for that there physic, or bain't thee?" savagely demanded Black of the girl, as his customers disappeared: for their entrance and exit had brought in a rush of cold air, and set him coughing frightfully.

"I be a going now," she answered, swilling the last dish in the cold water, and pushing it, splashing, into the rack.

"Thee'll put away the muck first," roared Black.

The "muck" meant the tub and the pail and the dirty water. Black need not have reminded her. With all her failings, she was a tidy housewife.

In a coarse red shawl—or, as it was called then, "whittle,"—and a smart bonnet, and shoes up at heel, Emma Geach started. It was she who did all the errands, for there was no ostler kept at the place since the death of the one who had been there so long—Joe. If by chance a stray horseman rode up to the inn, Black himself attended to the steed. Miss Emma was not accustomed to hurry herself when on these errands: and Black was often well-nigh inclined to strike her for the delay. It made not the smallest difference—if she felt inclined to stay out, she did stay out.

Hastening down Harebell lane at full speed, she came to a sudden stop at Beechhurst Dene gate. Captain Clanwaring was leaning over it still. Reviewing gloomily his difficulties, financial and otherwise, he had never moved from the place.

"Where are you off to?" asked he, taking the pipe from his mouth.

"He have sent me down to old Priar's for his physic," replied the girl, her naturally free tone having become almost shrinkingly timid.

Jarvis looked at her. The light eyes, generally glittering with a peculiar kind of hard brightness, had taken a soft, pleading look; the cheeks were rosy with a delicate flush. Never had Emma Geach looked prettier than at this moment.

"He is in a daze o' rage," said the girl. "The night afore last, nothing 'ud do but I must go up to his bed-room—he'd heard me come in, and shrieked out for me like mad. When I stood it out that I'd not got to see you cause o' visitors at the Dene, and so couldn't deliver his message about the money, he roared out at me 'twas a lie."

"I've sent him up a note," said Jarvis.

"It haven't done no good," said the girl. "He swears he'll have the money whether you've got it, or no. He said it out before Tom Clanwaring."

Jarvis, who had begun to puff at his pipe lest it should go out, glanced up with a start. "Before Tom Clanwaring! Black's a fool."

"No harm," returned the girl. "Were it money owing for 'bacca, says Mr. Tom a thinking, he says, as the letter were only to order some. Yes it were money owed for 'bacca, says Black, after he had stared a bit in t'other's face. Tom Clanwaring took it in. Good-bye," added Miss Emma suddenly, as the voice of the tenant of Harebell Farm, Philip Tillett, was heard on the other side his hedge, talking with one of his labourers: "Good bye t'ye." And she went on at a fleet pace. Jarvis Clanwaring sauntered indoors, finishing his pipe. Lady Lydia, writing a letter in the library, when he got in inquired whether he had been to Arde Hall.

"No," returned Jarvis, in his most sullen manner.

"But I thought you were going there this morning, Jarvis."

"Time enough."

"Look here, Jarvis: you must make good play with Mary Arde if you are to win her," returned Lady Lydia in as urgently serious a tone as woman can well use. "Don't waste the time—don't waste the shadow of a chance. Go you down at once, and call there."

It was not bad advice. Captain Clanwaring brushed

himself up a little, so as to look more of a fascinating dandy than before, and started.

Alas for human hopes! for human contrarieties! Miss Mary Arde descried the approaching visitor from a window, and made a precipitate retreat to her own room. Mr. and Mrs. Arde were out, and her maid came up to summons her. It was Susan Cole still. But Susan grown into a middle-aged woman.

"Captain Clanwaring, Miss May."

"I can't go down to him, Susan," said Miss May, colouring violently; "I won't go."

"But I told him you be at home," remonstrated Susan. "He's a waiting for you i' the drawing-room. You must go, Miss May."

"I tell you I won't go," persisted the young lady, fond of taking her own way as she had been when a child. "I *won't*. There. Let him come again when mamma's at home."

Susan stood in a dilemma: she liked her own way also. "What excuse be I to make for ye, Miss May? After saying as you was at home!"

"Oh, say anything," carelessly returned May.

"It's uncommon bad behaviour," debated Susan, standing her ground. "I can't go and tell him as you *won't* come down."

"Say I am ill. Now you go, Susan."

"That's a fine thing, Miss May—inventing a illness at a pinch! He'll know it's nothing but a excuse."

May laughed pleasantly. She rather hoped he would.

"I'm sure I can't think of nothing to say," obstinately persisted Susan, pushing back her cap.

"Say I've got the mumps, Susan. My compliments to Captain Clanwaring, and I'm sorry not to be able to see him; but I can't talk, from an attack of mumps."

CHAPTER XXV.

MISS EMMA GEACH.

THERE was discord at Beechhurst Dene. Christmas week —that is the week following Christmas—is generally regarded as one intended to be social and festive; but this one at Beechhurst Dene was especially unpleasant. The days, as they went on were full of discomfort; each day worse than the last. The Lady Lydia seemed to be doing her work well—that of getting Tom Clanwaring out of the house. Not only out of the house and neighbourhood did she intend to send him, but out of the country. She was devoting her whole energies, her great influence, to the task. Circumstances favoured her in rather a remarkable degree, as will be seen presently: they were to favour her more ere the week should be out. Dissension reigned. It was the whole household against Tom, and Tom against the household. Some insults were put upon him that stung him into retort. Petty charges were brought against him: trifles in themselves, but magnified into grave offences by the manner in which they were repeated to Sir Dene Clanwaring; and in these might lie just enough of truth to render them plausible, and, at any rate, hard to disprove. Graver charges were soon to be whispered—and Tom might not have been able to refute them, even had the opportunity been allowed him. But it was not.

Sir Dene was keeping his room. Full of pain both of mind and body, he was more irritable than he had ever been known to be. His anger against Tom, for having absented himself and gone to Simmons's (as he was led to think) on Christmas evening, rankled within him. He felt too vexed, too proud, it may be said, to speak of it to Tom: and Tom, knowing nothing, and suspecting nothing, could not, of course, refute it. Be you very sure Lady Lydia did not—and therefore the false impression remained with Sir Dene. The new feeling against Tom was augmented by these other charges: they rankled in the baronet's mind also: and there was great discomfort. Never for a moment was Tom allowed to be alone with Sir Dene: Lady Lydia with her specious contrivance managed that—and nobody suspected there was any contrivance in it; least of all, Tom.

One day Tom was stung into retaliation. He was insolent to Lady Lydia; he retorted on Captain Clanwaring; he took something like a high tone with his grandfather. The lion within him was aroused at last; the patient bearing of years, the calm enduring, gave way before a moment's passion. It was his grandfather's changed manner to him that stung him into this—not the insults of the others. Had Sir Dene brought any specific charge against him, Tom could have answered it quietly: but nothing of the kind was done; and, all the young man knew and saw was, that his grandfather at length turned against him, out of, as it seemed, very caprice. But the grievous state of worry this disturbed condition of things kept Sir Dene in can be better imagined than described.

The private arrangements Lady Lydia had been engaged in succeeded. They were now complete, ready to be acted upon; and she disclosed the matter to Sir Dene. She had been negotiating with some of her relatives in Ireland, and had got Tom an appointment there to manage the land of a large estate. It was really a good post of its kind, and the salary would be fair. To a young man seeking an opening in life it certainly was an opportunity not often to be met with.

Nevertheless, Sir Dene turned a deaf ear. The very idea of Tom's leaving Beechhurst Dene startled him.

"I'd not like it, my lady," was his short, imperative answer. And by the words " my lady " it might be known that he felt resentment to her, rather than gratitude.

She was not to be put down for that. She pointed out how excellent the chance was, how fitted Tom was for the post, and how great the returning peace his departure would bring to the Dene. She had even found a man able and willing to replace Tom on the estate—one Mr. Weston: a humble cousin of the Miss Dickereens, who would be glad of the post.

But no: Sir Dene wholly negatived it. Dining at the gamekeeper's on Christmas Day, and turning on the household since when they quarrelled with him, did not constitute sufficient offence to entail banishment, he said. Lady Lydia sighed and bit her lip, mentally telling herself that she must have a little patience yet, but that, *go* Tom should. Little did even she think how very soon it would be.

There's an old axiom—that people rarely accomplish any great amount of evil alone. Two certainly can do more harm than one. Wild beasts hunt in couples. It takes two to quarrel and fight; it takes two to make an evil bargain. When a man commits a murder, or a succession of murders, the first public thought is—he must have had a helping companion. Thus, in the ill-odour that latterly had attached itself to Miss Emma Geach, the discerning neighbours had been not so much asking whether she had a helpmate in ill-doing—that went for a matter of course—as speculating who that helpmate might be. Whatever it was she had done, or was suspected of—whether she poached game, as Black did, or robbed a house, or set a church on fire—the fact of her having had an aider and abettor was very sure and certain.

Public curiosity was always on the whet as to who this other might be: and the untoward circumstance, that no one in particular could be fixed upon, was, to say the least, mortifying. Harry Cole, the farrier and veterinary surgeon—a good-looking, fairly well educated man, who had succeeded to his father's business—would be talked of one day; Sir Dene's groom, James, the next; a smuggling acquaintance of Black's who was often at the Trailing Indian, the third, and others; but when the utmost grounds of suspicion attaching to any one of these men came to be summed up, it was found to consist of one sole fact—that they might be seen on occasion openly talking and laughing with Miss Emma. Not quite enough this to justify an accusation of arson, or what not. So that, in point of fact, the tantalised public considered themselves ill-used in the matter, and kept their eyes and their curiosity agape.

Seeing Tom Clanwaring perched on the table at the Trailing Indian, familiarly located there with Mr. and Mrs. Black and Miss Emma, would have been nothing: young Dene might have done as much himself, for he had just the same sociable kind of nature, for sitting on tables, or elsewhere, as Tom: but taken in conjunction with the private meeting and whispering between Tom and Emma Geach on Christmas night, that both Dene and Otto had been a witness to, it looked like something. The interview in the grove wore all the appearance of a secret one, of premeditation: and if young Dene joked a bit about the look of things, and Otto nodded assent in his steady manner, it was not to be surprised at. They had taken up the notion that Tom might have been the man who had helped to—fire the church, let's say. Not that he *was;* they did not go so far as that; only that he might have been. Certain things were laughed and joked over more freely in those days than they are in these; were, in fact, regarded as but venial errors. Dene talked and laughed about it indoors: and soon the only members of the household to whose ears the new suspicion had not penetrated, were Tom himself, Lady Lydia, and Sir Dene.

Strange to say, the sole one to reprove was Jarvis. "Hold your foul tongues!" cried he, savagely. "Any way, it's no concern of yours." Which reproof only set Dene laughing worse than before. And thus the week progressed, each day bringing more of discomfort and drawing matters nearer to a crisis. On the Thursday, Dene the heir and his brother

Charles took their departure for Scotland, to spend New Year's Day with their mother.

Friday came in, a morning bright with sunshine. The snow, threatened on the Monday, had cleared itself off without falling, and the weather was really lovely. Somewhat frosty; but calm, fresh, and clear.

Talking together over the low gate of the narrow side avenue leading to Arde Hall, stood Tom Clanwaring and the Hall's heiress; she inside, he out. As he was passing up from Hurst Leet, she happened to be there, in her scarlet-hooded cloak and white muff, the hood of the cloak drawn round her bright face and bright brown curls. Fashions changed less capriciously then than they do now—or perhaps economy made things last longer. Tom's mother had worn just the same kind of cloak; but the cloaks had not gone quite out, even yet. There they stood: Tom oblivious of his business, May of the passing of time.

"I'm so glad he's better," said May, alluding to Sir Dene —for Tom had been telling her that his grandfather was downstairs again. "Mr. Priar came in to tea last night, and was talking about him. He thinks he is changing so very much."

"He has certainly changed in the last few days, for he has been irritable with me without cause—that is, when he notices me at all," replied Tom. "For the most part he turns his head away from me, and when I speak gives me short and snappish answers."

"Have you offended him?" asked May.

"I suppose so: but I cannot imagine how. Altogether I have not had a pleasant week of it, May. They are trying me tolerably hard just now."

He laughed as he said it. Sunshine was always in his heart, let be what would. The young make light of troubles, May Arde's sweet brown eyes sparkled brightly in sympathy.

"When people are ill, they feel cross without knowing why, Tom. I suppose Dene and Charley have gone?"

"They started yesterday morning."

"I like Dene. Charley too, for that matter. But I like Dene better than—yes, better than anybody else at Beechhurst Dene," she added, casting a saucy glance at the handsome face bending towards hers. "Dene is always—oh Tom, look here!"

A clatter and commotion in the road caught her ear, and the glittering silver of the sumptuous Clanwaring liveries caught her eye. The Beechhurst Dene cortége was approaching at a gallop. It was the custom then to pay morning calls in more state than royalty observes now. Two outriders rode first; and then came the large carriage with its four horses, and the postilions' jackets laced with silver, harmonizing with the liveries of the outriders and the two standing footmen behind. Sir Dene did not drive four in hand. Tempted by the fineness of the day, my Lady Lydia had come out visiting: her daughter, Mrs. Letsom, sat next her, Jarvis and Otto opposite.

"Tom, I do *believe* they are coming to the Hall!" cried May under her breath.

Even so. The outriders took the sweep round that would bring them to the carriage entrance, running nearly side by side with the narrow beech avenue. Knowing, or suspecting, the feeling obtaining in Lady Lydia's mind towards them, both Tom Clanwaring and May might have preferred to get out of sight, had there been means of doing it; but the trees were bare in winter, affording no shelter. As the carriage swept round like lightning, almost close to them, Tom lifted his hat to Lady Lydia and Mrs. Letsom. My Lady answered the courtesy by a hard stare.

"What a pace they are going at!" exclaimed Tom. "Shall you have to go in, May?"

"I must. Of course, I must. Tom, he has been here every day this week," she cried in impulsive agitation, her bright eyes lifted for a moment, and then cast down again. "Every blessed day, as Susan phrases it. And mamma is beginning to like him so very much!"

"Every day, has he," returned Tom, pushing back the breast of his velveteen coat, as if he were too hot.

"I would not come down to him one day: Susan was in such a temper over it. Papa and mamma were out, and so I could do as I liked. When's he going away to join his regiment again?"

"*I* don't know, May. He will have to do it soon, I should imagine, or else leave it altogether."

"I'm sure he has got up his strength quite enough now."

"Strength?—Oh, it's not that, May. There's an attraction in the way. If he joined his regiment, he could not come down here at will."

May understood quite well—that she was the attraction. Deep in thought now, she was looking away, seeing nothing.

"I *wish* I had not any money of my own!" she whispered, really more to herself than to Tom. "It's that miserable twenty thousand pounds of mine. Perhaps he'd not care for me without that. If my dear little sister had but lived, it would never have been mine."

"True," said Tom.

"Susan Cole used to tell me when I was naughty that Master Tom—meaning you—would never care for me as he did for that little sister," went on the young lady.

"Did she?" said Tom, a great merriment in his deep-set blue eyes, so marvellously beautiful. "I loved that child dearly: I remember it still. I must have been very old when she died, May: nearly four."

"I *must* go; or they'll be sending for me," cried Miss May, shrinking from the expression of the said eyes. "Good-bye. To-morrow's New Year's Day, you know. Don't forget it."

"No danger," replied Tom Clanwaring. "Good-bye, May."

An ordinary shake of the hands, and away went Tom, striding quickly to make up for lost time.

"New Year's Day," that May had reminded him of, implied a meeting. A meeting for them. Just as it had grown into a custom for the Ardes to eat their Christmas dinner at Beechhurst Dene, so had it for the Clanwarings to dine at the Hall on the first day of the new year. If nobody else looked forward with a heart-spring to the morrow's festive gathering, the two who had just parted did. Parted reluctantly—for they would have liked to linger away the whole morning together.

Rather surprised was Tom, upon going up Dene Hollow, to see a few people congregated there; half a dozen, or so. A cart had come to grief on nearly the old unlucky spot. It could not this time be charged on the "Shadow." The linchpin had disappeared from one of the wheels: and the cart, which had contained grains (on their way to be conveyed to Mr. Tillett's pigs), was overturned. The sweet-smelling grains lay scattered on the highway; Hodge, Mr. Tillett's waggoner—for the cart was Mr. Tillett's—standing by with a most rueful face.

The accident had occurred just as the Beechhurst Dene cortége was passing; it had startled the carriage horses, and sent them flying downwards at such a rate as to put the outriders to the gallop, and threaten another accident. Lady Lydia, ignoring chances, always went the way of Dene Hollow when she could: its level road and fair scenery were pleasant to her.

"Which accounts for the sharp pace they came round at," thought Tom, as he listened to this, and recalled the speed of the horses.

Leaving the cart and grains to their unhappy fate, he pursued his way, and turned into Harebell Farm. Not to tell of the disaster particularly, but because he had some business with its master, Philip Tillett. Mr. Tillett, however, was not at home, and Tom stayed a few minutes talking with Mary Barber.

For Mary Barber, the thoroughly capable and earnest-minded woman—somewhat hard and superstitious though she might be—had never quitted Harebell Farm. William Owen did not want her when he migrated to his new home: he meant to marry, and did do so shortly afterwards: and Mary Barber remained with Mr. Tillett and his motherless young daughter. She was called housekeeper, but was treated and respected as one of the family; having two maids under her, instead of one as in Mrs. Owen's time. When Tom went in she was seated in the parlour, hemming a white cravat of Mr. Tillett's.

"Bless my heart!" she exclaimed, staring at Tom through her tortoiseshell-rimmed spectacles when he told the news. "The wheel off, and all the pigs' food a-lying in the road."

"Every grain of it," said Tom. "Cole's man had got the wheel in hand, beginning to tinker it up."

"The wheel bain't much. The grains is the worst. And for you to be a-laughing over it, Mr. Tom!"

"Oh, they'll get the grains up again. You'd laugh yourself, if you had seen it, Mary Barber. Hodge's face was better than a picture."

"There's no luck with our pigs this year," lamented she. "I said so to the master the other day. That last lot o' wash made for 'em got put into a new painted barrel, through one o' the men's carelessness, and a'most poisoned the pigs."

"Only not quite," put in Tom, always looking on the sunniest side of things.

"Well now, Mr. Tom—what caused the mishap to-day?"

"Why, I told you, Mary. The wheel came off the cart."

"'Twarn't that, sir."

"But it was that," returned Tom, looking at her.

"*'Twarn't* that," came the emphatic repetition. "'Twas the Shadow."

"Nonsense! Rubbish!"

The retort nettled Mary Barber. The Shadow was there, and would be always there, she said solemnly: and she put it to him plainly whether horses were, or were not, in the habit of starting at that place. Tom, half laughing, confessed they were, saying no more about the cart-wheel, intending to drop the argument altogether. Not so Mary Barber. Laying down the cravat and her spectacles on the table, she bent her face a little forward.

"What is it that frightens the animals, pray? Tell me that if you can, Mr. Tom."

"I'm sure I don't know," said Tom, "unless it's the shadow of the branches, cast on the road by the sun."

"It's not that, sir; you must know it's not. The Shadow's one of another sort. I give it a different name in my own mind."

"What name?"

"A curse."

"A curse!"

"A curse," she repeated, in her solemn tone. "Why, what else is it, sir? Hasn't it been as a curse to a good many folk? Sir Dene coudn't have thought it nothing less when he saw his blooming grandchild a-lying dead afore him."

Tom made no rejoinders now. His cousin Margaret's sad death had indeed brought grievous sorrow. To none worse than to him. To him, who had been the one to pick Margaret up.

"We thought it was the ice that made the horses slip. There was ice on the road, you remember, Mary Barber."

"Bother the ice," irreverently responded Mary Barber. "'Twas the excuse made, I know: but who believed it?"

Very few, Tom might have answered—had he chosen. Mary Barber resumed, her voice impressive again, hardly raised above a whisper:

"That time when my poor mother spoke to me o' the Shadow—dying she was, though I didn't see it—it sounded but like so much gibberish in my two ears. But that I knowed her to be sane, I'd ha' thought her mind was a-rambling. The next day, when she was dead, the words come back to me in a different way: for I've been a good deal with the dead and dying, Mr. Tom, and I know that what they speak just afore the soul departs is sometimes like a prophecy. And as I stood at her grave i' the churchyard while the parson was reading the bur'al over her out o' the Prayer-book, and thought o' what it was that had sent her to it afore her time, there come into my mind a kind o' light. A light o' conviction, one might call it: that mother's dying words were true —and that a curse lay on the fine new road that had killed her. It's a lying there to this day."

The less superstitious and more practical among the neighbours were apt to smile at this fixed belief of Mary Barber's, and call it her "crotchet." Her master, Mr. Tillett, a man of good sound sense, told her to her face that she would go mad upon the foolish point some day, if she didn't take care. Perhaps Tom Clanwaring shared Mr. Tillett's scepticism, for he took up his hat to depart without comment of any sort.

"Tell the master I'll look in again to-morrow, Mary Barber. If he'll consent to make the alteration, Sir Dene will go halfway in the cost. But we must have an answer. Good day."

Meanwhile the Lady Lydia paid her visits, a round of them. Mrs. Arde's was the only one near home; the rest lay at a distance. While the afternoon was still bright, the outriders came cantering round the corner by Cole the farrier's, and took the old hilly road that led to Beechhurst Dene, the nearest way from whence they were coming. The carriage followed close upon the outriders; and my lady, inside it, felt tired to death. As it whirled round the corner—rather a sharp turn, that, by Cole's—two people stood talking outside the forge—having met accidentally a minute or two before. Tom Clanwaring was one; his occupation had taken him to some land that lay out there: the other was Miss Emma Geach. A traveller, whose horse became suddenly disabled, had ridden in for refuge at the Trailing Indian, and the girl was despatched to fetch Cole. Nothing loth, she: especially as she seized on the opportunity to attire herself in her Sunday-going things.

A gay gipsy hat upon her abundant hair, gleaming and glistening in the winter sunlight, and some blue ribbons flying amidst it, stood she. Otto Clanwaring looked from the carriage and made some remark to his brother in a low tone. Not so low, however, but that its sense struck on the ear of Lady Lydia.

"What?" she exclaimed. "What's that you say, Otto?"

He answered by a light word or two, as if the matter he spoke of were of no serious moment. Assuredly he did not do it in ill-nature. "I don't affirm it, you know," he said: "but appearances certainly are against Tom."

Ay, they were, unfortunately. A dusky red light, telling of emotion, shone in my lady's dark face: she leaned out and looked back. Tom was striding onwards then, and Miss Geach was exchanging compliments with Cole. The disclosure struck her quite as a revelation. She had shared the curiosity of the public as to the doings of Miss Emma Geach. Otto would have dismissed the subject with a few careless words.

"What are your proofs, Otto?" she asked, leaning forward to speak in his ear.

"Proofs? Oh, I don't know about proofs," was the answer, still carelessly indifferent. And then he just mentioned what he and young Dene had seen.

My lady was virtuously indignant—of course. To do her justice, she believed the story: and began talking of it in private with her eldest son when they got home.

"Let it drop," said Jarvis, curtly.

"Drop!" she retorted. "I'll let it drop when I have told Sir Dene. He can let it drop if he will."

"Confound it, madam! can't you hold your tongue!" savagely cried Jarvis.

"No, I can't, Jarvis. This was just what was wanted to get the fellow away."

"Eh? what?" returned Jarvis, a sudden gleam awakening in his sly dark eyes.

"Why, don't you see that it is? I knew how worthless he must be; but the difficulty was to bring proofs of it to Sir Dene."

Jarvis drew a long breath. He began to discern a little light of way. Lady Lydia resumed.

"Putting all other considerations aside, Sir Dene *could* not allow him to remain here now. It seems quite like a Providence, Jarvis. I thought something or other would turn up. It's what I've been waiting for."

Not until the following day, the first of the new year, did Lady Lydia get the opportunity of conveniently speaking to Sir Dene. Their interview was a long one. What she said at it never was known, but we may be quite sure of one thing, that she did not tell her tale by halves. Otto—to his own intense disgust—was called in to testify to it.

"I'll be shot if I'd have dropped a word to her had I thought she was going to make this row over it, and do him damage with the old man!" mentally cried Otto, in wrath.

But—always speaking the truth if called upon to speak at all —he corroborated all, so far as he had cognizance of it. It appeared to be conclusive to Sir Dene: as might be seen by the look of utter sorrow on his pale face. In spite of all, he had loved Tom; had trusted him utterly; and this struck upon him as a cruel blow, rendering him unjust. What he ought to have done was to question Tom himself: and this he did not. His outraged pride, worked upon also by Lady Lydia, forbade it.

How the day went on, even Lady Lydia hardly knew. Never had one of greater unpleasantness been spent at Beechhurst Dene. Tom came in during the afternoon: and Jarvis picked a quarrel with him. For once he succeeded in putting Tom in a passion—and there were rare moments, as was previously said, when Tom could go into a passion with the best of them. When he was in this white heat, Jarvis unwisely (or wisely as the reader may decide) ventured on a word of insult more stinging than customary. In his cool, supercilious, contemptuous manner, he threw in Tom's teeth a reproach of the accusation they were whispering against him. It was but a hint, a syllable; but quite enough. Tom Clanwaring lifted his hand and knocked the gallant officer down. Sir Dene was a witness to it: it occurred in his own bay parlour, which he was just entering. That brought on the climax. Smarting under one thing and another, Tom the scapegoat appeared in that moment to Sir Dene as a very offshoot of Satan; and he swore a round oath that he should be out of Beechhurst Dene before night. The Lady Lydia had received an opportune letter that very morning, urging Tom Clanwaring's immediate acceptance of the post offered him, or else it must be given away elsewhere.

Verily, as my lady had remarked, it seemed that Providence was especially at work, ordering things in favour of the interests of herself and Captain Clanwaring!

CHAPTER XXVI.

AN EVENTFUL EVENING.

NEW Year's Evening. The reception rooms at Arde Hall were in a blaze of light; not with stifling gas, as is too much the fashion in these modern years, but with wax candles, cool and pure. It was Mr. and Mrs. Arde's custom to give a grand dinner the first day of the new year to as many guests as their dining-room would conveniently hold : and that was four-and-twenty. Four-and-twenty had been invited for to-day ; but only two-and-twenty came : Sir Dene Clanwaring and his grandson Tom were absent.

Sir Dene sent an apology for himself : he had hoped to be well enough to come, but quite at the last moment found he was not. For Tom little was said—he was altogether too insignificant to waste speech on. Lady Lydia spoke a few obscure words about going a journey ; and Captain Clanwaring, stroking his handsome moustache, made a supercilious remark in May's ear as he was taking her into dinner, to the effect that Sir Dene found Tom could not longer be tolerated. That was all. Tom's absence caused neither grief nor comment ; nobody missed him or cared for it. Nobody, save one ; and she might not show that she did. May heard Captain Clanwaring with a bright eye and smiling face, but her heart was sick with disappointment. The sunshine of the evening had gone out for *her* : too keenly she felt it, sitting through the long dinner.

The ladies rose to quit the dining-room ; May went out last, following her mother. Captain Clanwaring whispered something to her as she passed—for it was he who bowed them out. May laughed in response : a sufficiently light laugh to listening ears. But her step grew slow and heavy as the door closed. They were all within the drawing-room before she was at its door.

"Miss May!"

Turning round at the whispered words, she saw Susan Cole. The woman had a folded slip of paper in her hand.

"Mr. Tom Clanwaring is outside, Miss May. There's something wrong, I'm afeard. He asked me if I could manage to give you this without anybody's seeing."

Opening the paper, she stood underneath the hall lamp while she read it. Susan Cole, her mission executed, vanished.

"I am going away, Mary ; probably for years, possibly for ever. Will you come out to me for one minute ? I am at the avenue gate.—T. C."

Her brain was confused ; her heart was beating with its wild pain. Going away for ever ! Showing herself for a minute or two in the drawing-room as a matter of precaution, May caught up a woollen shawl, and ran out at the hall door. The avenue gate was only across the lawn. It was a starlight night, cold and frosty, but she did not at once distinguish any one, for the shrubs grew thick there.

He had his back against the gate, but he stepped to meet her as she advanced. Involuntarily, in her deep agitation, she put out both her hands. He clasped and held them fondly to him, his agitation as great as her own.

In moments of agony—and these were nothing less—the mind is for the most part in a state of bewilderment. It was so with Mary Arde; it was so with him. But a confused impression was retained by her afterwards, as to what was said at the interview. Perhaps the fault lay chiefly with Tom Clanwaring, for in his angry excitement he was less clear than he might have been. Those who had always been against him, trying to get him sent out of Beechhurst Dene, had done their work at last, and ruined him with his grandfather, he said. He was being sent away, Heaven knew where; certainly with little prospect of ever being allowed to return. He had to depart for Bristol at once by the night-mail, and wait in that city for orders on his way to Ireland.

She leaned against the gate for support: she would have pardoned him had he taken her to his arms and held her to his sheltering breast. But Tom Clanwaring, honourable as ever, dared not. Many and many a time had the warm words of love rashly trembled on his lips, and he had turned them off with some light jest: if he had put a restraint on himself then, how doubly needful was it that he should do so now! Even his own poor quasi-position in the baronet's household was torn from him, and he was being sent into the world adrift, a real servant, to work for his living. The inconsistency of *his* attempting to think of Squire Arde's daughter was more palpably present to him that night than it had ever previously been.

"I would have liked to wish Mr. and Mrs. Arde good-bye, May; but I cannot encounter the crowd they've got here to-night. So the will must go for the deed."

"But what is it that you have done?" she gasped. "*Why* are they sending you away?"

"I hardly know myself, May."

"Oh, but you must know," she said, thinking it was an evasion, made to spare her pain. "What is it, Tom?"

"You will hear no end of charges against me, I doubt not," he said, and the vagueness of the reply, as if it were still an evasive one, did strike on her memory afterwards. "I don't know what they may say: and I don't think it is of much use asking you not to believe them. I was always the scapegoat, you know; I shall be so to the end. May, I can no longer battle against the stream—and if I could, what end would it answer? It may be better for me that I should be away: but for leaving my dear old grandfather, I'd say there could not be a question of it. Think of me as kindly as you can, Mary."

The tears were streaming down her cheeks. "Only tell me, Tom, that you have done nothing very wrong," she whispered, her mind a chaos of confusion, of fear. Fear, she knew not of what: and perhaps his own want of clearness led to it. Mary Arde had never believed it possible that Sir Dene could turn against Tom to the length of discarding him—without some ample cause.

"If I have they have goaded me to it," was his answer, spoken in the moment's reckless irritation, as he recalled the passion he had been in, the flooring he had given the captain: for he attached no meaning to May's words, or suspected that she could really believe ill of him. "God bless and be with you always, Mary! I cannot stay longer; neither ought I to keep you out here. But I could not leave the place for good without seeing you."

"Why—why do you say it is *for good?*"

"Be you very sure that they who have procured my banishment will take efficient care I don't return, May. That's why."

"Are we to part—like this?" she wailed, her voice in its anguish rising almost beyond her own controlling calmness.

"Mary, my darling, don't tempt me. Do you know what it is costing *me* to part like this?—to stand here and say quietly to you, I am going? Have you not known for some time past that if I had dared—There, I must not go on: another moment and the temptation to speak will be greater than I can resist. You understand well, I fancy, Mary. Circumstances cast a wide barrier between us, and I may not presume to think of ever passing it. If there were but the least prospect of my achieving any position in the world, I might say to you, I will hope, without forfeiting all honour; but there is none, and I do not."

She put out her trembling hands once more; she lifted her streaming eyes to his. To those wonderful, blue ones in their deep caves, whose beauty the night could not wholly hide. The temptation was too great, and Tom Clanwaring bent his face on hers.

"It is but a cousin's kiss, Mary," he murmured: "we used to call ourselves cousins when we were children—taught so by Susan Cole. Surely none will grudge it us in parting. When I return—if I ever do—no doubt all danger will be over."

"Danger?" she breathed, questioningly.

"The danger that the scapegoat might forget himself and his honour by speaking of love. When you are the wife of a more lucky man than I, I may come back, May. Never before, unless my grandfather recalls me."

"You give me up, then?" she exclaimed in her pain: in the mortification that the renouncement undoubtedly brought to her.

"I do. I have no other resource. My parting blessing be upon you, May."

She drew her hands from his with a petulant gesture, and sped across the lawn, one bitter sob breaking from her lips: one more than bitter question from her heart—Did he care for her? When girls love as romantically as did Mary Arde, they are apt to fancy that all else should give place to it. Tom Clanwaring was Sir Dene's grandson—and May resentfully thought he might have been content to wait and see whether fortune would not be kind before he renounced her. He knew *she* had money—so they should not have starved! A few minutes alone in her chamber, effacing the traces of the tell-tale tears, and then she was in the drawing-room, quite unnaturally gay, whirling through a mazy country dance with Captain Clanwaring.

There was one other person that Tom Clanwaring would not omit to say farewell to before he left the neighbourhood: and that was Mary Barber. In striding up to Harebell Farm, he met Cole the farrier at the turning of the lane. It will be remembered that this was the son of the man spoken of as Cole the farrier in the first portion of this history. Young Cole and Tom had always been good friends.

"Good night, Mr. Tom," said the man as he was passing.

"Good night, and good-bye," replied Tom. "I am going away, Cole."

Cole wheeled round on his heel. "Ay, sir, so I gathered at the Dene this evening. But not just yet, are you?"

"In an hour's time. James drives me in the gig to catch the Bristol mail at Worcester. Good luck to you, Cole!"

"Stop a moment, sir—I beg your pardon. The servants

said something about a quarrel with Captain Clanwaring: is that the reason you've got to go?"

"I suppose so."

"Nothing has happened *since* that to send you?" continued Cole, with an emphasis, as marked, on the one word.

"Nothing, whatever. Fare you well, Cole. I've no time to lose."

As he went on up Harebell Lane, Cole stood and looked after him, as if in some hesitation. Finally, he continued his way towards his home.

Mary Barber was alone in the kitchen when Tom went in; her mind intent upon a curious incident that had occurred to her earlier in the evening, her hands busy with some preparation of cooking for the morrow. To say that she was struck into herself with the news—that Tom was going into banishment in Ireland—would be saying little. Ireland, to the imagination of quiet country people, represented something like the opposite end of the world.

"It can't be!" she exclaimed, dropping the fork from her fingers, and leaving the eggs to beat up themselves.

"I'm going this very night, Mary. This very minute, I may almost say; for in a few minutes I must be off."

Mary Barber stood quite still. Like Miss Arde, she thought he must have done something ill to turn his grandfather against him to this extent. Banished to Ireland! The very extremity of the measure brought its own revulsion in her mind.

"It won't be for long, Mr. Tom. Sir Dene 'ud never keep you all out there. 'Twould be like transportation."

"I have got to go, Mary: whether it's for long or short."

"What on earth 'll be done wi' the land? Who'll look to it?"

"*I* don't know," he replied. "They'll get somebody, I suppose."

"Not they," dissented Mary Barber. "You'll be sent for back to't, Mr. Tom. And a nice kettle o' fish I dare be bound you'll find things in! You away, and Sir Dene laid by—fine times it'll be for the men!"

Leaving her in this comforting belief without contradiction, Tom crossed the lane and went in home. The time for his departure was at hand: James waited in the gig to drive him into Worcester, to catch the Bristol night-mail, coming through the town on its way from Birmingham. He had been in hopes of seeing his grandfather once more.

"It's o' no good, Mr. Tom," said Gander sorrowfully. "Sir Dene he give orders he was not to be disturbed no more to-night on no account whatever; and he locked his room when he went up to bed. Your portmanteau and other things is in the gig, sir."

"Then there's nothing more to keep me here. Turned out like a dog! Good-bye, Gander," he added, shaking the man's hand heartily as he went out to the gig.

"I'll drive, James."

The groom handed him the reins and took the seat by his side. Gander watched the gig until the night hid it from his view. There came into the man's remembrance the turning out of his father, Geoffry Clanwaring. A prevision lay upon Gander that Tom would never come back, to be forgiven as Geoffry was.

The departure of Tom Clanwaring took the neighbourhood by surprise: and the more especially so because the precise cause of his banishment could not be ascertained. Sir Dene had issued a sharp general order to Lady Lydia and her family that nothing should be spoken of abroad—meaning in regard to ill-doing Miss Emma Geach. For once Lady Lydia was glad to obey him: her object was gained; Tom was gone, and she could well concede the rest. Jarvis was silent from policy; Otto from vexation: and Dene and Charles Clanwaring were away. So that scandal was buried; never, Sir Dene hoped, to be unearthed again. But there was another sin, or rather a frightful suspicion of it, brought against Tom: on which it might be well, for the honour of the family, to be silent also.

By the time service was over on the following day, Sunday, the second of January, the fact that Tom Clanwaring had been sent from Beechhurst Dene in disgrace was pretty generally known abroad. Servants will talk: and the news had spread. Lady Lydia and her children talked, for that matter, telling the fact that he was gone. Certain hints and innuendoes were dropped by them (not by Otto) imparting a confirmed notion that Tom must have been guilty of some conduct too bad to be spoken of, and which for the sake of the name he bore had to be hushed up. How near they were to the truth—or, rather, to what was supposed to be the truth at Beechhurst Dene—few guessed.

But, of all, none felt more surprise than Squire Arde. In his secret heart he not only liked Tom Clanwaring but thought well of him: and he could not imagine Tom could be guilty of any really bad conduct. In candour it must be added that the Squire had not the remotest suspicion of any attachment existing between Tom and his daughter: in his pride he would have deemed it utterly impossible. May had not spoken of Tom's visit of the previous night.

Leaving his wife and daughter at their own home after service, the Squire went on with Lady Lydia to Beechhurst Dene. Sir Dene, only just up, and looking very ill, opened his heart at the sight of his friend of many years, who stood, as may be said, in the light of uncle to Tom the scapegoat. And, in point of fact, the relationship, if it may be called so, of the Squire Arde to Tom had always stood rather as a barrier in my lady's plans against him. During the walk home she had talked in the most motherly way of Tom, lamenting his deplorable sins after the manner of a pitying angel. Not even out of her did Mr. Arde get at the nature of the sins: but she did drop a hint that he had shamefully wronged his grandfather in some money transaction in the hour of his departure. Mr. Arde asked the baronet point-blank what this wrong was.

"Why did Lydia speak of it?" rejoined Sir Dene, a shade of bitter mortification rising in his pale, sad face. "Ungrateful as he has proved himself, unworthy the name of Clanwaring, I'd not have it talked of abroad for the world. All this past night, in spite of his conduct in the other bad affair, I've been saying to myself that it surely cannot have been he. To steal money is not the work of a Clanwaring."

"What other affair?" questioned Mr. Arde, noting the words.

"Never mind—nothing," returned Sir Dene sharply. "That at least may be sunk in oblivion from henceforth. He has got his dismissal for it, so let it be."

And on this point Mr. Arde found it was useless to question further. So that he was no wiser than before as to the true cause that had led to Tom's disgrace. They told him of the other: as Lady Lydia had hinted at it, Sir Dene thought it might be as well to disclose the whole. The baronet just mentioned the heads, hating every word that fell from his lips, and my lady supplied the details.

The facts were these. After the explosion had taken place the previous afternoon, and Tom had been made to understand he must quit the place that night, Sir Dene, terribly upset by the disturbance, shut himself into the bay-parlour. The agitation had made him too ill to think of keeping his dinner engagement at the Hall, and he charged those who were going to say so. My lady and Mrs. Letsom went up betimes to attire themselves for the visit: Captain Clanwaring, reviving from the effects of his overthrow, and Tom's blow, was engaged with a visitor. One of the two gentlemen who had dined there on Christmas Day had again driven over from Worcester. It was Major Fife. He declined to come indoors, saying he had no time, but asked the captain to walk about a bit with him out of doors. So they made their way round to that side of the house where the trees and shrubs were thick.

While Sir Dene was thus sitting alone in the dusk, almost dark, Gander presented himself, saying that Mr. Parker had called to pay his rent. Rather glad to receive it—for the rent, half a year's, had been due since Michaelmas—Sir Dene bid Gander to show him in. Mr. Parker entered, making many apologies for not having been able to bring the money before. Sir Dene, always considerate to his tenants, especially the small ones, heard him with good-nature, and filled in a receipt—some of which he kept ready written in that upright piece of furniture, the secrétaire—by firelight. The money, forty-five pounds, was handed to Sir Dene in a canvas bag generally used for samples of barley, the farmer observing that twenty pounds of it was in gold, and the rest in notes on the Worcester old bank, and that Sir Dene would find the amount correct. Sir Dene nodded; he had no doubt of that; and put the bag on the table unopened. Mr. Parker, declining refreshment, left, being in a hurry, saying he would call for his bag in a day or two and drink a glass of ale then. After his departure, Sir Dene sat a few minutes in thought; and then with a deep sigh, stood up, undid the bag, and counted the money. He was putting it back in the bag and tying the tape round the neck when Tom Clanwaring came in. The sight of him disturbed Sir Dene afresh. Hastily thrusting the bag into the secrétaire, the lid of which had stood open, he was about to lock it, when, either from agitation or accident, he dropped the key. Tom stepped forward and picked it up, to save his grandfather stooping. Sir Dene locked the secrétaire, but did not take the key out: for Tom had begun to speak, and he turned quickly to confront him in his anger, pointing imperiously to the door.

"Quit my presence, sir."

Not on the instant did Tom obey. He had come in to speak his contrition for the heat he had displayed an hour before, the passion given vent to in the presence of him, his grandfather. Not a syllable would Sir Dene hear: and by way of summarily cutting short the discussion, he went out of the room, leaving Tom in it. Gander, standing at his pantry door, accosted his master as he was passing on to the dining-room, to say that Cole the farrier was craving a minute's speech of Sir Dene.

"I can't see him; I can't attend to anything just now," interrupted Sir Dene. "Let him come later."

Gander had no need to repeat this to Cole, for the man was standing behind him and heard it. Cole had been regaled in the servants' hall with the account of the explosion, and that Mr. Tom was turned out. Saying he would call again towards night, he took his departure.

After pacing the dining-room for three or four minutes in much perturbation, Sir Dene returned to the bay-parlour. It was empty then—as he expected—the door was shut and all things were apparently undisturbed. Remembering that he had left the key in the lock of the secrétaire, Sir Dene took it out before he sat down.

Rather a remarkable circumstance it was, taken in conjunction with another remarkable circumstance to be told of immediately, that Sir Dene did not again quit the bay-parlour, but remained in it for the evening. He took nothing but a basin of soup for his dinner; and that he caused Gander to bring to him: the family, you remember, going to dine at the Hall. Between seven and eight o'clock he sent Gander to summon to his presence Tom Clanwaring, who was then upstairs packing his things. This was to be the last interview. Very coldly and distantly did Sir Dene speak to Tom, gave him a few concise instructions as to how he was to proceed to take the mail that night as it passed through Worcester on its way to Bristol; and thence travel to the latter place, where he would wait at an inn for instructions from Ireland. Taking out his pocket-book, he handed him a sum of money in notes for his journey, and something over, shook hands with him by way of farewell, and dismissed him, wishing him, as a parting injunction, better behaviour in another place than he had latterly displayed at Beechhurst Dene. Tom would have lingered. He earnestly desired to say a word in his own defence

—though, be it always understood, he was entirely ignorant of any particularly grave offence being attributed to him—to plead this cause and ask *why* his grandfather was taking this extreme measure of discarding him. But Sir Dene stopped him at the onset: he refused to hear a word, and told him that he would not. And this was their final leave-taking. Tom completed his packing, and then went off to seek the interview with May Arde. Sir Dene sat on, alone.

Between eight and nine, Cole came again, and was admitted. His business was to get the prescription for some famous new horse medicine: of which Sir Dene had spoken to him a week before, and promised him the loan of. Sir Dene went at once to the secrétaire to get the paper, telling Cole to hold the light. The first thing that struck Sir Dene on pulling down the lid, was that the bag of money was gone. In his astonishment he spoke words which disclosed enough to Cole—the circumstances of the loss and the amount of money in the bag. Even as Sir Dene spoke, the thought flashed over him that it could only have been taken by Tom—that no one else had had access to the room: and in his horror and fear lest such a disgrace on the name of Clanwaring should be published, he first of all enjoined the man to silence, and then strove to smooth the matter by saying it was possible the bag was not lost, but had been removed to the safer quarters of his own chamber upstairs. Cole took his cue, and affected to believe that his Honour would there find it. The horse doctor was a keen man; and some muttered words of Sir Dene's, "What! has he done this in addition to the rest!" almost made him doubt whether suspicion might not be turning on Tom. However, it was not a business that he could presume to intermeddle with. Thanking the baronet for the prescription, Cole said good night with the most unconscious look in the world.

Then Sir Dene called Gander in, and bade him shut the door. "When I went out of this parlour to the dining-room earlier in the evening—do you mind it, Gander?" began he. "It was when you told me Cole had come up, and I said I could not see him. D'ye mind it, I ask?"

"Yes, Sir Dene."

"I left Mr. Tom in this parlour. How long did he stay in it? Did you notice him when he came out?"

"He didn't come out this way at all, Sir Dene. He must have left it by the window here."

"How d'ye know?"

"Well, sir, he was not in here when you came back again—I followed you in directly, if you remember, with the candles. And I'm sure he had not come out at the door while you were away, Sir Dene. If he had I must ha' seen him. Mr. Tom oftener goes out by this here glass door-window nor any other way, when he's a-wanting to go straight out o' doors."

Sir Dene paused. "Who came into the room besides, while I was away from it?"

"Not a soul," replied Gander.

And that exactly accorded with Sir Dene's own impression. As he had not shut the door of the dining-room, he thought he must have seen them if they did. Nevertheless, he *hoped* it was the contrary, and spoke accordingly in his mind's exasperation.

"Somebody did, I know."

"Somebody didn't, Sir Dene," returned Gander, with the familiarity of an old servant. "They couldn't. I never was beyond sight o' the door."

It was true. Gander's pantry and Sir Dene's door were within view of each other on opposite sides of the passage. It was simply impossible that any one could have entered the bay-parlour during the short interval in question unseen by Gander.

"Did you see Mr. Tom when he came into it?" resumed Sir Dene—as if willing to put the extent of Gander's sight to the test.

"I watched him in, sir. 'Twere just after Farmer Parker left. As Mr. Tom came down the passage, he asked me whether Sir Dene was in the bay-parlour; I said yes, and he went in. I could hear him and you talk together for half a minute, Sir Dene, and then you come out on't. Mr. Tom he didn't come out at all: he must ha' went through the glass doors."

And with this conclusive evidence, what was Sir Dene Clanwaring to think but that Tom was the culprit? It was as clear as though they had seen him do it, reiterated the Lady Lydia.

Such was the story told to Mr. Arde. In the impulse of the moment he took up the belief as warmly as they did, assuming Tom could not be innocent, except by a miracle; that he had been driven into crime at last. And though he regarded it with nearly as much horror as Sir Dene—for was not Tom connected with him?—he yet felt a large amount of pity. "Turned out nearly penniless, I suppose; and so the temptation was too great," thought the Squire to himself, as he went out of the presence of Sir Dene. But this feeling of pity Lady Lydia unconsciously crushed.

"And yet, I can hardly think he'd do it!" burst forth Mr. Arde, a revulsion of opinion setting in as he stood outside the front door, talking with her.

My lady glanced round, making sure they were quite alone, and sank her voice to a whisper.

"You'd not say so if you knew all. The other thing he has been guilty of is worse than that."

"*Worse* than that!"

"At least—if not worse, it's something very bad indeed of another nature. People estimate offences with different eyes, you know, Mr. Arde. I think theft might only have been expected from a man given to low tastes and low associates as is Tom Clanwaring."

"But what is the other thing that he has done?" resumed the Squire. "Can't you tell it me?"

"I cannot tell you, dear Mr. Arde. The probability is that you will hear of it before long—for I should think the neighbourhood is sure to get hold of it; but Sir Dene has forbidden it to be spoken of by any of us. My good son Jarvis, too, has begged me to be silent for the young man's sake. Ill as Tom Clanwaring has behaved, Jarvis is yet considerate for him."

Away went the Squire, the words burning a hole in his curiosity, and puzzling him mightily. For he was no wiser than ever, you see, as to what had driven Tom from Beechhurst Dene. "He must have turned out an awful scamp of some sort," was his mental thought.

"Well, what have you learnt?—what has led to his abrupt dismissal?" eagerly questioned Mrs. Arde, as her husband entered. Most excessively curious on her own score, she had been waiting with impatience the result of his visit to the Dene. Mary, standing by, held her breath as she listened for the answer.

"I can't come to the bottom of it," said Mr. Arde; "neither Sir Dene nor my lady seems inclined to speak out. There has been a series of general misconduct, I fancy; petty ill-doings one after another; Lady Lydia says no one can imagine what they have had to put up with from him, and how forbearing they have been. But"—and Mr. Arde's tones fell to something like fear—"whatever his petty offences might have been, he need not have capped them with a crime."

May's trembling lips parted. "A crime!" echoed Mrs. Arde.

"He went off with a bag of money belonging to Sir Dene. Stole it from the secretary."

"No," passionately cried May. "That he never did."

Mr. Arde turned his eyes upon her in surprise.

"What are you frightened at, child? It does not affect you. I called out No, just as you have done, until I heard the facts."

"And was this what he was dismissed for?" inquired Mrs. Arde.

"No, no; did you not understand me? This occurred after his dismissal—as he was going away. I tell you I can't get at the truth of what he was sent away for," continued Mr. Arde: "Lady Lydia says it is too bad to be spoken of. I don't think they'd have told me about the theft of the money either, but for a word my lady let drop; and so I asked Sir Dene point-blank. But, mark you; though it has been disclosed to me, this theft—I am connected with the fellow, unfortunately, and that makes a difference—not a syllable of it must be breathed abroad. Lady Lydia, incensed though she has cause to be against Tom, begged me to bury it in silence, for his own sake. As if I should proclaim it! The disgrace d reflect itself on me almost as much as on the Clanwarings."

Miss May metaphorically tossed her head, incipiently rebellious. "It's all of a piece," ran her mental thoughts. "A 'long series of petty ill-doings,' finishing off with something too bad to be spoken of, and a bag of money! Oh the wicked slanderers! They may just as well go and say that I had done it."

But that was destined to be an eventful night in more ways than one, and there's something else to be told of it. Somewhere about the hour that the money must have disappeared—that is, during the short interval Sir Dene was absent from the bay-parlour—a little earlier or a little later as might have been, Mary Barber went over on an errand to Beechhurst Dene. Neighbours in rural districts borrow household trifles indiscriminately of one other: when no shops are within convenient reach, this is almost a matter of necessity. Harebell Farm happened to be out of a very insignificant commodity—lemons. Mr. Tillett, coming home in the course of the afternoon from attending the corn-market at Worcester, the first market of the New Year, told Mary Barber that he had in-

vited some friends to spend the following day at the farm, and
particularly desired that a lemon pudding should be made.
Vexed at her own forgetfulness, she made no demur, thinking
she could borrow the lemons from Beechhurst Dene. Sometimes the Dene borrowed things of her. So at dusk, Mary
Barber, putting on a shawl and bonnet, went across the lane
on her errand. She had just entered the gate when a man
came dashing down the path right upon her, and laid hold of
her, as if for protection from some pursuing evil. Very considerably astonished was Mary Barber: and not the less so
when she recognised the intruder through the dusk to be
Randy Black. Randy in mortal fear. The man was completely unhinged: his face white, his hands shaking, his
breath coming in gasps. In the moment's abandonment he
confessed the cause of this—which he most assuredly would
not have done at a calmer time. He had just seen Robert
Owen.

The assertion startled Mary Barber into nearly as much
terror as his own. It was so long, too, now, since anything
of the kind had been talked of. Black, it appeared—at least
this was his own account—was going to the Dene to try and
get speech with Captain Clanwaring. He was about half-way
down the path to the house when some man (as he first took
it to be) glided out from between the trees and stood facing
him. The next moment, Black saw that it was Robert Owen.
Black turned tail and took flight in awful terror; and so met
Mary Barber. Mary Barber, listening to this, looking at the
gloomy path before her, the dark winter trees around her,
decided to let the lemons be just then, and send somebody
else for them by-and-by.

They passed out at the gate together, Black sticking very
close to her.

She went back to her own gate; he went too: it actually
seemed as if the man dared not just then be without some
companionship. He was getting better of his illness, but was
very ailing still, and Mr. Priar had ordered him not to go
out. Which order Black paid no manner of attention to. The
carter's boy at Harebell Farm, leaving work for the night,
came through the Farm gate in his smock-frock, whistling.

"If ye'll go up along o' me to the inn, and bring down a
physic bottle as I wants took to Dr. Priar's, I'll give ye a sixpence, Ned Pound," said Black. And Mary Barber could
not help noticing how the man's voice shook still.

"I'll go, and thank ye," replied Ned Pound after a pause of doubt as to whether so astoundingly munificent an offer could be real—for the boy had never had a sixpence of his own in his whole life. "I say, what makes your teeth rattle so?"

"It's this confounded cold night," replied Black: "enough to freeze one's bones it is. Come along."

Mary Barber looked after them as they went up the lane, Black's hand on the lad's shoulder. The extreme terror, displayed by such a hardened man as Black, struck her, and always had struck her, as being marvellously strange.

"He didn't care to go on by hisself," thought she: "that physic bottle's nought but a lame excuse. A whole sixpence to give!—Ned Pound'll be rich. And now—what should ha' brought back the poor master again? I'd thought he was laid."

What indeed! But, in this one instance, Black's sight and fears misled him. The figure he had taken for an apparition was no other than one of flesh and blood—Major Fife's. It will be remembered that Sir Dene Clanwaring and Gander both noticed the striking resemblance that Major Fife bore to the late Robert Owen.

It happened that Major Fife had come over from Worcester that afternoon to press his claims again on Jarvis Clanwaring. Totally declining to be put off any longer with vague promises, which Jarvis could alone give, the major, not caring in his own interests to proceed to extremities, discussed the face of things as they walked together about amidst the winter trees, both of them smoking. To appeal to Sir Dene—as Major Fife half threatened to do, there and then—would not serve the cause, Jarvis assured him, but the contrary; most probably destroy all hope from that quarter for the future. Jarvis offered to give him a legal undertaking to repay a portion of the money, if not all, by that day fortnight, the fifteenth of January. It was the best he could do. You can't get blood from a stone. Captain Clanwaring was tolerably candid about the state of his affairs: and the major, clearly seeing that there was no chance of making better terms, was fain to accept these. While Jarvis went in to write the document, the major, preferring still to remain where he was and finish his tobacco, strolled in and out among the trees and down the path: and thus ensued the encounter with Black. The man's extraordinary conduct, evidently the result of terror, astonished

Major Fife not a little. He mentioned it to Captain Clanwaring on his return with the paper. The captain fancied, by the description given, that the intruder must have been Randy Black. But his behaviour he could not account for. Neither then nor later did it come to Jarvis Clanwaring's knowledge that Major Fife bore a resemblance to the deceased man of whom he had often heard—Robert Owen, of Harebell Farm. Major Fife at once departed in the gig; which James the groom had been taking charge of at the front entrance.

And as Ned Pound was coming down Harebell Lane with the physic bottle and the promised sixpence, he met Captain Clanwaring striding up to the Trailing Indian.

CHAPTER XXVII.

AT SIR DENE'S SECRETAIRE.

IN a day or two there arrived two letters from Tom Clanwaring, dated Bristol. Very good and proper and nice letters, both of them. The one, written to Mr. Arde, expressed his regret that he had been obliged to leave without saying farewell to himself and Mrs. Arde, but that he had not liked to intrude upon them when they were engaged with their dinner-guests. It alluded to his abrupt dismissal, stated that he knew not the cause of it, and was unconscious of any offence of his that could have led to it, unless it was the quarrel with Captain Clanwaring in the afternoon, when he confessed that he had allowed himself to fall into undue passion. Not a word did it breathe of any sense of injustice, or cast the slightest reflection upon man, woman, or child; the sweetness of Tom Clanwaring's nature was never more unconsciously displayed than in that farewell letter. Squire Arde read it over once, and then began it again.

The other letter was to Sir Dene. Tom earnestly begged his grandfather to believe that he had not consciously been guilty of any offence towards him, or been willingly ungrateful. Nothing, he said, could be further from his thoughts. His greatest prayer and hope now was that Sir Dene should sometime be convinced of this; would see how much he had always loved him, how he had done his best to serve him, and how bitterly he was feeling the separation. Tom added some directions in the last page as to certain matters connected with the business of the estate, so that trouble might be saved to those who should succeed him in its management. It was a long letter, every word of it breathing the sentiments of a kindly and honest gentleman, and of the affection he felt for his home and his grandfather.

Too kindly, too honest to be allowed to fall under the eye of Sir Dene. Lady Lydia—who had taken the precaution to break the seal and skim the contents—might put no belief in the good faith of the letter: but she was by no means sure it might not act so far on the old man's tender feelings as to induce him to recall Tom. So she dropped it into the fire and held her tongue about its arrival. The opening of other people's letters was a grave offence in those days, not only against the code of honour: but who observed any kind of code to the humble dependent Tom Clanwaring?

And Sir Dene never knew that he had written.

Now Squire Arde possessed a conscience. Before the letter arrived, he had begun rather to veer round to Tom again and doubt whether he had really been guilty of any grave offence; that letter only served to increase the feeling and the doubt. He could not always forget that poor Tom, so hardly used among them, was the nephew of his dead wife; and he suddenly determined to go to Bristol and see him. It was understood that Tom was waiting at Bristol, according to instructions received from Ireland, until some agricultural implements should be ready, that he was to take over with him. Saying nothing to anybody, except his wife—and to her only that business called him away for a day or two—Squire Arde sent his servant to Worcester to engage a place in the Bristol mail, and departed himself the same night for the latter city, as Tom had previously done.

He saw Tom. He listened to his version of matters (given in answer to authoritative questioning), of what his treatment had been at Beechhurst Dene, especially in the past week; and Mr. Arde came to the conclusion that Tom had been more sinned against than sinning. But when he came to speak of some grave offence or crime, such as Lady Lydia had hinted at, but would not explain, Tom declared she must have been mistaken, for he had committed none. Mr. Arde, thinking it impossible she could have been so far mistaken, pressed the point; but Tom adhered to what he said.

"It does not matter," he lightly observed in his good-natured way. "I don't claim to be better than other people, sir." He had never called Mr. Arde "uncle;" had not been taught to do so. It might have been different had his own aunt, Mr. Arde's first wife, lived. The last thing Mr. Arde spoke of was the money.

"By the way," began he in a careless tone, "there has been a loss at the Dene since you left: or, rather, the evening you were leaving. A bag of money—forty-five pounds I am told it contained—that Sir Dene put into his secretary, disappeared in a mysterious manner."

"Was it the bag I saw him put in?" cried Tom, raising his honest eyes fearlessly to the Squire's face. "What a strange thing! It can't be lost."

"Yes, I believe it was that same bag. Sir Dene said something about your having been present when he put it up. It seems he left the key in the lock, and was absent from the room three or four minutes; not more. During that time the bag disappeared."

"Who went into the room?"

"There it is. No one went in, save Sir Dene and Gander. They did not see you come out, either."

"I? Oh, I went out by the glass doors. The truth is, I was so grieved at Sir Dene's refusing to hear a word of what I wanted to say, that as he went out one way, I turned out the other to walk my vexation off."

"Well, they both declare that no one whatever went into the room. Sir Dene——What now?"

A sudden light, as of awakened remembrance, shone in Tom Clanwaring's eyes. "Halloa!" he exclaimed, "I saw——" And there he stopped short.

"Saw what?" asked Mr. Arde.

"No," said Tom, "I'll say no more. The fact is, I thought I remembered to have seen somebody go into the room: but perhaps I was mistaken. I daresay I was mistaken."

"Go in by which door?"

"No, sir; I'll say no more."

"You ought to say. The money was stolen."

"I never will, sir. I'd not say it, if I were certain. No, not though I had seen it taken: which I certainly did not. Let people fight their own battles."

"And suppose they were to suspect *you* of taking it?"

Tom burst into a laugh. "Suspect me of taking money! Not they. They know me better than that, all of them."

"Suppose they were to *accuse* you of it?"

"Accuse me to whom, sir? Not to Sir Dene: it would be

waste of trouble. He knows that his money would be as safe with me as it is with him. I am his grandson, Mr. Arde."

Mr. Arde looked at the open countenance, at the blue eyes, so full of earnest truth, and he mentally saw that whoever else had stolen the money, Tom had not.

"Were it told you that you had been accused of this thing, you would surely speak, Tom Clanwaring!"

"I don't think I should," was Tom's answer. "I'd rather do a man a good turn than a bad one, be he friend or enemy. That is the only safe way to get on pleasantly in this life. It all comes home to us, sir. If we sow flowers, we are repaid by the perfume; if we plant nettles, they must spring up and sting us. I don't believe a man ever did the smallest kindness, but it was in some way returned to him; I feel sure that for every injury a man or woman designedly inflicts on others a worse evil is returned. Mrs. Owen taught me these truths when I was a little child, and I have seen them exemplified scores of times since."

But, though Mr. Arde felt at rest on the score of Tom's misconduct, he could not effect his return to the Dene. The edict of banishment was gone forth, and it might not be revoked. Neither did Mr. Arde see any urgent reason why it should be. He considered that some experience of the world might be of benefit to Tom rather than the contrary: and instead of telling Tom he would help him to return, he urged him not to "kick" against the new place in Ireland, but to do his best and make himself useful in it. Things might brighten, he observed; they generally did by dint of a little patience and perseverance. Tom replied that he had no intention of kicking against it: he was turned adrift, and it appeared Hobson's choice—go there, or starve.

"No need to starve," retorted the Squire: "you've got health and strength to work, and a good share of brains. There's not a man in England, or Ireland either, knows land better than you do, Tom. And look here: I've brought a bit of money for you."

It was a hundred pounds that he took from his pocket—to Tom's intense astonishment. The Squire explained. He had been putting it by for him bit by bit ever since Tom was a child. Foreseeing perhaps that Beechhurst Dene might not be a home for him always, that the time might come when he would be thrown upon his own resources, Mr. Arde, recognizing that Tom had some kind of claim upon him, put by this money by degrees for the rainy day. Had he found Tom to be worthless he would have kept it in his pocket: hence his journey of inquiry to Bristol.

"Put it safely up, Tom, and take care of it. Don't use it unless you really require it. Should you never get your recall to Beechhurst Dene, it may be useful to you."

Tom thanked him with all his heart; his earnest eyes, his expressive face, betraying his gratitude better than words could do it. Throughout his life he had been singularly responsive to kindness: probably from the little of it that was shown him.

On the morning following this, after Mr. Arde had quitted Bristol, Tom received a letter from Cole the farrier, saying that he had not been able to get his address before, and now only surreptitiously through Gander's good-nature, he wrote to tell Tom that he had seen some one (whom he mentioned), standing at the open secretaire that evening, just at the time the money must have been taken: and that person was no doubt the thief. The reason of Cole's writing this was that a hint had reached him, throwing some suspicion on Tom Clanwaring—though, in his delicacy, he did not expressly say so. Tom immediately sent the following letter back to Cole:—

"Thank you for writing to me, my good fellow: your motive was a right one, and I think I discern the prompting cause. But say no more to anyone. *You may be mistaken.* Keep silence. Even if you had *proof* as to who it was took the money—which you have not—there may be private reasons why it should not be told abroad. As to me—for, what I conclude is, that you have heard my name brought in—my back is broad enough to bear anything put upon it by idle report: and you must know, and I know, that no one whom I care for or who cares for me, would suspect me of such a thing. Sir Dene knows me better, and so do others. *Be silent.* I rely upon you to be so. Let people fight out their own battles: it is no affair of yours; I do not intend to make it mine. Good luck to you, Cole, in all ways.

"Sincerely yours, T. C."

Tom Clanwaring was right. Not for long did any one who knew him continue the suspicion as to the money. A complete revulsion of feeling set in with Sir Dene: and he called himself names for having allowed his mind to entertain such a suspicion for a moment. Even Lady Lydia, upon sober reflection, grew to think that it could not have been Tom—for nothing in his past life had led her to suppose he would descend to be a thief. Make the worst of him, and of the sins she had been fond of attributing to him, he would scarcely sink so low as that. No. Had there been nothing else against Tom, he might have been recalled instanter. But there was. Not to speak of those general petty sins, there was that other grave charge, not easily refuted. It was *that* that troubled Sir Dene: he had always believed Tom to be as morally good a man as his father Geoffry was: and the discovery to Sir Dene was bitter. No chance of that being refuted yet awhile: if it ever was, or could be.

It must be remarked that Lady Lydia did at first believe Tom had taken the money. In the teeth of the one great assumed fact—that only he had been in the room—she could not well think otherwise. The possibility that anyone else had stolen in through the glass-doors, did not then occur to her or to Sir Dene. But it was the theory taken up now: though whether she would have arrived at it of her own accord is uncertain.

On the Tuesday, the day following Mr. Arde's departure for Bristol, Mrs. Arde and Mary Barber met accidentally in Dene Hollow, the latter with a big market-basket in her hand. The two invariably held a gossip together when they met: and on this occasion Mrs. Arde (who considered Tom Clanwaring belonged to Mary Barber at least as much as to anybody else) chose to ignore her husband's injunction to secrecy, and whispered to her in confidence the story of Tom's misdoings: that is, of the one crowning act of them. Mary Barber's hard face took a harder hue in her astonishment; her grey eyes fixed themselves with a stare on Mrs. Arde's.

"Steal a bag o' money! *You* don't believe it of him!" she continued, fiercely and abruptly.

"But I can't help believing it, impossible though it seems that he could do such a thing," returned Mrs. Arde. "There was no one else near the room, you see."

"He went out at the glass-doors, did he?" quietly observed Mary Barber.

"They say so."

"Which proves he must have left 'em undone, for they don't fasten from the outside," reasoned Mary Barber. "What was to prevent somebody else from going in and helping theirselves to the money?"

Mrs. Arde paused: the notion had not struck her. They were not altogether conjurors in those parts: besides, the accusation of Tom, assumed to be a certainty, had kept suspicion from being directed to other quarters.

"I fancy there could not have been time for anyone else to get in," said Mrs. Arde, revolving matters.

"A thing like that's soon done—you must know it is, ma'am. Thieves be deft o' fingers."

"Of course it might be so," spoke the lady slowly. "But —was any ill-character likely to be close up at the house at that hour?"

"There's tramps and ill-folk about always at dusk, a-watching what they can put their hands on," said Mary Barber. "A couple o' gipsies, big strong men, too, was at our house o' Saturday, a-wanting to sell iron skewers. One on 'em might get up to the Dene from Harebell Lane quite easy. And if none o' the servants was on the look out, why he——"

The woman stopped. Stopped as if a shot had taken her. There had flashed into her memory one whom she saw flying from the house at dusk on Saturday; flying in terror. Not a tramp; but a man who would put his hand to worse deeds, if report might be trusted, than any tramp in the three kingdoms.

"What time was it exactly that this here theft happened? Do ye know, ma'am?" she presently resumed.

"I don't know exactly. Some time between four and five. Nearer five, I should think, for it was quite dusk. Why do you ask?"

"Well I—I was a-wondering," returned Mary Barber evasively, saying no more in her prudent caution. She wanted time to reflect first.

"Any way, Mrs. Arde, don't you go on a-suspecting Mr. Tom Clanwaring," were her parting words, spoken emphatically. "He'd no more touch what's not his own than you or me would. He's a gentleman to his fingers' ends; ay, and a right noble one. Warn't their sending of him off to that Irish Botany Bay enough for 'em, but they must bring up this?"

Mrs. Arde continued her way. Mary Barber put her back against the railings to think. It happened to be in that part of the Hollow where her poor mother's cottage had stood: her feet were pressing what might once have been the kitchen floor, on which she had played in infancy. The cottage was gone, and her mother was gone, so long ago now that its very remembrance was growing dim: and she and Sir Dene Clanwaring were drawing nearer and nearer to that other world, to which so many connected with this history, and younger than they were, had passed on before them.

Not that any of these thoughts were in Mary Barber's mind then; it was otherwise occupied. What she wanted to recall was, the precise time at which she had gone over to the Dene on Saturday night. And, try as she would, she could not. All she was sure of was that it was dusk; not dark: but she had not taken note of the time. The cuckoo clock (that had passed with the other things into Mr. Tillett's possession from William Owen) was getting old like herself, out of order often. On Saturday it had stood still all day.

The more she reflected on it, the stronger grew her conviction that the criminal was Black. Black, and nobody else. One thought led to another. She began to doubt whether Black's state of terror had not arisen from a fear that he was being pursued; that his assertion of having seen the apparition of Robert Owen, was all an invention to account for the fear. And this was the more likely from the fact that some years had elapsed since any report of the ghost had been raised: Mary Barber had been living in the agreeable assurance that time had "laid" it. Turning back, for she had been on her way to Hurst Leet, she went straight in at the front gates of Beechhurst Dene.

"It's right that they should know I saw Black where I did," ran her thoughts, "and specially if any on 'em be a really accusing Mr. Tom. Not as I believe *that*. Black, he's a nasty one to make a enemy of: so I'll just say I see him, and no more. Let Sir Dene and them do what they like in it."

Considerably astonished was Jones the footman, when he flung open the door of the grand entrance, to find nobody at it but Mary Barber. The woman knew proper manners as well as Jones did, perhaps better, and apologized for not going round to the side, on the score of her time being "precious" that morning. But she did not get to see Sir Dene: he was very poorly, Jones said, and not up yet: would Lady Lydia do? Mary Barber considered, and then saying that my Lady would do, put her basket down. But she would rather have seen Sir Dene. So she was shown into the library to my lady's presence, and to that of her two sons, who happened to be with her. My lady's curiosity was a little raised, as to what the woman could want—she had heard her come to the grand entrance. She sat near the window, working at some silk patchwork for bed furniture: Jarvis and Otto were talking together by the mantelpiece.

Standing, for she was not asked to sit, Mary Barber told what she had come to tell. Barely had she finished when Otto Clanwaring brought down his hand on the table with emphasis, as he turned to his mother and brother.

"That's it. There's the clue. I told you from the first what a shameful wrong on Tom it was, to suspect *him*. And you accuse Randy Black!" he added, approaching Mary Barber.

"Sir, I accuse nobody. Randy Black's one that I'd not like to accuse myself—he might be for drowning me in return—as perhaps he drowned somebody else, years agone. I only tell you where I see him o' Saturday evening—a coming out o' the back grounds here in a pucker o' fear. He give me a plausible cause for his fright—which has nothing to do with it, and don't matter: it mightn't ha' been true. I couldn't keep this back on my conscience, hearing that you suspect Mr. Tom Clanwaring."

"*I* never did," spoke Otto. "It was too ridiculously absurd to those who knew him."

"Both to them as knew him and to them as didn't," amended Mary Barber. But at this moment Captain Clanwaring stepped forward, pushing aside his brother.

"We are much obliged to you, of course, Mrs. Barber, for this information," said he in his pleasantest tones—and the captain's could be soft and pleasant when he chose to make them so. "It is very good of you to come. But now—will you add to the obligation by keeping this doubt of Randy Black to yourself, at least until it shall have been enquired into? The fact is," he added, meeting the woman's questioning eyes, and speaking slowly, as if with unwilling reluctance, "that my suspicions have been directed to a different quarter."

"Do you mean to Mr. Tom?" independently demanded Mary Barber.

"Oh dear no. We are sure it was not he." And as the positive words fell from Jarvis's lips, Otto, put into the background, looked hard at his brother.

"Well, Captain Clanwaring, as to keeping my doubts of Black to myself, I'll readily promise you that, for it's just what I mean to do," answered Mary Barber. "I don't say the man was guilty: he might not ha' been anigh Sir Dene's window: I must leave you to be the judge o' that. Seeing him where I did, a rushing pell-mell down the path, in a mortal fright, it was my duty to let you know on't. That's all."

"But—how did he account for this state of fear himself?" interrupted Otto. "Surely you may tell, Mrs. Barber."

"Well, Mr. Otto, what he told me was, that he had seen something to frighten him amid the trees," she rejoined, after a slight pause. "As I say, it might ha' been just an invention of his own. Good day to you, my lady; good day to you, sirs."

Lady Lydia nodded in reply to the salutation: she had not spoken one word throughout the interview. Otto civilly went to the front door with Mary Barber, and she made him a curtsey as she took up her basket and departed. Short though the interval was before Otto returned to the library, he found his mother and Jarvis talking fast, almost disputing. On my lady's mind there rested not a doubt that the offender was Black: her son would not admit it.

"This must be kept from everybody, Otto," spoke Jarvis, wheeling round on his brother. "From Sir Dene especially."

"And why?" asked Otto, honestly. "I should take it to Sir Dene at once, and clear Tom."

"Tom shall be cleared with him so far, never fear. In fact, Sir Dene's own mind has cleared him already. Look here, Otto: I must beg of you not to interfere in this. It is essential to me—I have been telling Lady Lydia so—not to exasperate Black just now. The fact is," added Jarvis, mentally anathematizing his brother's straightforward turn of mind that obliged the explanation, "I owe Black money, and can't pay him; and I believe he'd do me an ill turn were the opportunity afforded him. If we accuse him of this, it would bring on an inconvenient climax for me, for he'd be safe to come off to Sir Dene with the debt. I wish the devil had all money!"

"What do you owe money for to Black?" asked Otto, in some slight wonder.

"Tobacco," shortly answered Jarvis. "A tough score. Been accumulating for ages."

Otto knitted his brow. In his heart of hearts he despised his spendthrift elder brother. It might be detected in his voice as he spoke.

"It is no just cause for the information, that this woman has given us, being withheld from sir Dene."

"That's only cause the first, and personal to myself," resumed Jarvis. "There is another reason, and a weightier one. I don't believe Black had anything to do with taking the bag. I suspect some one else—you heard me say so to the woman—and I want to follow up the suspicion privately. Accuse Black wrongfully, and he is sure to make a row over it, and my efforts will be defeated."

"But who is it that you suspect, Jarvis?" cried Lady Lydia, impatiently. And the barrister's eyes were asking the same question.

"Just at present I cannot tell you, from the same motive. Be content to leave it with me for a little while, mother—and I'll do my best to unravel it. It is a man you would never think of—nor Otto either. Of course I may be mistaken; but I've got just a little clue, and I want to follow it up. It will take time to do it—and not a word must be said. As to Black, it was certainly not he. Bad as the man's character is, in this I could almost answer for his innocence. Accuse him wrongfully, and his anger would know no bounds. He'd come straight off to Sir Dene in revenge and tell him of the heaps of tobacco I've had, and the long amount I owe for it. There's brandy as well. Sir Dene—you know the awful fuss he makes about our keeping clear of debt round about here—he is put out with me already, as it is: and he might just send me adrift as he has sent Tom. On my *honour* I have reason to believe it was not Black; and I ask you, as a favour to myself, Otto, to bury what the woman has said in silence."

That Captain Clanwaring was terribly in earnest in this request; that he was moved almost to agitation in putting it, both his hearers saw. My lady heartily gave into it without further question, and told him it should drop. Otto tacitly did the same, mentally washing his hands of the affair altogether. It was nothing to him individually: and at the end of the week he was going back to his work in London.

CHAPTER XXVIII.

BACK FROM BRISTOL.

PACING the two rooms with slow and measured steps, from the bed-chamber to the sitting-room, from the sitting-room to the bed-chamber, his air not only that of a man pre-occupied with his own thoughts, but as if utterly weary of this life, went Sir Dene Clanwaring. Time was telling on him. Life and its events were telling on him. Is it true that, according as our course has been smooth and easy, imposing no check on our own imperious will and pleasure, so will a period of days more or less dark, more or less short, set in before life shall finally close? It had certainly been the case with Sir Dene Clanwaring.

That he had felt his wife's death years ago, and his favourite son Geoffry's death close upon it, as keenly as might be, was indisputable. But these events are of a class that we cannot avert; they come direct from God: we recognise them as such, and the wounds heal again. With these two exceptions Sir Dene's life had been altogether one of prosperity and enjoyment. He reigned supreme in his own neighbourhood; he took his pleasure abroad at will, in the metropolis or elsewhere; he had an ample income; no trouble disturbed him. And this desirable state of things continued until he was past his seventieth year. If ever and anon at odd moments a thorn pricked his conscience touching that old affair connected with the widow Barber, it soon disappeared again. But, almost in proportion to the extreme ease of his long life, so had been the tormenting discomfort of the past year or two.

The greater portion of Sir Dene's love had been concentrated on his grand-daughter, Margaret, the eldest child and only daughter of his eldest son. In her earlier years, when she was not of strong health, and it had appeared a doubt whether she would be reared, the physicians had recommended that she should live always in the country air; and therefore Beechhurst Dene became nearly entirely her home. She was a fair, gentle girl, merry of spirit, tender of heart, a favourite with all. How deeply Sir Dene grew to love her, he was perhaps not conscious of himself, until all was over. Tom was very dear to him, but not so dear as Margaret. As a rule, men never experience the same fondness for boys that they do for girls. It was Margaret who made Sir Dene's home like one ever shining beam of sunlight: he grew at last not to care to leave it, because she was there. In age there was not much difference between hers and Tom's, she being some few months the younger.

The day of the end was a day in January, two years ago this very month, when she was in her twenty-second year. Sir Dene was recalling it all as he paced the carpet. He was busy in his bay parlour with Mr. Tillett, who had come over from Harebell Farm to pay his rent, when Margaret put her bright face inside the door to disturb them. She wore a blue velvet gipsy hat, and her overdress was of soft blue cashmere with ermine fur about it.

"We are going, grandpapa," she said. "Good-bye."

"Good-bye, my darling," responded Sir Dene, fondly kissing her smiling face. "Don't stay out too long."

"We shall only go there and back, grandpapa."

A young girl of sixteen, Charlotte Scrope, was visiting at Beechhurst Dene at the time, and Margaret was going to drive her as far as Henwick to see her governess—for in that healthy suburb of Worcester, Miss Scrope went to school: a matter of two miles or so from Beechhurst Dene. It was not the custom for ladies to ride on horseback then; the few who did were called masculine women; but they sometimes drove a chaise or gig in the country for convenience sake. It was a fine, clear morning, the roads frosty, with bits of ice here and there; and as the pony-carriage took its way out of Beechhurst Dene, Margaret driving, and a mounted groom behind them, Gander, watching at the hall door, said to himself they'd have a nice morning of it.

A nice morning! In the field skirting Dene Hollow, the field that had once been the widow Barber's, Sir Dene's team was out, ploughing. Tom Clanwaring, riding through it on horseback, halted to say something to the ploughman. As the man, whose face was towards the road, raised his head to answer, his words faltered on his tongue, and his eyes dilated.

"Hullo! What's up? Look out yonder, sir!"

Tom turned, and was just in time to see the pony-carriage racing away as if flying for its life. Just in time to see some one jump from it, and fall in the road. He was off his horse, had leaped the railings, and was up with Margaret—for she it was who had jumped—almost as quickly.

She lay still in her blue garments, her lifeless face white as snow. Tom raised her in his arms, but the head fell: fell as he had never seen a head fall in this world. Afraid, he dared not think of what, he knelt down and let the poor head rest upon him; and, lifting his own white face, shouted out to the ploughman to mount his horse and gallop to the Dene.

The pony stopped presently of its own accord. Charlotte Scrope, who had sat still, was neither injured nor (she acknowledged) much frightened. The groom, leading the pony back again, the young lady still in her seat in the little carriage, said he could not imagine what had frightened the pony, that it should have put down its ears, and backed all of a sudden, and then, giving a leap, sprung off at a gallop.

"I cannot *think* why Margaret should have been so frightened as to jump out," cried Miss Scrope. "Has she fainted, Mr. Clanwaring?"

Alas! as the reader has foreseen, it was worse than fainting. Margaret Clanwaring was dead. Her neck was broken. But there were two things that would remain, and did remain, a marvel on thinking minds: why, as little Charlotte Scrope put it, she should have been so frightened as to jump out at all: and why, jumping from that low carriage, her neck should have broken. Mr. Priar talked in rather a learned manner, giving suppositions: that the head must have struck here or struck there: but people wondered for all that.

Sir Dene came speeding down from Beechhurst Dene with the rest: he could run still, for all his more than seventy years. The first thing that particularly caught his eye was the strangely piteous aspect of Tom's face. It served to startle him.

"She's not hurt much, is she, Tom?"

"I—I—better not disturb her, sir, please," was Tom's distressed answer. "We must get something flat to lie her upon."

Seven days afterwards, as Sir Dene Clanwaring stood over her grave in Hurst Leet churchyard, the thought that had been making itself more or less heard all the week, came rushing full upon him with overwhelming force. Ashes to ashes, dust to dust, read the clergyman. Ay: but Sir Dene surely saw, and took home to him, the one great, indisputable fact, indisputable to his conscience, that the curse of retribution lay on the road, Dene Hollow; and that this culminating punishment had come direct from God. The sudden cutting off of this favourite and most beautiful flower, who had become the best solace of his declining life, was only the righteous judgment of Heaven. Just as Mary Barber, when consigning her poor oppressed mother to the grave, in the same churchyard, had felt a sure and certain conviction that nothing but a curse could lie on the fine new road which had sent the aged woman to that grave before her time, which had been made, as she at times expressed it, out of her blood and tears; so did the conviction of his mistake and folly and sin lay hold on Sir Dene as he stood over Margaret's. It was the retribution coming home to him, he mentally said; the curse working itself out.

From that hour Sir Dene Clanwaring was a changed man. The pleasantness in his days seemed to have dried up; all their sweet apples had turned to bitterness. Instead of enjoying life carelessly, looking not beyond it, he began to see how very near, in the course of nature, his own grave must be drawing: he began to realise that he had not, in this short world, been living for, or thinking much of, the eternal one beyond. A kind of shadow, something like that which was reported to lie on Dene Hollow, lay on his own heart perpetually; the shadow of a vast sorrow. Sir Dene saw quite well that it would lie on his life to the end. The time went on. Instead of shaking off petty cares and annoyances as of yore, they clung to him and told upon him in an almost unnatural degree. There were hours still when he seemed to be full of life and animation, to enjoy the social intercourse with his family as much as ever; but on the other hand, there were times of depression, when he could truly say the evil days had come, and he found no pleasure in them.

Such an hour was this. Pacing his carpet with heavy and lagging tread, Sir Dene was dwelling on the two great sources at present embittering his life, the one a thing of the past, the other very recent—Margaret's death, and Tom Clanwaring's base ingratitude. He could not have believed that he should feel the departure of Tom as keenly as he was feeling it, or have wished him back again so ardently. We never know the worth of a thing until we have lost it. Had Tom come back now, and thrown himself at Sir Dene's feet in all humility to confess his sin, and said, "Grandfather, forgive me," Sir Dene would have read him a lecture, and stormed a bit, and then hugged Tom to him in very happiness. The sin, be it always understood, by the reader, was that one Tom had been unconsciously accused of in conjunction with the young lady at the Trailing Indian. No other rested on the mind of Sir Dene.

It is a bitter trial to be deceived in one whom we wholly trust. Sir Dene had trusted Tom—had believed him to be of conduct good and honourable—and the awakening brought very sharp pain. Loose conduct was not thought over-much of in those days, by Sir Dene, or by anybody else. It was not that in itself; it was the deception Tom had practised on him: been very black when he had appeared to be wholly white. If Tom had deceived him in one point, he had perhaps in others: at any rate, instead of being a young man of honour, open and candid and upright as the day, he must have been a very sly one, argued Sir Dene. And never to have written! Five days now since Tom's departure, and not a line from him. What though he had turned him out with harsh words of anger, Tom ought to have allowed for the passion, and condoned it: he was a young man, his grandfather an old one. Waiting at Bristol, nothing to do with his time there, and yet he could not write one word to the poor old man who had reared and loved him! Had Sir Dene been told then that Tom had written, written a gentle loving letter, and that my lady suppressed it, he had probably turned *her* out in his fury. And there he was, telling over Tom's sins and ingratitude as he paced the carpet, and lashing himself into a state of rage about it all, when Squire Arde was shown in on his return from Bristol.

"Tom did not take that bag of money, Sir Dene," said the Squire, impulsively, after explaining in two or three words where he had been to, and that he had seen Tom.

"No, that he did not," was the somewhat unexpected but emphatic answer of Sir Dene. "I was enraged against him at the time, Arde, or I should never have thought it. Mad, I think, I must ha' been. Poor Geoff was the soul of honour, and Tom takes after him."

"It's a great pity, Sir Dene, that the suspicion was caught up against him. Of course he did not take it. But who did?"

"There! Let the dratted dross go. I sha'n't make a stir over it. Perhaps the rats—sink 'em!—got at it. Much good may it do 'em!"

The explosive answer proved how very much Mr. Arde's comments, coming upon his own previous state of mind, told on Sir Dene's temper. It was the custom in those days for country gentlemen—and town gentlemen also, for that matter —to use far broader terms of speech than these. Sir Dene had usually been a notable exception, save at some rare moments when passion o'ermastered him. It appeared that passion could sometimes be in the ascendant still.

"Are you ill?" asked Mr. Arde, wondering at the irritability.

"I don't know. Ill in temper, I suppose. I miss Tom. Things go cross without him. That Weston that they've put on has been in three times this very day, asking this and asking t'other. Three times! I shall have my life bothered out. Tom was my right hand, Arde; I didn't value him when he was here, but now I look round for him every minute of the livelong day."

"Have him back," suggested the Squire.

"Not just yet. Lady Lydia would say I did it to affront her. He *was* insolent to her: there's no denying it. And there's that other thing lying always against him. He forgot his honour there."

"But what *is* that other thing?" questioned the Squire, thinking he was about to have his curiosity gratified at last. "Tom declares he knows of nothing."

"Let it pass," snarled Sir Dene, putting up his hand impatiently to enforce the words. "I'll never give utterance to it as long as I live: I'd rather open a running sore. Tom's been a confounded fool—and that's enough. No, Arde: I can't recall him yet to Beechhurst Dene."

"A spell of absence and of Ireland will do him good," remarked Mr. Arde soothingly—for he had rarely seen Sir Dene put out so grievously as this. "It will give him the experience of the world that he'd never learn at home: and a dose of roughing it is always serviceable to young men. In regard to that money——"

"Hang the money!" roared the old man. "I won't hear any more about the money. But for thinking he had helped himself to it—and I was an idiot for my pains—I might never have let him go. When it came to the last interview, why—things might have taken a turn. I never intended *that* to be the last—when I gave him his instruction and funds for his journey. Close upon that the loss was discovered, and I locked myself up in these rooms, so as not to see him again, and gave my orders to Gander."

"I was only about to say that some one might have come

in through the window, and taken it from the secretary," quietly pursued Mr. Arde. "In my opinion there's no doubt it went that way; I think Tom has none, either. For all you know, Sir Dene, some one may have been concealed amid the shrubs outside and have actually watched you count the money. Have watched all that passed."

"Let it go, Arde. With one thing or another, you'll drive me mad. Of course that's how it went—have I no brains, d'ye suppose? And to think how I slandered Tom!—my own boy's son! Bury the money! I wish Parker had been buried before he'd brought it here that afternoon!"

In all this, Mr. Arde could but discern one prevailing desire: a longing to have Tom back again. The next minute, Sir Dene unconsciously confirmed it in a singular degree.

"Margaret gone; gone in that awful manner; and now he is gone; gone in disgrace! What's the good of my life to me? They were the two I cared for."

"Not much difficulty, I fancy, in getting him back again before he reaches Ireland at all," thought the Squire. "You'd like Tom to be here, I see, Sir Dene," said he aloud.

"Better, I daresay, than he cares to come!" retorted Sir Dene. "Never to write a word to me!—it's too ungrateful, Arde."

Mr. Arde thought of the very nice letter he, himself, had received from Tom, and wondered. During that interview at Bristol, the subject was not started, and Tom did not happen to mention that he had written to his grandfather.

"But—has he not written to you, Sir Dene?"

"Not a word. He is bearing malice, you see. I didn't think it of him. Or else he's ashamed to write. There: let it go, I say. Come in at five and eat a bit o' dinner with me, Arde. Goodness knows I'm dull enough! We'll have it up here alone together, you and me."

"Tom shall get a private hint from me not to hurry away from Bristol, and to write to the old man forthwith," mentally decided the Squire, as he accepted the invitation. "In a week's time he'll be back at Beechhurst Dene."

Would he! If things did but go according to our wishes, well-laid plans might succeed. The first link in the chain of events, destined to frustrate Squire Arde's good intentions, was woven even as he left Sir Dene's presence.

Turning in at the library door, to say how d'ye do to the family, and to tell them he had been to Bristol, Mr. Arde came upon Otto. Otto alone. He was leaning back in an arm-chair, his feet on the fender, reading some dry law book. The barrister was going up to London by the morrow's night mail from Worcester: a letter, received that morning, was taking him away a day or two earlier than he had intended. Putting the book down, he rose from his seat to shake hands with Mr. Arde.

"I'm heartily glad you've been to see him, Squire," spoke Otto earnestly, as they stood over the fire, and he listened to the details of the Squire's journey. "In my opinion Tom has been shamefully used among us."

"Sir Dene wants him back already; I see that plainly," returned the Squire. "As you say, he has been badly used."

"Fancy his being accused of taking that bag of money!" continued Otto. "Great asses they must all have been to think it!"

"Ay. But now—who could have taken it?"

"Who! Why Randy Black."

"Randy Black!" echoed Mr. Arde, in great amazement.

And the exclamation caused Otto to remember what in the impulse of the moment he had quite forgotten—his brother's earnest injunction not to speak of Mr. Randy. He set himself to repair the damage in the best way he could.

"Look here, Squire. I ought not to have spoken of this," he said, dropping his voice. "Jarvey has got some idea in his head as to another man—not Black—and has sworn us all to silence in the interests of justice. Don't let it go any further."

The Squire nodded. "Do you happen to know who the other is?"

"Jarvey won't say: it might defeat inquiry, he thinks. For my own part, I privately believe there's no doubt it was Black. Not to speak of the man's bad character, appearances are nearly conclusive against him."

"Do you object to tell me what they are?"

"Not at all—as I've told you so much. But mind you keep counsel."

"Of course I'll keep it," said the Squire. "I'd not help to defeat the ends of justice for the world."

And Otto Clanwaring, perfectly satisfied of that, with or without the assurance, related what had come to their knowledge. About the time the robbery was committed, Randy Black was seen to fly down the side path, leading direct from the bay-window, in what seemed to be an agony of terror.

"Which terror might, of course, have been caused by a fear of pursuit—and most probably was," concluded Otto.

"But who saw this?" questioned Mr. Arde.

"It was Mary Barber. She was coming across here, it seems, to borrow something of the cook; and met Black in this state. I never knew any case that looked more like a circumstantial evidence of guilt in my experience," continued the barrister, with as much assumption of dignity as though he had been the Lord Chief Baron of the realm.

Mr. Arde agreed. In his own mind he deemed this evidence perfectly conclusive against Black. "Sir Dene does not know of this, does he?" he asked.

"Not yet. Jarvis wants to follow up his suspicion first in quiet: if Sir Dene were told, he would be sure to make a stir in it, and accuse Black. And that would—would spoil sport," concluded Otto, after a slight pause of consideration, during which he had remembered that he had no right and no need to allude to the other motive given by his brother for keeping Black's name from Sir Dene—the debt.

"Any way, whoever it may turn out to be, I'll answer for it that it was not Tom Clanwaring," concluded Mr. Arde, as he shook hands to leave.

"I'd have answered for that myself all along—and told them so," was the reply of Otto. "Mind you keep counsel abroad, Squire. Above all, don't let out to Jarvis that I've said anything. He'd think at once it was going to be proclaimed to the parish."

Squire Arde nodded. "All safe. Trust me."

He went slowly down the front avenue with his hands in his pockets. The Squire was in no hurry: upon arriving at his home that day he had found his wife and daughter absent. Not expecting him—in fact, not knowing when he would return, or where it was that he had gone—they had driven over to spend the day with some friends, living in the neighbourhood of Powick. One of the children at the lodge—it was a fresh generation there now—ran out with a smiling face, and held open the small gate for the Squire: for which he patted her head, and dropped a halfpenny into her blue cotton pinafore.

"How's mother?" asked he.

"Mother's a getting better, thank yer honour," said the child, bobbing straight down. "Dick, he says we shall ha' some snow-balling afore to-morrow," gratuitously added she, her eyes brightening at the prospect.

"Maybe," returned the Squire. "There. Run in."

Outside the gate he stood, revolving what he had heard. A slight covering of snow lay on the ground, just enough to make the fields and roads white. The little girl, peeping from the door, thought his honour was contemplating the landscape in reference to the tempting prospect of snow-balling. Mr. Arde was debating whether, instead of turning home at once, where nobody waited for him, he would not rather go on to Harebell Farm and question Mary Barber. He felt half inclined to continue his walk also, from thence to the Trailing Indian.

"All safe. Trust me," the Squire had said to Otto Clanwaring; and said it in perfect good faith. He would no more have gone talking of this matter to a stranger than he would have set the Worcester bellman to cry it in that city the next market-day: but it never occurred to him to think that he might not speak of it privately to the only one to whom (apart from Beechhurst Dene) the incident concerning Black was known—who had been the one to witness it, and to carry it to the Dene—Mary Barber. Rather, he considered, it was a secret lodged between himself and her; one that concerned him in whom they were both interested, and of whose innocence both felt equally sure—Tom Clanwaring.

"I'll go," decided the Squire. "I've got plenty of time on my hands, and a longer walk this sharp day'll do me good. Precious cold that homeward journey was: one's feet get frozen, travelling such weather as this."

"Good day, Squire. So you're back again, sir!"

The salutation came from Cole, the farrier, who met the Squire as he was wheeling round.

"Just back," returned the Squire. "I've been to Bristol."

A light shone in Cole's eyes. The words revealed to him that he had been to see Tom Clanwaring.

"Is he really a-going to Ireland, Squire?"

"That he is, Cole. According to present intentions."

"What a shame it was, their suspecting him about that bag of money!" resumed Cole. "As if Mr. Tom 'ud do dirty work o' that sort!"

"Pooh, that was all nonsense," said the Squire carelessly. "It's known it wasn't him."

"Ay, sure: or else I might ha' put a spoke in the wheel for him myself," returned Cole, in a significant tone that caught the Squire's ear. "I saw somebody that same evening not a hundred mile off Sir Dene's bay-parlour."

"I know!" cried the Squire in his incautious impatience. "'Twas Randy Black."

Cole glanced keenly at the Squire, as if in some slight surprise: and then his eyes went straight out into the far-away horizon. It was only that morning that he had received Tom Clanwaring's letter, enjoining silence.

"As to Randy Black, if all tales be true, he's capable o' worse things than stealing money," returned the farrier, carelessly. "But I'm not going to mix myself up in his affairs. Good day, Squire."

"Good day, Cole."

CHAPTER XXIX.

MISS EMMA GONE.

"ALL of a shake, he was, and his face whiter nor this here kerchief I've got on," said Mary Barber, in answer to Mr. Arde's confidential questionings, as she stood, cloth in hand, and her gown drawn through its pocket-hole: for he had disturbed her when she was hard at work in the best parlour, "beeswaxing" the bright old mahogany furniture.

"There can't be a doubt that it's what he had been after—that bag of money," returned the Squire. "The very absurdity of his plea for accounting for the fright; that he had seen—had seen Robert Owen, would be almost enough evidence, without anything else."

Mary Barber did not immediately reply. She had thoughts and thoughts. Dwelling upon the matter very much, indeed, as she had done since her visit to Beechhurst Dene, she had come to a somewhat different conclusion from that which she had mentally drawn then.

"Squire Arde, I think he saw the poor master. Any way, that he fancied he did. Because——"

"How can you talk such nonsense, woman?" interrupted Mr. Arde—who had never liked the report at all. "I thought that fools' gossip had died out long ago."

"So did I," said independent Mary Barber. "But it seems it hasn't: though what on earth can bring him above ground again—if he is above it—is more than I can tell. Look here, Squire: that terror of Randy Black's last Saturday night was real terror: and I don't believe it was caused, or could ha' been caused, by anything but what he said. Supernatural terror is different from other terror, say that caused by the fear o' pursuit. Had Black been running from pursuit only, he'd not have had his face ghastly, and his teeth a-chattering, and his skin in a clammy sweat. He'd ha' been flying stealthily, too, with steps as hardly dared touch the ground for 'fraid o' being heard and tracked: not with a great bustle and noise, as he was."

She paused, and gave a moment's vigorous rub to the table, as if to enforce the argument. Squire Arde stood, knitting his brow. Leaving the cloth where it was, she resumed:—

"Randy Black 'ud no more have showed that mortal fear to living man or woman, if 'twasn't real, than he'd confess himself a thief. It's the sort o' fear men be ashamed to own to: and they never would own to it but for being took unawares like, in the minute that the fright's upon 'em. Why, Squire, he was *beside* himself with fright! He a'most clung to my shawl for company! If he'd only been a-taking the money, would he have give Jack Pound's boy a sixpence to walk up Harebell Lane with him, because he didn't dare to go alone? No; he'd rather have slunk off somewhere by hisself, and hid away from pursuit. Randy Black saw the old master on Saturday night, Squire," she concluded emphatically, "or thought he saw him, as safe as that my name's Mary Barber."

"All the same he might have helped himself to the bag of money."

"He *might*," she answered, with a stress on the word that indicated doubt. "I don't feel so sure of it as I did in the first burst o' the thing. Maybe time 'll tell, sir."

And somehow, Mr. Arde, a rather impressionable man, did not feel so sure of it, either. Instead of returning home when he left the farm, he walked across the fields towards the Trailing Indian. The narrow path between the grove and the fence, from whence poor Robert Owen had fallen (as was supposed) to his death; the pond in the lane underneath; the old cowshed in the two-acre meadow—all were there just as they used to be a quarter of a century before. Squire Arde, passing the familiar objects, had his thoughts back in that bygone time. He remembered, as though it had taken place but yesterday, that visit he and his relative, the quaint old Squire, and Geoffry Clanwaring had made to the Trailing Indian the day after Robert Owen's disappearance, and his own vague doubts of Black. If the landlord had really had any hand in Mr. Owen's death, it might account for these fits of superstitious terror, that had occasionally assailed him since.

Silent and deserted as usual looked the Trailing Indian when Mr. Arde approached it. But no sooner had he entered the yard gate than a stout young fellow of eighteen, Sam Pound, came rushing out of the stable. His smock frock was rolled up round his middle, he wore no hat, and he had altogether the air of being at home and at work.

The Pounds were enough to puzzle people—there was such a flock of them. John and Matty Pound, at whose cottage, as may be remembered, the Widow Barber died, had fifteen children. This young man, Sam, was the youngest of them; Jack, the eldest of the bunch, was the father of the little lad who was carter's boy at Harebell Farm.

"Is it you, Sam Pound?" exclaimed Mr. Arde. "What are you doing here?"

"I be a come to live up here, Squire," was the answer—and the young man appeared proud of having to say it, and pulled his hair, that was like nothing in the world but tow. "That there stable be in a rare muck o' pickle, so I were a cleaning of it out a bit."

"Come to live here?" repeated the Squire slowly, thinking it strange Black should take on a man when so little business was doing to require it. "Are you to be ostler?"

"Man of all work, indoors and out. Randy Black, he sent for old feyther to come up yesterday, and they made the bargain atween 'em. Five pound a year I be to earn and my witl's and lodging. There be nobody but me to do nothing for 'em nohow," added Sam Pound, who possessed about the readiest tongue within a ten-mile radius. "Landlord, he be bad of his cough; and missis, her's bad; and Miss Geach, she've been and went off."

"Where's she gone to? What's she gone for?" questioned the Squire.

"Well, I take it her didn't care to stay no longer i' the face and eyes o' folks," returned the shrewd young man. "After cocketing up of herself above the parish all these mortal years, and a turning up of her nose at decent, hardworking young men like our Jim, a fine market she've been and went and brought her pigs to. And Jim, he's a doing better nor any on us, and could ha' give her a good home, wi' a side o' bacon in't!"

"But where's she gone?" repeated Mr. Arde.

Sam Pound shook his head to indicate his ignorance upon the point; shook it resentfully too.

"Her stopped the stage coach as it druv along the highway yonder yester morn, missis says, and got up atop, and sot herself down on't; her, and her big ban'box o' clothes alongside of her."

The first object Mr. Arde saw on entering the inn was Black himself, groaning and coughing, and choking over the kitchen-fire. Whether Black's disobedience of the Doctor's injunction to stay indoors, had tended to bring on a relapse, or whether it might have been the adventure in the Beechhurst Dene grounds that was telling on his nerves, certain it was that the man looked very ill; ominously so. The poor ailing wife, worse than usual that day, was lying in bed upstairs. Mr. Arde sat down, his stout umbrella held out before him.

Now, Squire Arde had not gone to the inn to accuse Black outright of the theft; rather, he intended by a series of delicate pumpings, to glean what he could in an incidental manner, and thence deduce his own judgment of things. But nearly at the first, he found himself foiled. Black evidently could not understand him; and when Mr. Arde spoke out more plainly, the man's surprise was so great, and apparently so genuine, that Mr. Arde was fairly puzzled.

"Don't you know that Sir Dene lost a bag of money out of his secretary on Saturday night?" pursued Mr. Arde.

"I never knew a word on't," returned Black emphatically, turning his white face (white from sickness) full on the Squire's—and for once both face and tones seemed as truthful as an honest man's. "What sort of a bag was't—how much money had it got in't?"

"Well, it was just a little sample barley-bag; and the sum was forty-five pounds," replied the Squire, giving him gaze for gaze.

"Notes or gold, sir?"

"Both."

Black slowly turned his eyes on the kitchen fire, and seemed to be thinking. It must be owned that he had not the air of a guilty man.

"Hearing that you were met flying out of the grounds about the same time, Black—that is, at dusk—I was wondering whether you had seen anything of the robbery," continued

Mr. Arde, thinking he was opening the ball with charming finesse. "Any suspicious-looking people round the bay window, for instance?"

Black shook his head. "I warn't anigh the bay-window, Squire. I never got more nor half way up the path to'ard it."

"What put you in that state of fright, then? You had, I believe, all the appearance of a man flying from pursuit."

"Well, because I got a fright, Squire. It don't matter what 'twas. I——"

Black stopped short, turned sideways, and looked at his visitor questioningly, the sickly face growing a little dark. Mr. Arde thought the man had suddenly divined that he was suspected of this thing.

"I had got a fright," he repeated sullenly.

"Fancying you saw Mr. Owen's ghost!"

"Did you hear that there from Mary Barber?" questioned Black after a pause.

"Well—yes. That's near enough. What a foolish coward you must be, Black, to fancy anything so ridiculous!"

"I see him as plain as I see you at this moment, Squire," burst forth Black in excitement. "He stood i' the pathway right in front of me, and I were close up again him afore I knew what 'twas, a-standing there i' the dusk. I swear I saw him. I'd swear it if 'twas my last breath."

The recollection, even now, seemed to bring out a cold sweat on Black's face. Mr. Arde, his hands leaning on the top of his umbrella, and his chin on his hands, could but look at him. For some moments nothing was to be heard but the ticking of the eight-day clock, standing in its upright case against the wall by the chimney-piece.

"Never a thing did I see i' the grounds but the ghost o' Robert Owen," resumed Black, with the same amount of earnestness but with less excitement. "Nothing frighted me but that. As to the theft o' money from Sir Dene's parlour, I saw nothing on't, nor nobody about to help theirselves to't. And I'll take my oath as I never heered o' the loss till this minute."

Had it been anybody but Black, the Squire would have given to this the most implicit credence. Being Black, knowing the man's habitual cunning and ruses—his assertions of innocence when accused of poaching and the like, every word of which was always a deliberate lie—he knew not what to think. A question suddenly occurred to him after he had risen to depart.

"What brought you in the Beechhurst Dene grounds at all, Black?"

"I was a-going to ask leave to speak to Captain Clanwaring," replied the man readily. "He's owing me a trifle for baccy, him; and I thought I'd go across, and ask him for't."

A very reasonable plea, presenting neither doubt nor difficulty to the mind of Mr. Arde. Sometimes he owed for tobacco at the Trailing Indian himself.

"I hear that Emma Geach is gone away," he remarked, the door in his hand.

"Drat her, yes!—and I be glad on't," exploded Black, in a very different tone. "I'd sooner have her room nor her company."

"Where's she gone?"

"Her didn't tell me. Took French leave, and was off afore I got out o' bed! Let her go!—go where her will. Dratted baggage!"

A sense of failure, in regard to the result of his expedition, lay on Squire Arde's mind as he and his umbrella went down Harebell Lane.

"I don't know what to believe, and that's the fact," he told himself. "Every word the man spoke seemed true. But then—who can trust Black? But for Otto Clanwaring's strict injunctions to be silent, I'd ask the captain who the other one is that he suspects. As it is—well, it's of no good for *me* to meddle further in it. Tom's cleared among 'em, and so let it go."

Sir Dene Clanwaring and the Squire spent a pleasant evening together, Gander waiting on them. Sir Dene avoided the topic of Tom Clanwaring (and indeed all topics connected with home troubles), but ever and anon a chance word would drop from him inadvertently, by which Mr. Arde gathered how much Tom was missed. At nine o'clock he took leave, for the host was weary, and wanted to go to rest.

"Sir Dene feels Tom's absence very deeply," innocently remarked the Squire to Lady Lydia, when he looked into the drawing-room, where she was sitting alone. Captain Clanwaring and Mrs. Letsom were dining abroad; Otto had gone out to post a letter. "Sir Dene wants him back again."

"Wants him back again!" repeated my lady, letting fall her knitting.

"That he does," cried the blundering Squire—who was one that could never see an inch beyond his nose. "I think we shall have him back, too, before a week, or so's, gone over.

Every drop of blood in Lady Lydia's veins seemed to stand still as she listened. Have the scapegoat back again!—after all her trouble! but she was a thorough diplomatist; and she smiled sweetly on the Squire as he stood before her.

"You have been to Bristol to see him, I hear."

"Aye, I thought I'd better go. And really, Lady Lydia, I must say, I think he has been sent away unjustly. Tom assured me that he had done nothing to merit expulsion, as far as he knew."

"You are so kind-hearted, dear Squire; and so unsuspicious! Of course, Tom Clanwaring would not proclaim his naughty deeds to you."

"The question, my lady, is—has he done any?" was the somewhat blunt answer.

Standing beside him on the hearthrug, glancing round as if to make sure that they were indeed alone, her voice quite affectionately low, her smile sweet still, my lady breathed into the Squire's ear, a whisper of Miss Emma Geach.

"No!" broke out the Squire. "That never was Tom."

"Yes, it was. *Tom.*" And then she told what she had heard from Otto. Woven into a tale (as she had been weaving it in her mind this past week) it seemed to be a charming history of proofs, one fitting into another. Lady Lydia, herself, fully believed in it.

The Squire gave vent to a long, dismal whistle. "I'd never have believed it of him," he cried, his mouth falling. "What a confounded hypocrite he must be!"

"Believe me, dear Mr. Arde, it is better that he should be away than here," she plaintively said. "Better for the peace of this house; better for that miserable girl at the Trailing Indian; better for you, especially better for your daughter. Rely upon it, all things are ordered for the best."

"What difference does it make to my daughter?" demanded Mr. Arde, opening his eyes at the words.

"Ah—what! But perhaps I ought not to speak out so fully," she added, in her candour. "I should not to any one but yourself. He was a presuming, designing villain, dear Mr. Arde. He dared to fall in love with May—there's no question of it; there's no doubt he dared to cherish the prospect of making her his wife. Yes, even he, Mr. Tom Clanwaring!"

The Squire's eyes dilated: the Squire's eyes grew round with horror. *He!*—the penniless obscure scapegoat, Tom Clanwaring?

"Make up to Miss Arde—to my daughter!" he stuttered. "Why the fellow must possess the impudence of Belial! Is he mad?"

"But that your own eyes must have been held, you would have seen it for yourself," she said. "I think Mrs. Arde saw it. There's no knowing what he might have beguiled May into, had he remained—a secret marriage, possibly: girls are innocent and persuadeable. Secret marriages run in his race, you know."

It was a side fling at poor dead Geoffry and Maria. Mr. Arde, overwhelmed with a conflict of feelings, wondered whether he was awake or asleep.

"Believe me, Squire, it is good for us all that he should be at a safe distance. Once in Ireland, the sea will flow between him and us. *Let him stay there.*"

Squire Arde acquiesced with his whole heart, and with a few strong words. He would have moved heaven and earth then to keep Tom Clanwaring and danger away, rather than help to recall him. *His* daughter!—and her twenty thousand pounds on her wedding-day, coveted by him! He began to see that he *was* a scapegoat, and nothing less: he began to think it likely that he *had* taken that money; all the enormities of which Tom Clanwaring had been accused found a willing echo in his mind. So prone is frail human nature to be swayed by self-interest.

Going down the avenue on his way home, and stamping as he went, as if to throw the flakes of snow off his boots, in reality to stamp off his indignation, whom should he meet just before he got to the lodge but Otto Clanwaring. In a few angry words the Squire stormed out the news he had heard, and compared Tom to the arch-enemy.

"Confound it! I wish I had lost my tongue before I'd ever mentioned the thing," was Otto's sharp retort. "We are none of us so white ourselves, Squire, I dare say. As to that Geach girl and her native impudence, *she's* not much to make an outcry over."

"It's not that," foamed the Squire: "it's the two-faced hypocrisy of the fellow altogether. I believed in him a'most as I believed in myself, Otto Clanwaring."

And away he went; stamping furiously amidst the snow-storm.

CHAPTER XXX.

SELLING OUT.

THE days and weeks went on. Tom Clanwaring's departure got to be a thing of the past. Tom was in Ireland, hard at work, filling the post he had been sent to. It was no sinecure. He had been pretty active on his grandfather's estate; he had to do a vast deal more now; and his personal responsibility was greatly increased. The rumour, that he had stood in the relation of sweetheart to Miss Emma Geach had become public property—but I think this has been said before: and Hurst Leet concluded that Sir Dene—or perhaps my lady—had banished him by way of punishment. Considering the light estimation anything of sweethearting was then held in, and the lighter estimation in which Miss Geach was held, Hurst Leet came to the conclusion that the punishment was harder than it need have been.

In January, when Otto Clanwaring returned to London, the captain ran up with him, having, as he said, business there. But Jarvis was soon back again. Sir Dene, responding to some dexterous persuasion of my lady's, helped Captain Clanwaring temporarily with a tolerably fair sum. It ought to have set him on his legs. Perhaps everybody thought it had, save the captain and his creditors.

In one thing the wise captain showed himself unwise. Unwise as a child. No sooner was he down at Beechhurst Dene again, than he made an offer of his hand to Mary Arde. In the whole, Tom had not been gone three weeks; the remembrance of him and his shallowey disguised love was full on May; and Captain Jarvis Clanwaring's own sense (for he certainly suspected the love) might have told him so. May refused him, with a few pretty words of thanks. What else could he expect? Privately cursing his precipitancy, the gallant captain made her a soft bland speech, intimating that his love for her could never die; and that he was willing to wait and work for her as Jacob (to whom he compared himself) did for Rachel, and think it no hardship. To this May replied that she begged he would not think of waiting for *her;* she had made up her mind not to marry at all. They parted good friends, apparently on the same terms that they had been beforehand.

After this, Captain Clanwaring divided his time pretty equally between London and Beechhurst Dene. No lover could ever pay his court more silently and unobtrusively than he did to May, hoping to rectify that first mistake. Not a day passed but he was at the hall: but he pressed no more attentions on May than he did on her mother. He had made up his mind to win her, and win her he would, but he knew that he could not do it by storm. Lady Lydia made the best play for him, especially with Mr. and Mrs. Arde.

And in Mr. Arde's great fear lest his daughter should be beguiled by Tom Clanwaring and bestow herself and her twenty thousand pounds upon so miserable a scapegoat (for over that twenty thousand pounds Mr. Arde had no control whatever), he looked with something like favour on the pretensions of Jarvis Clanwaring. Captain Clanwaring was not a particular favourite of his: he had disliked him as a boy, he did not much like him as a man; and he would not have preferred a soldier for May. Still the captain seemed strangely desirable by the side of Tom. We estimate all things by comparison, and shall as long as the world lasts. Mr. Arde knew no particular ill of Captain Clanwaring: it was generally believed that the captain had a few debts; but debt was so common an appendage at that day to young men of fashion that Mr. Arde did not give that a second thought. Lady Lydia whispered that Jarvis would inherit a large amount of Sir Dene's savings, and all of her own. What her savings might be, or whence they came, she did not state: but Mr. and Mrs. Arde, both single-minded people in the main, never doubted her word.

To his wife, and his wife alone, Mr. Arde had whispered the tale of Tom's evil-doings, of the incredible manner in which they had been deceived in him, of the infamous hypocrisy he must have carried on. Rushing home that January night through the snow-storm, he found his wife, just returned, sitting over the fire in her bedroom, and he told her all. Mrs. Arde was shocked. She had a high esteem for Tom: putting aside that semi-fear as to her daughter, she liked him excessively; and she could not at first give credit to the tale. Her husband assured her it was positively true: having no doubt of it himself, you see. They agreed to keep it from May; it was not suitable for her ears; never to breathe it to her, save in the extremity of necessity. May gathered that Tom had done something or other frightfully wrong—a vast deal worse than having knocked down Captain Clanwaring in a passion; but when she asked her mother what it was, Mrs. Arde replied that it would not bear talking of.

Just a word here about Miss Emma Geach. She was supposed to be hiding her diminished head in some shelter, near or distant, as might be convenient to her; taking rest, and gathering fresh strength and (as the people put it) brass, against the time that she should come forth again to adorn the world. And that she would come, and live amongst them as usual, Hurst Leet made no sort of question of. And thus the time went on.

The next news was that Captain Clanwaring had quitted the army—sold out. Lady Lydia was the first to carry the tidings to Arde Hall; Jarvis being in London completing the negotiations. Two causes had induced him to take the step, she said: the one was, that he could not bear to separate from May—as he must have done, for he was unable to get a further extension of absence; the other, that he knew Mr. Arde would like him better if he were not a soldier. In reference to May, Mr. Arde certainly would: but he observed to Lady Lydia that he thought it a pity: young men were so much better with some occupation than without it.

The same reasons were assigned to Sir Dene Clanwaring, upon whom the news came with intense surprise. Sir Dene was rapidly failing in health. Both body and mind were now so weakened that a state of something like apathy had set in; and he rarely took much note of anything. This selling out of Jarvis's, however, aroused him in an extraordinary degree, and he stormed over it as he had been wont to storm over annoyances in the days gone by. Lady Lydia quietly shut the doors while it lasted, then answered his questions and set herself to soothe the tempest. How did the fellow think he was going to live, flinging up his profession in that mad way, demanded Sir Dene; and my Lady calmly answered that he was going to marry Squire Arde's daughter, and would succeed to the Hall (as a matter of course) in the lapse of time. Sir Dene shook his head, only half convinced—half convinced of the wedding project, not at all of the expediency of the selling out—but his physical powers were unequal to maintain either passion or contention long. Dear Jarvey had quitted the army because of this contemplated marriage, she urged; he would for the present take up his abode at Beechhurst Dene, and make himself useful to his revered grandfather.

Such was my lady's specious whispers. But what, in all sincere truth, were the real inducing facts of his selling out? Simply, that he could not keep in. Captain Clanwaring was so deeply involved in debt that he was obliged to get the proceeds of his commission to extricate him—or, rather, partially to extricate him; for it would only go half way to it. Assistance he must have to avoid exposure and disgrace. In some way or another, he had managed to stave off the evil day until now: when it could no longer be staved off by any mortal contrivance known in this world, save some of its golden coin. There was but one way of getting it, and that was by selling the commission. Lady Lydia had absolutely none to give him; and Sir Dene it was of no use asking. My lady had sounded the baronet in a delicate way, and found him more inexorable than a flint. Not another pennypiece should Jarvis have from him, he said—nay, swore—as he buttoned up his breeches pockets emphatically; he had let him have too much already for his own good. Press it, Lady Lydia dared not; still less might she hint at the embarrassment her son was in; lest Sir Dene should talk of it to Mr. Arde (as he would be sure to do), and Jarvis's hopes be ruined with May.

So the commission was disposed of, and Captain Clanwaring —retaining his title by courtesy—took up his permanent abode at Beechhurst Dene. Weston, the new superintendent of the estate, had not proved a very efficient successor to Tom Clanwaring; my lady, my dint of prayers and tears, and almost going on her knees to beg it, got Jarvis to ride out on the land once a week, or so: and regaled Sir Dene's ears with dear good Jarvis's anxious industry in Sir Dene's interests. Sir Dene took no notice: thoroughly put out with the ex-captain, he was barely civil to him.

Grating ever on the baronet's mind was the one bitter fact of Tom's ingratitude. Not a line had he received from him since his departure. He concluded—as what else could he conclude?—that the young man had shaken off the ties and obligations of years as we shake off an old garment when it has served our turn, and abandoned him, his grandfather. Never was there a greater truth written than that of Shakspeare's—" Blow, blow, thou wintry wind; thou art not so unkind as man's ingratitude;" and Sir Dene was feeling it to his heart of hearts.

But now—what was the fact? If Tom had written one

letter to Sir Dene, he had written ten. All had been confiscated by Lady Lydia as that first one was, sent from Bristol. At length Tom wrote to *her*: asking how it was he did not hear from Sir Dene; or, indeed from any one. My lady answered him forthwith. Sir Dene was poorly and ailing, too much so to be crossed or troubled, she represented. He was still incensed against Tom, and she did not wonder at it, remembering what discomfort he had caused in those latter days at the Dene: she added (in a parenthesis) he could not *bear* to see one of Tom's letters arrive, caused them always to be put in the fire unopened; my lady therefore counselled Tom not to write again.

To suppress letters or to present them to their owners, was an equally easy task for Lady Lydia, since they were delivered at Beechhurst Dene in a closed bag, of which she now kept the key.

Another person that Tom had written to again, was Mr. Arde. When he had been about a fortnight in Ireland, he wrote to tell him what the place was like, what he had to do, and so on; he also once more thanked him for his unexpected liberality. Now, what did Squire Arde do on the receipt of this letter? He went into a passion and sent it back again. Snatching a sheet of paper, he penned a few strong words, commenting on Tom's rascally presumption in daring to address him, forbidding him so to offend again, wrapped the letter inside, and despatched it to Ireland, unpaid. So, between them all, Tom got hardly used.

And now things went on swimmingly. Captain Clanwaring, in feather as to cash, at least, temporarily, was the gayest of the gay. He was a fairly good-looking man, popular in the county, and he made the most of his attractions. The report, whispered by Lady Lydia—that her son Jarvis would inherit all, or nearly all, of Sir Dene's property not entailed—the entailed portion of course descending to young Dene—spread everywhere; and people, judging hastily, took it for granted Jarvis would be rich. Mothers far and near courted Captain Clanwaring; daughters ran wild to get from him only a look. He was the fashion; the one cynosure of society; and that, in a country district, and in the long-past days we are writing of, implied a great deal. But he had only eyes and ears for May Arde; his tender words, his sweetest smiles, his fascinations altogether, were lavished upon *her*. Mrs. Arde favoured the Captain's pretensions far more than the Squire did. Good looks, good family, irreproachable name (and for all the Squire or any of his friends suspected, the captain's was sufficiently irreproachable), devoted love, and the star of fashion are all good things in their way, but they do not entirely compensate for lack of an assured position, of a safe income, or for a kind of innate dislike that the Squire could but be conscious of. But these objections of his were not absolutely insurmountable. Whoever married May would obtain by the act present money and future position, for Arde Hall would descend to May: and in regard to liking or disliking, that was May's affair more than her father's. Altogether, the Squire was at length brought to say that if May set her mind upon Captain Clanwaring, he would not hold out against the marriage. Captain Clanwaring in answer (for the concession was spoken to him personally) seized the Squire's two hands in his, and thanked him with deep emotion, his dark eyelashes wet with tears.

"I think the fellow has some good in him," decided the Squire.

And so, once more, all things being propitious, the captain tried his chance, and had another fling with the die. It was a lovely day in June, and Mary was sitting outside the window on the lawn bench, under the walnut tree, reading a new book. She wore a dress of some thin pink material, its low body and short sleeves (still the fashion) adorned with white lace. Her brown eyes were bright, her pretty hair was tossed back, her cheeks had a radiant blush. Something in the book had called up the signs, for the story put her in mind of her own story and Tom Clanwaring's—a rich heroine was constant to a poor lover. May in her heart was just as constant to Tom, and meant to be; but the secret was buried five fathoms deep within her breast.

"How I long to peep at the end! I know it must all come right there!" she softly said, turning over some of the leaves. "But, no, I'll not: it would spoil my pleasure in reading. And something else will come right, if we only have patience. I wonder what he is thinking all this while. If—oh, my goodness, here comes that other one!"

The other one was Captain Clanwaring. Glancing round in desperate hopelessness of escape, May could only sit on where she was. The captain, decked out in nankeen trousers and all the other fashionable adjuncts of the period, was kissing the tips of his tan-coloured glove to her, as he advanced, flourishing his cane. May wished the grass-plot would open and let him in.

Not at all. He came on safely, and sat down beside her. Possibly seduced to it by the sweetness of the summer day—the balmy air, the rich hues of the flowers on which the bees hummed and the butterflies sported, the scent of the new-mown hay in the side-field, the universal loveliness of all things around—or perhaps by the winning beauty of May herself. Captain Clanwaring again spoke the few magic words to her, that many another girl in the country might have given her ears to hear. "May, will you be my wife?"

"Oh—thank you—thank you very much," responded May, in a desperate flutter. "But—I—can't."

"Do you mean that you *won't*, May?"

"I—can't—thank you; I don't want to marry," stammered May. "Please, Captain Clanwaring, don't ever say anything about it again."

She had risen to escape; but he caught her hand and detained her. Holding her before him while he poured forth his love-tale, her face so pretty in its distress, the blushes chasing each other across it, was more than he could withstand; May suddenly found his handsome black moustache bent upon her lips, and a kiss taken. With a sharp wrench of her hands out of his, and a cry of pain, May got away from him and ran indoors.

Susan Cole, putting her young lady's things to right in the wardrobe, was astonished to see her dart into the chamber, fling herself on a chair, and burst into tears.

"What on earth has took you now, Miss May?"

"I wish I could run away somewhere! I wish I could!" exclaimed Miss May, passionately. "It is a wretched world!"

"Indeed, and I think it's a very good world, for them that like to make the best on't," said Susan.

At that moment some lines of an old song were heard through the open window; a tolerably old song even in that day. The singer was probably unconscious that he had an audience.

> "Don't you remember a poor carpet weaver,
>   Whose daughter loved a youth so true.
> He promised one day that he never would leave her,
>   Down in the vale where violets grew.
> Never, he told her, would he be a rover:
>   She fondly thought he told her true.
> Ah, how shall this maid his truth discover?
>   Ah, will he plight his vows anew?"

Susan Cole's head went cautiously out. "It's Captain Clanwaring, Miss May!" she whispered, bringing it in again. "He's a-sitting on that there seat below, under the walnut tree."

"And I wish he was hanging on the tree instead!" returned Miss May.

CHAPTER XXXI.

BETTER TO HAVE LET THE DOUBT LIE.

STILL as a statue, her face white and rigid, almost like one that is carved out of stone, sat Mary Arde. There's an old saying, "Desperate causes require desperate remedies"—and a desperate remedy had just been applied to Mary's obstinacy. In the vexation brought to Mrs. Arde by her daughter's second refusal of Captain Clanwaring; in the worse vexation inflicted by the full persuasion that the rejection was caused solely by the young lady's liking for Tom, Mrs. Arde suffered herself to impart some hints to May, which she would have been sorry to do under less exacting circumstances.

It could not be (to go back a few months) but that the gossiping charges, laid to the door of Miss Emma Geach, should have penetrated the ears of Squire Arde's daughter. Not a man, woman, or child in the place but heard the comments freely bestowed upon that young person's ill-behaviour, and May amidst the rest. But that Miss Emma's doings, good or bad, could by any possibility concern her, or any of her friends or acquaintances, never crossed the mind of May Arde. How should it? May—to confess the truth—had always liked Emma Geach; with May the girl was never impudent, but pleasant and good-natured; and May had thought her very pretty. So that, when she grew to be talked of, May's feeling on the point was one of intense sorrow; and very little of blame. Indeed, as sensible people remarked, the wonder was, not that the girl had gone wrong now, but that she had kept straight so long, reared amidst the disreputable influences of the Trailing Indian.

Nothing whatever had been heard of Emma Geach since that black January morning when she took her abrupt departure by coach from the inn. As the months went on, and she did not make her re-appearance, as expected, people grew tired of looking for her. They regarded her prolonged absence as a

Y

kind of slight offered to their curiosity, and resented it. Where was she? What had become of her? Surely she had had time enough and to spare, to repose herself in her retreat! Who was she with?—what was she doing? All the gossips in the parish asked it one of another. But for any answer that ensued, they might as well have put the questions to the moon.

Late in the spring; nay, at the commencement of the summer; a kind of solution came. There arose a rumour in the place that Miss Emma's retreat was discovered. It was affirmed that she was in Ireland, paying a friendly visit to Mr. Tom Clanwaring.

This clinching assertion could not at first be traced to any one person in particular. Z heard it from Y; Y from X; X from W; and so on; but to get all the way back to A, step by step, seemed impossible. At length it was said that Black at the Trailing Indian was the authority, and that his wife had received a letter from Ireland from Emma Geach. Upon that, all eyes were opened in a most wonderful and convincing manner; and people asked one another how they could have been so obtuse as not to discern that when she went off by the stage coach it must have been because *he* had gone before, and that she probably went straight to Bristol, the horses' heads being set that way. High and low, up and down, went this report: to Beechhurst Dene and its grieving master; to Mr. and Mrs. Arde; to the village shopkeepers, to the peasants in the hay-fields.

"The girl in Ireland?—It cannot surely be true!" cried Mrs. Arde, aghast.

"Nay, but it is true; there's no doubt of it," replied Lady Lydia—for it was she who had first carried the news to the Hall. "Jarvis went up to the Trailing Indian, and put the question direct to Black."

A charming dish of well-seasoned hash, all this to tell May. Or, rather, to hint to her; for Mrs. Arde, respecting her youth and innocence, did not speak out very plainly. And there sat May alone in her chamber after the communication, feeling more dead than alive.

Tom Clanwaring worthless—and *so* worthless! Tom Clanwaring whose love she had fondly thought was given alone to her, and who had, and knew that he had, her whole heart! Oh, what a simpleton she had been! What a poor, soft, deluded simpleton.

On the past Christmas night—barely six months—but

which seemed to May, looking back, ages and ages—she had been so intensely happy as to wonder whether anything in life could ever look cloudy again; now, sitting there in her miserable chamber, with that most miserable blow weighing down her head, that utter despair her heart, she felt that life, no matter how long it might endure, would never emit for her one ray of brightness.

"Poor child!" exclaimed sympathising Susan Cole, who divined what the nature of the interview between mother and daughter had been as sharply as though she had made a third at it. "It's too bad o' missis to ha' told you *that!*"

May looked up with a start: her frame shivering, her cheeks hectic. She could not have spoken openly of the trouble for all the world; she would have died rather than let it be suspected how it was trying her. But, to this woman, who had nursed her in infancy, scolded and kissed her at will, her heart yearned for what none could impart—consolation.

"I don't think you know anything about it, Susan," she said, speaking in the lightest tone she could call up. "I don't know what you mean."

"Not know about it! Why, Miss May, every soul i' the parish has knowed about it for months past, but you. After keeping it from you so long, I say it might ha' been kept always.

"It can't be true, Susan!"

"Miss May, don't you try to go again common sense," reprimanded Susan. "Facts is facts. And, now that you've been made to hear 'em, it's o' no use to hope to shut your eyes again 'em. There's nobody i' the whole place as does, but one: that there brother o' mine, down at the forge."

A light as of half-hope shone in May's eyes. "Does *he* not believe it, Susan?"

"What, Harry Cole! Not he. If he see Mr. Tom Clanwaring a setting his neighbour's rick afire, Harry Cole 'nd shut his eyes, and only believe in him all the more. He swears by Mr. Tom Clanwaring; he do."

"Do *you* believe in it, Susan?" breathed May, quite hating herself for stooping to put the question. But, in great misery, it is something to have even a straw to catch at.

"I should be a soft sawney if I didn't," was Susan Cole's answer.

"It is very dreadful," sighed May, with a sob of the breath.

"Oh well, of course it *is,* Miss May," came the only half-acquiescing rejoinder. "But young men *be* young men, all the world over. For the most part, you may just trust 'em as far as you can see 'em. I be bound poor Mr. Tom had a rare example set him by Captain Clan'ring—in smoking and chaffing and what not," continued Susan, tossing her head. "The one manages not to get found out, and the t'other can't manage it; that's the chief difference, I expect, Miss May."

Susan whirled away from the room with as little ceremony as she had used in whirling into it. May sat on with her sorrow.

But, thinking here and thinking there, a reaction took place in her mind. All the deep regard and esteem given to Tom Clanwaring for years could not thus be set aside in an hour's time. May began to remember how unjustly Tom Clanwaring had been traduced, always; and to ask herself what *proof* there was of this new charge; to question whether there could be any.

"Susan," she said, when the maid next entered, "all this may be only a tale. Where's the proof of it?"

"Proof?" returned Susan. "Well, there's only two people 'i the place can furnish that, Miss May—Black and his wife at the Trailing Indian."

"How I wish I dare ask them!" thought May in her desperation.

For three days and nights May brooded over the question—*might* she ask them? And what at first she began by answering to herself "decidedly not," ended in "I will." During those three days and nights she neither ate nor slept: hope and fear alternated, the latter greatly predominating: and the whole time was as one long mental agony.

Perhaps she might never have gone, but for a rather singularly good opportunity, of doing so, presenting itself. These opportunities are the occasion of half the good and of half the evil that takes place in the world. On the third day, in the afternoon, Mr. and Mrs. Arde went to a dinner-party, a drive of seven miles, leaving May at home alone.

It was one of those lovely summer evenings, when the moon is rising just as the sun sets. Bright, warm, still, the world seeming to be at rest, under its flood of golden light. It had been too hot for walking in the day; May had sat about in garden seats and under trees, nursing that hidden weight that lay on her heart. A wish to go for a walk now arose suddenly; and with it an impulsive thought that it should be to the Trailing Indian.

"I shall go out, Susan," she said in her pretty imperative way. "Put your things on."

As Susan Cole had no objection to this, but rather the contrary, she obeyed; and they started.

Behold them emerging from the Squire's grounds on the upper road. Miss May in a pretty hat trimmed with a garland of roses, and with a green parasol held against the light in the west where the sun had set; Susan Cole in her every-day bonnet, which was just the shape of a big coal-scuttle, and made of black silk: and in a spotted cotton kerchief crossed upon her shoulders. May had some dainty white frilled affair on over her summer muslin, and black lace mittens that went to the elbows. The young lady turned to the right on reaching the road.

"Going *that* way!" exclaimed Susan Cole, in an accent of surprise mingled with a little tartness. "What on earth for, Miss May?"

"Because I choose to," answered Miss May.

Susan Cole gave a sniff. The way did not please her. She liked to meet sociability and gossip when she went out. To the left there were houses and cottages and men and women. To the right, the way Miss May had chosen, there was nothing but the solitary road; Sir Dene Clanwaring's park wall bounding it on one side, the landscape beyond Dene Hollow on the other; and not a chance of encountering so much as a waggoner.

"Well, this is a lively way to take," cried Susan disparagingly. "Be you agoing to call at the Dene, Miss May?"

"Not if I know it, Susan."

Another sniff or two, particularly crusty, and Susan Cole stepped on, in her tied shoes and white stockings, at the young lady's side. Her cotton gown, a buff-coloured sprig upon its light ground, reached nearly to the ankles. By the very way she walked, long strides, and her feet planted firmly upon the path, May saw she was in one of what the young lady was wont to call "her tempers." All things considered, May thought it might be well to conciliate her. If Susan set her face obstinately against the expedition, they might never get there.

"I am going to the Trailing Indian, Susan."

The avowal took Susan aback. Abstractedly she had no objection; for to get a word or two of gossip with Black and his wife was better than getting none. But her mood just then was contrary.

"And what i' the name o' wonder should be a taking you there, Miss May?"

"I'm going to see how poor Mrs. Black is. And," she added, partly in her straightforward honesty, partly because Susan would be sure to know the true motive just as well as she did, "I shall ask whether that thing is true that has been said of Mr. Tom Clanwaring."

"And why need you want to know whether it's true or not?" demanded Susan Cole provokingly.

"Oh—because I think it is a great shame of people to raise reports behind his back, when he cannot refute them," her face turning as red as the crimson sunset. "We were children together, and I can't forget it: cousins you know. That's why."

"You'd a deal better let it alone, Miss May."

May's countenance took a defiant turn. "You think so, do you! And why, pray, Susan Cole?"

"Black be the only folk i' the parish able to confirm the story, and say as it's true. Nat'rally *they* must know—as the girl lived at their place. Better stop i' the doubt, Miss May, nor hear as there's no doubt about it."

But this was just what May did not intend to do. For, in her heart of hearts, she believed that a word of inquiry might prove Tom innocent instead of guilty.

In silence they proceeded up Harebell Lane, shady and gloomy in even the bright summer evening, round by the pond, and on to the inn. Seated on a wooden stool before the closed side door, was Black; while Mr. Sam Pound sauntered about the yard with a moody look on his face and his hands in his pockets, thereby looping up on either side his smock frock. Whether May's courage failed her at seeing Black, when she had hoped to see only his wife; or whether she would not let it be thought she was coming up expressly, certain it was that she went on past the house. Then, turning suddenly, she came across to Black.

"How is your wife?" she asked. For Mrs. Black's chronic state of ill-health was such that people rarely failed to inquire after her. Black, instead of answering—as if he neither heard the question or saw his visitor—lifted his face towards the upper part of the yard, and shouted out to the young man in the smock-frock.

"Hang ye, Sam Pound! Get off, will ye, and fetch that there mare in. What d'ye mean by slouching about there, a doing o' nothing?"

"Be the mare to come in to-night?" responded Sam Pound. For which apparently dissenting question, his master gave him some abuse; and Sam went off. The mare belonged to a traveller, who had left it for a week to the care of the Trailing Indian.

"What did ye ask—how the missis be?" resumed Black to Miss Arde, at his leisure, after this. "Her bain't no great things. Her never be."

"We should like to go in and see her," said the young lady timidly, "if you please."

"Ye can't then. Her bain't to be seen."

"Where's your manners, Randy Black!" put in Susan Cole sharply. "Is that the way you answer the Squire's young lady?"

Randy Black took no notice whatever of this. Stooping down, he picked up a dirty pipe that lay on the ground beside him, got some tobacco from his pocket, and began filling the bowl. The man looked somewhat better than he did in the winter; but his sallow face had strangely haggard lines upon it. He was seated so immediately before the door that they could not attempt to go in, unless he moved. Of late, the door in front, facing the road, had not been used; it was hardly ever unlocked.

"'Tain't o' no good your stopping," he suddenly said, just as Susan Cole was on the point of another explosion. "The missis be abed. I bain't agoing to let her be disturbed at this time o' evening." And as Black was not a man to be persuaded by any means, but always stuck to what he said, good or bad, May knew that all hope of seeing Mrs. Black was over. Susan Cole caught the look of depression that took her face.

"Look here, Randy," said Susan, diplomatically coming round to a kind of hail-fellow-well-met tone, "as we be here, I may as well have a word with you about Emma Geach. How was she getting on when you heard from her?"

"'Twarn't me as heerd; 'twere the missis," ungraciously returned Randy.

"Well, how was she?"

"Tolerable, I b'lieve. Baby were dead."

"'Twas a sad pity for her it should have happened, Randy,"

continued Susan, as if all her best sympathies were in full play for Miss Emma.

Randy gave an ungracious grunt. "Her made her own bed, and must lie on't."

"And—was her sweetheart really Tom Clanwaring?" asked Susan, dropping her voice to so low a tone that even May scarcely caught it. The young lady suddenly turned her back, as if she saw something passing in the lane.

"Why, who else should it ha' been?" retorted Randy, lifting his eyes in surprise at Susan Cole.

"One was slow to believe ill of *him*, you see," she observed with something like a sigh.

"So one is o' most folks as have carried white faces—till they be found out," said Randy, pressing down the tobacco with his dirty little finger.

"And is it true again that she's with him over in that there place o' bogs—Ireland?"

"Where else d'ye suppose she is, Susan Cole?"

"And that she went straight off to him at Bristol when she run away from here?" continued Susan Cole, her own interests in the colloquy getting high.

"I dunno about her going off straight to him," was Black's answer. "Should think her'd not be such a fool as that, for fear o' being tracked. He'd never ha' been such a fool as to let her."

"Any way, she did go to him; then or later."

"In course she did. And I wish 'em joy o' one another's company!"

"Are you going to talk all night, Susan?" came the interrupting voice of Miss Arde at this juncture—and no one living had ever heard her speak so sharply. "We must be getting homewards."

"And so we must, Miss May. Well, good evening, Randy Black. Tell the missis my young lady called in to ask after her. Good evening to *you*, boy," civilly added Susan, as they turned out of the yard, and encountered Sam Pound bringing in the mare.

Back down the lane in the same silence that they had come up it, went they. May's face was white, her frame shivering: this confirmation of the worst was to her more than death. In passing the pond, Susan spoke in a half-whisper.

"Miss May, I told you it might be better for you to let doubt alone."

"No, it is best as it is," she resolutely answered, biting her poor lips to get some colour into them. "Best that the doubt should be set at rest."

Dingy and gloomy seemed the lane, now; not as much as a glimmer of the moon shone through the trees: but it was not so gloomy as May's heart. They stepped on side by side, saying no more.

"Well, I'm sure!—is it you, Susan Cole? And you, Miss May! Good evening."

The salutation proceeded from Mary Barber. She stood at the gate of Harebell Farm in her white cap and crossed kerchief, that might have been the fellow one to Susan's.

"What be you doing up this way?"

"We've been to fetch a walk—'twarn't possible to go out afore, this sultry day," replied Susan promptly.

"It *have* been sultry," assented Mary Barber. "I'm a standing here to get a breath of air. The heat's made you look pale, Miss May."

"Has it?" carelessly returned May. "How is Fanny Tillett, Mary Barber?"

"She's nicely, Miss May, I'm obleeged to ye. We've got her two cousins a staying here; the Miss Tilletts from the Wych. Nice merry-hearted young ladies, they be: one of 'em, Miss Eliza, sings like a nightingale."

The dull pain at Mary's own heart seemed very bad just then. Merry-hearted! She envied the Miss Tillets.

"Fanny's going back to stay with them when they return," continued Mary Barber. "The master, he——Why, who's this now, a clamping down the lane?"

The "clamping" proved to be from the heavy hob-nailed boots of Mr. Sam Pound. That gentleman was coming along at full speed: his hands swaying, his smock-frock flying behind him, his shock of hair waving on his bare head. He made direct for the gate and Mary Barber, touching his hair to Miss Arde and the company generally.

"Ud ye please to let 'em ha' the loan of a candle up there, missis?" he asked, jerking his head towards the Trailing Indian.

"The loan of a candle," repeated Mary Barber. "Be you out o' candles up there, Sam Pound?"

"We be. Our last bit, it were a' burned out i' the night; and the master, he clean forgot it till just now. He'll a got some in to-morrow; he telled me to say so; and ye shall have it back."

Not being particularly interested in the subject of the candle borrowing, Miss Arde and Susan said good night, and walked on. Mary Barber stood on at the gate; the fresh air, gently fanning her face, was grateful. Sam looked at her.

"Be you a going to lend us that there candle, please, ma'am?" he asked again in a minute or two; and his voice had a kind of pressing urgency in it.

"I'll fetch it directly. Be you in such a mortal hurry, Sam Pound?"

"*I* bain't, but the master be," was his answer. "He can't abear to be i' the house wi'out a light a'ter dark."

"Can't he," retorted Mary Barber, with composure. "How's the missis?"

Sam Pound looked about before he answered, as if to make sure the hedges would not hear, and dropped his voice to a low key.

"I think the missis be a dying, I do."

"What!" exclaimed the startled Mary Barber.

"I does," he said. "She ha' been right down bad this two days, just a turning about in her bed like one as can't keep still. All sorts o' things she've been a calling out—about hearses, and diamonds, and lace, and murders; a reg'lar hodge-podge on't. When Black found she was a talking like that last night, he bundled me down stairs, a saying as she was off her head. "Look here," added the lad, lifting his eyes, full of a kind of fear, to Mary Barber's, "it bain't right for her to die up there all by herself. I don't like it. She've been a moaning to-day like anything. I heered it down in the kitchen."

"Has Dr. Priar been fetched to her?" questioned Mary Barber.

"Nobody haven't been fetched to her: Black says the doctor can't do her no good. Fact is," added shrewd Mr. Pound, "Black don't want nobody to hear what her talks of. I say, d'ye mind hearing talk of a pedlar as was lost up there? 'Twere afore my time."

Mary Barber nodded.

"Last night the missis was a calling out about him. "Oh! don't hurt the pedlar! Where be the pedlar? What ha' you done wi' him?" Black, he turned the colour of a grey horse and shoved the blanket over her head. But——'tain't right for her to lie there all by herself to die, and not a Chris'n anigh her. Black, he stumps up a bit now and then, and he've sent me up wi' things to-day: but mostly she'll be all alone, a moaning like a poor hurted animal."

Mary Barber, making no comment, turned to go indoors, leaving Sam where he was. She came back with two candles held between a bit of paper, and her bonnet on.

"You run on down to Dr. Priar, Sam Pound, and ask if he'll be so good as to step up to the Trailing Indian, and say I sent ye. I'll take the candles on there myself."

Sam Pound hesitated. He thought the Trailing Indian might not approve of seeing Mr. Priar, and that he himself should have to bear the blame of it.

"Now you just be off," cried Mary Barber. "The sooner you be gone, the sooner you'll be back again. Don't stand staring like a stuck pig, Sam Pound."

Thus urged, Mr. Pound clattered off on his errand. And Mary Barber made the best of her way to the inn.

It was quite dusk indoors, and moonlight out, by the time she entered it. Black, regardless of the heat, had made up a roaring fire in the kitchen, for the sake perhaps of the light, and sat before it in his old wooden arm-chair fast asleep. Seeing him thus, a thought prompted Mary Barber not to wake him; but rather to go up in unmolested quiet to Mrs. Black. An iron candlestick stood on the table, put ready, no doubt, for the return of Sam Pound. She slipped into it one of the candles she brought; lighted it at the blaze, and stole up stairs.

The sick woman lay on her bed—a low bed in a lean-to room—in utter stillness. She was not dead; but that she had not many hours of life left in her Mary Barber saw. The light of the candle, or perhaps the stir, caused her to open her eyes: she looked quite sane now, whatever she might have been in the hours preceding. Mary Barber knelt down, and took the thin crippled hand that lay outside the clothes.

"I'm afraid you be very bad, poor thing," she said, in her least hard tone.

"Ay, I have been. It's a'most over."

"I've sent to tell Doctor Priar. He'll be up presently."

"No good, no good," said Mrs. Black, feebly attempting to shake her head. "Black, he'd ha' sent for 'm, had it been o' use. My time's come."

Mary Barber, looking at her countenance, believed it was true —that no doctor could have done her good this time, or prolong her days. The dying woman resumed.

"Mine has been a weary life, and I be glad to go. I'd like to ha' gone years back—but the Lord, He knows best. I hope he'll remember what I've had to bear here, and gi' me a little corner in heaven."

"And so He will; never fear," said Mary Barber heartily. "I'll send for the parson and he shall come to say a prayer to ye."

"I've said it for myself," said the woman, closing her eyes. But her feeble fingers held the strong ones gratefully. There was a pause.

"Look here," said Mary Barber, breaking it, her thoughts recurring to that one great—and in its surroundings most unsatisfactory—calamity of the past, that was never entirely absent from them long together, although so many years had gone by, "look here. Have ye never a word o' certainty to say to me about the death o' the master?"

Mrs. Black opened her eyes and stared, evidently not understanding. Her perceptions were becoming dim.

"My poor old master, Robert Owen o' the farm. Did ye know at the time anything about his death?"

The meaning was caught now, caught vividly. Mrs. Black's face assumed a look of terror, and she caught hold with both hands of Mary Barber.

"I've lived in mortal dread o' seeing him," she cried, with a sobbing of the breath; "I've not dared to go out i' th' gloaming all them years."

"Ah! But was he murdered?"

"I don't know. I never did know. Oh, it have been a fearsome life for me—fearing this, fearing t'other, and knowing nought. I'm glad it's ended."

"Who the plague be that, a cackling upstairs?" called out Black at this moment, his voice not at all the steady voice of a man at ease.

"It's me, Black," said Mary Barber, tartly, going to the head of the staircase. "I've come to see if aught can be done for your wife. Just bring up a drain o' wine if ye've got it, and some fresh cold water."

Before the astonished Black could find words strong enough to growl out his wrath at this summary invasion of his domestic privacy, Mr. Priar came in. Sam Pound had encountered him turning out of the gates of Beechhurst Dene.

But the surgeon could not prolong the life of Black's wife. Her poor, worn spirit, crushed by care and fear, flitted away as the summer's morn was dawning.

CHAPTER XXXII.

SEEN THROUGH THE VENETIAN BLINDS.

CONTINUED dropping will wear away a stone. During the whole of the summer months, poor Mary Arde, her heart dragging along always its heavy weight in silence, was subjected to a species of amiable persecution, the chief agents in which were her mother and Lady Lydia Clanwaring. The praises of Captain Clanwaring were being ever said or sung; the disreputable conduct of the scapegrace Tom reiterated. Not openly reiterated: that might have defeated its ends: just a hint of this thing and a hint of that, something or other ever looming out to his discredit. Mr. Arde was not quite so active an ally. But it was hardly right of him to let his daughter tacitly think there could be no doubt of Tom's catalogue of crimes, the stealing of the money amidst the rest. Mr. Arde believed quite enough against Tom without letting her remain in the assurance that Tom was guilty of much that he, the Squire, knew he was not. Self-interest makes some of us wink at deceit enacted in its cause: as it did Mr. Arde: and he was on the brink of incurring a life-long penalty as his reward.

May fought against the influence as long as she could; and then she yielded to her fate. At least, yielded to it so far as conditionally to accept Jarvis Clanwaring and promising to be his wife. The captain was ever near her; but so kind, so gentle, so unobtrusive in his claims and attentions, that she felt ashamed even tacitly to show that she could not reward his love. A saint himself might of late have believed in Captain Clanwaring: Mr. and Mrs. Arde sang his praises every meal-time. May's own feelings prompted her to take the captain in spite of her repugnance to him. She was but a woman; and she longed for a bit of revenge on Tom, who had been so disgracefully false to her in secret, and who allowed young persons to pay visits to him in Ireland. It was but in accordance with human nature that she should pant to show the false deceiver she cared for somebody else as well as he did, and show him she would, whatever the cost to herself.

It was in September that she accepted Captain Clanwaring. The promise she gave was full of hesitation, her manner provokingly listless. "As good Jarvis Clanwaring as any other, if marriage it must be," the refrain of despair kept beating in her heart. The captain, all tender kindness and impulsive gratitude, ventured to press for an immediate union. But here May rebelled: absolutely refusing not only to fix a speedy epoch, but to give an idea of when any such epoch might be fixed.

Now, nothing upon earth could have been more untoward for the captain; nothing have caused him greater inconvenience than this. The proceeds of his commission had kept him afloat for a short while; but during these summer months he had not known what to do for money. The back claims that he had been unable to pay pressed more heavily upon him day by day; and in this September month, the month that witnessed May's promise, his condition had grown desperate. Many an anxious hour did he and his mother spend together, plotting to see what could be done. Once let an exposure come, and the probability was that May would seize upon it as a plea for retracting her word, and the Squire uphold her. Lady Lydia was her son's only confidante: and she but a partial one. Jarvis gave her no details; and did not tell her the worst of his embarrassments. My Lady had been at her wits' end many a time before, contriving how to do the best for him in his troubles; but never so completely as now, when the glorious prospect of the marriage with the heiress had become a certainty, and must, by hook or by crook, be allowed to go on to completion. To get money out of a flint stone would have been as likely a result as the attempt to get any, now or hereafter, from Sir Dene. Nevertheless, got it must be, even though the means used were desperate. Desperate causes (the reader must pardon us for repeating a proverb quoted before) require desperate remedies.

The bright sunshine of September lay on the London streets, as a lumbering hackney coach passed on its slow way from a fashionable hotel at the West End towards Lincoln's Inn. It drew up before a door in Old Square; and Captain Clanwaring stepped out of it. His black moustache was charmingly curled: his whiskers shone; his appearance was altogether that of a stylish buck of the day.

Flinging his fare to the old coachman—who had on a heavy great-coat with about fifteen capes to it, in defiance of the weather's heat—the captain began to toil to the topmost chambers of the house. He anathematised the way a little as he went up, and struck his cane round once or twice angrily.

Arrived at the last flight, a door faced him, bearing a barrister's name on its panels. "Mr. Otto Clanwaring."

Otto Clanwaring worked just as much during the vacation as he did in term time.. Jarvis, going straight in without the ceremony of knocking, found him with a law parchment of some kind spread out before him on the table, and his head bent over it between his hands. Seated sideways to the door, and supposing it was only his clerk who had come in, Otto did not look round.

"What a deuced long way it is, up these stairs, Otto! It's my belief you've got another flight added on, since I was here last."

Up went Otto's head with a start. "Why, Jarvis!"

Laughing a little in his surprise, the barrister rose and held out his hand to his brother. Jarvis resigned to it the tips of his fingers encased in their delicate straw-coloured kid. The contrast between the brothers was remarkable. The one tall, handsome, elegant, attired in all the height of the fashion; the other, little and plain, his clothes of homely grey, and somewhat shabby.

"How hot you feel up here!" remarked Jarvis, sinking languidly into a chair on the other side of the table.

"Rooms up in the roof are always hottest," replied Otto.

"And highest. Why don't you move down lower?"

"This suits my pocket best, Jarvis. When did you come up to town?"

"Night mail," shortly answered Jarvis.

"All well at the Dene?"

"Passably," yawned Jarvis. "Old man gets more crotchety than ever. Shuts himself up in his chambers for days at a time. Lets nobody go in at all hardly but Gander."

Otto, who had resumed his seat, bent his head on his work again. That Jarvis never condescended to trouble his chambers unless for some purpose of his own was a long-ago proved fact; and Otto knew he had only to be still to hear it. He would not inquire: not at all approving of these missions of Jarvis. The probability was that he had come now to try and borrow money, or to badger him to accept a bill. In the latter, Jarvis had never succeeded yet: the barrister was too cautious.

Leaning a little forward on his chair, and lightly tapping the table with his cane, sat the captain. Either he had nothing to say, and had actually come from the West End merely to while away an idle moment, or else he was taking a long time to say it. Tapping here, tapping there, he happened to tap a letter lying amidst other letters, and the tap flirted it upwards and turned it over. The direction was uppermost then, and caught the eyes of Jarvis, somewhat awakening them from their lazy indifference.

"That's Tom Clanwaring's writing, Otto?"

Otto quietly lifted his face. "That? Yes. I got the letter this morning."

Jarvis curled his lip. "I wonder you suffer *him* to correspond with you!"

"He is welcome to correspond with me if he likes. That's the first letter, however, that I have had from him."

Jarvis wished to know what the letter was about, but did not ask. His brother had a civil way of declining to give information, if it suited him not to give it. The next moment, Otto spoke; quite readily.

"Tom writes to ask me if I will tell him how things are going on in his old home. He says he can get no news whatever. Nobody writes to him.

"What does it concern him, how things are going on?" growled Jarvis.

"I suppose he possesses common remembrances and affections," returned Otto, pushing up the cuff of his grey coat. "The way Tom was treated among us all that time was an infernal shame."

"You didn't do much toward the treatment at any rate," retorted Jarvis. "Given you your way, and you'd just have shut your eyes to everything, and kept the fellow where he was."

"Of course I would. And I've not forgiven myself yet for having been the means of letting out that thing about the Trailing Indian. No, and not forgiven some of the rest of you either, for taking it up in the manner you did. 'Twas a cowardly shame."

"Perhaps you'd like to say it ought to have been hushed up? That the fellow should have been let off scotfree?"

"One man may walk into the house while another may not look over the hedge," remarked Otto. "Had you or I been found out in a bit of a scrape, Jarvis, nothing would have been said. Not that *I* have anything to do with such scrapes, thank goodness."

Which almost sounded as if Jarvis had. The latter answered sharply.

"He had been the bane of our house long enough. 'Twas time he went out of it."

"Well, I see no reason for his being sent to Coventry, now, in the way you all seem to be sending him. Just an answer to his letters once in a way, telling him how Sir Dene is, would not hurt any of you."

Captain Clanwaring threw back his head and waved his scented handkerchief; as if to wave off anything so low as Tom Clanwaring, that might come between the wind and his nobility.

"I would not condescend to write to the goat if he were dying. One would think you might employ your leisure better, Otto!"

"It's not the first time my leisure will have been taken up in doing work neglected by others," quietly replied Otto.

"Just as you please, of course," was the rejoinder of Jarvis, scornfully delivered, as if the subject were altogether beneath him.

A silence ensued. The Captain leaned back in his chair, softly whistling. Otto turned over a leaf of his parchment, and made a pencil mark on its margin. Presently he spoke again.

"Has that Emma Geach come back, Jarvis?"

"I've not heard of it."

"I wonder where she is."

"Don't know. There was a report in the summer that she was in Ireland."

"Oh," said Otto. And went on with his reading again.

"How is it you've not been down at all this year?" asked Jarvis, tapping his boot.

"I have had a good bit of work one way or another, and thought I could not do better than stick to it. Holidays run away both with time and money: I cannot well afford either yet. Talking of money, Jarvis—has that thief been discovered yet?"

"What thief?"

"You know. He who stole the bag out of Sir Dene's secretary on New Year's Day. You were going to follow up some suspicion upon the point. Did you?"

"No. At least—I did what I could, but it was not enough. Nothing has come to light."

z

"And nothing will until Black confesses," observed Otto. "He was the thief. If I were down there, and Sir Dene would let me have the handling of it, I'd risk my reputation on bringing it home to the man in a week."

Jarvis pushed his dark face forward, and looked hard at his brother. The indifference on his countenance had given place to what seemed quite like alarmed interest.

"*Don't meddle with it, Otto.* You might do incalculable harm. At least, the harm of condemning the thing to remain for ever in its present obscurity. It was not Black. It was no more Black than it was you or me."

"Have you still an interest in warding suspicion off Black?" questioned Otto.

"I! Why what interest did I ever have in doing that?" retorted Jarvis, as if he had forgotten so much of the past.

"That tobacco debt of yours."

"Oh—that! Ay, I remember. That has been settled long ago, and a fresh score run up," added Jarvis slightly laughing. "See here, Otto," he continued seriously, "I have a private reason of my own for wishing the facts connected with that matter to be brought to light. In my own mind I am as sure who it was as though I had seen the money taken. Give me time and I'll track it home to the right one yet."

"Can't you tell me who it was?"

"No. No. And if I did, it would not particularly interest you."

"Black's wife's dead, I hear."

"Went off two or three months ago," carelessly rejoined Jarvis. "I don't think Black will last very long. He seems to be on nearly his last legs."

"And how are the Arde Hall people?" continued Otto, privately wishing his idle brother would betake himself away, and leave him to his work. "How's May?"

"They are all right. May is engaged to me."

"No!" exclaimed Otto, darting a quiet glance at the Captain.

"She is. Why need you be so surprised?"

"Because, to tell the truth, I thought she'd never consent to have you," said Otto, candidly. He did not add the other thought, though, that lay in his mind: "She cared only for Tom Clanwaring."

"Much indebted for your good opinion," derisively spoke Jarvis. "She has consented, and so you were wrong, you see. As for me, I'm glad the matter's set at rest: I have been dangling after her long enough."

"I congratulate you, Jarvis. May Arde is the sweetest girl I know."

"Thank you. Yes, the prospect is not bad," complacently continued the Captain. "Ten thousand pounds settled on her; ten thousand pounds to be handed over to me on the wedding-day. And all the rest of the property, including the Hall, when the old people fall in."

"A widely different prospect from mine—who have to work hard for my bread and cheese: and probably will have to work to the end," returned Otto, with good-natured cheerfulness. "You were born, I take it, under a luckier star than I, Jarvis."

Jarvis slightly nodded his head, and took another look at his handsome boots. In his opinion there could not be a more unlucky star than one that entailed work of any sort. They were interrupted by a knock at the door.

"Come in," called out the barrister.

A little bald-headed gentleman dressed in black, with a broad-plaited frill standing out from the bosom of his shirt, and a heavy bunch of handsome seals hanging, answered the mandate.

"Oh! I'm so glad to find you in, Mr. Clanwaring," he said, standing with the door in his hand. "Don't disturb yourself. The serjeant is obliged to forestal the hour fixed for the consultation, and name an earlier one. Four o'clock instead of six. Will it suit you?"

Otto considered. At four o'clock that afternoon he had intended to proceed elsewhere on business. It was, however, no appointment, and he could take another time for it.

"I suppose it must suit me, Mr. Lake," he said aloud. "Yes. I'll be over at the serjeant's chambers at four."

"That's all, then, Mr. Clanwaring. Four o'clock precisely, please. I've been to the other two. Good morning."

"That was the great Serjeant Sterndale's chief clerk," observed Otto to his brother. "Lake is the cleverest little man in Lincoln's Inn. Three parts of those written opinions of the serjeant's, so renowned for their depth and wisdom, are his. It's said he gets twelve hundred a year salary."

Silence set in again. Captain Clanwaring was sunk in a brown study; the barrister went on with his parchment. A glint of hot sunlight took a corner of the window and threw its rays on the table almost like a burning-glass.

"I am in an awful mess, Otto."

The acknowledgment sounded so strange after the former declaration of glowing prospects, and perhaps so unexpected, that Otto looked across as if he hardly believed his ears.

"Debts again?"

Jarvis nodded. "Nearly done to death with 'em."

"That's what he has come about, is it," thought Otto. "I can't help you, Jarvis," he said aloud, forestalling any request of the sort. "It's as much as I can do to get along and pay my own way."

"Nobody asked you to," retorted Jarvis. "I believe I shall be able to help myself."

Otto silently wondered how.

"Do you know anything of a man named Pale?"

"Pale the money-lender? Yes, I know him."

"Had transactions with him yourself, perhaps?" went on Jarvis.

"Never. Not in the way you mean. Why do you ask about him?"

"I want you to tell me, if you can, whether, or not, he is a man whose discretion may be depended on. Is he one who would keep a client's counsel?—or would he go blabbing of business to other people?"

"I should think his discretion might be entirely depended on. It is the impression he gives me. I don't know much of him."

"Might be trusted then, you think?"

"Yes, I do."

Jarvis lifted his cane on the table again, and stirred about some papers that lay in the glint of sunlight. His manner was very absent.

"What's his precise ne of business, this Pale?"

"Lending money.'

„ Of course. But what upon? Postobits?—and promissory notes?—and—"

"Upon anything," interrupted Otto. "It's all fish that comes to Pale's net."

"Just what I heard. Has heaps of property in his hands. Plate and diamonds, and things of that kind."

"I dare say. Sure to have."

"Exacts hard terms, no doubt?"

"They all do that. I don't suppose Pale's worse than others. For what he is, they say he is tolerably fair-dealing."

"Where does he live, this man?"

"His rooms are in Pall Mall."

"Got a heap of clerks there?" questioned Jarvis, his face assuming a moody look, as if it did not please him that Mr. Pale should have "a heap" of clerks. "Eh?"

"Got some, I suppose. I have never been there."

"Why I understood you to imply that you had done business with him!" exclaimed Jarvis, lifting his eyes.

"My business with him had nothing to do with money-lending. It was of so strictly private a nature that I preferred to find him out at his own residence, rather than go to his public rooms."

Jarvis paused a moment. "Where is his private residence?"

"In Goodman's Fields?"

"Where the deuce is Goodman's Fields?"

"East-end way. Towards Whitechapel."

"Oh," said Jarvis.

"Are you going to get money from him, Jarvis?"

"Well, he——" another pause. "He has been recommended to me as a man likely to lend some. I think I shall try him."

"He'll want a first-rate security. I warn you of that."

"As if the fraternity didn't all want that—and be hanged to 'em!" growled Jarvis.

"Shall you be able to give it?"

"I shall give him a bill at three months backed by a good name," replied Jarvis, after stopping to consider whether he should answer the question or not. "An undeniably good name; safe as the Bank of England."

"And how do you propose to take up the bill at the three months' end?"

"With some of the money that will come to me on my marriage. The knot will have been tied before that."

Otto Clanwaring laid down his pencil and looked at his brother. Every feeling of justice within him felt outraged.

"Jarvis—it is of course your business; not mine. But I would suffer any trouble rather than so foredestine Mary Arde's money. 'Twill be desecration."

"She'll never know it. You needn't preach. I should not do it but for being compelled."

"Suppose the marriage should never come off?"

Jarvis turned blue with anger at the supposition. "Suppose yon sun never sets?" said he, wrathfully. "Keep your croaking for yourself, Otto. And, here—tell me how I am to ferret out this house of Pale's. If I don't find him in Pall Mall, I may go there."

Otto wrote down the directions, his brother standing beside him to look on. "And you think he may be trusted to keep dark?" repeated Jarvis, as he took the paper.

"Certainly I do. Most money-lenders may be trusted for that. It is their interest to be silent," added Otto. And the Captain departed without the ceremony of saying good morning.

"Curious that he should harp so upon secrecy when secrecy's the rule," thought the barrister as the other went down. "He must have some especially urgent motive for wishing it. I should like to know whose that other name is. Curious, too, that I should be going to pay Mr. Pale a visit myself to-day or to-morrow."

But that he was so reticent by nature, and perhaps also that he could not hold his brother in any favour, Otto might have mentioned the latter fact. He was engaged in the friendly office (not as a barrister) of striving to establish the innocence of a young man upon whom a suspicion of forgery rested. Mr. Pale could materially aid him if he would, but to get him to do so was difficult. It was altogether a matter of great delicacy.

The day went on. At four o'clock, Otto Clanwaring attended the chambers of Mr. Serjeant Sterndale. The consultation therein lasted until six, after which Otto took his dinner, consisting of two lamb chops and potatoes, supplied by his laundress. To save cost, he lived in his chambers. Then he indulged himself in his pipe, sitting at the open window in the twilight while he smoked it, and glancing, while he thought, at the redness left in the western sky after the setting of the sun.

With his methodical habits, his industry, and his anxiety to make use of every minute of his time, the barrister's evenings were generally appropriated beforehand to some work or other. This evening was an exception: the changing of the consultation hour had put things out of their regular groove. When his pipe was smoked, Otto sat on, feeling himself entirely at liberty for the evening, and accordingly something like a fish out of water.

"Why should I not go down to Pale's now?" he suddenly exclaimed. "I will. He's nearly sure to be at home. And it will save time to-morrow."

Descending the stairs and passing out of the square, he got into the line of principal streets, preferring their cheerful route to that of the more obscure ones. A good many people were abroad that genial evening: hot London strolling out for a breath of air. Some of them jostled Otto as they passed: he bore steadily on, and jostled in his turn. Half-way down Cheapside there was a stoppage on the pavement, caused by a crowd gathering round a man who had fallen down in a fit, or pretended fit. Otto was elbowing his way through it, just as a girl was elbowing hers the other way. They met face to face, in the broad glare of a silversmith's shop, and Otto Clanwaring exclaimed aloud with surprise. It was Emma Geach.

"Whence have you sprung?—from over the seas?" he asked, the little bit of information given him by Jarvis that day, as to her being in Ireland, flashing into his mind.

"From over the seas or out of the earth," she answered in her customary light and free manner. "How are all the folks in your country, Mr. Clanwaring?"

"What have you been doing with yourself, and where have you been hiding all this while?" returned Otto, passing over her joking question for what it was worth.

"I've been in a trance," said the girl, saucily. "Just come out on't."

"Do you know that your old home has had a loss?" continued Otto, determined to ask no more questions and get chaffing answers. "Black's wife is dead, poor thing."

"Yes, I know it," replied the girl, her voice and face both passing into sadness. "I should ha' liked to see her again. But she's better off."

"When are you going back to the Trailing Indian?"

"That's amid the doubtfuls, sir. Maybe sometime, maybe never. I get a bit o' news o' the old place once in a way; but I don't get much. It have been told to me that Sir Dene's breaking up fast."

"I fear he is."

"How be the Ardes?" she suddenly asked.

"Oh, they are all well. Miss May's thinking about getting married."

"*Is* she?" was the remark, evidently given in surprise. "And who be it to, sir?—Young Squire Scrope?"

"Can't tell," shortly returned Otto, for it was by no means his wish to talk of family matters to this damsel: indeed, the remark about May had slipped from him unintentionally, as it were. "Are you living in London?"

"I be lodging in it—just now. And there's my landlady a-waiting for me, and looking cats and dogs at this hindrance," she added, "for we be in a hurry to get home. Her son met with an accident down at the docks to-day, and she asked me to go along of her to see him."

Otto Clanwaring turned at the words, and saw a decent woman standing a few paces off. Before he could turn his head back, Miss Geach had slipped away, and joined her. They passed up Cheapside together, the girl flinging a nod and a good night back to Otto in her freedom. He went on his way, his mind full of the encounter.

"I suppose she has been in Ireland and come back from it," ran his thoughts. "She's looking well, wherever she may have been."

Pursuing his route on foot, by the time he got to his destination, which lay in the neighbourhood of Mansell Street, he felt somewhat fagged, and devoutly hoped Mr. Pale would be at home, so as not to have had the walk for nothing. The money-lender's house was little to look at outwardly: it made the side of a small paved court, the opposite side of it being a dead wall. The court was no thoroughfare, and nobody had any business in it, unless it was with Mr. Pale's homestead. In fact, it was altogether as private a place as might be found in the heart of London. The door, level with the pavement, was in the middle of the dwelling, a parlour window on either side of it.

"Oh come, I think he is at home," said Otto Clanwaring, seeing a strong light shining behind the white blind of the first window, as he turned up the court. For Mr. Pale was a bachelor, and the family consisted of himself alone.

Now, perhaps for the reason that the court was considered safe from passers-by who might look in; or else through some careless inadvertence of the attending servant, the white roller blind behind had not been drawn to its full extent. Venetian blinds ran across the bottom of the window; and the white blind left about three or four inches of the space uncovered. The staves happened to be turned straightwise, so that the room was exposed.

Otto Clanwaring halted, and glanced in. Not from any

intention of slyly spying—whatever might be the failings of some of his family in this respect, he was too honest for it—but simply to assure himself that the money-lender was at home. Yes. There sat Mr. Pale ; his grey hair close to a shining and brilliant lamp. At the same small round table sat another man, to whom Otto's eyes naturally turned. It was Captain Clanwaring.

It is to be feared that Mr. Otto Clanwaring burst out with a most unorthodox word. Very far indeed was it from his purpose to interfere in any way with his brother's affairs; he would a great deal rather keep aloof from them : and he certainly had not cast so much as a thought to the possibility that Jarvis might choose this night hour for a visit to Mr. Pale. After all, Otto felt that he might have taken his walk for nothing.

"If I thought that his business was likely to be over soon, I'd wait about in some back street and come again after he is gone," soliloquized Otto. "It wouldn't do to let him see me; he'd jump to the conclusion that I had come down to spy upon him: Jarvis was always suspicious. Wonder if he'll be long ? "

Still with no idea of prying, only to gather a hint, if might be, whether the interview was, or was not, coming to an end, Otto looked in again. They were seated facing each other at the table, sideways to the window, and very near it, for the room was small. It almost seemed as if Otto made a third at the meeting, so close and plain was everything.

He gave a sudden start. A start of simple, disbelieving astonishment in the first place. Mr. Pale, lifting something into the lamp's rays, and gently waving it, a great flood of dazzling light flashed forth. Otto recognized the family diamond case with Sir Dene's arms upon it, and the family diamonds.

Only astonishment at first. It was succeeded by a sensation of dismay, bringing pain and shame. Too surely he drew the right conclusion—Jarvis was raising money on these, the Clanwaring diamonds.

Valuable diamonds. Worth at the least some two or three thousand pounds. They had not seen the light since the death of Sir Dene's wife, so many years before. They went with the title, and would lapse to young Dene when he should come into it.

"Has he *stolen* them ? " wondered Otto bitterly, wiping his face from the moisture which shame had brought out there. But no: only for a moment did he think so ill as that: good sense led him to what was in fact the truth—Lady Lydia had lent them to him for his temporary need. But she must have done it without the cognizance of Sir Dene; so it was not much better than stealing, after all. Otto felt that he would rather have had his arm cut off than see this.

The impulse crossed him to go in, denounce Jarvis for a villain, and secure the jewels from desecration. Only for an instant. He saw how impolitic and impracticable such a course would be; how much worse it would make it all. No, there was nothing for him but to be silent; to be a tacit party to the transaction, and to hug his shame.

He continued looking. He saw no meanness in that now. Mr. Pale clasped up the case again—Otto heard the sharp click where he stood—put it inside a small bureau, and brought back some bank notes from the same receptacle. Not many; three or four. Then he wrote out a cheque; and handed both cheque and notes to Jarvis. What the amount in the whole was Otto could not see—and he resented it. The next thing, Jarvis wrote something, which Mr. Pale took possession of. This seemed to complete the transaction; Captain Clanwaring rose, and was coming swiftly forth.

The barrister glided out of the court, and bolted into a dark passage of a friendly shop that was putting up its shutters. It was a blow that had struck home to the family pride of Otto Clanwaring.

CHAPTER XXXIII.

BEEN WITH THE OLD SQUIRE IN THE NIGHT.

KNOCK, knock, knock!

The knocking, very gentle, was at Sir Dene's chamber door. Gander stood there, in the dull light of the November morning. "If my bell does not ring, call me at nine o'clock," were Sir Dene's orders to Gander the previous night. Very unusual orders indeed.

For Sir Dene, unless he was actually ill, liked to be up betimes as of yore. The once hale old man was breaking up fast: more than age was telling upon him. Generally speaking his bell rang for his shaving water long before eight.

He had felt out of sorts the previous day. "Not ill—out

of sorts," he answered when questioned. News had come in of a sad stage-coach accident on the awkward old bridge at Powick: and it had recalled to Sir Dene all the back trouble of the accidents of Dene Hollow. Not that the trouble needed recalling: more or less, it was ever present with him.

Knock, knock, knock. Rather louder.

"Come in, then. Can't ye hear?"

By which irritable answer Gander found his master must have spoken before. The feeble voice had failed to catch his ear. In went the old serving-man—for Gander was himself getting tolerably old now—in the striped jacket he always, winter and summer, wore in the morning. Sir Dene, a cotton nightcap on, with a hanging tassel, raised his head on the pillow.

"Where's the hot water?" For Gander had come empty-handed.

"I've not brought it, Sir Dene. I thought maybe ye'd take a bit of breakfast afore stirring."

Now Sir Dene was feeling weak, shaky, feverish: almost as though he should like some breakfast first. But he had an unconquerable aversion to giving way.

"I don't know, Gander, I'd like to be up and doing as long as I can."

"It's a regular stinger of a morning, master. Wind nor-east, and enough to cut one in two. Air bleak, and as dull as ditchwater."

"Is it? We don't have the fine weather we used," remarked Sir Dene—as many another old man is apt to say and think. "There's no good bright days now, Gander: no sparkling, crisp, sunshiny frost. What's become of 'em?"

"It have been a dull autumn; and it seems to be a setting in for a dull winter," returned Gander. "I'll fetch you up a cup o' tea Sir Dene. It'll do ye good."

Quitting the chamber before Sir Dene could make any denial, he speedily reappeared with a small tray of breakfast. A cup of tea, hot buttered toast, and an egg. Sir Dene sat partly up, drank some of the tea, and then lay down again.

"You'll try a bit of the toast, sir?"

A slight wave of the hand answered him. Gander, who must have been ill indeed not to relish his own breakfast, pressed it with concern.

"You'd relish it, I think, Sir Dene. It have got plenty o' butter on't."

"I've no appetite, Gander. I think my time's coming."

Gander understood the allusion—that he meant for death—and felt a little uncomfortable. As he stood looking down at Sir Dene, he saw that the once fresh and healthy face had an unusual pallor on it. Between the white nightcap and the white pillow it looked nearly as white as they did.

"You'll be better after breakfast, Sir Dene. It's this nasty grey east-winded morning, as is upsetting everybody. I wish you'd try the toast."

"Squire Arde came and paid me a visit in the night, Gander. I think we shall soon be together again."

Gander could not make out what Sir Dene was rambling about. He had drawn up the blinds and now glanced round to the grey skies he had been talking of—as if that would help him.

"The old squire, ye know, Gander. He looked just as he used to look; he'd got his pepper-and-salt suit on, and the little old drab over-coat atop. We were having a comfortable chat together, him and me. 'Twas like old times."

"It must ha' been a dream, master."

"Well, I suppose it was. It seemed like reality. As happy as kingfishers, we were, us two, chatting together. It seemed good to be with him."

"This toast 'll be cold, sir. I know a bit on't 'ud bring you round."

"Won't be long, I take it, Gander, before I go to him. It's getting a'most time. God, He knows best. But I don't think it'll be long."

Drinking up the rest of the tea, Gander dexterously put some toast into the old man's hand in exchange for the cup. Sir Dene eat it up: perhaps half unconsciously. Nevertheless, he did seem better after it, and then said he would take some more tea.

"It was that dratted coach, a overturning of itself on Powick Bridge, as upset him," soliloquized Gander, going out with the cup to replenish it. "But there's times now when he's not a bit like himself. Fancy his saying he've had a visit from old Arde!"

The postman's ring echoed through the hall as Gander crossed it: and the locked bag was taken up as usual to Lady Lydia. In going back with the tea, Gander halted at my lady's door to inquire if there were any letters for his master.

Two. Sir Dene looked at their handwriting as he sipped his tea. They were from two of his grandchildren: Dene the heir, and the barrister Otto. Laying them on the counterpane unopened, he began to eat another bit of toast, the faithful servant standing by.

"Ay. They think it's right to show the old grandfather that they don't forget him, these young blades! But there's one of 'em that doesn't write, Gander."

Gander knew quite well to whom this alluded. Sir Dene was in the habit of talking to him of things that he never mentioned to other people.

"Well, Sir Dene,—I've said it afore, and I says it again—my opinion is, as Mr. Tom have wrote, and his letter must ha' dropped into the sea a crossing it."

"Nonsense!" peevishly cried Sir Dene, "Letters don't get lost like that."

"'Tain't like Mr. Tom to bear malice; and I know he *don't* bear it. I'd write him a word, Sir Dene, if I was you, and tell him to come. Likely, he don't dare to make no move without a word from you."

It was just what had been, off and on, hovering in Sir Dene's mind for some weeks past—to write and summon Tom. Perhaps it wanted but this word of urging to put it in practice. "I think I will," he said. "He has been banished long enough for punishment. I'll do it as soon as I'm up, Gander."

And, having an object to accomplish, Sir Dene got up at once. When shaved and dressed, he sat down by the blazing fire in the next room, and penned to Tom a letter of recall, short, kind, and peremptory. His hands shook, but the words were clear. Folding it up, as letters were folded in those days when envelopes were unknown, he sealed it with a big red seal and stamped it with the Clanwaring arms, Gander holding the lighted taper. When the seal was cold he dipped his pen in the ink and began to address it.

"Tom Clanwaring, Esquire." Thus far had Sir Dene proceeded, when he looked up.

"What's the direction, Gander?"

"I'm sure I don't know," said Gander. "I heard it once—a place with a crackjaw name."

Sir Dene laid down the pen in consternation. Was Tom in some unknown region of Ireland where he could neither be written to nor got at? Reassurance came to Sir Dene.

"My lady must know, Gander. It's where some of her people live. Go and ask her for it."

Away went Gander. Never a suspicion of any treachery on my lady's part, in regard to Tom, had occurred to this simple man and his simple master. Simple in all confiding honour. My lady and her eldest son were cosily sitting together at a well-spread breakfast table, by a blazing fire. My lady in a kind of brown "saque," the pattern of which might have been taken from a pillow case; Jarvis in a flowery dressing gown. Their conversation was brought to a sudden standstill as the servant went in.

"My lady, will you be so good as to give me Mr. Tom's direction?"

For answer, my lady, a little taken to, stared at Gander up and down.

"Sir Dene has sent me for it," added the man.

"What does Sir Dene want with it?" she questioned.

"I b'lieve it's to address a letter to him," said Gander, who never was too obliging to my lady. "Sir Dene is waiting for it now, please."

Quite equal to the occasion was Lady Lydia, without the help of that interchanged glance with her son. "I must search in my desk for it, Gander. My best regards to Sir Dene, and I'll send it to him almost immediately."

"The goat is being recalled," remarked Jarvis when they were alone.

"I daresay. He is not coming, though."

"'Twould hardly be policy. You must fail to find the address."

"I'll give one that won't reach him," whispered Lady Lydia.

She soon appeared in Sir Dene's room, and found him restlessly waiting—for he retained a great deal of his old impatience still. On a piece of paper in her hand was written a long address that Gander might have decidedly pronounced to be "crackjaw."

"Dear Sir Dene! How are you to-day? Tom's address, do you want? Here it is."

Sir Dene read it over, and slowly copied it on the letter.

"You take care of this and post it when you are at Worcester to-day, Gander," said he, handing the letter to the man.

"It can go in the bag, Sir Dene," interposed my lady. "I shall have letters myself to send off to-day."

"Gander's going to Worcester: he'll post it there," persisted Sir Dene, really from no other motive than a spice of obstinacy. And Lady Lydia turned green as she thought how very near the letter would have been to reaching Tom, but for her precaution in regard to the address.

"Have you been writing to Tom at last, Sir Dene?"

"I've been writing for him to come home, Lydia: he has been banished long enough. I can't help it if it offends you. I don't think——I don't think I shall be very much longer among you all, and I'd like to have him here. He was poor Geoff's legacy to me you know."

"Oh, Sir Dene, don't say that. You'll be among us for years yet, I hope."

"It strikes me not. I've been with old Squire Arde three parts o' the night: a token, I take it, that I shall soon be with him in reality."

Lady Lydia stared a little, and glanced at Gander.

"I've not got much to keep me here now," went on Sir Dene. "But I should like to live to see Tom come home."

"You have your letters from Dene and Otto," observed Lady Lydia, by way of drowning the last remark. "What do they say?"

"They don't say much. Dene and Charley are coming for the wedding. Otto——Well——I——have not read Otto's, have I, Gander?"

"I didn't see you read it, Sir Dene," replied Gander, who was busying himself about the room. "The letter's at your elbow, sir."

"It's not often Otto writes," remarked Sir Dene, breaking the seal of the barrister's letter. "His time's too well taken up: if Jarvis had only half his patience, 'twould be better for him, Lydia. Otto will make a name in the world, once he can work himself into note—get on to be a judge, I shouldn't wonder."

"He was of a plodding nature, even as a boy," rather scornfully rejoined Lady Lydia. She had no superfluous love for her son Otto.

"Now, look here!" cried Sir Dene, as he read his letter. "Here's Tom been writing from Ireland to Otto to ask how I am, and saying he cannot get to hear a word of Beechhurst Dene from anybody. That was two months ago, Otto says. So Tom doesn't quite forget the old man!"

Lady Lydia, taking in the sense of the words as well as her

anger allowed, felt that she should like to annihilate that blundering fool Otto.

"But why the deuce doesn't Tom write direct, and ask?" burst forth Sir Dene, rather explosively. "It's his temper keeps him from it; that's what it is. He must have got a touch of the Clanwaring obstinacy, after all; though poor Geoffry hadn't. Any way, he'll have my letter now as soon as the post can take it to him. Don't you forget it, Gander."

"No danger, Sir Dene. I'll be too glad to see Master Tom back at home myself, to forget it," added bold Gander for the particular benefit of my lady. "The house have never been the same without him."

"And see that his room is got ready, and all that, Gander, mind."

"It's always a' ready and waiting for him, Sir Dene."

"What else does Otto say, Sir Dene?" inquired Lady Lydia, with an impassive face.

"What else? Well, he says he shall hope to be down at the wedding. There: you may take his letter away and read it if you like."

The wedding, thus mentioned by Sir Dene's grandsons was that of Captain Clanwaring. For May Arde, yielding to persecution (as she regarded it) and fate, had at length been won over to fix the probable time. When told by her father and mother that it must take place before the year was out, and bade to say *when* she answered in her desperation, "After Christmas, then."

Her conscience smote her as she said it; smote her of sin. For, down deep in her heart lingered vividly as ever the image of that scapegrace Tom: and in spite of her secret prayers, her tears, her strivings, she could not thrust it out. Since that summer evening's visit to the Trailing Indian, not a doubt had rested on her mind of Tom Clanwaring's disloyalty to her, and of his utter worthlessness; and yet—love him less she could not. "I may be able to forget him, once I am married, she said to herself—over and over again: and as good marry Jarvis as anybody else!"

And in a short while after making the concession, May absolutely began to regard it as a boon, and to look forward to the marriage with something like a satisfaction. Not in the marriage itself, poor girl; but as a release from uncertainty. The unrest of her life was so great as to be absolute torment. Thus matters were arranged to the satisfaction of everybody : other people were all agog with pleasure : and on May's part there was no thought of drawing back. Sir Dene liked the proposed union immensely. He privately deemed May a great deal too good for Jarvis: but that was the Ardes' business, not his. Lady Lydia was in the seventh heaven of delight; and the Squire's wife wrote sundry letters to intimate friends, apprising them of the completion of the contract of marriage between Captain Jarvis Clanwaring and her beloved daughter, Millicent Mary Arde. The reader will therefore readily understand how objectionable would be the return of Tom Clanwaring to upset, or possibly to upset, the onward stream of events, coursing along so smoothly.

"Once get the wedding over, and he shall come, if it so must be," said Lady Lydia to Jarvis; "but that must take place in safety first."

Jarvis resented the intimation. It was as much as to insinuate that May cared for Tom still, more than she did for him: his hair and his temper alike bristled up. The Captain was a very attentive lover; never a day passed but he would be at the Hall once or twice. But any attempt to enter on the endearments lovers suppose they have a right to offer, was so promptly discouraged by May; in fact, he saw they would be so evidently distasteful, that the gallant Captain prudently confined his display of affection to warm hand-shakes. Now and then he ran up to town for three or four days; and May would again feel free as a bird in the air.

In the afternoon of the cold and bleak November day, spoken of above, May, well muffled up, returned to the Hall in her father's open carriage, having been with him to Worcester. Whether it was her chronic state of low spirits and the inanition they caused, that rendered her chilly, certain it was, she now always felt more or less cold. Her errand to Worcester had been to the dressmakers; to try on certain of the dresses that were being prepared for the wedding. Mrs. Arde, suffering from some temporary indisposition, had remained at home.

"You look cold, May," said the Squire, as he gave his hand to help her down.

"Do I, papa? It is cold. I think I will run about a bit to warm myself, before going in."

May's "running about to warm herself" consisted in a listless kind of slow sauntering. She was not in spirits to run. Walking about the premises, back and front, buried in her over-sad thoughts, she was about to turn in at the gate leading to the kitchen garden, when she saw Cole, the farrier, turn out of the stables. A favourite carriage horse of the Squire's was ill at the time. May waited at the gate till the man came up.

"Is old Jack better?" she asked.

"Not much, Miss May. I've been giving him another ball."

"What a cold day it is!" cried May—and she shivered a little as she spoke.

"Coldish," returned the man. "It strikes me we shall have a hard winter of it, Miss May."

"I hope not—for the poor's sake," was May's answer. Her sweet brown eyes, with a whole flood of sadness lying in their depths, went straight out to his. Cole and Miss May had been on quite familiar terms always, so to say: the result of his sister being the young lady's attendant. When Miss May was a little tottering damsel in back-strings, Harry Cole, the good-natured, laughing stripling, would toss the little lady "up to the moon." They were great friends still.

"I hear Mr. Tom's sent for back, Miss May."

At the unexpected words, a rush of crimson dyed May's face. Harry Cole, who had more innate delicacy than many gentlemen, had stooped to get some spots of mud off his trousers at the ankle, and missed the sight.

"Indeed," said May, constraining her voice to indifference.

"While I was at the Dene just now, Gander got in from Worcester. He told me he had been posting a letter for Mr. Tom, that Sir Dene has wrote to call him home again. It's too bad to have kept him over in that Irish place so long, Miss May."

"They say it has been for punishment," returned May, fiddling with the latch of the gate.

"I know they say it. Any way, Miss May, that does for an excuse. Punishment for what, I wonder?"

"All kinds of things were laid to his charge."

"Well, so they were, Miss May. But they didn't go down with them that knew him."

May felt as if her life's blood were coursing about anyhow. As Susan said, Cole had never been able to see a fault in Tom Clanwaring.

"There was that bag of money, you know. That *was* absurd."

"Oh dear, yes," answered Cole, with a laugh. "And lots more beside that. Some things are believed in to this day as if they were gospel. Mr. Tom's one person, and I be another, Miss May: but I know this—that if it had been me, I should have come back and faced my enemies long ago. Any way, I hope he'll soon be here now."

"Susan has got the toothache," said May, by way of turning off the subject.

"Serve her right: why doesn't she get it took out?" said Cole, who had none too much sympathy with Susan: she, in the right of her superior years, having been accustomed to domineer over him from his childhood upwards in the most unscrupulous manner. "I've told her, Miss May, and others have told her, that she'll get no proper rest till she's got rid of the tooth: but she's just as pig-headed over it—"

"Is that you, Harry Cole? Come here."

Cole turned at the calling voice, to see the Squire. Touching his hat to the Squire's daughter, he hastened away.

"Sent for at last, is he!" mused May. "But I don't think he will dare to come. Oh dear! what an unhappy thing this life is!"

She went indoors at once, too miserable to stay out. Utterly wretched was she, half reckless; and felt that she would give all the chance of future happiness in this life to get away from marriage and Jarvis Clanwaring. Not that there was the smallest thought that she *could*. Fate was fate, and she might not turn aside from it. Susan Cole, her apron held up to her cheek, came forward to meet her in the hall.

"Here's Captain Clanwaring a waiting for you in the little parlour, Miss May."

CHAPTER XXXIV.

OVER THE CLARET CUP.

"It seems very odd, Gander."

"Never a answer to it of any sort, Mr. Otto; neither of coming nor writing. Never no more notice took on't than if it had been dirt."

"Well, I cannot understand it."

The glitter of plate and glass was on the supper table, at which Otto Clanwaring sat. He laid down his knife and fork to talk to the old serving man, the butler at Beechhurst Dene, who stood close to him. Gander's eager face was bent forward with excitement, under the wax lights.

It was the Wednesday before Christmas, and Otto Clanwaring had just arrived at the Dene for two purposes; to kill, as may be said, two birds with one stone. The one to spend, as usual, the Christmas-tide; the other to assist in celebrating the marriage of Captain Clanwaring.

The wedding was fixed for Tuesday, the twenty-seventh of December. Miss Arde had held to her original determination—not to be married before Christmas. Captain Clanwaring pleaded for an earlier period in vain: and was at length fain to show himself grateful for the tardy one ultimately fixed. So the preparations were put in hand, and the invitations sent out.

Christmas Day would fall this year on a Sunday. This, you understand, was the week preceding it. On Monday, the nineteenth, Squire Arde went to London on business connected with his daughter's settlements, and also to procure the marriage licence. He intended to return by the Thursday night's mail so as to be at home on Friday morning; which would be the day before Christmas Eve. The Hall was in full swing of preparation for the festivities attendant on the wedding. Beechhurst Dene had made ready, too, in anticipation of its expected guests.

Mrs. Letsom and her children had accompanied Otto from London. It had not been Otto's intention to quit his work until the Friday, but his sister appealed to him to accompany her; and she would not start later. Colonel Letsom was in India with his regiment. They took the day coach to Worcester, and thence drove over to the Dene: reaching it as the clocks were striking ten, amidst a sharp fall of snow.

Sir Dene, weak in health, subdued in spirit, but dressed with extreme care as usual, his coat blue, his fine white hair (scanty now) powdered, sat in the large drawing-room to receive them. Lady Lydia was with him, and also a shrunken-looking little lady in grey silk with hair as white as Sir Dene's, and a close white net cap on, with satin bows. It was Miss Clewer: sister of Sir Dene's late wife. The reader had the pleasure of once seeing her—at that stormy interview that witnessed the turning out of poor Geoffry. She was considerably turned seventy; but she had come posting over in her carriage and four from her residence in Gloucestershire, to be present at the first marriage that was to take place amid her grand-nephews. The nephews and Louisa Letsom called her Aunt Ann, just as their fathers had done.

During the commotion caused by the entrance of the travellers, Jarvis came in, the bridegroom elect; came in from his usual evening visit to the Hall. In spite of the elaboration of his getting up, the curled hair, the shining mustache, and all the rest of the attractions, Otto thought he looked strangely haggard. Almost as much so as Sir Dene. And Sir Dene's looks had struck the barrister painfully.

"How dreadfully he is changed, mother," whispered Otto, under cover of the bustle.

"Changed!" repeated Lady Lydia, her eyes and thoughts on her well-beloved son, the gallant Captain. "Who's changed?"

"The poor old grandfather."

"Oh. He. He is getting on for eighty, Otto. You cannot expect him to be blooming for ever."

"It's not exactly that—blooming. There's so intense a sadness on his face. He looks just as though he were worn with sorrow."

"Did you ever see such a shrivelled-up mummy as old Aunt Ann!" returned my lady, behind her fan. "If you'll believe me, Otto, she has brought a cat and a parrot with her and two maids: one for herself, the other for the animals."

"She has never had children, you see, mother," was Otto's considerate answer. "When we live a lonely life, we are apt to make pets for ourselves."

Gander had supper ready laid in the dining-room. Mrs. Letsom—her head aching intolerably from the cold and the very long journey, for they had left London at six in the morning—declined to take any, saying she would rather go at once to bed: so Otto went in to his supper alone. During which he and Gander had a dish of confidential chat together, after the custom of old times. They were talking of Tom Clanwaring. The summons sent to Tom by Sir Dene had brought forth no response whatever: as Gander was telling.

"I don't believe he ever got it," exclaimed Otto.

"He must ha' got it," exclaimed Gander resentfully. "Don't I tell ye, Mr. Otto, that I put it myself into the slit o' the box at Worcester? As good suppose that the mail didn't go out, as that there letter didn't go along of it. Try a bit o' that raised-pie, sir."

Otto shook his head. Pies so late at night were too heavy

for him. "If he did get the letter, and could not respond to it in person, he might have written to Sir Dene."

"That's what Sir Dene says. It have tried him more nor anything a'most that went afore it, Mr. Otto. For days and days, ay and weeks, after there was time for Mr. Tom to get here, Sir Dene was waiting and watching for him. 'Perhaps he'll be here by morning, Gander,' he'd say to me when he went to bed at night; and i' the morning the first question 'ud be, 'Gander, has he come?' It has just been like a heart-break to him."

Otto Clanwaring, his supper finished, leaned back in his chair. There was something in all this that greatly puzzled him.

"To be recalled was all he wanted; I am sure of it," remarked the barrister. "I cannot think why he should not have come."

Neither could Gander. Neither could Sir Dene. Neither, truth to say, could many other people. Sir Dene supposed that Tom was too conscious of his unorthodox doings in connection with the Trailing Indian to show his face again yet awhile: and Sir Dene resented it accordingly.

The Chinese have a noted proverb: "To expect one who does not come; To lie in bed and not to sleep; To serve and not to be advanced, are three things enough to kill a man."

It would almost seem as if the non-arrival of his favourite grandson were killing Sir Dene. But the yearning wish to see him, the deferred hope, the grievous disappointment, were giving place now to angry implacability.

"I never thought as Mr. Tom was one to resent affronts in this fashion," spoke Gander, beginning to remove the supper things. "Poor Mr. Geoffry wouldn't ha' done it."

"Nor I. He has the most forgiving disposition in the world. Besides ——"

Otto stopped. The door was pushed open, and Sir Dene came tottering in, leaning on his stick.

"I hope you've got what you like, Otto. There's been nobody to take it with you."

"I've done famously, grandfather. No, thank you: no more. I never dare take much late at night, or I should get in for a headache on the morrow. Gander and I were talking about Tom, sir. It seems a very strange thing that he ——"

"Don't speak of him to me; don't mention him in my presence," roared Sir Dene, lifting his stick menacingly at an imaginary Tom in the distance. "If he were to attempt to enter Beechhurst Dene now, my servants should thrust him forth. Never again: never again."

"There's something or other wants explaining in all this," thought Otto. "However, it is no business of mine," he mentally concluded, with his usual rather selfish indifference to other people's interests.

Gander brought in some mulled claret in a silver cup, and Sir Dene and Otto sat over the fire and sipped it. Little things troubled Sir Dene now: and he began mentioning the state of expectancy he had been in all day, looking for his two eldest nephews, Dene and Charles. Eldest in point of precedence, youngest in age. They were to have arrived at the Dene that morning from Scotland: and had not come.

"Sure they've never been so foolish as to take ship—which Dene's fond of doing in summer," said Sir Dene, rather fractiously. "They might be kept out at sea a couple of weeks, if they've done that."

"They'd be sure to come by land, sir, at this season of the year; and with time limited," returned Otto. "Is their mother coming with them?"

"She can't," said Sir Dene. "I'm sorry for it; for she's a great favourite of mine, and I've not seen her for these two years. There's more things than one going contrary just now, Otto."

"But why can she not come, sir?"

"Because she's ill. I believe it's intermittent fever, or something of that. D'ye think the boys can get here to-night, Otto?" he added, after a pause.

"Well—of course it is possible," replied Otto, in some consideration: and he felt sure now that the old man was sitting up, expecting them. "They'd come by coach, no doubt, to the nearest place to this that the stage touches at, and then post on. I don't think they'd be likely to come so late as this, grandfather. We shall see them in the morning."

"Ay, I suppose one must give 'em up for to-night," conceded Sir Dene. "And how is the world using you, Otto? Are you getting on?"

"Yes, I am getting on, grandfather," returned Otto, proud in his independent spirit of being able to say it. "My name is becoming known, and business drops in. No fear now but I shall make my way; and make it well."

"Ay, I always said you would, give you time, though you have been so kept back by struggles and expenses," observed Sir Dene. "You have been steady and hard-working from the first, Otto; and those who are so are sure to get on. It is the conviction that has lain on my mind of your steady perseverance, my lad, that has induced me to help you so readily in your embarrassments."

Happening to be holding the claret cup to his lips at that moment, Otto looked at Sir Dene over its brim. He did not quite understand.

"I have had no embarrassments, sir," he said, as he put it down.

"Well, expenses then: I suppose I ought not to say embarrassments. Whatever they were, I only felt they were legitimate. And I let you have the money with a very different feeling from any I ever let your spendthrift brother have; I can tell you that."

Less and less did Otto understand. "I have not had any money from you since you first started me in life, grandfather. There are moments," he added, with a slight laugh, "when I feel proud of that fact. At least I am thankful for it."

"What do you call your first starting in life?" cried Sir Dene, looking hard at his grandson.

"After I had kept my terms and was called to the bar, you generously put a cheque for five hundred pounds into my hand, sir. To start me in my profession, as you called it."

"Well?"

"Well, it did start me, grandfather. I set up my chambers with it—that didn't cost much: for all the furniture in them, bed included, is not worth twenty pounds. And the rest I husbanded, and lived as economically upon as I could until work came in. I have never had cause to ask you for more, grandfather; and I never have asked it."

"Don't quibble, my lad. If you've not asked yourself for it, you have had it."

"Had what, sir?"

"Had what—why money. And I say, Otto, I have given it you with more satisfaction than any ever given to Jarvey."

"But, grandfather, I have not had any from you at all, I am happy to say. Except that first five hundred pounds."

Sir Dene and his grandson were staring at each other with all their might. Sir Dene openly. Otto covertly: for he thought the poor old man's imagination was solely at work: that his memory was rambling.

"Five or six times at the very least, Otto—more I think; my books will tell—have I helped you to money within the last two or three years. Sometimes for large sums. Why should you wish to deny it?"

"It must be all a mistake, sir. I have had none."

Sir Dene leaned back in his chair, his lips compressed. Were *all* his grandchildren turning out false? He had believed Otto to be so strictly truthful.

"How dare you say this to my face, young man?"

"It is the truth, grandfather. I don't know what else to say." And so earnestly did Otto say it, that Sir Dene almost began to wonder whether he himself was dreaming.

"Only a month or two ago—'twas sometime in October—I sent you up a cheque for a hundred pounds. Sent it up in a letter direct to your chambers. Come! What do you say to that?"

"I received it, sir, all safely, and acknowledged it to my brother, as he desired I should," quietly answered Otto. "I paid it away the same day, in conformity with his instructions."

For some moments Sir Dene did not speak. A light seemed to be breaking upon him.

"Paid it away for yourself, or for Jarvis?"

"Oh, for Jarvis."

"I see. Just tell me what you know about it, Otto."

"I don't know much, grandfather. Two letters were delivered to me that morning, each bearing the Worcester post mark. The one contained a few unimportant words from you to myself, hoping I was well, and that, and a cheque for a hundred pounds. The other was from Jarvis: saying I should receive such a cheque, and if I would kindly pay it away to a person (a lawyer) who would call on me in the course of the day. The lawyer called; and I paid it to him."

"One more question, Otto: and yet, my boy, I hardly need to ask it. Is it true what you say—that you have never had any money from me since that first five hundred pounds?"

"It is perfectly true. Neither have I asked you for any, sir."

"No: but others have, in your name."

"Jarvis, I suppose."

"Once or twice. Your mother, chiefly, Otto," continued the baronet, bending his fine old face forward, and sinking his voice to a troubled whisper. "She'd sell her soul for that first-born son of hers. It's my belief she'd sell her soul."

There was an ominous silence. Sir Dene sat, half beaten under the discovery; his head bent in thought, lifting this hand, lifting that, as he recalled the false pleas pressed upon him from time to time—Otto's non-success in his profession, his heavy expenses, and urgent need of money to rub on with, so as to keep his head above water. Never had the conduct of Captain Clanwaring appeared so flagrant as now. A groan burst forth from the old man.

"Otto, I hardly know whether I ought to let this wedding take place. Whether in honour I should not show the Squire what a false man he is,—a spendthrift,—a coward."

"There's no doubt, sir, that Jarvis ran recklessly and foolishly into debt while he was in the army, and that he has been driven to his wits' end to find money to stave off the embarrassments it entailed upon him; but marriage may make the turning point in his life. I should say it would."

And Sir Dene groaned again in very bitterness of spirit, as he rose to go up to his room for the night, leaning on the held-out arm of Otto.

The morning brought disappointment, in the shape of a letter from Dene, the heir. He wrote to say that a change for the worse had taken place in his mother. She was becoming so dangerously ill that neither he nor his brother could think of leaving her, even to attend the wedding. The letter concluded with a half-jesting wish that Jarvis might find a better groomsman. For young Dene (considered as first and foremost in the Clanwaring family, after its head) had been solicited by Jarvis to undertake that office. Jarvis, with rather an ill grace, observed to the barrister that he supposed the honour must fall to his lot now: and said it as if he grudged it to him.

"It's none such an honour—as I look upon it," was the significant retort of Otto Clanwaring.

CHAPTER XXXV.

AN ARRIVAL AT THE TRAILING INDIAN.

THE snow flakes were falling, large and thick. Falling on the hat of Mr. Sam Pound, swinging by one leg on the gate of the Trailing Indian. His master was out. Black had gone down to Hurst Leet on some urgent private business: no doubt connected with certain poaching friends of his who lived there. At least, such was the conclusion drawn by young Mr. Pound, who was tolerably shrewd. Finding it rather lonely indoors as twilight appeared, for not a soul was in the dreary inn but himself, Mr. Pound had stepped out to have a look at the lane, by way of taking a slight change.

"Mother Goose be a plucking of her geeses," quoth he to himself, raising his eyes to the floating feathers that filled the air. "Us han't had a reg'lar snowy Christmas for this ever-so-long. Bids fair for't now."

This was Friday. On and off since Wednesday the snow had been falling; so that the roads were already pretty thick with it. Regarding a fall of snow chiefly as a medium for the recreative exercise of snowballing, and especially of snowballing some unsuspicious individual, whom the blow caught unawares, Mr. Pound was extremely satisfied with the propect before him.

"We shall ha' the morris-dancers here," cried he, sucking up his breath. For he was very fond of the morris-dancers: and thought them, next to snowballing his friends and enemies, the best things brought by a hard winter.

Swinging to and fro on the gate was rather slow work, particularly as the snow had got into the gate's hinges and prevented it swaying quickly. Taking his foot off, he picked up a handful of snow, and sent it bang against the opposite hedge of holly. A sure marksman he, when a snowball was the weapon hurled.

"Hul—*lo!*"

This exclamation was caused by surprise. Just as Mr. Pound was manipulating a second ball to fling after the first, a huge mountain of snow—and it looked like nothing else—loomed slowly into view on the high road that crossed the end of the lane. Peering at this extraordinary phenomenon as well as circumstances permitted him—that is, between the fading daylight and the storm of snow—Mr. Pound at length made it out to be the "waggon."

"Well, I never!" cried he. "That there waggin haven't hurried herself!"

In those days the waggon was an institution in England; and was used for the conveyance of parcels and passengers from one town to another. This particular waggon in question was in the habit of passing along the road weekly, generally at dawn on a Friday morning—for waggons travelled night and day. They could not afford to halt by night on the road; not they: on they blundered, crawling and creeping, and dragging their slow length along. A distance that a stage coach might take twelve or fifteen hours to accomplish, the waggon would get through in a week. That this one had been a tolerably long time on its journey was proved by the mound of snow collected above it.

"Black, he said as he hadn't a seen the waggon go by, and I telled him it had went byafore he was up. Thought it had. Hullo! it be a stopping!"

The stopping of the waggon opposite the lane was less surprising to Mr. Pound than the sight of the waggon itself had been; for it sometimes brought parcels for the Trailing Indian. Now and then it let out passengers at that place, to claim the inn's hospitality, or to go on to Hurst Leet. Strictly speaking, this was what might be called a cross-country waggon, communicating with the London and Worcester waggon, the London and Gloucester waggon, and other waggons of importance. Mr. Pound began to trudge towards it, to receive anything that might be there for his master. He could not resist the temptation of sending a snowball or two at the horses.

"I'll lay a twopence as it have brought that there box o' baccy from Lunnon!" thought he as he advanced. "Black have been a growling over it this——"

Mr. Pound's words failed him in very surprise. Of all the surprises brought by the waggon, this was the greatest. Instead of the expected "box o' baccy" disinterring itself from the inside, there appeared, helped out by the waggoner— Miss Emma Geach.

Mr. Pound's first movement was to halt where he stood and give vent to a low whistle; his second, to turn tail, scutter home, bang-to the inn door behind him, and slip the bolt. The return of this young person displeased him excessively. Of the two, he would rather the waggon had brought a wild bear. Miss Geach was at the door almost as soon as he; rattling at it in an authoritative manner, when she found it fastened.

"Now then, Sam Pound, open the door! What do you mean by this?"

So she had recognized him, in spite of the falling snow and

the twilight! Not seeing his way particularly clear to keep her out, Sam unbolted the door.

She came in with her old warm cloak drawn round her, worn and shabby now, and a ragged shawl tied over her bonnet. She had gone away grandly by coach, plump, blooming, her big bandbox of clothes beside her: she came home humbly in a waggon, thin and cross-looking, and with no luggage at all—unless a handful of things tied up in a cotton handkerchief could be called such. Sam Pound, backing against the rack behind the door, made his observations in silence.

"Take a cup o' beer to the waggoner, Sam Pound. And be quick over it."

Whatever Miss Geach had lost in the way of looks, she had kept her tongue. Sam would no more have dared to disobey the imperative order than he'd have attempted to fly. Drawing the beer, he went out with it, walking as slowly as he could, and sullenly kicking up the snow before him. In the first place, Sam held Miss Geach in no favour: her scornful treatment of his brother Jim excited his resentment, and he also disliked her on his own account. In the second place, suppositions were crossing his mind that now she was back, he might no longer be wanted at the Trailing Indian: and, as it was a tolerably idle service, it just suited Mr. Sam.

When he returned indoors, and he took his time over the errand, Miss Geach had been upstairs to her room, had put on a gown of hers that had stayed all this while at the inn, and was down in the kitchen again, making some tea. Brushed up a little from her cold journey of several days and nights, she looked tolerably the same as usual; a little thin, perhaps, but quite as good-looking.

"Toast this bread, Sam Pound."

Sam Pound's mind was so entirely stunned by her proceedings altogether, that he complied mechanically, and stooped to toast the bread. Two rounds of it, off the quartern loaf. When toasted, Miss Geach put on plenty of salt butter, drew the table closer to the fire, and sat down to her tea.

"Where's Black?" she asked then.

"He's a went off to Hurst Leet."

Sam had squatted himself on his hams against the wall on the other side of the fireplace, and sat facing her, his hands clasped round his smock frock and legs. The reflection of the flame played on the red bricks; the kitchen looked homely and comfortable in the fire light.

"Wonder when her had any tea last?" thought Sam, as he watched the eagerness with which she ate and drank. "Shouldn't think 'twas o' one while."

"And how's the place going on, Sam Pound?" demanded Miss Emma, pouring out another cup of tea and beginning upon a second round of toast.

"Mortal dull. Us haven't had a customer in all to-day, not for as much as a pint o' beer."

"Who was asking about this here inn? I mean the place out o' doors. Hurst Leet and that."

"It be as it al'ays is, for what I see," returned Sam, ungraciously determined to give no more information than he could help.

"Anybody dead?"

"The missis here be dead."

"Don't I tell yo I warn't asking about this here house, Sam Pound?" was her answer, given wrathfully. "How's Harry Cole, down at the smithy?"

"He've had a bad wrist, he have, through a beast of a horse what up and kicked him a being shoed. It be got well again."

"Is Mr. Tom Clanwaring come back?"

"The face her must have to ask *that*!" thought Sam, as he sat and stared. "No, he bain't back, he bain't."

"I suppose the rest of 'em be a coming to the Dene for Christmas. The heir and his brother—be they here?"

"I ha'n't seed 'em."

"Be the Lunnon lawyer here yet?"

"I dun know," shortly answered Sam. "Them there quality folk don't concern me: nor me them."

Miss Geach was not to be repressed.

"The Captain—be *he* come yet?"

"The Captain ha'n't been away, as I've heerd on," growled Sam.

"Not away!"

"No, he ha'n't. He lives at the Dene now, he do."

"I'm sure he don't."

"I'se sure he do. There."

Miss Geach, about to drink up a saucerful of tea, paused, with the saucer to her mouth. "Who says he do, Sam Pound?"

"I says it, for one. All the parish knows he do. Bain't he about the place everlasting?"

"Be you sure?"

"Be *you* sure as that there's buttered toast you be a swallowing of?" was Sam's conclusive retort. "The Captain have lived along o' Sir Dene and Lady Lyddy a most a year now, he have."

A peculiar kind of light stole slowly over Miss Geach's face as she at length took in the assertion, making it look very hard. Sipping up the tea deliberately, she filled the saucer again.

"And the Squire's people, how be they?" she resumed, but with an air of pre-occupation and of utter indifference to the question. "Is Miss May married yet?"

"Not as I've heard on," said churlish Sam, more than ever resolved to tell nothing of his own accord.

"And how be your own folks a going on since I left these parts, young Sam?" she continued, condescendingly.

"They bain't dead yet, our folks bain't, and there bain't none of 'em married," was the spoken response. "Nasty greedy gut!" mentally continued Sam, for his own private benefit. "Her's a gobbling up all that there nice toast, her is, and never offering a fellow a bit! *Soaking* in butter, it were!"

Miss Geach had "gobbled up" the first half of the last round, and was beginning the second half. Also she was now stirring the sugar round vigorously in her third cup of tea. Sam, who was inordinately fond of good things, did not know how to suppress his ire.

"Where's the young 'un?" suddenly asked Sam.

"What young 'un?"

"That there babby o' your'n. Left it on the road?"

At this most unexpected and insolent close questioning, Miss Geach dropped the spoon and some of the tea together. Sam quailed before her hard look.

"Why, what do you mean, Sam Pound? What babby?"

"Oh well,——I thought—as you might ha'—bought—a babby, you know, since you've been away."

"Did you! Who gave you leave to think, pray? Me bought a babby? What should bring me a buying of a babby?" she continued, peering hard at Sam's countenance, and wondering perhaps how to take his words, and whether he was as simple as he was just then looking. "I haven't bought a babby; nor haven't sold one; nor haven't got one nor had one. There! Be I married, d'ye suppose, that you should set on and ask me that daft thing?"

Sam had sundry retorts ready at his tongue's end: but he deemed it prudent to let them stay there. In the old days she used to think nothing of slapping his ears. She had hard hands of her own, too.

"Take and fish out the biggest lump o' coal you can find i' the coal-hod, and put it on, Sam Pound. After that, you may shut the shutters and light the candles."

The final piece of toast was being bolted—to use Mr. Sam's private expression—as he slowly rose to obey her. He had a great mind to tell her to put on the coal herself—but it might not be policy. Suppose she took and turned him out that night?

"Mother used to say her had as much stock as Old Nick," thought the young man. "Her've got more on't now, her have. Wish the waggin had froze her, I do!"

He had his ten fingers in the large wooden coal-hod, searching for a big lump of coal, when the door was pushed sharply open, and a rush of air, a cloud of snow, and Randy Black burst in together. By the evident haste the latter displayed, one might have supposed he had been seeing another ghost.

"Well, Black, and how be you?"

In the hurry of his arrival, he had not at first noticed her presence. The salutation brought him up, and he stood without motion. Had she been a ghost herself, he could not have gazed more intently.

"It's me, Black. You needn't stand stock still, a staring, as if you didn't know me."

"I might well stare, to see *you*," retorted Black, in no pleasant tone. "You impudent huzzy! How dare you come back here in this bold way?"

"Because it's my home," returned she with equanimity, as she began to wash up the tea-things.

Leaving them to the battle—which Miss Emma Geach would be tolerably sure to gain; for Black, in his failing health and strength, was no match for her now—we will go on to Beechhurst Dene. Something a little curious was happening there this self-same evening.

Sir Dene, dressed for guests, was standing in the bright light of his sitting-room fire. He was thinking that, what with one non-arrival and another, things were not going as pleasantly as they might have gone. The disappointment about the heir and his brother was still felt by him, and now he had just heard a report that Squire Arde had not returned from London. Gander gave him the information while helping him on with his coat. Captain Clanwaring, just come in from the Hall, said its master had not arrived. There was this snow, too!

One of the grandest dinners given for many years at the Dene, was to take place this evening. All in honour, of course, of the coming wedding. Invitations had gone out to the first people in the county, including some of its resident nobility, and were accepted. The entertainment was to be on a grand and lavish scale: amidst other things, a band was engaged to play in the hall during the banquet.

On Sunday, Christmas Day, the Ardes would dine quietly at the Dene as usual. On Monday there would be a grand dinner at the Hall. Not so grand as this one to-night: Arde Hall was not foolish enough to attempt to vie with Beechhurst Dene, or put itself into the same scale of pomp and expenditure. And on Tuesday, the wedding-day, of course the Hall gave a breakfast.

With all his heart, Sir Dene wished this evening over. Truth to say, his strength was not equal to the entertaining of guests: though, in his old-fashioned courtesy, he intended to try and do it as in his best days. But if his old friend and neighbour were to be absent, half of its charm, for him, would have left it. Squire Arde was to have been home certainly that morning. Sir Dene thought it very hard that he had not come.

"I hope the carriages will be able to get along the roads," thought he, as he went to the window and looked forth on the snowy landscape, shining far and wide in the light night. "It is a long drive for some of 'em: they'll be twice as long doing it as they would if the roads were clear. Hope they'll take care to set off in time!"

It was past five now, and the dinner hour was seven. As Sir Dene stood, looking and thinking, the door was tapped at, and Captain Clanwaring put his head in.

"Mr. Arde is not back, sir."

"And why's he not back?" retorted Sir Dene in a tart tone. The tartness not meant for the absent Squire, but for Jarvis himself. Sir Dene had taken his resolution—not to speak at all of the deceit in regard to money matters that had come to his knowledge through Otto; at least, until the wedding should be over. But the fact lay solely on his mind and had rendered him barely civil since to either the Captain or Lady Lydia.

"He couldn't get his business done in time to leave London last night; he leaves to-night, and will be home to-morrow," said Jarvis. "Mrs. Arde has just had a letter from him."

"A letter at this time o' day! What d'ye mean?"

"It was delivered about three o'clock this afternoon, sir. The mail was, no doubt, late at Worcester: and the road is very heavy just now between there and here."

"There's no uncertainty about it, then—that he won't be here to dinner?"

"No, sir: he can't be."

Sir Dene turned his back, and Jarvis retreated from the room. By-and-by, when the old man was dosing in his easy chair by the fire, he was woke up by a resplendent vision kneeling at his feet.

It was Mrs. Letsom. She was in a pale pink silk, richly trimmed with lace; but she wore neither flowers nor jewels; her fair neck and arms were bare.

"Grandpapa, I have come with a petition," she coaxingly said, winding her pretty white arms about him. "Oh, if you will but grant it!"

"What is it, my dear?" he asked, bending to kiss her. For he loved her very well: though not as he had loved Margaret. She kept his head down to whisper in his ear.

"Let me wear the diamonds to-night."

Up went Sir Dene's face with a jerk. A jerk of puzzled surprise.

"The diamonds, Louisa. What diamonds?"

"Yours, grandpapa. The Clanwaring diamonds."

Sir Dene shook his head. "Those diamonds have never been got out, except to be looked at, since my wife died."

"Then I'm sure it's time they were aired," returned the young lady.

"Our diamonds are never worn, you see, but by the wife of the reigning baronet, Louisa," he explained, with a touch of the pride that was not yet at rest within him. "They will go to young Dene when I die; and be worn by his wife when he shall marry."

"But why need you be so exclusive, grandpapa? Dene's not married yet; nor likely to be."

"It is our custom, child. Your mother once attacked me on the subject of the diamonds; trying to persuade me to let her wear them. If I remember aright we were going to the ball at the Worcester Music Meeting, with the Foleys, and others. But I gave her to understand, once for all, that it could not be."

"That was different, grandpapa. This would be only in our own house, just for to-night. If you would let it be the necklace only, then!"

"I don't like to break through the rule, Louisa. Dene might not like it, either."

"Dene's not here. Besides, he has no business to like or dislike anything of the kind, as long as you are with us. I think Dene would be the first to say I should wear them, grandpapa.

Sir Dene remained silent, as if considering. Mrs. Letsom rose, and began turning herself round in the light of the fire, her hands held out.

"My dress looks well, doesn't it, grandpapa? It's new on to-night."

"Very well, my dear."

"But don't you see that I have neither bracelets nor necklace on? I'll tell you why. While I was dressing just now, my maid discovered the calamity that my jewel-box had not come. Not that there was much value in it, except the pearls. I have nothing to wear to-night, grandpapa."

"Your mother has jewels. Borrow some of her."

"I'd not wear any she's got—wretched old trumpery! Oh, grandpapa, if you would! Just the necklace only. You would enjoy the pleasure of seeing it worn on a neck once again."

And Sir Dene yielded. With the fond face kissing his, and the white arms entwined about him, he could but yield. But only the necklace, he said; he was resolute in that. Only the necklace.

"Ring for Gander, then, Louisa."

The diamond case was kept at the bottom of a chest in the next room, Sir Dene's chamber. Getting his keys, Sir Dene unlocked the chest himself; and Gander dived down with his hands to get it out, in somewhat the same manner that Mr. Sam Pound had just dived into the wooden coal-hod at the Trailing Indian. He had to remove sundry things; Sir Dene's military orders (he had one in his coat to-night); parchments belonging to the estate, and such like. Mrs. Letsom, her face and fingers alike eager, stood by and held the light.

But the case of diamonds was not there. *It was not there.*

Sir Dene sunk down in a chair speechless. Gander raised a hullabaloo.

For once the faithful old man-servant lost his wits. He flew out into the passages, shouting out wildly, "Thieves! Thieves!" Louisa followed, wild too, screaming in her turn, and whiffling the candle about.

It brought out the people who were attiring themselves in their dressing-rooms. Lady Lydia, Aunt Ann, Captain Clanwaring, and his brother Otto. The Captain demanded whether the house had gone mad.

"No," said Gander, "it's the diamonds that be gone. We've had thieves in."

"The beautiful Clanwaring diamonds," shrieked Louisa. "And I was to have worn them to-night."

Otto stood, half paralyzed. He looked at his mother, he looked at his brother; but they both went suddenly into their rooms again, and shut the doors. Going up to Louisa, he caught her hand.

"Say no more now, Lousia," he whispered in some agitation. "Hush it up. Hush it up, by any means in your power—if you value this house's peace and good name."

"Hush it up!" retorted Louisa Letsom, in a loud tone of rage. "Hush up the theft of our diamonds! You cannot know what you are saying, Otto Clanwaring."

CHAPTER XXXVI.

THE SNOW STORM.

A DARK, thick night, that of Friday, the twenty-third of December. The London and Worcester mail was toiling its slow way along towards the latter city under difficulties. Snow was falling heavily: snow had been falling, more or less, for some days. The coach was unusually laden. Although in was the Royal Mail, and carried his Majesty's letters, it was not on that account exempt from parcels, especially at the busy Christmas season; and it was crammed with presents from people in London to their friends in the country.. Baskets of codfish, barrels of oysters, small hampers of wine; and passengers' luggage. Never had the Worcester mail been more weightily charged.

Four passengers sat inside; none out. People had not cared to risk the cold journey for so many hours outside when they could get an inside place. Of the passengers, one was a lady; the other three were gentlemen: and they leaned in their corners, well wrapped up, wishing the night was over, and inwardly grumbling at the tardy pace to which the state of the roads condemned them.

Slower and slower went the horses. After leaving London, the mail had got along pretty well and kept its time tolerably at the different halting-places for the change of horses: it was only within an hour, or so, that the roads had become what they were—nearly impassable. The poor horses toiled and pulled: never a handsomer team to look at than those four bright brown steeds; but they could not get along. The coachman—himself half blinded by the drifting storm—alternately coaxed and whipped them. The guard rose perpetually, in his seat behind, to look out on the white mist, so far as he could see of it in the light given by the mail lamps. Then he would put his horn to his mouth, and blow a blast; sometimes short and snappish, sometimes patient and prolonged. To what end? It only went shrieking and echoing away to the lone country, its sound losing itself in the snow.

The horses came to a standstill, and the coachman turned his head to speak, from the midst of his mufflers. "Light your lantern, Jim, and see whether I *be* in the road."

The guard got down with his lighted lantern, and at once sunk up to the knees in snow. "This can't be the highway," he muttered to himself. "If 'tis, the storm must have fell here kindly."

It was impossible to tell whether they were in the road or not. Snow was everywhere. So far as could be seen of the limited space on which light was thrown, the look-out presented nothing but one white plain: and those small white mountains, revealing glimpses of themselves in places, might be heaping drifts that had gathered, might be hedges that were covered: no human being could tell. The horses, panting after the laboured exertions they had made, tossed their heads to the reins and tried to shake themselves free: but the leaders would not go forward of their own will, and to urge them might bring death.

"It is o' no use, Smith," spoke the guard to the coachman at length, from the depths of his many capes and comforters. "We can't go on."

"What's us to do, then?"

"May I be pressed if I know!"

Meantime the inside passengers were gradually awaking from their state of semi-sleep to the fact that they had come to a standstill: that the mail was not progressing at all. Two of the gentlemen wore white cotton night-caps; the third had a purple silk handkerchief tied on his head; the lady was enveloped in a quilted bonnet. In those days of long night stages, it was the custom to prepare for sleep inside the coaches with as much regard to comfort as circumstances permitted. One of the windows was let down, and the purple handkerchief, together with the head wrapped in it, thrust itself out to ascertain the cause of the delay.

"What's the matter?"

The guard with his lantern trod his way to the window at the call, as quickly as the depth of snow allowed him.

"We can't get on, sir."

"Not get on!" came the half angry, half authoritative rejoinder, in tones that are familiar to the reader. For the traveller with the purple silk handkerchief was Squire Arde.

"No, sir," repeated the guard, "we can't get on at all. The snow has been uncommonly heavy here, and the horses are not able to make their way in it. It's coming down now as thick as ever I saw it: getting worse with every minute."

The startling news fully aroused the whole of the passengers. As many of the four heads as could come out at the two windows, came out, their faces presenting various phases of that undesirable emotion—consternation.

"We must get on, guard," spoke Squire Arde, with a stress on the "must" and the authority of one who is accustomed to command.

"I can't see how it is to be done, sir," civilly replied the man. "The leaders refuse to move of their own accord, as 'twere; and Smith dare not force 'em on. We don't know that we be in the road."

"But we must get on," pursued Squire Arde. "To-morrow will be Christmas Eve; and I—I—I have engagements at home that I cannot break or put off."

"To-day is Christmas Eve, sir," corrected the guard: "morning has been in some time. But we cannot get on any the more for that."

"Whereabouts are we?" was heard from a passenger who was unable to get his head out.

"Not such a great sight off Chipping Norton, sir," was the lucid answer. "Halfway, may be. But it's all guess-work."

"Is there any danger, guard?" called out the lady, in her quick, pleasant voice.

"Not as long as we keep still, ma'am."

"But surely we are not to keep still all night! Good gracious, guard! Why suppose—suppose another coach comes up and runs over us?"

"Another coach couldn't any more come up, ma'am, than we can get on," returned the guard; who seemed as much at a loss and as full of dismay as his passengers. "We might have done well to stop at Woodstock: the ostler there told Smith it would be a wonder if the mail made her way to Chipping Norton."

The gentleman with the largest cotton night-cap was striking his repeater. By the hour it gave back, he knew they could not hitherto have been very seriously delayed.

"Oh come, guard," said he, "it's not so bad. I dare say we can get on with a little perseverance. The snow must have drifted just here."

"That's what it is, sir. If it had been as bad before, we couldn't have got along at all. But it's of no use trying to get through this."

"What is to be done, Smith?" roared Squire Arde at the top of his voice to the coachman. "What is to be done?"

"Nothing so far as I see," was the substance of the coachman's reply, given with equanimity. "If I tried to force the animals on, it might result in a upset down a bank, and cost all on 'em their lives, men and cattle too."

Even Squire Arde's impatience would not wish to risk that result. But he urged a cautious trial: as indeed did his fellow travellers. They thought it possible that the great drift of snow was confined to this one spot, and might be got through.

An effort was made. The guard and the passenger of the repeater went to the heads of the leaders; and for a short space and with great caution some few yards of the way were surmounted. But the snow got deeper: or rather, they got deeper into it. The coachman's decided opinion was, that they had lost the road; and that even this cautious moving was extremely perilous. So they desisted: life is sweet, and none of us are willing to risk it lightly. There appeared nothing for it but to remain as they were—stationary.

And, remain so, they did, until morning light. None of the passengers ever forgot that night. The fame of it went abroad; and it is talked of to this day in the counties of Worcestershire, Oxfordshire, and Gloucestershire.

When day dawned it was found that the coachman's conecture was correct. They were off the road: and how they had penetrated without accident to the spot where they found themselves was a marvel. Inside a ploughed field stood the coach, its previously broken fence having removed the barrier between it and the highway. *But the fence was broken only for a very short space, not much more than enough to allow of the horses and mail getting through.* It was this that rendered it remarkable—that they should have passed through at that one particular spot. The snow fell incessantly: the road, even could they have got back to it, was utterly impassable; to attempt to go on to Worcester out of the question for the present. By dint of exertion and skill, they reached a lonely farmhouse beyond the field; and, within its hospitable walls and stables, man and beast obtained the most welcome rest and shelter that any of them had ever enjoyed in their need.

I must beg you to note the days: for there was a singular romance attached to this detention of the mail and its passengers. People interested in the fact, were wont to say that it had been stopped by the Finger of Heaven. This day, Saturday, was Christmas Eve; Sunday would be Christmas Day: and Monday, the 26th, would be the eve of Miss Arde's wedding-day.

When Mr. Arde went to London on the Monday, putting up at the Castle and Falcon, it had been his full intention to quit it by the Thursday night's mail, so as to reach Worcester on Friday morning, and his own home in the course of the day. But when Thursday came, he found he was not able to do this; and he wrote to his wife saying he should be home on Saturday. As we heard in a previous chapter.

This delay in London rather vexed him. For one thing, it prevented his joining the state dinner given by Sir Dene Clanwaring on Friday: and Mr. Arde was fond of good dinners. The fault was his lawyers'; they were preparing Miss Arde's marriage settlement, and did not get it ready. He blew them up sharply: and on the Friday morning the deed was handed to him. On the Friday afternoon he was at the Bull and Mouth, and put himself into the Worcester mail—which in those days started early, either at four or five in the afternoon. He had with him the marriage settlement, and the marriage licence: a fine cod-fish, and two barrels of oysters.

So the mail set off on its journey cheeringly enough; and traversed part of the distance only to find it could not traverse the rest. Mr. Arde, when writing to his wife, had said he should be home on Saturday "without fail." But, here he was instead, snowed up in that lonely farmhouse, somewhere in the unknown regions about Chipping Norton: and, on the whole, glad that a farmhouse was there to be in.

Nevertheless as the hours on the Saturday went on, and there appeared to be no chance whatever of their moving, for the snow continued to come down heavily at intervals, Mr. Arde chafed at the delay: showing some irritation on the point to his fellow-travellers, and telling them that urgent business awaited him at his home in Worcestershire. Very true; it did so. But had the business been ten times as urgent, had it involved life or death, he could not any more have helped the detention. When the elements set themselves against man, man is powerless to contend with them.

Beds were improvised for the travellers on Saturday night. The farmer and his family were hospitable to the last degree, and did their best in every way to make their unexpected guests comfortable. The mail-coach, covered well with sacks to keep it dry, stood out in the snow; the horses were in the stables; the coachman and guard made themselves happy with the farmer's servants, and no doubt secretly enjoyed the holiday as an interlude of rest from their life's occupation.

Many were the anxious looks cast out on the weather when the travellers rose on Christmas morning. One sheet of white presented itself everywhere, and there was at least no chance of their getting on that day. The farmer feasted them right royally with turkeys, and other good things incidental to the season; amidst which appeared Mr. Arde's large cod-fish, and one of his barrels of oysters: a rare treat to the farmer and his people. They drew round the fire for dessert, to make merry, telling anecdotes and stories; and for a time Squire Arde forgot his vexation. Some friends in the locality, who were to have partaken of the family's hospitality, dinner guests, could not get there for the snow.

On Monday, matters out of doors remained in the same state, and the prisoners had to be prisoners on that day still. Worse still, there seemed to be no indications that things would alter; and Mr. Arde was at his wits' end. He chafed, he fumed, he marched to the doors, he opened the windows, he took counsel with the coachman and guard. All to no purpose. The rest rallied him; the lady laughed at him good-humouredly: cheerful-hearted herself under all circumstances of existence, however untoward, she merrily told him that the adventure was agreeable, rather than otherwise, and would serve them to talk of the remainder of life. Mr. Arde at length disclosed the reason of his impatience—his daughter, whose wedding was fixed for the following day, could not be married without him, as he bore the licence and the settlements. They allowed the plea: agreeing with him that the detention was unfortunate: but they were unable to speed him onwards.

"Only think if I should not be home by to-morrow morning!" cried Mr. Arde in accents of fear at the very thought.

"They would only have to postpone the ceremony for a day or two," cheerily pointed out the lady.

Squire Arde shook his head. "I don't like weddings postponed," said he. "Old wives say it bodes ill-luck, you know, Mrs. W——. We must get away somehow to-night."

And out he went again in his restlessness, to see the guard and coachman.

Must get away to-night! Squire Arde might as well have said he must go up in a balloon and get the clerk of the weather to change the aspect of affairs. There was as much possibility of his doing the one as the other. Monday wore on. The travellers sat by the fire, and played cards, and the good farmer feasted his guests again. Not one of them in after life forgot his genuine hospitality and kindness. For I am recording only what took place in actuality. Up to this time; all Saturday, all Sunday, all Monday; they had been detained. So prolonged and heavy a snow-fall had not been known in the country for years and years.

Tuesday morning. Squire Arde was the first to gaze out anxiously. It was the wedding-day—or ought to have been—and he was nearly rampant. For though a very easy man in general, it was in Mr. Arde's nature to put himself fiercely out when anything went wrong on great occasions: and perhaps the consciousness of the very fact that in his heart he did not cordially like Captain Clanwaring for his daughter's husband, made him all the more impatient to get the marriage over and done with. Doubt would then be off his mind. Ever and anon in the past few weeks a voice had been whispering to him that he and his wife might be wrong to have urged Jarvis Clanwaring upon Mary: she was young enough and could have waited to make another choice. However, what was fixed, was fixed: and the Squire now only wanted to be at home and get it over. But this snowstorm was preventing him.

As an imprisoned bird flutters his wings against the bars of his cruel cage, vainly endeavouring to escape from it, so it was with George Arde. He chafed as before, he fretted, he fumed, all to as little purpose as the poor caged bird. As the one cannot break his wire bars, neither could the other his fetters. What mattered it to Mr. Arde though the weather on this Tuesday morning was changing—giving evident signs of a speedy break up! It did not serve him. Had the roads between that farmhouse and Hurst Leet been instantaneously rendered, by some miracle, clear as a bowling-green, he could not have reached home in time for the ceremony: no, not by the help of the fleetest horse. Mrs. W——, good, trusting woman that she was, then, and throughout all the trouble that was destined to come to her in later life, said to him that these vexatious impediments sometimes intervened only to answer some wise end. But Mr. Arde wholly refused to see it in this instance, and chafed amazingly.

By Tuesday night the high road had become passable for large vehicles: and the mail, leaving London that afternoon for Worcester, absolutely passed on its way. Nothing of this was known at the farm. News certainly did come in that the highway was tolerably clear. What of that?—it only served to exasperate Mr. Arde the more. For this mail of his, this miserable mail, embedded deep in the ruts and snow, could not as yet be got by any manner of means to the highway. And thus another night passed, and the prisoners were prisoners still. Squire Arde decided that fate and fortune were alike against him.

CHAPTER XXXVII.

AT BEECHHURST DENE.

IN Gander's pantry, a sociable kind of room panelled with oak, stood over the fire Otto Clanwaring and the butler; the latter in his usual striped morning jacket, which he wore summer and winter, and with a tea-cloth in his left hand. Gander was frightfully discomposed. In all the years that the man had lived with Sir Dene, he had never been so put out as he was now, at the disappearance of the case of diamonds. It was Saturday morning, and Christmas Eve, for we have to go back a little to record what had been taking place, during the snow-storm, at Beechhurst Dene and elsewhere. The grand dinner, as may be remembered, took place on the previous night, Friday; and Sir Dene, fatigued with his exertions as host, was not yet up.

"No, Mr. Otto, you had better *not* go in to see him," Gander was saying with quite the same amount of decisive authority that he had used when the barrister was a boy. "When my master says to me 'Gander, you'll take care that I am not disturbed for a bit,' why it's my place to take care he's not, sir: and Sir Dene knows that I shall take care."

"I should be the last to disturb him against his will, Gander."

"Yes, I think you would be, Mr. Otto."

"The dinner was too much for him, that's the fact," observed Otto. "A courteous-natured man, as my grandfather eminently is, exerts himself at all cost to entertain guests when they are around him: and a state occasion like that last night involves a continual strain on the exertion, mentally and bodily. Sir Dene should have given up the presidency to—to Captain Clanwaring; and sat, himself, as a guest."

"He'd not do that," disputed Gander. "While he's able to appear among 'em at all, it'll be as head and chief. Quite right too. To Captain Clanwaring he never would give up," boldly added Gander: "he don't like him well enough. I can't tell but what he might ha' give up last night after what happened, had the heir, Mr. Dene, been here."

Otto said nothing to this. Whatever might be his own private contempt for his elder brother, he did not choose to speak of it to the butler.

"What a snow-storm we are having, Gander!" he cried, turning his eyes on the white landscape outside the window, by way of changing the conversation.

"'Twas not the entertaining o' the folks, Mr Otto; my master's equal to that once in a way yet; though I think it'll be the last time he'll ever attempt it," resumed Gander, disregarding the remark about the snow. "'Twas that awful upset just as the company was arriving. It shook him frightful. My wonder was that he sat down to table at all. I'm sure I didn't know whether I stood on my head or my heels all the while I waited."

"Yes," said Otto, looking close at the fire; "it is not pleasant to miss one's family diamonds."

"No, it's *not*," significantly spoke Gander. "Not a wink o' sleep has the poor master had for thinking on't. And he has been getting a notion into his head in the night about it that makes him feel worse."

"What notion's that?"

"Well, he thinks 'twas no common thief that took 'em," returned Gander, gently swaying his tea-cloth.

"No common thief!"

"No housebreaker, nor nothing o' that sort. 'Don't *you* be put out about it, Gander,' said he to me; '*you'd* not touch the diamonds'—for you see, Mr. Otto, 'twas an awkward loss for me, and I told him so; nobody but me, besides himself, having access to the keys that unlocked the box. He had been thinking it over in the night, the master went on to say, and he had come to the notion that somebody had took them diamonds to make money on 'em."

Knowing what he did know, the usually impassive face of the barrister turned as red as a school-girl's. Glancing up at Gander's clock he made some light remark about the hour. But the butler was not to be repressed.

"It have been nothing but worrying him for money this many a year past. Worry, worry, worry; I wonder sometimes that the master stands it, and so 'ud you wonder, Mr. Otto, if you were in the midst on't. My lady's at him perpetual: it's money for herself she wants, or for the Captain, or for *you*. As for the Captain, he have not dared to ask on his own score this long while, for Sir Dene 'll never hear him."

Otto Clanwaring opened his lips to say that none of the solicited money had been for himself; but closed them again without speaking. A shrewd doubt lay upon him, gathered from Gander's glance and from Gander's tone, that the man guessed it perfectly, or else that his master had enlightened him.

"And so, Mr. Otto, Sir Dene thinks, seeing lately he has not responded much to the demands, but just shut up his breeches pockets, that perhaps the diamonds have been took to make money upon. Borrowed, you know."

Again an idea crossed the mind of Otto Clanwaring, that Gander had his suspicions that he, Otto, knew something of this; suspicions drawn no doubt from his perhaps too evident efforts to hush up the matter on the previous night when the loss was discovered. Otherwise the man would hardly so have spoken.

"I can only say, Gander, that I have not borrowed the diamonds—as you call it."

"Not likely, Mr. Otto. But now you look here, sir. If them diamonds could be brought back, or if proof could be given to the master that they bain't lost outright—sold, say—'twould comfort him." Otto really knew not what to answer.

"I was thinking, sir, that perhaps we might ha' got up a little bit of a plot; you and me. If you could get the diamonds, I'd carry the case in my hand to Sir Dene, and say, 'Look here, master, at what I've done; at my poor old foolish memory;' and vow to him that I had put 'em elsewhere for safety when I was a-rubbing of 'em up, and forgot it.—Just as the widow Barber put away that paper of her'n years ago, and couldn't find it again, and had to turn out of her place in consequence."

"Are you suggesting this out of consideration for Sir Dene, or for others?" inquired Otto.

"Why, for Sir Dene, of course, sir," replied Gander, with an emphasis and a flick of the tea-cloth, that seemed to imply he'd not trouble himself to do it for others. "I'd spread the diamonds out before him to comfort him; and he'd believe, seeing 'em and listening to me, that they had never been lost, but in my stupid memory. 'Twould be a pack o' lies: but heaven 'ud forgive me for the sake o' the poor master. He's too old to have these tricks played him, Mr. Otto: and the loss o' them diamonds is just telling upon his mind: and I dun know what the end on't 'll be."

There was a pause of silence. The barrister had his head bent as if in thought; Gander and his cloth were perfectly still, waiting for an answer.

"Tell me freely why you are saying this," said Otto, looking up suddenly, his indifferent tone changing to a frank one. "You have something in your thoughts, Gander."

"Well, sir, as it's you, and you ask me, I think I will tell. Captain Clanwaring has got the diamonds."

An exceeding disagreeable sensation, resembling shame, seized hold of Otto on hearing this. He gave the man a word of reprimand and bade him not talk so fast. It was not Otto's duty to betray his brother.

"I am just as sure of it as that we two be talking here, Mr. Otto," persisted Gander. "After the company had gone last night, Miss Louisa—Mrs. Letsom that is—came into my pantry here, and began again about the diamonds, vowing she would have every nook and corner o' the house turned out, and every servant in it searched, them and their boxes. All in a minute, in come Captain Clanwaring. He seized hold of her and said—well, I hardly know what he said, Mr. Otto, and at the time he didn't see me, for I'd gone behind the screen there. Just a few words, it was, ordering her to be *quiet*, but they startled me. His face was as white as white paint when it's got varnish on't, a kind o' blazing white. He had took enough to drink, too. I knew then who had got the diamonds; and Miss Louisa, I fancy she knew, for she turned as white as he was, and never spoke another word. 'Twas my lady who cribbed 'em out o' the chest, I guess, Mr. Otto. Must ha' been. Nobody but her could get to Sir Dene's keys —save me."

Otto Clanwaring, the rising barrister casting glances towards a future chief judgeship, possibly to something higher than that, bit his lip almost to bleeding. How painful this was to him, a man of honour, his sharp accent told.

"Then it was you who instilled these suspicions into the mind of Sir Dene, Gander!"

"Not a bit on't, sir. I've never let 'em out o' my mind till this moment, and I shan't speak of 'em again. Sir Dene took 'em up for himself in the night, while he lay awake. Hinting at 'em to me this morning when I went in, I pretended to say that he must be mistaken."

"And you must be mistaken, Gander," spoke Otto, decisively. "Better not let Captain Clanwaring hear you."

"Let it go so, Mr. Otto," returned the man calmly. "But —if there's any means o' getting the diamonds back, *get* 'em back, for the poor master's sake."

"Sir Dene must talk to you very confidentially, Gander?"

"So he do, sir. There's been nobody else here the past twelvemonth for him to talk to but me, and he has got into the habit on't. You've all been away but the Captain; and the master wouldn't talk to *him*. If Mr. Tom was here 'twould be different."

The ringing of Sir Dene's bell broke up the colloquy. Gander threw his tea-cloth on a chair, and hastened up stairs: leaving Otto standing over the fire.

It was a painfully humiliating moment for Otto Clanwaring. That the affair had taken place exactly as the old serving-man had divined—his mother abstracting the case from the chest, and handing it to Jarvis—Otto felt as sure of as though he had seen it done. With his whole heart, he hated the clear-sightedness of Gander in this. Although the man had been in the family so many years as to have become almost like one of themselves, it was not pleasant that he should be cognisant of this disgraceful act.

"What a curse are spendthrift habits!" cried the barrister in his bitterness.

Quitting the pantry, he bent his steps to the library, where he expected to find his mother and brother alone. He intended to act on Gander's suggestion, and ask them to redeem the diamonds, if possible. The time had gone by for mincing the matter, in the opinion of Otto Clanwaring.

With the snowy landscape out of doors so suggestive of cold, and the blazing fire within, the library presented a picture of warm comfort. Lady Lydia and Jarvis sat on a sofa, and were evidently consulting together. Jarvis lay back against one of its cushions, yawning and stretching, and not looking any the fresher for the quantity of wine taken at the past night's dinner. Otto took up his stand before them; and in a low voice and in a few words said what he had to say. It brought my lady bolt upright. She told Otto he was mad.

"I know you have pledged the diamonds, Jarvis," went on Otto. "What did you get upon them?"

"It's a lie!" said polite Jarvis.

"Look here," quietly rejoined Otto, "this sort of thing will do no good. The job is a bad job altogether, but it's *done*; and all that remains now is to see whether it can be undone. Don't trouble yourself to deny it to me, Jarvis. I have known of the transaction all along."

"What an infernal lie!" amended Jarvis.

"Pale the money-lender holds the diamonds. I saw you leave them with him at his house; I saw you receive the wages.'

An explosive burst of abuse from Jarvis. Abuse of the money-lender, who must, as he concluded, have betrayed trust; fiercer abuse of Otto. Lady Lydia, fearing the noise might penetrate beyond the room, stood between them, praying them to be tranquil.

"It could not be helped," she said to Otto, finding how useless it would be to play longer at denial. "Jarvis was *obliged* to have money, and there were no other means whatever of raising it. The diamonds were lying there useless, not looked at from year's end to year's end; and I assumed to a certainty that they would be replaced before Sir Dene could find it out. There's no great harm done," she concluded in a slighting tone.

"As he has found it out, they must be brought back," was Otto's answer. "For Sir Dene's sake. Do you hear, Jarvis?"

"They can be brought back, and will be brought back, as soon as the wedding is over, without any of your confounded interference," spoke Jarvis sullenly. "But for the delay in that, they'd have been home before."

"Some days to wait yet!" remarked Otto. "Were the roads clear—but it's hardly to be expected with this continued fall of snow—I would go up to London and get them, if you could find the money."

Jarvis half laughed in derision. He find the money! When the ten thousand pounds to be allotted to him of Mary Arde's fortune should have passed with herself into his own possession, he would have more than enough money for everything. Until then he had not a stiver.

"What did you get from Pale on them?" asked Otto.

"Only a trifle. Three hundred pounds."

Three hundred pounds! In truth it was a sum far beyond any possible means to find. Otto imparted a hint that Sir Dene suspected something, but held his tongue about Gander. A great pity crossed his heart when he thought of Mary Arde. Tied to this spendthrift, what would her future be? But that Jarvis was his brother, and brotherhood involves obligations, Otto had certainly opened the eyes of the ruling powers at Arde Hall.

"It is nothing short of a fraud," exclaimed Otto.

"What is?" snapped his mother.

"The marrying Mary Arde."

My lady's eyes and tongue alike blazed forth their denunciation of Otto and his gratuitous opinion; and he was fain to hold his peace.

She went into Sir Dene's room as soon as she could get admittance, which was not until the baronet had dressed for the day, and was sitting by his fire. There she set herself, in her plausible way, to disperse any doubt that might lie on Sir

Dene's mind of Jarvis in connection with the diamonds. He heard her in silence, saying nothing, and whether she made any impression upon him, or not, or whether he really did entertain any doubt of Jarvis, she could not tell. Of course she was unable to speak out on the matter, or to defend Jarvis openly: it had all to be done by implication. That Sir Dene was looking unusually worn and ill that day, was plainly observable; he seemed to be nearly prostrate, sunk far in a state of apathy.

"I quite think with dear Jarvis, that it is no common thief who has taken them," remarked Lady Lydia: for she continued to pursue the subject long after Sir Dene's silence might have warned her it had been wiser to drop it. "As you said last night, Sir Dene, whoever took the diamonds must have known they were kept in the chest——"

"And known where my keys are kept too, my lady, when I have not got them about me."

It was the first time he had spoken, and the interruption was a quick one. My lady coughed.

"Ah yes, no doubt," she blandly said. "Those diamonds, I fancy, had not been looked at for a year. Perhaps not for considerably more than that."

No answer.

"There is only one possible solution of the mystery that occurs to me; and that may not be the true one. But you know, dear Sir Dene, we cannot help our thoughts."

Still no answer. Sir Dene was bending forward, his hands resting on his stick, his eyes bent on the carpet, as if he were studying its pattern. Lady Lydia brought her face a little nearer to his, and her low voice took a confidential tone.

"Did that worthless, ungrateful fellow, Tom Clanwaring, help himself to them before he went away? It is the question I am asking myself, Sir Dene. He knew where the keys——"

Not quite at the first moment had Sir Dene gathered the sense of the implication. It flashed across him now. He started up in fierce passion, grasping his stick menacingly. Perhaps the fact of his *knowing* Tom could have had nothing to do with the loss, rendered his anger at the aspersion the greater. For it happened that both Sir Dene and Gander knew the diamonds were safe six months ago. Searching the chest in the month of June for something wanted, they had seen the case there.

Rarely had Lady Lydia heard a similar burst of reproach from Sir Dene's lips. In spite of the animosity which he had been professing for Tom latterly, as well as really indulging, his true feelings for him peeped out now. How *dared* she so asperse his best grandson, the son of his dear dead son Geoffry, he asked her. Tom was a gentleman at heart, and would be one always; a true Clanwaring he, with all a Clanwaring's honour; and he had a great mind to despatch Gander to Ireland when the snow had melted, that he might bring him back to the Dene by force. Things had never gone well since Tom left. As to that bold baggage up at the Trailing Indian—it must have been her fault more than his; she was older than Tom, and had got ten times the brass. Many a light-headed young fellow had done as much in his hot blood, and repented afterwards, and made all the better man for it. Sir Dene was a fool for sending Tom away—did my lady hear?—a fool. A fool for that and for a good deal more.

Thus he went on, saying in his passion anything that came uppermost; but no doubt giving vent to his true sentiments. My lady became meek as a lamb, and metaphorically stopped her ears. Especially to the repeated insinuation that other folks knew where his keys were kept, and the diamonds too, as well as Tom: the "other folks" pointing indubitably to herself, if not to her son Jarvis.

When the storm died out, and Sir Dene had sunk back in his chair, exhausted, Lady Lydia made a pretence of gently tending the fire, talking about the snow, and the weather generally, and the past night's company while she did it; any safe topic that occurred to her. She then withdrew from the room and left Sir Dene to his repose. It would not do, she saw it clearly, to say too much about the diamonds while he was in this untoward frame of mind. That he had a doubt of *her* she felt convinced; but she was not so sure that he doubted Jarvis. With her whole heart she wished the wedding over and the diamonds replaced. Had it been in her habit to pray, she would have prayed that Tuesday might arrive on eagle's wings.

Meanwhile as the day wore on, some uneasiness was excited in the Arde family at the non-arrival of its master. The hall was in a vast commotion of preparation, not only for the wedding itself, but for the dinner entertainment that was to be given on its eve, Monday night. Towards Saturday night the non-appearance of Mr. Arde was explained. Some farmers, making their slow way home from Worcester market, brought word that the London coaches, including the mail, had not been able to reach Worcester, from the impassable state of the roads. Report spoke of "mountains of snow" in the low-lying lands around Moreton-in-the-Marsh. Mr. Tillett of Harebell Farm, knowing that Mrs. Arde was anxious and uneasy, called at the Hall to tell her this.

"Dear me!' she exclaimed, at the news. "Will the coaches not be able to get in to-day at all, think you, Mr. Tillett?"

Looking out on the snow, remembering what the signs abroad were, Mr. Tillett thought it hardly likely that the coaches could get in.

"If any one of them does, it will be the mail," he remarked. "That is sure to make its way when it can, ccount of the letter-bags."

"I suppose it is bad between this and Worcester?" said Mrs. Arde.

"Worse, madam, than I have ever known it. In places I hardly thought I should get my horse along."

"A pretty long while some of the people must have been getting home last night from the dinner at Sir Dene's!" exclaimed May.

Mr. Tillett laughed. "They'd arrive in time for breakfast, Miss May."

"Mamma," said May, in an eager kind of tone, after Mr. Tillett was gone, "if it's like this, we shall not be able to dine at Beechhurst Dene to-morrow."

"Nonsense, May. There can be no difficulty at any time in going that short distance. Besides, the upper road is not one for the snow to lie upon: it slopes slightly all along on the one side, you know."

May sighed. Only the not dining at the Dene on the morrow in the company of Jarvis Clanwaring, would have seemed a relief. Now that the union with him was drawing near, all her old horror of it had returned. She hated it and dreaded it in what seemed, even to herself, a most wicked degree. And yet—how was she to help it? She did not know, poor girl. Many and many a minute did she pass, praying on her knees to God, that He would pity her and help her to put away the sin.

CHAPTER XXXVIII.

A DISH OF TEA AT THE FORGE.

CHRISTMAS DAY. Before the morning had well dawned, the children from the gatekeeper's lodge trooped up to Beechhurst Dene, were admitted by the servants, and gathered themselves in a group at the top of the stairs near the doors of the best chambers, to sing their carol. It was a universal custom, this carol singing, in those days; and, as a rule, servants in every great house were up early, expecting it. Gander had been on thorns, wishing to get into his master's chamber to see how he had slept, and to take him some tea; but as Sir Dene chose to be first of all aroused on Christmas Day by the carol singing, almost as if it were a religious rite, and that nothing else should previously disturb him, Gander waited.

The carol chosen by the children this year—or rather chosen for them by older heads—was a new one, called "The Carnal and the Crane." It was tolerably long, and sung to a monotonous kind of chant. At the first verse of it, Mrs. Letsom's little ones, in their white night-gowns, were peeping down through the balustrades above. While below, collected near the foot of the stairs, stood all the servants, including Gander. Partly hiding themselves, however, that the sight of them might not daunt the shy young carol singers. The verses well through to the end, came the final benediction; spoken, not sung.

"Wish ye a merry Christmas, Sir Dene, and ladies and gentlemen all: and a happy new year, and a many on 'em."

The little white-gowned people above clapped their hands; the servants clapped theirs, and applauded. Now, it had been the invariable custom, during this applause, for Sir Dene's door to open from the inside and a small shower of sixpences, agreeing with the number of singers, to be pitched forth among them. Be you very sure the singers looked for this observance with eager eyes. But on this morning they looked in vain. The door remained closed.

"Come you down, dears," called out gently one of the head women-servants, breaking at length the waiting pause. "Come you down to your hot coffee. Sir Dene's asleep, maybe; he's not well just now. He'll send you out the sixpences later."

A good breakfast was always provided for the singers in the kitchen. And again on New Year's morning, with a second sixpence. For the same ceremony took place then. Only the carol chosen was a different one, and the after wish for a merry Christmas omitted.

In obedience to the call, the children went down as quietly as their timid feet allowed them. And Gander went up. "May be he's not well enough to get out o' bed himself," ran his thoughts in regard to his master, "and is waiting for me to fetch the sixpences. I know he had got 'em put ready last night."

Knocking gently at the door, and receiving no response, Gander went in. The chamber appeared to be just as he had left it the previous night, none of the curtains undrawn. Turning to the bed, he saw his master.

"The Lord be good to us!" ejaculated Gander.

For Sir Dene Clanwaring was lying with his face drawn, and apparently senseless. He had had some kind of attack, probably paralysis.

Mr. Priar pronounced the attack to be a very slight one, quite unattended with present danger. But there was no warranty that another might not succeed it: and the doctor enjoined strict quiet in the chamber and out of it.

"I'll lay a guinea as it comes o' the worry about them there diamonds!" was Gander's private comment to Otto Clanwaring.

There was no dinner company. A message was despatched to inform the Ardes of what had occurred and to stop their coming. Neither did any of the Beechhurst Dene people attend morning service, although it was both Sunday and Christmas Day, the snowy state of the roads preventing it as much as the state of Sir Dene. The Ardes and their servants went, but they were nearer the church. Mrs. Arde and May would dine quietly at home, Captain Clanwaring their only visitor. It was the Captain who had carried down the news of what had occurred, and then got his invitation. The Miss Dickereens were not sent for as on the previous Christmas Day: perhaps Mrs. Arde thought they might not care to encounter the snow. Mrs. Arde was thoroughly put out by the prolonged absence of her husband. His decision was wanted on many details connected with the wedding, and he was not there to give it.

As for May, in her heart she could very well have dispensed also with Captain Clanwaring. Never had she felt more wretched than on this day. Try as she would she was unable to rally her spirits. A weight, as of impending evil, seemed to lie upon her: and had the coming Tuesday been to witness her hanging instead of her wedding, she could not have looked forward to it in a more gloomy spirit. As she recalled the happiness of the last Christmas, a half groan burst from her lips: the contrast between that day and this was so great. *Then* she had wondered whether things could ever look cloudy again: *now* the secret cry of her heart was—that never again could they look bright. Ah, should not experience have taught her a lesson? That unclouded brightness had all too soon faded into a darkness as of night: might not the present darkness clear itself into day? Heaven however was at work for Mary Arde, though she knew it not.

"I suppose, Miss May, there's no reason why I may not run home," spoke Susan Cole, towards dusk in the afternoon. "They've invited me there to take a dish o' tea."

"What reason should there be?" replied Miss May with apathy.

"You won't want me, I mean? I thought you'd be out, you see, Miss May, when I promised to go. Mother, she's getting old now and looks out for one, once she expects one's coming."

"I shall not want you for anything, Susan," said May, rousing herself. "You'll have a fine snowy walk, though."

"I'll borrow a pair o' Mark's gaiters, and pick my petticoats up round me," was Susan's unceremonious avowal. "'Twon't hurt me."

"I am glad to dine at home, for my part, instead of at the Dene," remarked May. "Friday's dinner there was so tedious."

Susan shook her head. "Miss May, I don't like them break-ups to old customs. For ever so many years now, till the last, the Hall has dined at the Dene on Christmas Day; and the Dene with the Hall on New Year's Day. Last year 'twas broke through. The master here warn't well enough to go to the Dene, or thought he warn't, and so none of you went; and when New Year's Day come round, Sir Dene, he warn't well enough to come here. 'Twas odd that the custom o' both days should be interrupted. I said then 'twas like a break-up, Miss May; and so it have proved. All the rest o' Beechhurst Dene come here, but Sir Dene. He didn't though; and he's the master."

"The rest did not all come," said May, quietly.

"All but Mr. Tom. And he ceased to be one o' the Beech-hurst Dene folks that same night."

"Yes," said May. "Turned from it."

"Served him right," retorted Susan. "What did he get into mischief for?"

May's face took a sudden glow of colour, red as a fire coal.

"I wish I was over in Paris, or somewhere," she suddenly exclaimed after a pause, "and all this worry over."

"What worry?" questioned Susan.

"Of the wedding,——and the people."

"Weddings comes but once in a life-time. It's right to have a show and bustle over 'em, Miss May."

May, seated on a low toilette-chair covered with white dimity, for the colloquy was taking place in her bed-room, began scoring her blue silk dress across with her nail, and made no answer. Very pretty she looked. Her cheeks were somewhat thinner than of yore, but they had not lost their rose-colour: her beautiful, soft brown eyes were lustrous still, her hair was bright. The allusion to Paris meant more than the chance remark the reader may have imagined it to be. A visit to Paris was in those days a very uncommon thing: and Captain Clanwaring had proposed to take May there after the marriage. They were not to settle down in a home yet awhile, for some months, at least; but take their pleasure. In fact, the question of where the home should be was left in abeyance: Mr. and Mrs. Arde naturally wished it to be near them; Captain Clanwaring secretly wished they might get it. He could not live long away from London and its attractions, and did not mean to try to. "Once she's my wife, safe and sure, she will have to do as I please," he told himself. And —to prevent the question of their home being decided beforehand, he had ingeniously laboured to inoculate his bride elect with a wish to see Paris and its wonders, which he had never seen himself; as well as other places. Poor May thought that seeing wonders might help her to bear her lot—which in prospective was looking cruelly hard, whatever it might prove to be in reality. She had her private thoughts also as well as he. "Once I am his wife, I shall be able to put away all these old regrets—and longings—and misery. And the further I am away from here, the better chance there'll be of my doing it. Nothing like old associations for keeping up old feelings." So the proposal of sojourning in Paris, London,

Bath, and elsewhere, had been rather eagerly received by May. In summer they were to come on a visit to the Hall.

"Talking o' Tom Clanwaring, that there girl's back again at the Trailing Indian," cried free-tongued Susan, with her usual lack of regard to what was expedient to be spoken of, and what was not.

May lifted her head in a kind of quick surprise; and dropped it again.

"I come out o' church to-day with Matty Pound," continued Susan. "While picking our way through the snow in the churchyard, she began a telling me that Emma Geach was back—maybe, the sight o' Mr. Geoffry Clanwaring's gravestone put Matty in mind on't. Sam Pound called in at their cottage yesterday, and told 'em the girl got home o' Friday evening by the waggon. Sam's in a fine way over it, his mother says, afraid he won't be wanted at the inn no longer, now she's come. And a nice stock of impudence she must have, to take Black by storm in that way, without saying with your leave or by your leave, now she's got tired of Ireland!" added Susan on her own score. "Or perhaps it is, that Ireland have got tired of her."

"That's enough," coldly interposed Miss May, rising from her seat with a haughty gesture, on her way to quit the room. "These things are nothing to me."

Neither had Susan Cole supposed they were, or could be, anything to her now. But in Susan's insatiable love of retailing gossip, she had not been able to keep her tongue still.

"Won't you dress now, Miss May?"

"I shall not dress to-day more than I am dressed."

"Well, and I don't see that there's need on't," acquiesced Susan. "That's a lovely pretty frock, that silk is."

The frock—as a young lady's dress was invariably styled then—was of that dark bright blue colour called Waterloo blue, after the somewhat recent battle of Waterloo. It was made in the fashion of the day—low neck and short sleeves, each edged with a quilling of white net, a bit of drooping lace falling beneath. Only a young girl did May look in it: not much more than a child. Susan watched her down the stairs; the graceful head thrown back further than usual.

"It's a sore point still, I can see, about that Emma Geach," muttered Susan. "Why couldn't Tom Clanwaring have kept the wench there till the wedding was over and Miss May gone? He——"

The words were stopped by the return of May. "Susan, mind you give your mother that little present I left out for her: and take her some of our mince-pies," she said. "And tell her—tell her that I will be sure to come and see her the first thing when I am back here again in summer."

In her red cloth cloak and black poke bonnet, with her petticoats gathered up nearly to the tops of the beaver gaiters, thick shoes on, and no pattens, for pattens were only an incumbrance in the snow, their rings getting clogged continually, away started Susan at the dusk hour to partake of the "dish of tea" at her brother's forge. It was open road all the way, and less difficult to traverse than she had expected. The forge was waiting for Susan: though rather doubtful as to her coming. Mrs. Cole, the mother, a mild, loving woman always, doubly so now she was getting in years, sat in her arm-chair in the full warmth of the parlour fire, with her two sons: Harry, the prop and stay of the home and business; and Ham, who shoed the horses, beat the iron, and did the other rough work. They were good sons: and it was thought that Harry, so good-looking and popular, had kept single for his mother's sake. On the table stood a substantial tea: plum cake, cold savoury sausages, and plates of buttered toast that the young servant brought in. One guest had already arrived, uninvited: and that was Miss Emma Geach. In the old days Emma Geach had made herself tolerably at home at the forge: and after ill report had touched her name, gentle Mrs. Cole, willing to "think no evil," had received her and been kind to her as before.

"That's Susan!—I thought she'd come," exclaimed Ham, as a thumping was heard at the door, together with a stamping of feet. "She's knocking the snow off her shoes."

Ham (a contraction of his name, Abraham) ran to admit her, and took the opportunity of holding a whispered colloquy on the mat, the parlour door being shut.

"I say, Susan, Emma Geach is in there!"

"None of your stories, Ham!" cried Susan, sharply.

"She walked in just now, a saying she was come to have tea with us, if mother 'ud let her, for it was awful dull work up at the Trailing Indian," continued Ham. "She's just the same, Susan."

"What did mother say?" was Susan's indignant question.

"Say? Why nothing: except that she was welcome. You know what mother is."

"And Harry?"

"Harry's the same as mother for being civil to people," returned Ham.

"I've a good mind not to go in," said Susan. "Perhaps I might get telling her a bit o' my mind."

"I'd not do that, Susan—it's Christmas Day. Besides, her affairs isn't any business of yours. She has not harmed you."

"I'm not so sure o' that," disputed Susan sharply. "'Twas not by straightforward means she got Tom Clanwaring into her clutches, I know—and I nursed him all through his baby years. Is she going to stop to tea with us?"

"Well," said Ham, simply, "we can't turn her out. Neither mother nor Harry 'ud like to do it, Susan."

Susan, arming herself for any possible battle, went in with her head up. Miss Geach looked completely at home. Her out-door things were off; her abundant hair, well cared for, shone in the glow of the fire, and she was talking and laughing with Harry Cole in the old light and free manner. Susan, after greeting her mother, took off her things, and sat down to make tea. It might be, that her propensity for gossip and to have her curiosity somewhat appeased as to the past, induced her to postpone hostilities, for she nodded to Miss Emma without much show of disdain.

"And when did you get back?" demanded Susan, when she handed the young person her tea.

"Friday night," said Emma promptly.

"Oh! Had a stormy passage on't? I've heered it's mortal bad at sea at this season o' the year."

Whether Emma Geach did not understand the allusion, or whether she would not take it, remained a question. After staring at the speaker for a minute or two in silence, she tasted her tea and asked for another lump of sugar.

"And Ireland? What sort of a place might it be to live in?" began Susan again satirically.

Another stare from Emma Geach. She had got a saucerful of tea up to her mouth then, and gazed over the brim at Susan all the while she drank it.

"How should I know what sort of a place Ireland is?" she retorted, when putting the saucer down. Susan Cole looked upon it as an evasion, and was in two minds whether, or not, to tell her so. But at that moment her brother Harry kicked her under the table; and she knew it was as much as to say, She's our guest for the time and must be treated as such.

So the conversation turned on other matters. Sir Dene's seizure; and the non-gathering at the Dene for the Christmas dinner in consequence, which Susan told of. Next the prolonged absence of Mr. Arde came up, and the old lady expressed a devout hope that he would be home for the wedding on Tuesday.

"What wedding? Who's a going to be married?" enquired Miss Geach when she heard this.

"Why, my young lady, Miss May's a going to be married," said Susan, proud of relating so much. "Have you lived in a wood, Emma Geach, not to ha' heerd on't?"

"That there Trailing Indian's worse nor a wood now, as far as hearing news goes," was Emma Geach's rather wrathful answer. "'Tain't lively at the best o' times; but nobody cares to come up to it through the snow. Since I got into the place I've not seen a soul but Black and Sam Pound. Black, he's sullen and won't talk: and t'other knows he must keep his tongue still afore me, unless I choose to let him wag it. No fear as I should ha' got to hear of a wedding being agate from them two."

"We've got a grand dinner o' Monday night," spoke Susan, by way of continuing her revelations. "The Hall be a'most turned inside out. I can't think what'll be done if the Squire don't get here."

"Report says that no coaches are getting into Worcester," said Harry Cole. "It's to be hoped the roads 'll clear for the wedding."

"So 'tis," said Susan. "They be a going to Paris and France, they be, when the wedding's over. Miss May's full on't."

"My!" exclaimed Emma Geach. "It's young Squire Scrope, I suppose."

"Miss Charlotte Scrope's to be bridesmaid," went on Susan, her tongue too busy to heed the question. "She and Miss May's to be dressed all in white; only Miss May's to have a veil and orange flowers in her bonnet, and t'other not."

"I thought May Arde would have him some time if he stuck up to her well," remarked Emma Geach. "Though Tom Scrope isn't the man for every girl's money. Scrope Manor's a nice place: 'tain't a bad match for her."

"Who was a talking anything about Tom Scrope, pray?" loftily demanded Susan. "Tisn't *him*."

"No! Why who is it then?"

"Captain Clanwaring. That Trailing Indian *must* be a wood, for news, it must."

The revelation seemed to have some effect on Emma Geach. A piece of plum cake, being conveyed to her mouth, was summarily arrested half way: her face became of a burning red, and then changed to a deadly whiteness.

"Captain Clanwaring! It's not him that's going to marry Miss Arde!"

"Well, I'm sure! perhaps you know better than me," cried Susan. "It's Captain Jarvis Clanwaring, and nobody else, Emma Geach."

Emma Geach appeared to be making an effort to recover her surprise—or, at least, to hide it. She was eating away at the cake with a great show of appetite, and looking at it closely as if trying to count the plums.

"Once get away from a place for a few months, and all sorts o' changes takes place to surprise one," she said with an air of indifference. "Since when has *he* been a making up to her?"

"Since when?" repeated Susan. "Well, it's a'most a twelvemonth since he asked her first. She'd have nothing to say to him then: no, nor for a long while after. He's got her now, though; leastways will have her Tuesday next: but I don't believe any man ever strove so hard for a girl yet, as the Captain have strove for her."

"And a whole twelvemonth he have been trying for her?" casually remarked Miss Emma.

"Ay," assented Susan. "And he had begun it in secret afore that: only he didn't dare to say nothing. I say, mother, have ye heerd that Mr. Otto's to be his groomsman, through the heir not being able to come for't?"

"Mr. Otto, is he?" returned the old mother. "I wish 'twas better weather, Susan: I'd ha' liked to walk to the church to see 'em married."

"Won't it be full!" was Susan's answering comment.

Thus, one topic succeeding another, the sociable evening passed away. About eight o'clock Susan took her departure: absolutely forbidding either of the brothers to escort her. She'd not have 'em go wading through the snow that night, she said: and as her will had been law with them always, they obeyed her. Harry Cole was ten or twelve years younger than she, and Ham twenty.

So Susan set off alone. She had got a few yards down the

road when she heard footsteps after her, floundering quickly through the snow. Believing that one of the two must be coming in spite of her injunction, she turned round, a sharp reprimand on her lips. But it proved to be Emma Geach.

"I just want to ask you something, Susan Cole," she said, her voice sunk to a whisper, "I had my reasons for not saying more afore 'em at the forge. What did you mean by asking did I have a stormy passage over the sea, and how did I like Ireland?"

"Why shouldn't I ask it?" returned Susan. "It's Ireland you've been a stopping at, as all the world knows."

"I've not been a-nigh Ireland," said the girl earnestly.

"Not a-nigh Ireland?" echoed Susan, struck with truthful accents. "Everybody said you went there."

"Went for what?"

"Well—'twas said that you went with Mr. Tom Clanwaring from Bristol. Or else followed on over the sea after him."

Even in the starlight, Susan Cole could see the puzzled wonder that slowly spread itself on the girl's countenance. It seemed that just at first she did not understand the implication.

"Why what fools they must be!" she indignantly cried when the meaning dawned upon her. "They *couldn't* think it, Susan Cole."

"Everybody thought it; the whole parish, from one end on't to t'other, thought it," was Susan's answer. "And said it, too."

"Not everybody; 'twarn't possible. Not Black—nor Captain Clanwaring."

"Both o' *them* did," said Susan, emphatically. "'Twas Black, I b'lieve, first spread it, and the Captain retailed it after him. I've heered 'em both say it."

"They both knowed better."

A few minutes longer they talked together, regardless of the cold night and the depth of snow they stood in. Susan Cole went on her way at last with uplifted hands. She had heard something that nearly stunned her.

"May heaven have mercy on my poor young lady!" she groaned aloud to the frosty air. "What a sinner the man is! —what a good-for-nothing hypocrite! Letting the good name of another be blackened for his! Drat the ruts then!"

Paying no attention just then to where she put her feet,

Susan had sunk into a drift of snow up to her knees. Getting out of it as she best could, she shook her legs and petticoats, and went on again. A great question lay on her mind: ought she to impart what she had just heard to her mistress? —or keep silence on the point now that the wedding was so near?

Perhaps what really turned the scale was Susan's love of gossip. With a story like this burning her tongue, it was next to an impossible task for her to keep silence. After Mrs. Arde went to her chamber for the night, she found it invaded by Susan.

The woman whispered her tale, the substance of what Emma Geach had said, standing with her mistress on the hearth-rug. As the red light played upon Mrs. Arde's face, Susan saw it take a pale hue, a haughty expression. That she was overwhelmed with dismayed indignation at the first moment, was all too evident. The next, she had burst out laughing.

"The girl has been playing a trick upon you, Susan. How could you be so easily taken in? Captain Clanwaring indeed? Now, does it stand to reason?"

And, so prone to yield to persuasion is the human mind, that Susan Cole veered round to her mistress's impression. It called up her temper.

"The vile huzzy!—to try her tricks upon me! Let me come across her: that's all."

CHAPTER XXXIX.

THE WEDDING DAY.

SNOW, snow, nothing but snow. It lay on the ground as persistently as though it meant to stay with the world for ever. The tops of the houses at Worcester on one hand; the distant Malvern Hills on the other; the trees and hedges, the fields and dales intervening between each, and the whole vast surrounding landscape, presented a surface whiter than the whitest alabaster.

In the drawing-room at Mrs. Arde's was a motley company. Motley in regard to appearance. For, while some of them wore the gala attire suitable for a marriage, others presented quite an ordinary aspect. Take Captain Clanwaring, for instance: he was in the choicest of bridegroom's costume;

May, on the contrary, had on a homely dress of ruby stuff.
The Lady Lydia Clanwaring was resplendent in shining silk
and lace; Mrs. Arde and her sister were in morning gowns.
Otto Clanwaring was attired to match his brother; Charlotte
Scrope, the bridesmaid, a very pretty young girl, was plain
as the bride.

For this was Tuesday, the wedding morning; and the great
question agitating those assembled, together with two or three
other guests not necessary to mention, was—should the marriage take place, or not.

When the previous day, Monday, did not bring Mr. Arde,
and it was likewise known that none of the London mails or
other coaches, due some days now, had reached Worcester, the
Hall fell into real consternation. Captain Clanwaring protested
most strongly against the ceremony being delayed, even
though Tuesday morning should not bring the Squire; but
Mrs. Arde answered to this, sensibly enough, that without her
husband there could be no marriage, as he was bringing the
licence with him. May said little on the Monday, for or
against; nothing indeed; for she assumed to a certainty that
she could not be married under these drawbacks.

The dinner had been held at the Hall the previous night,
and was somewhat of a failure in its master's absence. Some
of the invited guests, too, could not get there for the snow.
Mrs. Arde presided; and her sister, who was staying with
them, helped her to make the best of it. And so Tuesday
came in, and had not brought the Squire. Mrs. Arde then
despatched hasty messengers to as many friends bidden to the
marriage as were within reach, to say it would not take place
that day. Sir Dene was progressing favourably; but Mr.
Priar, together with the physician called in from Worcester, enjoined the strictest quiet.

Captain Jarvis Clanwaring was on the wing early, on his
part. While it was yet dark, he quitted Beechhurst Dene,
rode into Worcester, and procured a licence. By ten o'clock
he was at home again, somewhat sooner than he had hoped,
and brought word that the weather was breaking-up.

"I cannot risk the chances of its being delayed even for a
day," he observed in some agitation to his mother, as he
went to attire himself for the ceremony. And my Lady Lydia
answered, "Of course not:" though perhaps he had no idea
of the imminent peril he was in. So Captain Clanwaring was
driven to the Hall in full fig, the licence in his hand; and my

lady, with the rest of the company at Beechhurst Dene, speedily followed. His dismay was excessive when he found his bride not dressed, and Mrs. Arde quietly saying there could be no wedding that day.

"It is cruel, cruel!" spoke the Captain to Mrs. Arde—and his agitation, that he could not quite disguise, spoke volumes in that lady's mind for the depth of his love. "There is no impediment now: here's the licence: and perhaps by the time we are at the church Mr. Arde will be here, for the roads are undoubtedly becoming traversable. Don't, *don't* put off the wedding: it always brings ill-luck. Let May dress!"

Mrs. Arde glanced at her daughter, as much as to ask what her decision should be—at least, the sanguine Captain so interpreted it.

May, calm as the snow outside, and perhaps as cold, shook her head. "No, no," was all she said.

"But May, my dear May, surely——"

"No, not without papa," interrupted May, cutting short the bridegroom's remonstrance—and this time her voice took a tone of fear. "I will not be married in this uncertainty. My father may not be safe."

In Captain Clanwaring's angry vexation, he gave vent to a word, spoken contemptuously. "Safe!" Recollecting himself on the instant, he softly implored her not to persist in her decision; not to invoke ill-luck upon their union. May remained quietly firm: and, to the Captain's angry fancy, it almost seemed that she was glad of the respite.

At that moment the church bells burst out, a merry peal. Mrs. Arde, though she had sent to the clergyman, had forgotten to send to the clerk. That functionary had gone to the church with the bell-ringers, expecting the wedding party every minute: and this was the result. Captain Clanwaring, unmindful of the cold, threw up the window at which they were standing.

"Listen, May! Surely you will not let them ring for nothing!"

"Indeed, and I think the wedding ought to be to-day, my dear," spoke up old Miss Clewer, from the depth of her large white quilted satin bonnet, and grey dress of twilled silk. "As my grand-nephew observes, a put-off wedding sometimes brings ill-luck: it has resulted, within my own knowledge, in there being none at all."

D D

An awful suggestion for the bridegroom, flushing his pale face to a hot crimson. Lady Lydia came to the rescue: not attacking the decision of May, but of Mrs. Arde. But that lady proved to be as firm as her daughter. She had never had any intention of being otherwise.

"My dear Lady Lydia, you ask an impossibility. I hinted to Captain Clanwaring yesterday, that the deeds of settlement were not signed: cannot be, until the arrival of Mr. Arde; and now you oblige me to speak out. Were it my daughter's own wish that the ceremony should be solemnised, I could not accede to it. She cannot marry until the completion of the settlements."

Mrs. Arde spoke very decisively. She had of course right on her side, and her child's interests to see to. Failing any settlement, all that May possessed would become the property of the gallant Captain. Even he and his mother could not decently urge that. No more was to be said. It would only be putting off the wedding for a day, as everybody agreed: say until the morrow: now that the weather was breaking, a few hours would no doubt bring the Squire. Captain Clanwaring, terribly glumpy, had to submit: but he did it with a bad grace, not caring to conceal his mortification. As to the barrister, Otto, he had not spoken a word, for it or against it.

And so the bells, clanging out in their innocence, clanged out still, unconscious that there was no wedding to ring for. It had the effect of calling innumerable gazers to the church from far and near. A report had gone about the previous night that perhaps the ceremony might be postponed if the Squire did not arrive: but when the bells were heard, it was assumed to be taking place.

"Do send to stop the bells, mamma!" pleaded May.

With her whole heart, Mrs. Arde wished her visitors would depart. It was an uncomfortable morning for her. No one seemed at ease; she least of any. Soon after twelve o'clock struck, when some of them were preparing to go, a party of morris-dancers came on to the green lawn. Of course all stayed then, and crowded the windows to look.

"Harriet," whispered Mrs. Arde to her sister, "I cannot stand this longer; my nerves have been on the strain all the morning, and are giving way. Do you play hostess for a bit."

She slipped out of the room, put on a warm shawl and

hood, and made her way to the foot avenue, that ran beside the lawn and the approach to it. The snow had been swept, and she paced it thoughtfully, lifting her face to the cold fresh air, and looking through the bare side branches at the morris-dancers. Fleet of foot and not ungraceful were those men; their white attire was decorated with all kinds of coloured ribbons, that kept time and waved about to their steps and their staves. The figures were prolonged; and the men did their best; at Arde Hall the morris-dancers were sure of a meal and a largesse, whenever it was a hard winter and they were shut out from their legitimate labour.

Though a tolerably common sight in those long-past winters, it was not a very frequent one, and idle spectators from the road were running in to gaze, quite a small crowd of them. The disappointed ones, who had been to the church and found no wedding, happened to be passing back again, and flocked in at the large gates. Mrs. Arde, pacing the solitary avenue, chanced to turn her attention from the dancers to these spectators, and saw amidst them Miss Emma Geach.

And yet, not exactly amidst them. They were thronging the gate and the railings before the lawn: this girl had drawn herself up close to the fence that skirted the side of the avenue, as if she did not care to be noticed. She stood there, leaning one arm against it, her old cloak muffled about her, and looking at the dancers with a listless air.

Obeying the moment's impulse, Mrs. Arde stepped through the beech trees and approached her. Putting aside the girl's naturally bold manners, Mrs. Arde always rather liked Emma Geach, and had pitied her isolated condition—isolated from all good associations—at the Trailing Indian. This alone might have caused her to accost the girl; but she had another motive. At the time that communication was made to her by Susan Cole on Sunday night, Mrs. Arde had fully disbelieved it, regarding it as a foolish scandal on Captain Clanwaring: but since then, a *doubt*, a very ugly doubt, had insinuated itself ever and anon within her mind: and instinct now prompted her to set it at rest.

"Is it you, Emma? I heard you were back."

"Yes, it's me," replied Emma, turning her head at the salutation. "I've been to the church to see the wedding ma'am; but it's said there is to be none."

"Not to-day. The Squire is absent."

"Can't get home for the choked-up roads," freely remarked Miss Emma. "I had a fine slow journey of it in the waggon."

"Where did you come from?"

"Well, I came from Lunnon. No need to hide it, that I know of."

"Not from Ireland?"

The girl's eyes flashed with quite an angry light. "Yes, I hear that *that* have been brought again me, but it's false as——"

"It has been said that when you left here you went to Bristol to join Mr. Tom Clanwaring," interrupted Mrs. Arde.

"When I left here I went straight to Lunnon town, as I was bid to go by him that led me wrong; and I've never been away from Lunnon till I took the waggon to come down here again."

Mrs. Arde gazed in the girl's face, reading it eagerly. There was a savage look in it, a passionate ring in her voice, that spoke too surely of the naked truth.

"It was Tom Clanwaring's name that was coupled with yours, you know, Emma, even before you left the place."

"Mrs. Arde, I never did know it. If I had, I bain't sure but I should ha' set it to rights then. 'Twas a shame on him for folks to say it. Mr. Tom!—why, he had always been as good as a brother to me from the time I was that high,"—slapping a lath that ran along the fence. "Leastways, as much o' one as a gentleman can be to a poor girl. Mr. Tom Clanwaring is just as good and noble and straightforward, as t'other is a cheating and lying sneak. Black and him must ha' put their heads together, and laid it on Mr. Tom."

"The other being Jarvis Clanwaring?" spoke Mrs. Arde.

"Him, and none other: Jarvis Clanwaring. When he got his turn served he just threw me over, Mrs. Arde. He did, the raskil; and I don't mind who knows it now. It's six months a'most since he've been to see me or sent me aught to get me a crust o' bread. I've been nigh upon starving. I might ha' starved outright but for a good woman whose room I lodged in: she helped me what she could."

"You are telling me the truth?" asked Mrs. Arde.

"It's the truth—as God hears me. I'd a mind to ha' told it out to Captain Clanwaring's face i' the church this morning when he was a being married: and I think I should ha' done't. 'Twas only the thought of one thing might ha' stopped me—and that's the trouble and pain 'twould ha' gave Miss May. When I heard 'twas him she was a going to marry I pitied her a'most to crying; a good-for-nothing knave like him can't bring her much good."

"You should have told of this before to-day, for Miss May's sake," said Mrs. Arde sharply.

"I knew nought about the wedding till the night afore last," spoke the girl; "I never knew as he was living down at Beechhurst Dene. He let me think he was about in places, a serving with his regiment: but it seems he have sold out on't."

"Where is the baby?" whispered Mrs. Arde.

"It died when it was born, ma'am. And a lucky thing too. Jarvis Clanwaring, grand as the world thinks him, is just a bad man, Mrs. Arde, made up o' deceit and heartlessness. Bring me to him, and I'll say it to his face. He have been up to his ears in debt, too, this long while. Perhaps you didn't know o' that, either."

Mrs. Arde made no answer. The morris-dancers had brought their performance to an end; and the spectators were coming away. Perhaps Mrs. Arde did not care to be seen talking to Emma Geach: for she wished her good morning, and turned towards home. What she had heard three parts stunned her. May came into her chamber almost as she was entering it.

"Mamma," she cried, her face pale, her voice beseeching, "you will not let this wedding take place before papa returns? Promise me! Captain Clanwaring is saying——"

"Be at rest, May," interrupted Mrs. Arde, bending to kiss her. "You shall certainly not marry before your father is here."

And the very emphatic tone, telling of strange anger, a little surprised Miss May.

Careering into the faithful city of Worcester, the coachman driving his four fine horses at a somewhat faster speed than their usual majestic pace, the guard's horn blowing blasts of importance, went the Royal Mail. Along Sidbury, up College Street and High Street, through the Cross, and on to the Foregate Street; where it finally drew up before the two principal inns of the town, the Hoppole and the Star and Garter. People had run out at their shop doors to see it pass; a small crowd collected round it almost before it stopped: for it was the first mail that had reached Worcester since the detention. The supposition prevailing was, that it was the mail known to have been so long on the road, the one that started from London the past Friday. The curious people, running up, were eager to learn what it had been doing with itself, and where the detention had been. Quite a chorus of questions assailed the guard and coachman as they descended from their seats: and then it was discovered that this was not the lost mail at all, but the regular mail that had made the journey in due course and without much delay; having quitted the Bull and Mouth the previous afternoon. In the check their curiosity sustained, they began to walk off again one by one. This was Wednesday morning.

The mail brought but one passenger: a sharp-looking active man, who leaped out of the inside, and had no luggage with him. He was a little stared at. It was concluded that his business must be of importance, to travel in that ungenial weather and risk being buried in the snow on the road.

"Didn't ye see nor hear nothing o' that there lost mail, that have been so long a coming?" questioned a bystander of the guard.

"No; nothing. It passed Woodstock, and it didn't get to Chipping Norton; so must be somewhere between the two places," was the guard's answer. "But whether it's above ground or dead and buried below the snow, and its folks dead and buried with it, is more than I can say."

"Had you much difficulty in getting along, guard?" questioned a gentleman.

"No, sir. The worst was between Woodstock and Evesham. In places there we a'most stuck fast; but——"

"Can I charter a horse and gig from this hotel, guard? I want one immediately."

The interruption, spoken in a sharp, gruff, imperative tone, came from the passenger. Finding that he could charter a horse and gig, he ordered it to be got ready without any delay, and ran into the Star to drink half a glass of hot brandy-and-water.

"Wouldn't you like some breakfast, sir?—or luncheon?" asked the barmaid.

"I have not time for either."

The gig came to the door, together with a man whom the traveller had requested should accompany him: a tall, strong young fellow belonging to the Star and Garter stables. The landlord came out to see them start.

"Have you far to go?" he asked.

"About three or four miles, I fancy," was the reply. "I am a stranger in these parts."

Away they started; he taking the reins himself, and whipping the horse into a canter; turning down Broad Street, onwards over the Severn bridge, and so out of the town that way. In due course of time he came to the neighbourhood of Beechhurst Dene, and there arrested Mr. Jarvis Clanwaring. It was accomplished without the slightest trouble.

On the Tuesday evening a note had been delivered to Captain Clanwaring at Beechhurst Dene from Mrs. Arde. It stated in unmistakably decisive terms that until the return of Mr. Arde there would be no marriage; all things must remain in abeyance. The Captain could do nothing—save relieve his feelings by a fit of hot swearing in his chamber. On the following morning there was still no Mr. Arde; but in the course of it Captain Clanwaring walked over to the Hall. He did not get to see the ladies—which he considered very strange. Susan Cole brought him a message that Miss May was very poorly with a headache (" and not to be wondered at!" put in Susan in a parenthesis), and her mistress was busy writing letters. So Captain Clanwaring, rather discomfited, took his way back home again. He was crossing the upper road in a sauntering kind of manner, his eyes moodily bent on the ground to pick his way over the snow, which was still lying there, when a passing gig came to a sudden standstill, its driver leaped down, and Jarvis Clanwaring, gentleman and ex-captain, found himself in custody.

"Curse you, Rilling!" was all he said, gnashing his teeth with impotent rage. For he knew the capturer very well.

"'Twould have been done an hour or two earlier, Captain, but for the snow keeping the mail back," was the man's equable answer. "A fine tether you've had of it altogether."

The arrest was for a very large sum of money, and it was of no use to fight against it. Persuasion and resistance would alike be futile, as the unfortunate Captain knew. Fate is stronger than we are. The public arrest had been witnessed by at least two people, one of whom chanced to be Mark, the servant at the Hall, the other, Sam Pound; and the news went about with a whirr.

The captor and the captured, the gig and the supernumerary, proceeded to Beechhurst Dene. Jarvis was in an awful fever to get free: we should have been so in his place. There was only one way by which it could be acomplished—the paying of the money; or else by bail that was as good as money. It was possible, though not very probable, that Sir Dene might have settled the matter could he have been appealed to; but the state in which Sir Dene was lying, partially if not quite insensible, put any appeal to him out of the question. The heir, Dene, was not there; nobody was there but the barrister.

"You will give bail for me, Otto?" said the crest-fallen Captain, who felt as if he would very much like to shoot somebody—perhaps himself.

"Couldn't take Mr. Otto Clanwaring's bail," interposed Mr. Rilling, gruffly; for nature had endowed him with an uncommonly gruff voice. "Couldn't accept anybody's undertaking, except the baronet's, Sir Dene."

"But Sir Dene is ill, you hear; paralysed," remonstrated the unhappy Captain.

"Yes, Captain. More's the pity for you."

"If my brother gives you his undertaking it will be as sure as Sir Dene's, Rilling," urged the Captain. "He———"

"I could not give it, Jarvis," interposed the cautious barrister. "You must know that I am not in a position to take a debt upon me that might prove an incubus for my lifetime. And where should I get the money from, do you suppose, if called upon later to pay it?"

"It will stop my marriage," breathed Jarvis, biting his feverish lips. "I have been looking to that to save me from this gulf. Those cursed roads! But for Arde's delay, I should have been married and safely away. Otto! stretch a point for me."

"The counsellor's promise would be of no more worth than yours, Captain—begging pardon of him for saying it," reiterated the sheriff's officer. "Besides, there's more behind this," was the candid avowal.

As Otto Clanwaring had felt fully sure of. If this one debt on which Jarvis was arrested were settled, a host of others, on which judgment had been obtained, lay behind it. In fact, it was pretty plain that Captain Clanwaring's career was for the time over.

"And my marriage?" he groaned. "What's to become of that?"

"You could not think of marrying Miss Arde now, though you were free," urged Otto, in his strictness. "At least, without informing them of the facts. It would be a most dishonourable thing, so to deceive the Arde family."

"Hold your cant," retorted the exasperated prisoner.

There was no loophole of escape for him; none, in later weeks, when Sir Dene was cognisant of the affair and able to converse upon it, he said that Jarvey's sins had come home to him. Mr. Rilling and the extra man and the Captain all took their departure together in the gig; the latter wedged securely in between the two others.

When the Lady Lydia Clanwaring got home towards dinner-time—for she, with Miss Ann Clewer and Mrs. Letsom, finding there would be no wedding that day, had driven over to spend it in Worcester—she found what had taken place. Her beloved son, of whom she had made a very idol, and would have willingly offered up all the rest of the world in sacrifice at his shrine, had been ignominiously conveyed away a prisoner; and was even then on his road by night coach to be lodged in one of the gaols of the metropolis! My lady rose the house with her frantic cries.

Somebody else got home the same evening—and that was Squire Arde. For the long-detained mail had contrived to free itself that day, and reached Worcester at last; causing a hubbub and congratulation that some of the old citizens may yet remember. The first thing the Squire heard when inside his own doors, was—the news of Captain Clanwaring's arrest, and of his heavy embarrassments. Many-tongued rumour had been exceedingly busy with the unfortunate Captain's fame all the afternoon; and facts, hitherto unsuspected, had come out in a remarkable manner.

Captain Clanwaring arrested!—and taken off a prisoner to the Fleet!—and over head and shoulders in debt and embarrassment! Captain Clanwaring, who but for those heavy snow drifts would now be Mary's husband! Squire Arde turned hot and cold as he listened.

What an escape it was for Mary! How Jarvis Clanwaring had managed to stave off the evil day so long and to conceal the true state of things, was a mystery. The selling of the commission had been forced. It was a stop-gap for the time; since then, Lady Lydia and others had helped him, including those harpies, the London money-lenders. The indignant Squire found that his daughter's money was indeed required; that there was urgent need of the marriage being hastened on.

"What an escape!" aspirated the Squire in solemn thankfulness. "And I—Heaven forgive me!—murmured rebelliously at the delay caused by the snow-storm, little thinking that it was the saving of my child! Perhaps God sent that detention expressly in His love for her!"

Within the privacy of their own chamber that night, sitting over the fire, Mrs. Arde whispered another item of news in her husband's ear—that which was connected with Miss Emma Geach. For some little time the Squire would not take it in; but when convinced of its truth, he began stamping about the room in wrath so great and loud, that poor Mrs. Arde was fain to beg him to be still, lest the household should think he was beating her.

"Let 'em think it!" roared the Squire. "The desperate villain?—And he would have made a wife of my innocent child!"

Hardly giving time for morning dawn well to set in, the Squire stamped up to the Trailing Indian, to "have it out" with Black. He told that worthy inn-keeper that he was a base villain, and not a shade better than the other villain; that they had sacrificed the good name of Tom Clanwaring, and nearly sacrificed the life's happiness of Miss Arde.

And she, Mary Arde: how did she take the disappointment relative to her marriage?—To most young ladies the breaking off of a marriage is, to say the least of it, mortifying. Not so to Mary Arde. She was as one released from a weight of despair. She warbled about the house like a freed bird. Susan Cole, who could not have kept her tongue silent had she been paid to do it, disclosed to her lots of things. The lightness came back to Mary's steps, the colour to her cheeks: it was as if some special happiness had fallen on her heart from heaven.

"She could not have liked him!" cried the wondering Squire to his wife.

"She did not," said Mrs. Arde. "I fear she liked Tom Clanwaring too well for that."

The Squire frowned a hideous frown at the unwelcome name. Though Tom had been shamefully aspersed, and been proved innocent where he had been thought guilty, he was not the less ineligible to be "liked" by May. "And never will be," spoke the Squire hotly.

And that poor neglected scapegoat was never so much as thought of by the world, or by Beechhurst Dene. Tom Clanwaring was in the place deemed most appropriate for him: some remote district of Irish bog, working out his sins.

And so the weeks wore on.

CHAPTER XL.

THE LAST OF RANDY BLACK.

TURNING out of the gate of Harebell Farm, went Mary Barber. Rare, indeed, was the fact of her going abroad without any particular object; and yet she was doing so this late afternoon. It had been the monthly wash that week at the farm; but the weather had been favourable for drying, and the close of this day, Wednesday, saw all the things done up, and in their appropriate presses and drawers. Mary Barber, assisted by one of the women servants, had been ironing hard for many hours, and when the early tea was over, betook herself out for a walk, partly because she had no other pressing employment to get to, chiefly that she had an unusual feeling upon her of being stifled in-doors. So, putting on her every-day shawl and bonnet, away she went.

"Curious I should feel as if I wanted fresh air, me !" she said, half aloud. "I must be getting old; that's it: and I *be* getting old, for that matter. Well, I've had my health and strength better nor most people; and there's some good work in my arms yet. Suppose I'd had a weak heart, as my poor sister had !—and died of it as she did ! Them boys of hers be getting on like a house a fire: quite gentlefolk they be now, though me, their aunt, Molly Barber, can't be called much else but a upper servant."

Walking up Harebell Lane, she glanced at the budding hedges on either side, at the springing grass. It was only February yet, but the most lovely weather conceivable, warm enough for May. The prolonged and heavy snow storm of the previous winter seemed to have benefited the earth. They would have it cold again, no doubt; but just now the days were bright and beautiful. Mary Barber went along sniffing the air as if she could not enjoy it enough: shut up all day with the hot ironing stove, bending over the linen she ironed, the freshness was only too welcome. The setting sun threw his golden rays slantwise; birds were chirping their last song before settling down in their nests, all nature seemed glad. Primroses and violets nestled in the banks of the shady lane: hard Mary Barber actually stooped and gathered some.

She was feeling less hard than usual that evening. Life had been all prose for her, no poetry at all in it. Perhaps it was the unusual weariness that softened her: not exactly weariness of limb, but weariness of spirit. Her thoughts were running into a groove not at all customary.

"Says Richard Pickering to me t'other morning in Worcester, when I ran again him coming out o' the hop-market, 'You should not stay on at Harebell Farm, Aunt Mary'—a calling of me aunt for once, he did—'but have a nice little home of your own, and live comfortable in it.' 'Twas the old pride in part made him say it; neither him nor Willie have ever liked my being in service, specially him. 'We'd help you to the home,' he went on, 'I and William; we want you to have rest, Mary. And he's right, I say: for I am beginning to feel the need o' rest, and service is getting hard for me. But I don't care to be helped by them, and what I've saved isn't quite enough to keep me yet. Bother take it! What has set me on o' these thoughts this evening, I wonder? I think I'll get Priar to give me a dose o' physic to put me to rights. 'Twon't do for me to fail i' my work."

Approaching Harebell pond—which she did not do once in two years, as a rule; no, nor in four—the sad fate of her former master, Robert Owen: a fate which every one had long ago given up all hope of clearing: recurred to her. Every circumstance connected with it flashed into her mind as vividly as though it had passed but yesterday. The singular dream, when she and others, quite a crowd of them, seemed to be searching for him up this very lane and across the fields, all bearing for one point, the direction of the Trailing Indian; and the absolute later disappearance: and her visit to the inn in the morning, when Emma Geach was a wailing infant of a few hours old, and the mother lay in danger up stairs: and the commotion and uncertainty altogether, until the water gave up its secret: like the bits of glass in a kaleidoscope fixing themselves into their places one after another, so the past events rolled through her mind.

She passed the pond with a glance and a shudder, slightly quickening her steps. A few yards onward there arose a hazy kind of indecision in her purpose: whether she should go straight on through the gate, leading into some fields on Sir Dene's home farm that lay beyond; or continue her way up the lane—which here took the sharp turn to the right. Her feet, unprompted, as it seemed—for certainly she was not conscious of making any decision herself—chose the latter. In after life, Mary Barber was wont to say that an instinct from Heaven guided her.

"I'll go to the end, just as far as the turnpike road; and then turn back," she said to herself, finding which way her apparently purposeless feet had taken her.

This brought her, as the reader must know, to the Trailing Indian. Mary Barber turned her eyes upon that hostelrie in some curiosity: its past association rendering it always a place of interest. Since Miss Emma Geach's return to take up her abode in it, the inn had shown some slight signs of renewed life. That bustling damsel, ready of service, free of tongue, made a pleasanter hostess than Black and Sam Pound had made hosts; and stragglers were beginning to drop in again for half pints of ale or cider. As to Sam, his worst fears had been realized: he was dismissed.

The golden beams of the sun, partly below the horizon now, had turned to crimson, and the front casements caught the red glow. The side-door of the inn stood open, but there was no other sign of life or habitation about the dwelling. It looked very solitary, and everything around was still, including the evening air.

"She's out," thought Mary Barber, "else there'd be some clatter o' dishes going on; and her tongue with it. As to Black——"

The words were stopped by a startling sound. If ever Mary Barber heard a groan of agony, she heard one then. Whence did it come? She turned to look about her, and there arose another. No mistake now: they came from the house.

"Anything the matter?" she called out, making her way to the side door.

A succession of moans answered her: painful moans, telling of some awful calamity. Mary Barber was not timorous: she had seen too many ugly sights in her life for that, ghosts included; but it was certain that a tremor of fear seized on her then, and she would willingly have turned back, rather than entered.

"What be it?" she asked, halting outside the kitchen door.

Ah, what was it? Mary Barber groaned herself when she went in, and saw. Randy Black was stretched on the kitchen floor, bleeding from a wound in the side, his gun lying beside him.

He had got the gun about intending to clean it, unconscious that it was loaded. The charge went off and shot him. It appeared that he had lent the gun to one of his friends, James Thaxted. When the man returned it Black asked if it was charged, and Thaxted replied No. *He* had understood Black to say, Have you drawn the charge?—as was explained when too late.

Whatever ill had encompassed Black's life, Mary Barber could but feel the deepest compassion for him now. Something in his face would have told her that the injury was mortal without his confirming words, "It's my death! it's my death."

What could she do alone? Emma Geach had gone off to Worcester for the Wednesday's market, and to buy herself some gowns. While she was on her knees, doing what she could to staunch the blood, and nearly at her wits' end, young Cole entered; and Mary Barber said Providence had sent him.

"You be fleet o' foot, Ham. Put out the best speed ye've got, lad, and get Priar up here. And list ye," she added in a whisper, drawing the young man's ear down, "when Priar's come off, run round to the parson, and ask *him* to please to come. If ever mortal man wanted shriving when his soul was on the wing, it must be this 'un lying here."

Apparently Mr. Black was thinking somewhat of the same. Whence he gathered his deductions perhaps he could not have defined; but that death was close upon him he felt sure and certain. And strange though it may be to say it of this hardened and bad man, whose whole life had been marked by recklessness; who had laughed at death, and set it, and what must come after it, at defiance as a thing that could not concern him—he was now shrinking from it in a fright, the veriest coward. Such instances have been known: where this awful terror has assailed a soul at the close of an ill-spent life. It was not the life so suddenly cut short that the man was regretting; that appeared not to give him a thought; it was the dread judgment to which he was hastening.

Mary Barber turned him round, for he had been lying on the wound, and found a pillow to put under his head on the kitchen bricks, and gave him a sup of brandy which he asked for. The bleeding seemed to stop, and he was in less pain.

"When did it happen?" she asked.

"On'y just afore you come," groaned Black. "I'd got the gun muzzle upwards, and was a turning round to light a candle."

And then he gave vent to words and plaints and cries that surely would never have been wrung from him in health; ay, and *prayers*. Prayers that he would at all times have scoffed at. Prayers for mercy: prayers to be let perish for ever as a dog and be no more heard of after death. Mary Barber was horrified: she compassionated him with her whole heart; she knelt down, raising her hands together, and asked aloud for pardon for him, even at the eleventh hour. The man was beside himself with fear. He called for more brandy, and when she hesitated to give it him, he swore at her in some of the worst language he had ever used in his wild career. The next minute he was beseeching her and Heaven alike to forgive him. She administered a little brandy; not much, for she was afraid to do it without the sanction of Mr. Priar.

"Priar 'll be up soon, Black," she said. "You shall have more then if he'll let you."

The man's faculties appeared to be almost supernaturally clear; his intellect and memory bright as they had ever been in life; his reason as free: but a degree of physical exhaustion came on, and then he lay comparatively still. Mary Barber seized upon the interval to tell him about the Thief on the Cross, and Black hushed his voice while he listened.

"He had been bad, too, like you, Black, that man had; but the Saviour pardoned him. With the Lord it is only to repent, and ask, and have."

Black turned his head about on the pillow and moaned and sighed and muttered; but was still quiet. A thought came into the woman's mind, and she promptly acted on it.

"I'd like to ask ye one thing, Black, while there's time: 'twon't hurt you to answer it now, one way or t'other. The bag o' money stole from Sir Dene's parlour that New Year's Day—was it you took it?"

"Was it me took it?" retorted Black with a touch of his old fierceness. "What d'ye mean?"

"Some of 'em be a suspecting Tom Clanwaring on't still: as it strikes me," was her reply. "Only this very morning Squire Arde, who came up to the farm a wanting to see the master, stood by my ironing-board, a talking on't. I said 'twas curious Mr. Tom didn't come back now things again him had been cleared up: at that the Squire went quite in a passion, and said things again him were not cleared up, and the fellow was not wanted back. It could have been nothing but the money he was thinking of, Black: there's nought else lying again Mr. Tom now."

Black's eyes were cast up towards her; dark, and almost fierce as ever, were they. But he made no answer.

"Tom Clanwaring never harmed you, Randy. He showed himself friendly always, and did you many a good turn. If 'twas you took the money, you might confess to it now, for his sake."

"The man as took the bag o' money was Captain Clanwaring."

"What?" cried Mary Barber, interrupting the hoarse deep tones.

"The man as took the bag o' money was Jarvis Clanwaring," repeated Black. "I swear it with my dying breath."

Mary Barber peered into Black's face, believing his senses were deserting him. He saw the doubt.

"That there same Saturday night, soon after I got home here myself, up come Captain Clanwaring. He owed me money, and he had got frightened for fear I should let out things he didn't want let out—for in the morning I told him I'd do it if he didn't pay me. He gave me just half what he owed: and I wondered where he had got it from, for he was as hard up hisself as any poor devil——"

"Was it for bacca, he owed it?" she interrupted.

"No, 'twarn't for bacca," retorted Black, resenting either the question or the interruption. "'Twas put upon bacca, and that's enough. Just a few days after, Squire Arde was here, and began a fishing to know whether 'twas me took Sir Dene's bag o' money. 'Twas the first time I'd heered of any money being stole; and I knew at once who 'twas that had took it, and where Captain Clanwaring had got his money from. I see the bag in his hands and the notes and gold in it."

"That there Captain Clanwaring must have as many sins to answer for as you, Black," spoke Mary Barber, drawing a deep breath. "Perhaps more i' the sight of Heaven. Why didn't you tell o' this, and clear Tom Clanwaring?"

Black shook his head. "I couldn't tell o' the Captain *then*, though I'd used to threaten it. His interests was mine till I'd got my money from him in full. And he might ha' turned on me, he might, for he knowed a thing or two."

It appeared to have been a case of rogue cutting rogue. That Captain Clanwaring and Black were mutually afraid of each other, and had acted in accordance with it, there could be no question.

A perfect yell from Black startled Mary Barber out of her momentary reflection. His side had burst out bleeding again, bringing back all his terror. Perhaps in the past few minutes, feeling easier in himself, and believing the bleeding had stopped, he had been indulging some faint idea of recovery.

"I'd lead a different life, I would!" he aspirated, as if making a promise to the empty air.

The most welcome sound that ever greeted Mary Barber's ear, was that of gig-wheels. Mr. Priar and his apprentice had come speeding up. They were followed by Harry Cole and others. After apprising the surgeon of what had happened, Ham had gone on his way to impart the news generally. Mr. Priar speedily cleared the kitchen of the interlopers pressing into it. Mary Barber and Harry Cole alone being suffered to remain; and the clergyman when he came.

Alas! nothing could be done to save the life that was so swiftly passing. All the skill of the medical man was not able to prolong it by one hour beyond its allotted time. Black was not moved from his position. On the kitchen floor he had fallen, and on the kitchen floor he remained to die. Some blankets were gently slided under him to make it less hard; but he might not be disturbed further.

In the presence of the clergyman and doctor, of Mary Barber and of Harry Cole, he made a confession: some dim hope that it might serve him when he should stand before the Great Judge in that dread hereafter, urging him to do it. Petty sins were avowed, such as smuggling, and poaching, and receiving stolen goods; a whole catalogue of such doings, that appeared to have been always running on. These lighter offences Black did not himself seem to think much of; but there were others. Grave crimes; beside which the lighter sunk to little. As the eye estimates things as being large or small according to comparison, so does the conscience. Randy Black had the lives of three men on his soul: the pedlar, once or twice spoken of here; a gamekeeper; and Robert Owen.

The only one of them wilfully and deliberately murdered, was the pedlar. Stupefied by drink, perhaps purposely given him, he had been killed in the dead of night by Black's own hand, and afterwards buried by him and the ostler, Joe; his box of wares, some of them real gold and silver, being the inducing motive. The gamekeeper was shot by Black in a night fray, but not of deliberate intention; guns were going off on both sides. The third, Robert Owen had been wilfully assaulted, but not wilfully murdered.

That Black was telling the truth without disguise, in this, his dying hour, was all too evident; nay, he sought rather to make himself out worse than better. Once this awful hour comes upon hitherto careless sinners, there can be no playing at bo-peep with the conscience.

On that long-past Easter Sunday night, as may be remembered, Mr. Owen, after quitting his daughter Maria and Geoffry Clanwaring, had been traced to the two-acre meadow; the young man, Parkes, having watched him cross it on his way to the cow-shed. Subsequent to that no trace of him—in life—could be discovered; and this loss Black now supplied.

After leaving the shed, Mr. Owen went back across the meadow towards his home. In the narrow path, so often mentioned, between the grove of trees and the pond, he halted and leaned over the fence, whether without any particular motive, or from hearing some fancied sound that he would investigate, could never be known. Black, concealed in the grove of trees with a heavy stick, pushed out and dealt him a sudden and violent blow on the back of his head. It must have stunned Mr. Owen, for he fell more forward and did not lift himself: Black took him by the heels and tumbled him over into the pond. So he lay there and was drowned without a struggle, his senseless condition preventing his making any effort to save himself.

"As the Lord's above, and hearing me, I didna mean to kill him," gasped Black, when he had told this. "Owen o' the farm was spying on me and my doings, and I wanted to serve him out for't; break a arm or a leg, or crack his skull a bit, and so teach him not to come interfering in matters as was none of his. But I never meant to kill him. I thought he'd scramble out o' the pond sure enough; I run off home here a thinking it."

"But you must have gone out into the grove with the heavy stick to watch for and assault him," said the surgeon, in answer to this.

"So I did," was the ready avowal. "Things had crossed

me that Sunday, and I had a lot o' drink in me. I'd slep some on't off, but not all. While Joe was a shutting up, just after I woke, that dratted Owen of the farm came slap into my head. I thought I'd go and see whether he was a sneaking and peeping then; and I caught up my stick and went and hid i' the grove, and waited—I knew his cow was sick, and fancied he might be coming to't the last thing. But I swear I didn't think to kill him; and when I come home here and telled Joe, we both chuckled over the sousing he'd got, and I went up to bed a picturing of him trailing home through the lane like a drownded rat. Next morning, when Joe came creeping to my bedside, a saying that Owen hadn't turned up nowhere and was a being enquired for at our house here, I was hard o' belief, and telled him to his face he was a lying fool. No; I never killed him wilful."

Mary Barber threw her hands on her face, and sobbed a sob of emotion. Rarely had she been so moved. Memory was over busy with her. The vivid dream—not less vivid than when she had dreamt it—that had surely foreshadowed her master's death, passed through her mind for a second time that evening in all its details. He passed through it. She saw him walking in from church that Easter Sunday, after partaking of the Lord's Supper; she saw him seated at his table's head entertaining Sir Dene's son and his son-in-law, Geoffry Clanwaring; she saw him stand in the yard at sunset speaking to Joan: it was all before her now. The sun's ray's fell across his face, lighting up its remarkable beauty. Mary Barber had seen many a handsome man in her life, gentle and simple, but never a one whose form and face equalled his, Robert Owen's. She had suspected Black at the time, had suspected him since, for her dream had certainly, in some vague way, pointed to him and his home, the Trailing Indian, as being concerned in the disappearance: and now she found that her suspicions were true. If Mary Barber had wanted her belief in dreams strengthened, this would have done it.

But, if her faith in dreams of the night was confirmed, that in regard to the appearance of supernatural visions was destined at the same time to receive a shock. Robert Owen's ghost had not been a ghost. Knowing what Mary Barber knew, remembering the experiences of her earlier life, and what she had once seen in the Hollow Field—her sister on the stile there—no power, human or divine, could have shaken her belief in the possibility of the dead appearing to mortal eyes. In this one instance, regarding her late master, she found that she and others had been craftily imposed upon.

The strange figure, appearing to the world as a supernatural visitant, and popularly believed to be the unfortunate Robert Owen's spirit, was, after all, only flesh and blood. Black and some of his associates, including Michael Geach, set their heads to work, and turned Mr. Owen's death to good account. The happy thought was Black's. They improvised a ghost to represent him; the object of course being to keep undesirable people away from Harebell Lane, and that part of the Harebell fields that overlooked the lane. The men, who were in the habit of stealing up the lane to Black's with booty about them, had been seen so many times of late that they had grown afraid, and flatly told Black that they must give up the game unless something could be done to insure greater safety. Robert Owen's ghost effected this. It was far more easy to get up a ghost of him than it would have been of most people: for there were those most strongly marked features—the flowing, silvery beard, and the magpie cap. A silvery beard was procured, and another magpie cap: also clothes and a walking-stick similar to those used by Mr. Owen the night of his death. Michael Geach was the ghost. He was as tall as Mr. Owen, and had the same well-formed, handsome cast of features—though the shape of features cannot be seen very much of at a distance by moonlight. Arrayed in the clothes and the beard and the white-bordered cap, Michael Geach might have been sworn to in any moonlight court of law as Robert Owen. The best proof was that he deceived Randy Black himself.

When Black had burst into his house that unlucky night in a state of terror not easily imagined or described, and confessed that he had seen Robert Owen's ghost, his terror and his belief were alike genuine. That the man, hardened though he was in crime, had Mr. Owen's death somewhat on his conscience, various signs betrayed to those about him. Coming home from Hurst Leet that bright night, what with the natural loneliness of the lane, its weird shadows and its awful pond—awful to Black at night since what he had done there—it was only to be expected he should begin thinking of Robert Owen; a very unpleasant thought, which made him quicken his pace past the pond. Had it been to save Black's life, he could not have helped turning his eyes in a kind of dread fascination to the fence above, whence Robert Owen had fallen. And there—there stood Robert Owen himself; that is, his spirit, as Black took it to be; the white beard, and the magpie cup, and the coat he was drowned in, all conspicuous.

And now here was a strange thing—that that man, hardened in sin and in the world's worst ways, should have been stricken with this most awful terror. But that he was so, and this is no fiction, it would be scarcely believable. The idea that it was Geach never so much as crossed him; for he had reason to believe that Geach was a vast number of miles away, on the Cornish coast in fact, gone there on some secret mission connected with a privateer: that he could be in Worcestershire, even had the thought suggested itself, Black would have deemed an impossibility. Geach, however, had arrived at the Trailing Indian that night during Black's absence. While waiting for the landlord to come in, it occurred to him that he might make use of the hour to profit, and he arrayed himself in the ghost's coat, which was kept at the inn—and stole out to frighten the world, putting on the cap and beard when he was safe in the grove of trees. But that Geach saw the state of terror he sent Black into, and enjoyed it too much to speak, there could be little doubt of, though he vowed to Black afterwards that he did not recognise him. How all that might have been does not signify: there's the explanation.

Perhaps the strangest fact of all, connected with that strange business was, that Black retained his terror. Even when he knew, after the elucidation, that the apparent ghost was no ghost, but his friend Michael Geach displaying himself according to custom, the terror wholly refused to quit him. In spite of reason, in spite of knowledge, in spite of the great fact that Robert Owen's spirit had never really come abroad at all, Black lived thenceforward in a chronic state of terror: of terror lest he should see it. It was just as though some mental disease had been caught by him that night, and could never afterwards be eradicated. Time, instead of wearing the impression off, only seemed to increase it. He hardly dared go abroad at night; as the years went on, he cared not to remain alone in the inn after dark. The day of the ghost had, so to say, gone by: its remembrance had nearly faded out of the public mind; and yet Black retained his fear. The fear was never realized, and yet he retained it in all its force. Black thought it was realized once. When he saw

Major Fife at twilight in the dark walk of Beechhurst Dene, deceived by the resemblance, he mistook him for Robert Owen, and he was never undeceived.

And so, the mystery attaching to the dead master of Harebell Farm, mystery in more ways than one, was cleared up at last. Robert Owen had slept peacefully in his grave, and had never come out of it at all to disturb the community. The people connected with the Trailing Indian—meaning those who were not in the secret, and shared the popular belief in the ghost—might have noticed, had they been only sufficiently observant, that the apparition was never seen save during the occasional sojourns of Michael Geach at the inn, and not at all after his death. Geach once got up a seeming fit of terror on his own part. Late one night he rushed into the Trailing Indian in a fine state of agitation, and told a story to the gaping company of having seen the ghost in the lane.

But the prolonged fear that lay on Black, lasting for years and years, was so entirely devoid of reason, so utterly absurd, especially in a man like him, as to be almost incredible. It wore him to a shadow; it embittered his life; it left him no rest, sleeping or waking. Could it have been the finger of God that rested on him, working out the man's punishment? Mary Barber assumed so.

"It seems the Lord has been punishing you, Black," she observed compassionately, after listening to his confession of how dreadful his sufferings from this terror had been. "Let us hope that He'll be all the more lenient to you now, and mercifully hear the quicker your groans for pardon."

CHAPTER XLI.

WITH SIR DENE.

ADVANCING at a jog-trot up Harebell Lane, came a horse carrying double: a country yeoman, Charles Parker, (who, by the way, was first cousin to the Parker connected with the stolen bag of money) on his back, and Miss Emma Geach on a pillion behind him.

In those days it was nearly as common to see a horse carry two people as one; sometimes it was made to carry three. Mr. Parker was returning home from the Wednesday's market at Worcester, whither he had conveyed his daughter in the morning, and left her there on a visit. Happening to overtake Miss Geach on the road when returning, he good-naturedly asked her to get up and ride. The party had nearly reached the Trailing Indian when Mary Barber turned out of the inn, and met it. Emma Geach's loud laugh was echoing on the air; a musical laugh enough, truth to tell, and well known; otherwise Mary Barber might not have recognised her, for the night was rather dark. The woman made a motion for the horse to be stopped, and spoke.

"Holloa, why it's you, Mrs. Barber!" cried the yeoman. "Good evening t'ye."

"Looking for your sweetheart, Mary Barber?" asked free-tongued Miss Emma.

"If ye'll get down, girl, I'll tell ye what has happened; ye'll see then whether this be a time to be looking for sweethearts, even for them that's got 'em," was Mary Barber's answer.

There was a solemn tone in it that struck on the ears of both her listeners, and Miss Emma slid off the pillion to the ground. Mary Barber told of the accident. To give Emma Geach her due, she was sobered on the instant, and much concerned for Black.

"I heard Thaxted tell Black with my own ears that the gun warn't charged," she said, explosively. "What did the man mean by't?"

"That's what Black said," replied Mary Barber.

"Is his hurt bad?" resumed Emma. "Mr. Parker, I thank ye for giving me the lift to-night, and saving me the trapes home afoot. The devil take that there Thaxted," she added, preparing to hasten into the inn.

But Mary Barber put out her hand to detain the girl, willing to soften the shock even to her, and whispered how worse than "bad" the hurt was.

"'Tain't for death, sure!" exclaimed Emma, her voice taking a sound of fear.

"Ay, but it is," was Mary Barber's answer. "No good a beating about the bush any more, Emma Geach. Black's dead."

"Dead! Dead a'ready!"

"About ten minutes ago. Mr. Priar and a lot of 'em be there, men and women. I couldn't do no further good, and I come away."

Very much to Mary Barber's surprise, who had deemed her to be without feeling, the girl burst into a passionate flood of tears. All her days, Black had been to her but a cross-grained master, or whatever he might be called, and they had lived in perpetual warfare; but it seems she bore him some natural affection.

Leaving them to go into the house—for Charles Parker got off his horse to follow—Mary Barber went on down the lane. A project was in her head, that she should proceed at once to Beechhurst Dene, and request an interview with its master. Sundry things disclosed that night had surprised her not a little, and she felt it to be her " bounden duty " (as she put it to herself) to disclose them to Sir Dene.

"It's not too late for't," ran her thoughts; " it can't be much more than half after eight. Poor Black haven't been long agoing. The Lord keep us all from a sudden death like his!"

No; he had not been long. The wound had speedily done its work. Only about four hours—hardly so much, in fact—from the commencement to the close. It was a strange coincidence, that Mary Barber should have been present when both Black and his wife were dying, and it haunted her mind.

"'Twas no chance took me out, and *there*, this evening," she murmured. " I wonder how long 'tis since I went out for nothing but a walk—without having some object to take me? Why, years, it must be. Any way, I can't remember it. That feeling o' wanting to go abroad and get fresh air had never come to me afore. 'Twas just a good angel's hand guiding me."

Arrived at the gate of Beechhurst Dene, she stopped; hesitating whether to enter then, or wait until morning. An impulse was strongly prompting her to go in, spite of the lateness of the hour, spite of her working attire. The gown she wore was of lilac cotton; clean, but somewhat tumbled with her aidings of Black; her bonnet was the usual black poke of a country woman, the cap-border under it clean and full; her shawl was of fawn-coloured cloth, much worn.

"Sir Dene 'll excuse it all," decided she, opening the small gate. "Gander 'll know whether I can ask to see him to-night or not."

At that moment footsteps were heard in the lane, and she waited to see who might be following her. It was Harry Cole. Mary Barber leaned her arms upon the gate while they talked together of what had occurred.

" I never thought his hand was in Mr. Owen's death," remarked Cole. " Some of you fancied it at the time, I remember, but I didn't: he carried it off brazenly."

"He told me something else before you and Priar came," observed Mary Barber. "That money lost out o' Sir Dene's parlour—'twas Jarvis Clanwaring took it. Black says he was sure of it."

"So was I," laconically replied Cole.

"You were! Nonsense, man!"

"Well, I did think 'twas him; I thought it was, for certain. That same night, just at the very time the money must have been taken, I saw Captain Clanwaring at Sir Dene's secretary. Oh, 'twas the captain: no doubt of it."

"And why couldn't you have opened your mouth and said this, Harry Cole?" demanded Mary Barber, hotly.

"Because I was bid not to," was the sentence on Harry Cole's tongue. But he substituted another for it: "Because it was no business of mine."

"No business of yours! 'Twould have cleared Tom Clanwaring."

"Oh, nonsense," said Cole. "Nobody really suspected Mr. Tom. Well, good night, Mrs. Barber. This has been a sad evening's work."

Sir Dene Clanwaring had almost entirely recovered the seizure in December, and was himself again. It was thought that when the genial weather of summer set in, he might become as well as ever he had been of late years. Meanwhile, by Mr. Priar's orders, all topics likely to excite him were avoided, by visitors as well as servants; so that Sir Dene was living in a good deal of ignorance as to the doings of his neighbours. Jarvis Clanwaring he knew all about. That gentleman was languishing away his days in prison (in a rather jolly manner, probably, after the fashion of the time); for by no manner of persuasion could Sir Dene be brought to release him. Lady Lydia sighed and prayed her heart out over it, but Sir Dene was wholly deaf; flatly refusing to help at all, and calling him to Lady Lydia's face by any name but that of gentleman. Sir Dene resented the deceit practised on the Ardes. That a grandson of his, over head and ears in debt, should have palmed himself off as an honourable man, and attempted to marry Mary Arde, brought a blush of shame to his old cheeks. He knew all about the diamonds, too, and had got them home again; having furnished the money to Otto for their redemption. Altogether, Jarvis had done for himself pretty effectually, and Sir Dene assured Lady Lydia that the only fit place for him was the prison he was in. Which gave her the most intense aggravation.

"Can I say a word to Mr. Gander, please?" asked Mary Barber, of the servant who came to the door.

Gander happened to hear the question himself, and came forward. He and Mary Barber were great friends.

"See Sir Dene? Yes, and welcome," said he, in reply to her application. "'Twill be a bit o' change for him. Dull enough it is for the poor master, a sitting up there by himself hour after hour."

"Why don't my lady sit with him?" was Mary Barber's rejoinder. And Gander gave his head a toss.

"Sir Dene don't care to have too much of *her* company. She only gets worrying of him to loose the captain out o' prison."

"I say, I've had a rare shock to-night," said Mary Barber, as she and Gander ascended the staircase together. "Randy Black's dead."

"No!" exclaimed the butler. "Why, what has he died of? 'Twas only yesterday I saw him."

"Ay, so did I," she answered. "His gun went off and killed him. I'm a wanting to tell Sir Dene something that he said in dying."

But that they had reached the baronet's door, Gander might have asked further details, and what the something was: for he had his share of curiosity.

Sir Dene was pacing the carpet in his sitting-room, a favourite exercise of his always, and the only one he could take now. Mary Barber had not seen him for some months: and the change age and illness had made in him, perhaps trouble also, startled her. His once stately form was bent; he tottered as he walked, leaning heavily on his stick; his fine blue eyes were faded; his face was haggard and strangely grey. For a moment Mary Barber could not speak: she believed that if ever she saw death in a face, she saw it in his. Gander shut them in together.

"I made bold to come at this late hour and ask if I might see you, Sir Dene, having a matter to speak of to you," she respectfully said, curtseying. "Gander, he thought you'd please to see me, sir."

Even though it was but Mary Barber, Sir Dene, in his never-failing courtesy of mind, laid his hand on a chair near the fire, as he might have laid it for a lady, and motioned to her to take it. His own large arm-chair stood opposite; he sat down in it, and bent his head towards her, leaning both hands on his stick.

"I have heard to-night what has surprised me, Sir Dene: and I think you ought to hear it too," she began. "So I stepped here without loss o' time to see if I might get speech of you. And I hope, sir, that you'll be so good as to pardon my coming before you in my old things: there was no time to go in home and change 'em."

The probability was that Sir Dene had not noticed whether she wore old things or new. His sight and senses were alike getting dim for these trifles of existence. Two wax candles burned on the mantel-piece, and the fire threw out its blaze on every portion of the small, comfortable sitting-room.

"It don't matter," said Sir Dene. "The things look good to me."

In a low and cautious tone—for Gander had warned her not to startle his master—she imparted to Sir Dene the event of the night. Randy Black's accident and death; and then went on to the items of his confession.

"Poor Owen! murdered after all!" interposed Sir Dene. "But I always said that tale of his ghost appearing was the most ridiculous in the world. Fit only for children and simpletons."

"Well, sir, 'twas what drove my young master, Mr. William Owen, away," she returned. "That, and nought else."

"So I heard," said Sir Dene. "Squire Arde confided it to me after his departure. Had I known 'twas that before the young man went, I'd have tried to reason him out of his foolishness. Ghosts are all nonsense, you know, Mrs. Barber."

Remembering what she remembered—the ghost that she most undoubtedly had seen; ay, and more than that one, as she fully believed, during the experiences of her past life, Mary Barber's opinion was wholly different. And she was not one to shrink from expressing her opinion, even to Sir Dene Clanwaring.

"That the spirits of the dead visit this world sometimes, there's little doubt on, Sir Dene; but it ain't given to everybody to see 'em. I have seen 'em, and so can speak to't. I believe in dreams, too; that they come as warnings, and what not, of things about to happen."

"Ay, that's another thing—dreams," readily acquiesced the old man. "I've had a queer dream or two myself."

The little interruption over, Mary Barber went on to the matter she had come to relate: that it was not Tom Clanwaring who had taken the bag of money, but the captain. Sir Dene, who had been scoring the pattern of the carpet with his stick (also a habit of his), and following it with his eyes while he listened, lifted his head suddenly.

"Jarvis Clanwaring did that?" he cried, looking at her.

"Yes, sir. Black vowed 'twas him with his dying breath. Harry Cole, too, he confirmed it to me i' the lane: for he saw the captain at your secretary." And she repeated what both had said, word for word. It did not appear to surprise Sir Dene much.

"Look you, Mrs. Barber, that ill-doing grandson o' mine— that I'm ashamed to own, and think it a mercy his father was not spared to be pained by his goings-on—was hard up for money about that time; and that's how 'twas, I expect. For the matter o' that, I don't know when he was not hard up— as the world has since learnt. So he took the bag o' money, did he! He's a disgrace to the name of Clanwaring."

"But it's not me that would have intruded to speak of it to you, Sir Dene; I hope I know what respect means better than that——"

"You are welcome," interrupted Sir Dene. "He has been the town's talk."

"Only that I thought it my duty, sir, to clear poor Mr. Tom," she continued. "That bag o' money, sir, you know, was laid by some people to Mr. Tom's door."

"The people were fools," was Sir Dene's retort.

It took Mary Barber aback. She had recently felt so fully persuaded that it must be the one only matter lying against Tom Clanwaring and prevented his recall; for she knew of nothing else that could lie. This she said to Sir Dene.

"No, no," he answered. "My grandson, Tom, is a true Clanwaring: no fear of his thieving bags of money. Why, you ought to know him better than that, Mrs. Barber."

"And I do, sir. When the accusation was brought again' him, my bile went up above a bit. I a'most got a fit o' the yalla jaunders, Sir Dene."

"It's that other affair, up at the Trailing Indian, that has been on my mind," said Sir Dene, acknowledging more to this woman than he had to others: but reticence sometimes forsakes us at the last. "The girl has left Ireland, and is back, I hear."

Mary Barber's hard grey eyes opened with a stare. What was Sir Dene talking of?

"Do you mean about Emma Geach, sir?" she asked.

"Brazen baggage!" ejaculated Sir Dene. "Of course I mean it."

"But, sir," returned the woman, all the emphasis she possessed put into her tone, "that—that was not Tom Clanwaring."

"Was it me, d'ye think?" retorted Sir Dene, angrily, believing she wanted to impose on him in her partizanship for Tom. "It's not your place to tell white lies to me, Mrs. Barber."

"I've not told lies, neither white nor black, in all my life, Sir Dene, and I'm sure I'd not begin now," said independent Mary Barber. "The girl's sweetheart was not Mr. Tom: it was Captain Clanwaring."

"Why, what d'ye mean?" cried Sir Dene.

"Sir, it's gospel truth. That was Captain Clanwaring. Mr. Tom knew nought about it, any way: I don't suppose he have heard on't to this day. Sir Dene, I thought Squire Arde might ha' told you."

The two sat looking at each other. She unable to believe that he did *not* know it, fancying his memory must be in fault; he wondering whether he was listening to a fable.

Since the disclosure made by Miss Geach, the truth of the affair had become public property, what with the whispers of one and another, Susan Cole included, and had reached the servants' ears at Beechhurst Dene. But Mr. Priar's orders—Don't say anything of this or any other exciting matter to Sir Dene until he shall be strong—were very strict, and even Gander had not ventured to disobey.

"Is it possible you have not heard that Mr. Tom was cleared o' that, Sir Dene?" asked Mary Barber, breaking the silence.

"I have heard nothing," replied Sir Dene. "What is there to hear?"

Letting her ungloved hands, hard and worn with work, lie folded in her lap, as she sat bolt upright in her chair, Mary Barber recounted the facts to Sir Dene. She spoke in her usual deliberate manner: and before she was well half way through, he got up in trembling excitement, and stood facing her.

"And that sinning reptile could suffer the brunt of the

scandal to lie on my grandson Tom all the while, knowing 'twas himself?"

"He did, Sir Dene. Black confessed to't as well this very night. Don't ye see, sir, if the truth had come out 'twould have ruined Captain Clanwaring with Miss Arde."

Sir Dene gave a very hard word to Captain Clanwaring, and paced the room in tribulation.

"Poor Mr. Tom have just been a scapegoat among 'em— what he was always called—and nothing else, sir. He have had to take their sins on himself in manhood as well as childhood, and work 'em off. And as to his being ungrateful to you, Sir Dene," she continued, determined to speak out well now she had the chance, "I don't give credit to a shred on't. I'll lay my life that he has writ to you times and again, if it could be proved, and the letters has never been let get to you. Mr. Tom 'ud desire nothing better than to come back, I know; and as to that letter you wrote to him, calling him home, and Gander posted, rely upon't, sir, that it never went anigh him."

Whether the woman's decisive assertions, or the strong, good sense that shone out in every word she spoke, made impression on Sir Dene, certain it was, that a conviction of the truth took instant possession of his mind. The bitter wrong dealt out to Tom throughout his life by Lady Lydia and her family, seemed to rise up before him in a vivid picture. He *saw* how it had been, quite as surely as if he had read it in a mirror: it was as though scales had hitherto been before his eyes, and had suddenly left them clear.

All the old love for Tom, which had but been suppressed, filled his whole being again. He opened his heart to Mary Barber as it had never been opened to living mortal.

"The only child of my dear son, Geoffry!" he cried from his chair, the tears coursing down his cheeks. "And I have let him live away from me, an exile! Geoffry left him to me: you know he did, Mary Barber! and this is how I have kept the trust!"

The tears gathered in her own eyes, hard and cold and grey, as she watched the old man's sorrow. In her homely fashion she tried to soothe it.

"The meeting with him will be all the sweeter now, Sir Dene. Don't fret: 'twas not your fault, sir, but theirs that have kept him from the place. You needn't lose no time in getting him home, sir."

"Fourteen months!" bewailed Sir Dene, apparently catching no comfort from her words. "I've counted 'em one by one: him over there, and me here alone. Seems to me, Mrs. Barber, that my life has been nothing but mistakes that it's too late to remedy."

"There's not a single life, Sir Dene, but what has mistakes in it; plenty on 'em. Looking back, we see 'em; though we couldn't see 'em at the time, or should have acted different. It's too late, as you say, sir—we all find it so—too late, except for one thing, and that's just taking 'em to the Lord for pardon."

Sir Dene nodded twice, and passed his silk handkerchief over his face. Mary Barber was about to rise and make her farewell curtsey, when he resumed.

"The worst mistake o' my life was the cutting of that road, Mrs. Barber—Dene Hollow."

"Well, sir, if I differed from you that it was not, 'twould be just a empty compliment, and have no truth in't," was her straightforward reply. "Nobody can say the road have answered."

"Answered!" echoed Sir Dene, as if the word offended him. "Look at what it has done for people: and for me worst of all. But for that accursed road, my granddaughter, Margaret, would not be in Hurst Leet churchyard."

"My poor mother said, with her dying breath, that she saw the Shadow on it, you know, Sir Dene. She thought it was accursed."

"Ay; Old Mrs. Barber. I turned her out, and broke her heart. Did she curse the road?"

"No, no, Sir Dene. Had she cursed it, the curse might never ha' come. When we leave our wrongs and oppressions to *Him*—the wrongs that bring tears and blood, as 'twere—trying ourselves to bear 'em patiently, as mother tried, it's Him that sends the curse, sir."

"Ay, ay," returned Sir Dene. "Ay."

In the silence that ensued, Mary Barber rose. But again Sir Dene spoke, his eyes lifted up straight into hers.

"I've had her on my mind more than folks think for, Mary Barber. I've seemed to see her often. Sometimes she's in my dreams. If time was to come over again, I'd cut off this right hand rather than take her home from her."

"When things be much in our mind, we're apt to dream of 'em Sir Dene."

"True. If the dead are permitted to know one another up there," slightly lifting his stick to indicate heaven—"I'll ask her pardon for what I did."

"Oh, Sir Dene! Don't fear but what 'twas all forgave by her afore she died."

"Night and morning I ask God to pardon me for it, Mrs. Barber. It won't be long before I'm there, now."

"Indeed, Sir Dene, I hope you'll be spared to us for awhile yet."

"Not for long," he reiterated. "I've been with Squire Arde, lately—the old Squire, you understand. We have talked with one another as happy as crickets; and I know we are going to be together again. Three times 'tis in all; the third time was last night."

"Do you mean in a dream, sir?" she doubtfully questioned, after a short pause.

"Gander says so. I don't think it. Any way, it will not be long before I am with him."

"And now I must wish ye good night, sir," she resumed, dropping her stiff curtsey. "And I thank you for having been pleased to hear me, Sir Dene."

Sir Dene rose. Bending his weight on his stick with the left hand, he held out the other.

"You will shake hands with me, Mrs. Barber? And you'll not forget to carry in your mind what I've said about your poor mother: how I have repented all I did with my whole heart, and how it has come home to me."

He shook her right hand, and held it for a minute in his; not speaking, but gazing at her steadily and wistfully. Mary Barber felt like a fish out of water.

"The Lord give you comfort, Sir Dene!" she whispered "I thank you for condescending to me. And I trust, sir—if you'll not take offence at my saying it—that we shall all meet together in heaven."

He loosed her hand, and turned to the bell with a kind of sob. Gander, answering the peal, met Mary Barber on the stairs.

"I say, Gander, why in the world is it nobody has been honest enough to clear up Mr. Tom to Sir Dene?" she sharply asked.

"Clear up Mr. Tom of what?" returned Gander.

"Why, about that Emma Geach."

"Oh—that. Well, Mr. Priar stopped it. He said Sir Dene must get better first, and then he'd tell him himself."

"Mr. Tom has not had much fair-play among ye, as it seems to me. One good thing, Sir Dene knows it now."

"Will ye step in and take a sup of anything?" asked Gander, hospitably throwing wide his pantry door, thereby displaying its good fire.

"Me step in!—I've not time. They'll have sent all over the parish after me at home as 'tis, I expect, thinking I be lost. Good night, Gander."

CHAPTER XLII.

THE ORDERING OF HEAVEN.

"Who let the woman in?" demanded Lady Lydia Clanwaring of Gander.

"I did, my lady," was the butler's answer, given equably.

"And how dared you do it? How dared you allow her to go up to Sir Dene?"

"There was no reason, that I knew of, why she shouldn't go up. Mrs. Barber's respectable, my lady. Sir Dene's downright glad to ha' seen her."

My lady never got much good from Gander. The more imperious she was with him, the more indifferent to it was he. Next to getting her beloved son out of the London prison, the great wish of her present days was to get Gander out of Beechhurst Dene. And yet, she could not really hope to do it. Even were Sir Dene to have another seizure, a calamity which was expected to arrive sooner or later, and become utterly incapable of exerting authority, even were insensibility to set in, my lady could not hope it. For in that case, the probability was, that the heir, Dene, would take up his abode at the house as master, and he would be the last to suffer the deposal of the old serving-man.

"You take too much upon yourself," retorted my lady.

"I know pretty well when I may take things on myself and when I mayn't, my lady. If I had went up to my master last night, and said, 'Mrs. Barber, from Harebell Farm, is a asking to see you, sir, he'd ha' said, 'Show her up, Gander, show her up.' Said it eagerly, too."

The word struck on Lady Lydia's ears. "Eagerly! Why should he have said it eagerly?"

"Well, my lady, 'twasn't long ago that Sir Dene told me he should want me to fetch Mrs. Barber to him one o' these days; that he'd like to talk to her a bit afore he died. When I heard her voice at the door last night, asking to see him, the thought crossed my mind that her coming had happened just on purpose."

Where was the use of contending—of saying more? None: as Lady Lydia felt. The visit had been paid, and the harm done; and all the scolding in the world would not undo it now.

After the departure of Mary Barber, Sir Dene said nothing that night of what he had learnt. Gander, who helped him to undress, heard no particulars of the interview—and Sir Dene had grown more confidential with Gander than he was with any one. On the following morning, Thursday, this day that we are writing of, Sir Dene's bell rang early. While eating his breakfast, he quietly asked Gander why certain matters, known to all the parish, had been kept from him, whom they most concerned.

Gander, feeling perhaps a little taken aback, did not answer on the instant.

"I'd have thought you would tell me, Gander, if nobody else was honest enough for it," the old man continued in a pained tone.

"And my tongue have been a burning to do't all along, sir," burst forth Gander. "But Priar, he gave so many orders about your being kept quiet that I didn't dare to."

"But for Mrs. Barber I might have gone into my grave, and never had my best grandson cleared to me! What possessed Arde, that he could not tell me?"

"Squire Arde has got some grudge again' Mr. Tom, I know," observed shrewd Gander. "I told the Squire a week ago 'twas time you heard the truth, Sir Dene, but he charged me to be still silent."

"A pretty nest of conspirators you've all been against my poor boy! You ought to be ashamed of yourself, Gander!"

"Sir Dene, next to you there's nobody old Gander cares for like he do for Mr. Tom. But when it comes to a choice between ye—when it's his interests put again yours, meaning your health—why of course his has to go to the wall. And always will, sir, with me," added the man, stoutly.

"Here—move the tray away. I'll get up now."

"You have not took as much as usual, sir."

"I've had as much as I can eat. I want to write a letter."

Sir Dene's hands were flurried; Sir Dene's eyes seemed a little dim; he was longer dressing than ordinary, and also longer reading his Prayer-book after Gander had left him. About eleven o'clock he sat down to his desk at the sitting-room fire; Gander putting every article ready to his hand; pen, ink, paper; and he began the letter. It was the first he had attempted to write since his illness, and the progress was not satisfactory. His feeble fingers could scarcely hold the pen; the strokes were shaky.

"My dear Tom; my dearest grandson."

The date and this commencement had been accomplished after a fashion when the door was tapped at, and Lady Lydia entered. With the customary bland smile on her face, and the blandest tone she could subdue her harsh voice to, she was beginning to enquire after dear Sir Dene's health and how he had rested; but he stopped her in the middle.

All that he had heard the previous night, he repeated to her. It was Jarvis who had taken the bag of money; it was Jarvis who had given rise to the scandal talked of Miss Emma Geach. Sir Dene did not enlarge on the iniquity in itself; but he did on the dishonour of Jarvis in allowing the odium to fall, and rest, upon another. He said that *he* was ashamed of him—her son and his grandson—to his fingers' ends: that so despicable a scoundrel had surely never been suffered to trouble the earth as Jarvis Clanwaring.

Whether Lady Lydia had known of these facts before, whether not, Sir Dene could not judge; the revelation certainly fell upon her with a shock. Her face turned of a ghastly green; her spirit for the minute seemed to quail. Gathering some courage she attempted to dispute it; but Sir Dene stopped her in the midst. He knew it to be true.

"Where did you hear it?" she enquired.

He told her of his interview with Mrs. Barber. And then he bade her leave him that he might get on with his letter.

"Are you writing to Jarvis to reproach him?" she asked, rising from her seat.

"I'd not trouble my hands to write to him, madam; writing's a task for me, now, I can tell you that," was Sir Dene's answer. "Reproach *him*! A man, capable of acting as he has done, would but laugh if reproached."

"I thought you might be," she said, more humbly than Lady Lydia had ever in her life spoken at Beechhurst Dene.

"I am writing to my dear grandson Tom, my lady. Trying to tell him how keenly his old grandfather feels the pain of having doubted him. He'll not lose an hour after he reads the letter, I hope; but travel night and day until he gets here."

"That is, you are sending for him home?"

"I am, my lady. Never again to leave it while I last."

She quitted the room, carrying her mortification with her; and Sir Dene resumed his letter. It made not much progress yet. The mind and the slow fingers alike grew weary; and he was fain to put it aside when it was half written. In the fulness of his repentance, Sir Dene was writing more than he need, considering that he expected Tom would ere long be with him.

Meanwhile Lady Lydia was having it out with Gander down stairs, as we have seen. Gander was clearly to blame for all, she reasoned: had he not given admittance to the woman, Mary Barber, Sir Dene would have continued to live on in happy ignorance. And within the last week or two my lady had quite believed she was making some impression on Sir Dene on behalf of the incarcerated ex-captain! She knew that she should never do it now.

"I hate Tom Clanwaring, and I wish he was dead!" she breathed to herself. "He has stood in my children's light from the first hour I brought them here, and found him, a miserable unit, lolling on Sir Dene's knee in his frills and velvets. Jarvis has been a fool, and played his cards badly; but that other's an upstart interloper, and he shall never come here home to stay if I can drive him out."

Mr. Priar came in to see Sir Dene. He fully confirmed (but it was not necessary) what Mary Barber had said: and then talked a short while with Sir Dene about Black. An inquest was called, and would be held on the morrow. Sir Dene relieved his mind by a little self-reproach in regard to Tom: and Mr. Priar's answer was, that he had always wondered how anybody could suspect ill of Tom Clanwaring.

"I wish I had known it all when Arde was here yesterday afternoon!" exclaimed Sir Dene. "I'd have given him a bit of my mind. If other folks keep things from me, he ought not. Tom's his nephew, in a sort."

"The Ardes are all off this morning on their visit," observed the surgeon. "I saw the carriage go by."

"Ay. Off to Shropshire for a week or so."

Mr. Arde, with his wife and daughter, generally paid a visit once a year to some relations of Mrs. Arde's in the adjoining county. That they should happen to have gone now,

Sir Dene was to-day making a grievance of, as it obliged him to keep that "bit of his mind," intended for the Squire, unspoken for a season. He little thought that he would never speak it.

"What about the Trailing Indian?" suddenly questioned Sir Dene. "Is it shut up?"

"Oh dear no; it's not shut up," said Mr. Priar.

"Who's keeping it open?"

"Emma Geach. She has got Sam Pound and his mother up there for company. I'll look in to-morrow, Sir Dene, when the inquest's over, and tell you about it," added the surgeon, rising to depart. "The chief witnesses will be myself and Mary Barber."

Sir Dene got to his letter on the following day. While he was at it Mr. Priar came in to tell him the result of the inquest, just held at the Trailing Indian. "Accidental Death, with a deodand of two pounds on the gun." Had it been anybody's gun but Black's own, the jury would have put on five pounds. Talking with the doctor he grew fatigued, and resumed his letter late in the afternoon. As Sir Dene was folding it, the same difficulty occurred to him that had occurred once before: he did not know Tom's address.

"D'ye recollect it, Gander?" he asked, lifting his spectacles to the old serving-man, who was hovering by the table, nearly as much interested in the letter and in Tom's recall as his master. "If not, you must go to my lady again."

"It's down stairs in my pantry, Sir Dene. When Mr. Otto was here at Christmas, I got him to write it down in my cellar-book."

Sir Dene wrote Tom's name on the letter, and then took off his spectacles to ease his face while he waited. Gander came back his cellar-book.

"The letter can't go to-day, Sir Dene. It's too late."

"Too late, is it? I'll leave the direction and the sealing till to-morrow, then. I'm tired, Gander. Here; put it in, and lock up the desk."

Gander locked the letter inside the desk, and gave the key to his master. After that, Sir Dene had his dinner, and was more silent in the evening than usual.

"As sure as fate, she's dead at last!"

The exclamation was Gander's. Saturday morning was well advanced, and the postman had just left a letter for Sir

Dene, bearing a Scottish postmark. My lady no longer held the bag. It was in a strange handwriting, and had an enormous black seal. Gander was drawing his own conclusions as he carried it up—that "Mrs. Clanwaring," the heir's mother, was dead. He generally called her by the old name. She had continued weak since her illness at Christmas, but no danger had been recently apprehended. Gander had liked her always, and was full of sorrow accordingly. His master, feeling very ill that day, was remaining in bed.

"I'm afraid here's bad news come, Sir Dene," said Gander, going in to the chamber. "And I'd have ye be prepared for't, sir, afore the letter's opened. It——"

"Not from Tom!—Anything amiss with Tom?" tremblingly interrupted Sir Dene, catching sight of the great black seal.

"Tain't from Ireland at all, sir, but from Scotland. I'm fearing it's the poor dear lady gone at last, sir. Mrs. Clanwaring."

"It's not Dene's writing?" cried Sir Dene, rather in surprise, as he put on his spectacles.

"No, sir, nor Mr. Charley's, either. They'd be too much cut up to write; not a doubt on't. Both of 'em was rare and fond o' their mother."

Sir Dene, breaking the seal, fixed his eyes on the few lines the letter contained. It seemed that he could not read them. A look of horror stole slowly over his face, and he fell back on the pillow, motioning to Gander to take the letter.

"It can't be! It can't be!" he faintly said. "Look! Look!"

In surprise and some dread, Gander clapped on his own spectacles to read the lines. And, when the reading was accomplished, he was not much less overcome than his master.

Oh, it was grievous news. Not Mrs. Clanwaring; it was not she who had died; but her two brave sons, Dene and Charles. They had been drowned in one of the Scottish lakes. A pleasure party of ten young men, had set sail in the brightness of the early spring morning; an accident happened, and but two of them lived to land again. Dene and Charles were amongst the drowned.

Before Gander could at all recover his senses, or believe he read rightly, all his attention had to be given to his master. Sir Dene was exhibiting symptoms of another fit of paralysis.

"Good mercy avert it!" ejaculated Gander, ringing the

bell for help. "And who on earth's come now? That's a travelling chaise a rattling up the gravel!"

Clattering to the door of Beechhurst Dene was a rickety post-chaise and pair. It contained Otto Clanwaring, who had travelled down to Worcester by the mail from London. Otto had received the account of his cousins' melancholy fate earlier than Sir Dene. Poor Mrs. Clanwaring—we may as well call her by that name to the end—had been mindful of the old man even in the midst of her sorrow, and wrote to ask Otto to go down and break it to him in advance of the direct news. The barrister was not quite in time.

Leaping out of the chaise, Otto encountered the scared face of Gander.

"What has brought you here, Mr. Otto?"

"Sad news, Gander: grievous news," was the answer. "I have come to break it to my grandfather."

"Ye're too late, then, sir. We've had it in a letter, and I'm afeard Sir Dene's a-going to get another stroke. This chaise had better go a-galloping off for Priar."

"Priar!" returned Otto. "Priar is coming up now. I passed him as he was turning in at the lodge gates."

"Thank goodness for that! it's a great mercy!" was the old butler's answer, as he turned to run up stairs again.

Too true! Too true! Dene Clanwaring, the heir-apparent to the title and the estate of Beechhurst Dene, and his brother Charles, *his* presumptive heir, were no more. They had met their death by drowning. Full of health, and spirits, and hopes, and life, their career in this world had been suddenly cut short in its early promise, and they were called to meet their Maker. But one week later, had they been spared, they would have come on a long visit to Beechhurst Dene.

Lady Lydia was as one stunned. She had been wearing out her heart with futile prayers and wishes for the release of her son; but never were the wishes so feverishly earnest as now. Oh, if her best-beloved one, Jarvis, could but be there! —if he were but at hand to take up the lost heir's place with his grandfather!

"Send for him; send for him!" moaned Sir Dene, faintly, —and they were the first words he spoke. Lady Lydia, Otto, the surgeon, and Gander, stood around his bed. The threatening stroke kept itself off still; but not, as Mr. Priar thought, for long; and Sir Dene seemed weak almost unto death.

"I cannot send for him," bewailed Lady Lydia, in her

bewildered state of mind taking the words to be an answer to her thoughts, and dropping hot tears. "That is, it's of no use my sending, for he could not come! Oh, Sir Dene, don't you remember? He is in a debtor's prison—as I have been telling you every day for weeks."

Sir Dene looked at her with questioning eyes amid the surrounding silence. "Not he: not Jarvey," he said, when understanding dawned on him. "I don't want *him*. You know it, my lady. I want my own boy, Tom. My heir."

"Tom!" shrieked Lady Lydia. "*Tom* the heir! Tom!"

"Of course he is the heir, mother," put in Otto. "What are you thinking of?"

It was a positive fact that the obvious and to her most unwelcome truth had never crossed her brain. She refused to see it now that it was pointed out, and stared around with frightened eyes.

"Of course it is so," said Otto, answering what the eyes seemed to question. "Tom must come here without delay. I wrote to him before I left London."

"He never shall come! He never shall be the heir," hissed my lady, in a storm of passion. "A low-lived, mischief-making, working scapegoat! *He* the heir? Never. I'll not recognise him as such. I will not allow him to be received at Beechhurst Dene." Perhaps the barrister was not the only one in the room who wondered whether excitement was temporarily turning Lady Lydia's brain. He caught her hand, and drew her beyond the hearing of the invalid.

"Pray exercise your common sense, mother," he quietly said. "Tom Clanwaring is the heir in the sight of man and the country; as much the heir as was the poor fellow who is gone. A few days—I see it in his face," he whispered, indicating Sir Dene—"nay, more probably a few hours, and Tom will not be the heir but the master of Beechhurst Dene."

Gander deemed it well to put a spoke in the wheel. "There bain't no power that could keep Mr. Tom out on't, my lady. He comes in by the rightful law o' succession. The king and all his nobles couldn't do it."

Lady Lydia sank down on a chair with a low cry; it had despair in its depths. Tom Clanwaring the master! Was *this* to be the ending? Had she schemed, and planned, and toiled in her underhand way all these long years only for this? Even so. For once right had been stronger than might, and had come out triumphant.

But Sir Dene was speaking from the bed.

"It's a'most as it should be," he said—and they had to bend down to catch his accents. "In the old days I'd use to wish my dear son Geoffry was my heir, 'stead o' John: just as later I'd catch myself wishing 'twas Geoffry's son, 'stead o' Dene. For I never loved any of 'em as I've loved Tom. Dene was good and dutiful to me, and I loved him next best; but Tom I had here as a baby, you see, and he grew up in my heart. It has pleased the Lord to take Dene and Charley on before me to the better land—and I hope in His mercy we shall soon meet there, and dwell together for ever! Tom, he has got to fulfil Dene's duties here, and he'll do it well. It's not the ordering of man, but of Heaven."

CHAPTER XLIII.

THE NEW MASTER.

It was a very few days afterwards. Another visitor was arriving at Beechhurst Dene. Not thundering up grandly in a chaise, as Otto had done, but walking in all humility, and carrying his own portmanteau. Not any one so short and slight as Otto, this, but a tall, fine commanding man, his unconscious step the step of a chieftain, and a sweet smile on his fair Saxon face. For very blitheness of heart smiled he, in the joy of seeing the dear old familiar places again.

It was Tom Clanwaring. As speedily as wind and road could bring him after the receipt of Otto's letter, he had come. And the wind had been strong and favourable, filling the sails of the good ship, and sending her to a swift haven. Thence on across the country by coach; which brought him to within a mile of Beechhurst Dene. Otto's summoning letter had been brief and somewhat vague. "Poor Dene and Charles are *dead*, Tom. Come off at once to Beechhurst Dene."

It had been little more than that. In the surprise and shock, Tom really knew not what to think. He *could* not picture to himself any possibility so bad as that: there must be a mistake on Otto's part, he concluded: his worst fears did not point to the death of both. But on landing in England, a newspaper that had the account of it, chanced to fall in his way. He learnt that it was, indeed, too true, and that he was the next heir to Beechhurst Dene.

He could not realize it. Never once during the whole of his chequered life, had so wild an idea entered his imagination. The bare fact, that any remote contingency existed by which he might succeed, had been totally overlooked. He, the despised, humiliated waif who had been taught always to regard himself as not fit company for the other grandchildren, who had been put upon, neglected, made to work and earn his bread—*he*, the heir! In truth, it was next to incredible. Tom himself could not fully believe it until it should be confirmed by his grandfather; and it must be said that any gratification he might otherwise have felt at the prospect, was wholly lost sight of in his grief for the fate of Dene and Charles. The two boys had always liked him: since Dene grew up he had stood out well for Tom.

There was no hesitation in his steps as he approached the house, but there was doubt in his heart. Responding instantly to Otto's peremptory recall, from the habit of implicit obedience he had been reared in, Tom had not received with it any intimation that he would be welcome to his grandfather. During all the fourteen months of his exile, he had never once heard from Sir Dene; had never been told that Sir Dene's anger had turned, or that he wanted him home. Otto Clanwaring had once written to advise him to come and chance it: but Tom would not do that without a summons from Sir Dene. Sir Dene *had* sent him a summons, as we know: but my Lady Lydia had taken care it did not reach Tom. In short, had Ireland been a spot isolated from communication with the rest of the world, Tom could not have remained in much more ignorance of Beechhurst Dene and its doings since he left.

The windows of the lodge were closely veiled by their white blinds: he noted it as he passed. Generally speaking, they were gay with children's heads. It was the first corroboration his sight had received that his cousins' deaths were real, and it brought the fact home to him. "Oh, Dene, Dene!" he groaned in his heart. "If I could but see you running down the avenue to meet me, as you used to do!"

At that moment, the death-bell rang out at Hurst Leet Church. Very distinctly it came to his ears in the still spring air. Tom stopped and listened.

"It is tolling for Dene and Charles!" he softly said, with wet eyelashes. "Better that I, the friendless waif, had gone, than they, rich in all things that make life dear!"

At that time it was the custom for the bell to toll an hour

night and morning, every day between the death and the burial. Sometimes when the deceased was of high position at midday as well.

But this was not the regular tolling Tom had supposed it to be. It was the *passing* bell. After the three times three (for Dene and Charles, two, it would have been six times three), there rang out a succession of sharp quick strokes; the indication that a soul had just passed to its account. As Sir Dene, in the years long gone by, had stood that night in Dene Hollow, to listen to the passing bell for poor Maria, Tom's pretty mother, so Tom stood listening now; but he knew not for whom it was sounding.

Every window was closed in the house; he saw that as he neared it: every one. It looked like what it was—a house of the dead. Save that smoke was coming out of some of the chimneys, there was no sign that it had inhabitants. As he rang gently at the bell, a favourite dog came leaping round from the back, recognised Tom, and began to lick his hand.

"You are glad to see me at any rate, Carlo, old fellow!" was his comment, as he stooped to caress the dog. "I wonder whether anybody else will be? I wonder," ran on his thoughts, "whether they will give me house-room—let me occupy my poor old bed in the garret?"

It was Gander who gently drew the door open. In his tribulation at what had fallen on the house, Gander would not have allowed a footman to open that front door, lest he might make a noise in doing it. When he saw Tom standing there, he stared in utter astonishment.

"Don't you know me, Gander?"

"*Know* ye, sir! But we didn't think you could ha' got here so soon—and a-carrying of your own portmanta! I'm sure I expected to see ye come in a chaise-and-four."

Tom's hand was in the old man's, shaking it heartily. "I hardly dared to come on my feet, Gander," he said, in reference to the last remark. "As to chaises-and-four, they have been for my betters, not for me, Gander," he added, his unconscious pressure of the man's fingers, the feverish eagerness of his low tone betraying how much the question was to him. "Has my grandfather forgiven me? Will he receive me kindly?"

Gander looked at him. The great fact, making havoc of his heart, was so intensely real that he was slow to believe Tom could be in ignorance of it.

"Mercy light upon us, sir! Haven't ye heard? My master's gone."

"Gone! Gone where?"

"He's DEAD," burst forth Gander, with a sob. "Dead, Mr. Tom. And here's asking pardon for calling ye so, for you be Sir Tom now."

The fresh colour was deserting Tom Clanwaring's face. "I spoke of my grandfather, Gander," he said, in an accent that had in it ever so much of dread. "*He* cannot be dead?"

"He died at mid-day, Sir Tom. It's barely an hour ago. Yes, sir, it's true: my dear old master is dead and gone."

And Tom knew then that the passing-bell had been for Sir Dene. He sat down on one of the hall chairs, and burst into tears. The shock was sudden, and very bitter. In his whole life he had never been so unmanned; or his feelings so wrung as now. Otto Clanwaring, coming down the stairs, approached, and held out his hand.

"Oh, Otto! it seems very cruel. Not to have seen him! Could you not have sent for me in time?"

"It has been so sudden at the last," spoke the barrister. "When I wrote to you from London to come, there was nothing the matter with him. He died blessing you, Tom. He has charged us—me and Gander—with the most loving messages for you, the truest and tenderest words."

"But he never recalled me," returned Tom, his heart feeling as if it would break with the thought. "I have always lived in hope of it."

"He did recall you, Mr. Tom," spoke up Gander, forgetting again the new title. "He wrote months ago, asking you to come back to him, and 'twas me posted the letter. When the days went on, and you didn't come in answer, Sir Dene thought you bore malice, and wouldn't."

"I did not receive the letter," said Tom, looking alternately at Otto and at Gander, as if questioning where the fault could have been. "I have written to him from time to time, but never have had a line from him since I left."

"Why, in his last illness he said that he had never had a line from you, Tom," exclaimed Otto.

"And no more he never did," assented Gander.

"Then who has had the letters?" questioned Tom. "The last I sent was at Christmas. I wrote to wish my grandfather a happy new year. I wrote to you as well, Gander."

"We never got no letters from you, Mr. Tom; neither him

nor me. As to who had 'em, perhaps my lady'll be able to tell," added bold Gander. "'Twas her that used to unlock the bag."

And not one present but knew from that moment that the correspondence had been suppressed. Tom rose and took up his portmanteau. The action shocked Gander; he quite snatched it out of his hand.

"I ask your pardon, Sir Tom—a chattering here when I ought to be a waiting on ye! Here, Jones," calling to a servant at the back of the hall, "carry up Sir Tom Clanwaring's portmanta."

"Is it my old room, Gander?"

"*Old room!*" returned Gander, partly astonished, partly scandalized at the question. "It's the state rooms that have been prepared for ye, Sir Tom, level with Sir Dene's. Be you a forgetting who you be, sir?"

It seemed that Gander at least was not going to let him forget. In this most unexpected accession to place and power, a reminiscence of his familiarity with Tom in the old days was troubling Gander: he had observed to him no ceremony whatever—as he would have done always to the baronet's heir. The fact caused him to make more of Sir Tom now.

Stepping on before, up the stairs, his body turned sideways in respect, he marshalled Tom along the corridor to the state rooms, and flung the door open to bow him in, Jones and the portmanteau bringing up the rear. But for his sad heart Tom would have laughed at it. As the two men were returning, a door in the middle of the passage was unlatched, and Lady Lydia's face showed itself.

"What mean all these unseemly footsteps, Gander?" she tartly asked. "One would think the whole of you were running up and down stairs for a wager."

"The young master has just arrived, my lady. Jones and me have been a conducting him to his rooms."

"The young master?" she repeated, not catching Gander's meaning.

"The new master, my lady, I suppose I ought rather to say. Sir Tom Clanwaring."

It was the first time she had heard the title; the first time she had ever in her whole life *imagined* it. Sir Tom Clanwaring! Staring hard at the servants for a minute, like one on whom some great awe is falling, she shut the door in their faces, and gave vent to a low cry of pain in the privacy of her chamber.

Well, yes. Tom Clanwaring was the master of Beechhurst Dene to all intents and purposes—the new baronet of the realm. One had died; another had succeeded. But that it should be *this* one to succeed read like a page out of a romance.

During the few days that had intervened before his death, Sir Dene remained perfectly sensible. Very weak and feeble, at times not able to speak, but with all his faculties undimmed. He seemed to foresee, to know, that Tom would not arrive while he lived; and he charged Otto with all kinds of loving messages for him. One of the last things he spoke of was the road, Dene Hollow; regretting in much distress that he had ever made it. This was that same morning, not an hour before his death.

"When I wrote out my testamentary paper I thought it would be Dene to come in after me, you see, Otto," he feebly said, "and I charged him with the concern o' that road, and other things. You'll tell Tom to carry them out: it is he who must do it now."

"I will be sure to tell him, grandfather," replied Otto. "Who are your executors?"

"Eh? Executors? Oh, Tom."

"But surely not Tom alone!" returned the barrister in surprise.

"The other was Dene. And he has gone before me. The paper is written out in duplicate, Otto. One copy will be found in the bay-parlour; right hand secret drawer o' the secretary: the other lies at my lawyer's in Worcester."

As the old man spoke, a thought crossed Otto. It was not usual to make last testaments in duplicate: had Sir Dene done it as a security against fraud?—the possible fraud of his (Otto's) mother and brother? The barrister bit his lip hard, and strove to persuade himself that he was wrong in thinking it.

"Tom'll make a better master of Beechhurst Dene than any of you; better even than Dene would have made," murmured the dying man. "Just as Geoffry would have made a better one than John. Tom's a gentleman and a Christian; he'll do his duty to heaven as well as to man. There'll be no oppression from him: wrongs'll be righted, the poor cared for. God bless him! God reward him for all he has done in life for his poor old grandfather! God be with him always, his Guide and Friend, until He shall land him safely on the eternal shore!"

These were the last words heard from Sir Dene. He said

more to himself, but their substance could not be caught. An hour later, the stroke that had been waited for seized upon him, and in a few minutes he had ceased to exist.

When Tom came forth from his room, the travelling dust washed off, and his coat changed, Otto took him in to see Sir Dene. How sore his pain of heart was as he gazed down on the beloved old face, none save himself would ever know. He had so changed in the past year that Tom could scarcely recognize him. He would have given a great deal to have arrived a day earlier.

On a small table by the bed lay Sir Dene's watch, chain and seals. The same chain and seals Tom had played with as a child, seated on Sir Dene's knee—the same watch Sir Dene had many a time held to his little ear that he might note the ticking.

"They should not lie there, Otto," he said, involuntarily. "They should be put up."

"Yes. There has been no time to do anything yet. Here are the keys," added Otto, holding out the bunch that lay on the same small table. "You had better take possession of them."

"Why am I to take possession of them?"

"Because it is your right. I expect it will be found that all things are left in your power. In any case, you are sole master here."

How strangely it sounded in Tom's ear! The despised brow-beaten young man sole master of Beechhurst Dene!

"There's a letter for you in Sir Dene's desk, I believe," resumed Otto. "It was the last he ever wrote —indeed, the only thing he has written since his first illness. Before it could be posted, Gander had news of Dene's death and your recall."

Tom hastened to get the letter and open it. The kind loving letter—which it half broke his heart to read. Sir Dene told him in it that he had never in his whole life loved a son or grandson as he had loved him: he told him that though he had, through the machinations of others, banished him for a time, he had never in his heart believed him in any way unworthy.

"The luncheon's waiting, Sir Tom," whispered Gander, meeting him on the stairs. "I'd not let it be served till I thought ye were ready; and my lady's in a fine temper. A'most famished, she says."

A flush rose to his fair features as he advanced to Lady Lydia in the dining-room. She and her aide-de-camp, Dovet, had taken counsel together on the untoward state of affairs, and had come to the conclusion that nothing remained but to make the best of them. So my lady, tacitly eating humble pie, met Tom with one whole hand stretched out, and a smile on her vinegar face. Never before had she accorded him more than a frown and a finger.

Force of habit is strong. After Lady Lydia had moved to the table, Tom went to his old side-place, and was about to take it. He was pounced upon by Gauder.

"What be you thinking on, Sir Tom? This is your place now."

"This" was the seat at the table's head, formerly Sir Dene's. One moment's hesitation on Tom's part, and then he took it —took it almost with deprecation, the flush deepening on his face. And never once, either then or later, was Lady Lydia reminded by so much as a word or look, that his position was changed from that of yore. Sir Dene had rightly summed up Tom: "a true gentleman."

Only on the same afternoon had the Ardes returned home. The first tidings that greeted them were—that Sir Dene was dead. They could hardly believe it to be true: when they had quitted home Sir Dene had been so well. The Squire despatched Mark to Beechhurst Dene to inquire particulars of the barrister, who he was told was down; and waited impatiently, after his custom, for the man's return. May was with him: and the dusk of evening was beginning to draw on.

"Here's Mark, papa," said May, as she heard his voice in the hall. "He seems to have brought some one with him. It must be Otto Clanwaring."

Not Otto: not his slight figure at all: but a tall, graceful man, he who appeared when the door was thrown open. The Squire could see so much, as he peered through the dusk at his visitor, and at Mark who was showing him in.

"Sir Tom Clanwaring."

"Who? What?" cried the Squire, sharply.

"Sir Tom Clanwaring, sir," repeated Mark.

Ay, it was he; the *master* of Beechhurst Dene. The Squire felt something like a lunatic in his bewilderment: and the pulses of May's heart went on with a rush and a bound. Conscience was striking the Squire. He had long known how entirely worthy Tom Clanwaring was, how shamefully he had been traduced: but in alarm, lest he, the despised and penniless, should make way with his daughter, he had continued to abuse him. And now, here he was, the young chieftain, lord of all. Like Lady Lydia, Squire Arde was very content to eat humble-pie.

"Only to think of it, Sir Tom!—that you should have shot up above 'em all!" cried he, when the first greetings had passed. "I daresay the rest won't get much."

"I'll make it right for everybody as far as I can," replied Tom, with his warm-hearted smile. "And what about myself, personally, Squire?" he resumed, the smile becoming rather a mischievous one. "Am I still regarded as a general scapegoat with a peck of sins upon my shoulders?"

Squire Arde's voice was subdued as he answered, his countenance somewhat crestfallen. "Tom, I don't think anybody believed aught against you in their consciences: even Lady Lydia. Sir Dene has wanted you home all the while; he was never quite the same after you left. As to that bag of money——"

"Never mind about the bag of money," interrupted Tom.

"I was going to say that not long ago Harry Cole imparted to me a very nasty suspicion as to who it was really took it. He saw—saw some one at the secretary himself that night. When I blew him up for not avowing it, he said you had forbidden him. What do you know?"

"Never mind," repeated Tom. "We will let bygones be bygones."

The Squire was not to be put down. "Tom, I mean to have this out with you. Surely you may trust me! The thief was that villainous man, Jarvis Clanwaring. Did you know it was him at the time?"

"I could not help suspecting it. I was not sure. That night, as Sir Dene, refusing to hear me, left me in the bay-parlour, I flung out at the glass doors, I fear in a passion, and came right upon Jarvis Clanwaring looking in at a corner of the window. He murmured some excuse, which I did not stay to hear, and he went on in. Subsequently, after I had seen you at Bristol, I got a letter from Cole, who must have been passing the window immediately afterwards. It seems Cole took up a notion that I was suspected, and he wrote to tell me he had seen some one else at the secretary. I wrote back and silenced him."

"Why on earth did you do that?"

"What did it matter, sir? I knew Sir Dene would never suspect me: no, nor other people really; at least, none that I cared for. It would have been damaging Jarvis needlessly, you see."

"What do you mean by needlessly?"

"Well, without doing much good to me. My best friends would know I was not guilty. For the rest, my back was a tolerably broad one in those days. The appropriating a little money, when I was starting out to see the world, was but a trifling addition to its lump."

"How considerate you are, Tom!—how forgiving!"

"It is in my nature to be so, I think sir; I don't take credit for it. People tell me it was in my father's Let bygones be bygones in all ways," he emphatically added, rising and grasping the Squire's hand. "For my part, I mean henceforth to believe that the bag never vanished at all. I hope to do all I can for everybody. I hope to welcome Jarvis to Beechhurst Dene for the funeral, if he'd like to come."

"He had better not show his face within my doors," said the Squire explosively. "Jarvis Clanwaring is an unmitigated scoundrel. As to coming to the funeral, there's no fear of that. He is in prison."

"So I find. Otto is about to take steps to release him."

"At your cost?"

"It's hardly to be called that, sir. With Sir Dene's money."

There was an interval of silence. Mr. Arde's mind was full.

"Tom, we have never known you; never properly valued you."

"Then I hope you will value me all the more for the future, sir," answered Tom, slightly laughing. "May I see May?" he added after a pause, his tone serious now, and very pointed.

"She ran away as I came in."

"Go and look for her, my dear boy; go and find her," was the impulsive answer—and it spoke volumes to Tom Clanwaring's ear. "Ah me, how blind we have been!" continued Mr. Arde. "I worked against you with her, Tom, just as much as the rest did. I hope you'll forgive us all."

"You know, sir, we have agreed that bygones shall be bygones," he gently said, suppressing his emotion.

In the adjoining room, cowering before the fire on the hearth-rug, hiding her face from the light, was May. She started up as Sir Tom went in: she put up her hands in deprecation of his anger; she felt faint in her heart-sickness of shame and repentance. He said not a syllable of reproach; only took her in his arms and held her face to his.

"Oh Tom, Tom! I———"

"Hush, my child! I will not let you breathe a word of excuse to me," he fondly interrupted. "I know how it was. Otto has told me all the truth, and has not spared his brother. The battle against you waged fiercely; you were beset on all sides; you held out as long as your strength held out, and then yielded in helpless weariness."

"No, it was not that—the want of strength," she interposed, the hot tears streaming from her eyes. "I could have held out always, but for their making me believe—believe things against you."

"I know. It is all over now, my darling; and I am here not only to claim but to protect you. Look up, May; I must kiss these tears away. You shall never have cause to shed more if I can help it."

"But so ugly, so common a name—Sir Tom!" exclaimed Mrs. Arde, not knowing whether to laugh or cry for joy, and trying to get up some grievance as a set off to her gratification. Tom had gone away then, and she had her daughter to herself.

"So is May," replied that young lady, a remnant of the old sauciness cropping up.

"Nonsense, child! Your name is not May at all, you know. It is Millicent Mary."

"But I'm never called anything but May—hardly. O mamma, dear mamma"—and the glad tears again burst from her eyes—"do not let us pretend to *make* troubles; we have had too many real ones to bear. Think how good God has been to us! But for that blessed snow-storm, I should have been tied for life to Jarvis Clanwaring."

But, after all, Sir Tom Clanwaring was not to continue to be Sir Tom. As if some instinct or prevision had lain on Sir Dene, it was expressly stated in his testamentary paper that should any one of his younger grandsons succeed him, through mishap to his heir, he, the succeedor, should assume and bear the name of Dene. So that Tom had to take entirely the name of his grandfather, and become Sir Dene Clanwaring.

In this last testament of Sir Dene's—which, in truth, though legal, was not an express will, and was never called such, he expressed his regret for having made the road, Dene

Hollow; and gave directions in the strongest terms that it should forthwith be ploughed up. "For," ran the paper, "it had been made out of a neighbour's wrongs, and God's blessing had never rested on it." A good and pretty cottage, better than the one formerly pulled down, was left to Mary Barber for life—to her own unbounded astonishment.

An income was secured to Lady Lydia; the small amount of which, small especially in her own idea, nearly turned her dumb. Jarvis's name was not as much as mentioned; Otto had a substantial sum of money: Gander had a legacy of fifty pounds a year for life. And Tom—Tom was left residuary legatee, just as much to his own astonishment as the cottage was to Mary Barber; for the testamentary paper had been written while he was in Ireland and ostensibly lying under Sir Dene's displeasure. This, of itself, would have made Tom rich for life. Only the entailed estates and the contents of Beechhurst Dene would have come to the heir. Tom himself was sole heir now.

And, being on the subject of bequests, it may as well be mentioned that Mr. Randy Black left a will, after the manner of his betters. Towards the last years of his life it had been supposed that he was poor, living almost from hand to mouth upon the scanty profits of the Trailing Indian, or upon any less legitimate returns he could pick up by poaching. It turned out, however, that Mr. Randy Black had a few hundred pounds in store: the furniture of the inn, old but tolerably substantial, was also his. The whole of it, without reserve, was bequeathed to his "adopted daughter," Emma Geach.

So Miss Emma turned out to be an heiress in a small way.

CHAPTER XLIV.

CONCLUSION.

MIDSUMMER DAY had passed, and June was drawing to its close. The blue skies were without a cloud, save where the sun was setting in its golden light; the scent of the lying hay filled the still evening air. Out of doors nothing could be more calm and peaceful: within doors, at Arde Hall, all was bustle, preparation, and excitement. For on the morrow its daughter wa to become Lady Clanwaring.

Things at Beechhurst Dene had settled down into their routine, and Tom was as calm and efficient a chieftain as though he had been born and reared to it. Nay, far more so. Brought up in the pride and exclusiveness, in the expectations pertaining to their position, not one of them would have made the kind, considerate, and thoroughly capable master that Tom made. "Tom" to his friends still, "Sir Dene" to the world.

Some people said he would be too lenient, too good-hearted, in fact, for his own interests. Witness, for instance, his having granted a renewal of the lease of the Trailing Indian to Miss Emma Geach! Miss Emma, brassy as of old, had presented herself one day in the bay-parlour, where the young Sir Dene sat over his papers, and boldly asked for it. Would she be able to get a living at the inn, was Sir Dene's answering question; and she said, "Yes, for certain," and imparted a little news about herself. She was about to be married to Jim Pound. She should keep the inn going, and attend to the customers, while Jim would go out to his regular employment abroad as usual. And she intended to conduct the inn respectably, she added—and Tom saw she meant it—and not have the disreputable characters there that Black had favoured. She also purposed, if Sir Dene had no objection, to alter the name of the inn to the "Wheatsheaf," and to have a new signboard painted, showing a big sheaf of corn, well gilded. Sir Dene replied that he had no objection in the world; on the contrary, he thought the "Wheatsheaf" carried a more reputable sound with it than the "Trailing Indian." So he gave her the promise of the lease; and he shook hands with her for their early friendship's sake, when both were little Arabs running about Harebell Lane, and wished her prosperity with all his heart. As Mr. James Pound was a hard-working, steady, simple young man, who had never had but one idea in his head, and that was admiration of Miss Emma Geach, and would be sure to let her be mistress and master, Tom considered her prospects of domestic felicity were very fair.

Witness, too, what he had done for Mary Barber—furnished the pretty cottage for her in the nicest manner. At all this the parish shook its prudent head: clearly the young Sir Dene was not sufficiently awake to his own interests.

But, if he was not going in for his own particular interests, he undoubtedly was for his people's love. Tenants and servants had already found out how good he would be to them, how implicitly they might trust in his honour and generosity. The trials he had undergone throughout his life had been the best possible training for him: heaven, foreseeing things that we cannot, had no doubt been all the while fitting Tom Clanwaring for the lot in life he was to fulfil. Geoffry's dying prayer for his child's best welfare had been heard.

Jarvis Clanwaring, released from his debts by Otto (acting for Sir Tom), had declined to attend his grandfather's funeral; for he had sufficient sense of shame not to show his face again in the neighbourhood of Hurst Leet. A post was obtained for him in India, in which he might do well if he chose to be steady, even make a fortune in time: and he had already sailed for it. Lady Lydia had fixed her abode in London; Dovet, of course, being with her: and Tom generously doubled the amount of income bequeathed to her by Sir Dene.

The road, Dene Hollow, was a road no longer. A ploughed field existed where it had been. Just as that fine new highway in the years gone by had obliterated all trace of the Widow Barber's house, so the long ploughed field now obliterated all trace of the highway. But the convenience of Hurst Leet and its surrounding people was not lost sight of. Tom had talked to Mr. Arde, and persuaded that gentleman to allow another road to be cut through his property, Tom undertaking the expense. It was a better site for it than the other, and just where it ought to have been made at first. And so, the time had gone on to midsummer, and the wedding of Sir Dene and Miss Arde was fixed for one of these last days of June.

They stood together, he and his betrothed bride, on this their marriage eve, in the small side room of Arde Hall that had once been the young lady's school and play room. The servants were busy laying out the breakfast in the dining-parlour; Mrs. Arde was in the drawing-room, putting the finishing touches to the vases of flowers, Charlotte Scrope, again come to be bridesmaid helping her. Miss May had been wilful. Not an earthly thing, even to a blessed bit of ribbon, as Susan Cole angrily put it, that had been prepared for the other wedding, would she let serve for this. The attire, both for bride and bridesmaid, had to be bought anew. To the last hour of Susan's life she would not cease to grumble at the folly and waste. Even now, she had been giving Miss May a taste of her opinion, although the young lady was by the side of her bridegroom so soon to be.

It was but a shabby little room, but the only one free in the house that evening. The last rays of the sun shone on their faces, as they stood side by side at the open window, through which the hay sent in its sweetness. Still faces, this evening, both, and somewhat serious; but oh! with what quiet happiness underlying their depths! Squire Arde had been watching through his spectacles the men at work on the new road, but had now betaken himself from the room. Susan Cole, a basket of ribbon on her arm, a needle and thread in her hand, was ostensibly making up white favours, and passing in and out at will. Susan, for some cause not yet explained, was in a very explosive temper that evening; nearly everybody she came near being treated to a touch of tartness.

"They are putting up for the night," observed May, alluding to the road labourers beyond the side field.

"And for to-morrow also," added Sir Dene. For old and young, rich and poor, were on the morrow to rest from labour.

"How glad they must be when their day's work's over," said May, shyly, in the reminder. "They are taking away their tools."

"Glad to get the work to do, *I* should say," put in Susan. "Glad that folks is found to be at the costs o' new roads and give 'em work."

She whisked out of the room again, basket on arm, as abruptly as she had just whisked into it. Tom's blue eyes shone with a merry light.

"The new road has never altogether met with Susan's favour," he said. "She thinks I need not have gone to the expense."

"She is getting stingy in everything," returned May, remembering the reproof just tilted at herself about the wedding things. "Tom, do you know I fancy sometimes it's because she's—rather old."

"It's because she likes to stand out for her own opinion, May, my love. She is not old yet."

"It was quite right to make the road; and to do everything else that you are doing. Tom, we shall be dreadfully rich. I don't know how all the money will get spent."

He shook his head with a smile, playing with her brown hair. "I could spend twice as much, May."

"But not on ourselves?" she said in surprise, lifting her eyes to his.

"No. On others."

"There will be enough, Tom. This will be ours sometime, you know. Who could have thought the two properties would ever be united!"

"Who would have thought at one time, May, that you and I should ever be?"

"Who!—why, all along nearly——"

She stopped suddenly—with the brightest blush. His whole face was laughing.

"All along—what?" But Miss May grew very hot indeed, and bit her lips.

"All along what, May? Come. I am waiting to hear."

"Never you mind, Sir Dene. If you intend to take me up in this sharp way, you had better tell me so beforehand."

"And if I do tell you so?"

"Why then—I am not sure that I'll be married at all."

"No! That breakfast in the other room must be eaten, you know, May."

"I don't know anything about it, sir. And I think——"

What May thought was never spoken. An interruption stopped it in the shape of Susan Cole again. Flinging open the door, she put her basket and ribbon on the table, and came up to them, evidently armed for conflict.

"Look here," she began. "I'm a going to have it out. I can't help myself: I shall burst if I don't. And I never thought you'd be, either of you, ungrateful to me—yes, Sir Dene, I am speaking to you as well as to Miss May. Since my missis said what she did an hour ago, I don't know whether I've stood on my head or my heels. And I've went and cut up all the ribbon for the favours into wrong lengths! It's not my fault."

"Just say what your grievance is, Susan," spoke Sir Dene.

"I don't pretend to be one o' your fine stuck-up maids," went on Susan, never seeming to hear him, "and I know it's only reasonable to expect that Miss May, about to be My Lady, and a going to London to be showed off at the King's Court, and that, may want one that's fashionabler. All that was understood—that another was to be took on in my place: and I was agreeable. But when my missis says to me just now, when we was a measuring the white satin together (and I lost the measure on't later), 'You can always come back here, you know, Susan, if they should not continue to want you at Beechhurst Dene,' you might ha' knocked me down with a end o' the ribbon. Miss May—Mr. Tom—when I hear these things, I think it's time to ask you what footing I be upon," excitedly went on Susan. "I looked to fill another sort o' place, you see, at Beechhurst Dene, and never to be turned out on't."

"I'm sure, Susan, I don't wish to turn you out," said May, quite taken aback. "I never thought of doing it. What is the other place you would like to fill?"

"Why the nurse's of course, Miss May," retorted Susan.

"The nurse's?" repeated May, not taking the meaning.

"Yes, Miss May: nurse. Nurse to the babies when they come."

May stared blankly for a moment or two; and then her face turned to a crimson flame.

"How very absurd you are, Susan!"

"Me absurd!" echoed Susan Cole, her own face aflame with anger. "What's absurd? I nursed you, Miss May; I nursed Master Tom here; 'twould be a hard thing if I didn't nurse your children."

"So it would," put in Tom, biting his lips hard, to keep countenance.

"In course it would," repeated Susan, somewhat mollified by the admission. "And me a stopping single for your sakes! I had my sweethearts in those days, and my offers too—as you might ha' seen 'em a dangling after me when I'd got you out, if you'd been old enough to have sense in your eyes. But I didn't take 'em: I kept to you. First one of you in my arms, and a teaching of to walk and a keeping of out o' mischief; and then the t'other. A fine time on't I had with you, Miss May; for of all the ondacious children you were the worst: Master Tom, he was tractabler. Ever since he came home—Sir Dene—I've looked to nurse your babies. Who else has got a right to nurse 'em? It'll be an unjust thing if you don't let me!"

"So you shall nurse them, Susan," said Tom, laughing. "I promise it."

Susan gave a satisfied nod, caught up her basket of favours, and went away again. May was leaning from the window then as far as she safely could without pitching out. Tom went to her; but she would not turn round. He thought he heard a sob.

"Why, May! My darling! What is it?"

Gently raising her to him, she turned her face and hid it on his breast. He put down his own face and wanted to know what the sorrow was.

"Not present sorrow at all," she whispered. "It's not the first time since you came back that I've cried for happiness. While Susan was grumbling—and what a stupid thing she is! off her head, I think—some of the past sorrow flashed into my mind, and I began to contrast it with what is. God has been very good to us."

"More than good, May. We will—Who is this?"

May was away like a shot, demurely stretching herself beyond the window again. The intruder was Otto Clanwaring. He had come down to be Sir Dene's best man at the wedding.

They walked home together arm in arm, the two young men, talking soberly one with the other. Of the crowd expected in the church on the morrow; of Mary Barber's best grey gown, and the shawl with the border of lillies and roses that were to be worn at it. Of Harry Cole's old mother, who was to be driven down by him to the church. Of Mrs. James Pound's (no longer Miss Emma Geach) late smart wedding attire to be displayed at it. Of Gander's prominent place in the tail of the procession. In short, of the general satisfactory state of all things.

And the stars came out one by one in the clear sky, and the whole atmosphere, within and without, seemed redolent of peace. As they went on, up the avenue, and came in sight of Beechhurst Dene, its master lifted his hat, his lips moving silently. Otto thought Sir Dene might be murmuring to himself some words about the warm weather. In truth, the words were very different.

"God be thanked for the way He has led me since the day I was carried in here, an infant waif, my father's tears falling on my face! May He be ever with me to the end!"

My friends—in conclusion. Dark days have embittered the lives of some of us, just as they embittered Tom Clanwaring's. They will dawn for us again. Days when we look yearningly into the far corners of the wide earth for a gleam of comfort, and look in vain: there's not a ray in the sunless sky, not a star in the black over-shadowing firmament. But above this dreary earth, higher than that leaden sky, is Heaven. *There* sits ONE who sees all our cares, notes our oppressions, hears our sighs, pities our tears : and who will surely in His own good time cause the darkness to merge away in bright and loving light if we do but patiently trust to Him.

And so a new reign was begun at the Dene in all happiness. And Susah Cole got the post she fought for.

But Hurst Leet generally was never persuaded out of the belief that Robert Owen's ghost had " walked." Only people did not talk much about it abroad, as he was the grandfather of Sir Dene.

THE END.

J. OGDEN AND CO., PRINTERS, 172, ST. JOHN STREET, E.C

www.ingramcontent.com/pod-product-compliance
Lightning Source LLC
Chambersburg PA
CBHW022110300426
44117CB00007B/655